D1193459

SCENIC DRIVING
SOUTH
CAROLINA

JOHN F. CLARK
and
PATRICIA A. PIERCE

FALCON®

GUILFORD, CONNECTICUT
HELENA, MONTANA
AN IMPRINT OF THE GLOBE PEQUOT PRESS

L. E. SMOOT MEMORIAL LIBRARY
9533 KINGS HIGHWAY
KING GEORGE, VA 22485

This book is dedicated to our families, whose continued love and support make everything possible. To the Clarks—Jay, Jean, Kathy, Marion and Tom, and the Pierces—George, Margaret, Leslie and Virginia.

A FALCON GUIDE®

Copyright © 2003 by The Globe Pequot Press

All rights reserved. No part of this book may be reproduced or transmitted in any form by any means, electronic or mechanical, including photocopying and recording, or by any information storage and retrieval system, except as may be expressly permitted by the 1976 Copyright Act or by the publisher. Requests for permission should be made in writing to The Globe Pequot Press, P.O. Box 480, Guilford, Connecticut 06437.

Falcon and FalconGuide are registered trademarks of The Globe Pequot Press.

Photos provided courtesy of the authors.
Maps created by Topaz Maps Inc. © The Globe Pequot Press

ISBN 0-7627-1139-6
ISSN: 1545-1607

Manufactured in the United States of America
First Edition/Second Printing

The Globe Pequot Press assumes no liability for accidents happening to, or injuries sustained by, readers who engage in activities described in this book.

contents

THE SCENIC DRIVES

Acknowledgments

We owe much to many, without whose help this book would not have been possible. Special gratitude is extended to Leslie Pierce, for her many helpful suggestions and her enthusiasm to drive from dawn to dusk hammering out perfect scenic routes, and to John Dantzler, who co-authored *Hiking South Carolina* with John Clark and helped compile significant information used in this volume.

For assistance in many shapes and sizes, we extend our warm thanks to Kay Abernathy, Vaughan Alsbrook, Robert Barber, Kate Billing, Leann Brown, Jay Clark, Kathy Clark, Tom Clark, Heather Garren, Sonny Graves, Clara Heinsohn, Denton Lindsay, Ann McIntosh, Yvonne Michel, George Pierce, Margaret Pierce, Virginia Pierce, Ann Rentiers, Mary Riley, Tricia Tangney, John Tiencken, Gene Williams, Mike Winburn, Scott Winburn, and Jaco van Zyl.

Finally, we are most appreciative of the hard work, expertise, pleasant dispositions, and patience of our editors at The Globe Pequot Press, Mary Luders Norris and Hrissi Haldezos.

Wigington Scenic Byway

LOCATOR MAP

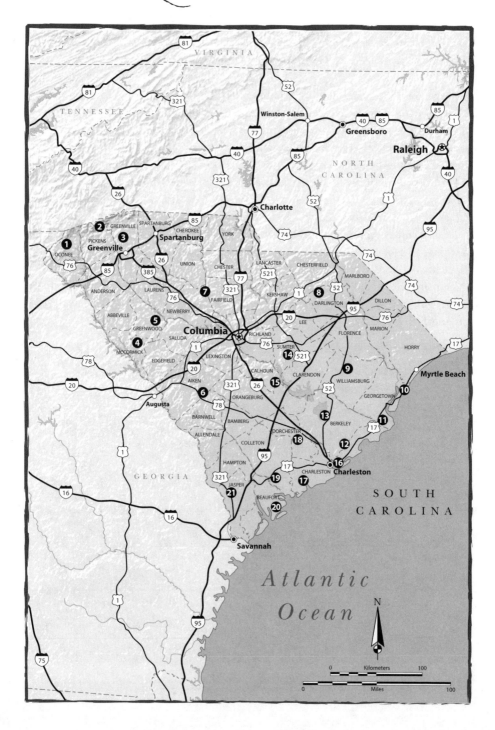

MAP LEGEND

Scenic Drive	▬▬▬▬	Lake	
Interstate Highway	95	Swamp/Wetland	
US Highway	17	Dam	
State Highway	35	Waterfall	
Secondary road	S-13-247	Mountain	▲
Forest Road	FR 710	Point of interest	◘
Surface street	Walnut St.	Campground	Λ
Railroad	┝┼┼┼┼┼┼┼┼┼┥	Small town	○ **Rockville**
State line	SOUTH CAROLINA GEORGIA	Large town	◉ **Newberry**
Park/Forest boundary	CAROLINA SANDHILLS N.W.R.	Major city	✸ **Columbia**
River			

State Champion Live Oak

introduction

South Carolina packs delightful variety into a relatively small area. The sliver of mountains at the northwest corner of the state features a dazzling array of gorges and waterfalls, as well as the wild and scenic Chattooga River, famous as the setting for James Dickey's *Deliverance*. Stretching from the mountains to the center of the state are rolling foothills. A belt of sandhills, remnants of ancient sand dunes, separates the foothills from the low, flat coastal plain, which covers the southeastern two-thirds of the state.

The state's population centers are Greenville-Spartanburg, the hub of the state's booming industrial sector; Columbia, the governmental and commercial center; and Charleston, one of the busiest seaports on the East Coast and a thriving tourism mecca. However, in spite of the growth of industrial prosperity and the three midsize metropolitan areas, South Carolina, due largely to its heavy agricultural heritage, remains primarily a state of small towns and communities and devotion to the rural lifestyle. South Carolinians revere their natural heritage.

The state's tourism industry is huge, hosting more than 30 million visitors annually. Most tourists come for the superb beaches, golf, tennis, entertainment, restaurants, shopping, and fine weather of the coastal areas of Myrtle Beach, Charleston, and Hilton Head. These destinations offer tremendous attractions, but the rest of the state of South Carolina offers the same seductive weather and much more. The Palmetto State presents charming small towns, quaint bed-and-breakfast accommodations, numerous historic sites (the state's recorded history dates back 500 years), beautiful natural resources, attractive farmland settings, and a variety of recreational opportunities.

This book features twenty-one of South Carolina's most scenic drives, offering more than 1,500 miles of riding pleasure. For the most part, readers are treated to little-known routes through small towns, rural countryside, and public lands. Exceptions are the Charleston and Waccamaw Neck drives, where nature, history, and people blend in unusually splendid harmony.

As you drive through South Carolina's back roads, you will see gracious old homes shaded by oaks and pines and surrounded by flowering shrubs, as well as prosperous farmlands full of cotton, tobacco, soybeans, corn, hay, and vegetables. Horse and cow pastures present idyllic settings, and prolific pecan, apple, and peach orchards decorate some areas.

One thing you will see often, in cities, suburbs, towns, and out in the country, is churches—lots of churches, rich and poor, new and old, and numerous gradations in between. You will also see very modest homes, ramshackle dwellings and farm buildings, and a fair amount of poverty. South Carolina is not a wealthy state, and a majority of the state's less developed areas are in rural counties. Part of the reason some of these areas are scenic is precisely because they are largely untouched by development.

The downtown areas of small communities are often intriguing. Some still manage to thrive, but many are simply ghosts of their glory days in the early and middle parts of the twentieth century. Quite a number center around railroad tracks, harkening back to a time when trains were the chief intercity carriers of both people and goods.

Public lands make up a fair proportion of the scenery along the routes in this book. State parks, state wildlife management areas and heritage preserves, national wildlife refuges and monuments, and national and state forests collectively preserve for posterity a great deal of South Carolina's bountiful natural resources.

REGIONS

Geologists divide the state into three (sometimes four) physiographic provinces, all of which extend into the neighboring states of Georgia and North Carolina. The **Blue Ridge** province, strictly defined, only covers the extreme northwestern mountainous edge of the state. The **Piedmont (foothills)** province, roughly the northwest third of the state, runs from the Blue Ridge approximately to the center of the state.

The **Sand Hills,** remnants of an ancient seacoast that provide evidence that the sea level was once much higher, stretch across the state's midriff in a belt from Cheraw through Camden, Columbia, and Lexington, and on to North Augusta. Some scientists consider them to be part of either the Piedmont or Coastal Plain physiographic province, while others identify them as a separate province.

South and east of the Sand Hills, the **Coastal Plain** province covers the rest of the state. It is characterized by very flat terrain and a plethora of wetlands. A subregion is the **Coastal Zone,** the narrow strip bordering the Atlantic Ocean.

Other observers identify geographic regions in South Carolina in a variety of ways. Frequently used regional terms include Foothills, Upcountry, upstate, Midlands, Savannah River Valley, Lowcountry, Pee Dee, Grand Strand, and the coast.

South Carolina's visitation promoters present the state in terms of ten tourism districts: Upcountry; Old 96 District; Olde English District; Thoroughbred Country; Capital City and Lake Murray Country; Pee Dee Country; Santee Cooper Country; Myrtle Beach and the Grand Strand; Historic Charleston; and Lowcountry and Resort Islands. Information on these districts is contained in Helpful Organizations, located in the appendix section of this book.

Names people use for South Carolina's Coastal Plain can be a bit confusing. Many South Carolinians refer to this entire area as the **Lowcountry** (also written Low Country, low country and lowcountry), but the boundaries of the Lowcountry are open to question. Some parties refer to the southernmost counties of the state as the Lowcountry, and sometimes the term refers to the historic plantation area around Charleston. Others use the term to refer to all of the area formerly dominated by river plantations, from the Waccamaw River wetlands above Georgetown all the way to Beaufort. The Lowcountry and Resort Islands tourism district is composed of Beaufort, Colleton, Jasper, and Hampton Counties, all south of Charleston.

The **Grand Strand,** the string of ocean resorts on the 60-mile coast centered on Myrtle Beach, is often thought of as a region in its own right. Adjacent to the Grand Strand, but inland, is the **Pee Dee** section of the state, an agricultural region comprising the watershed of the Great Pee Dee River and its tributaries.

Stretching from northern Charleston County to Georgia are the **Sea Islands,** once the home of substantial rice and cotton plantations. On these islands, a distinctive African-American culture survived and thrived, but this culture is threatened by resort and other commercial and residential development.

NATURAL RESOURCES

Rivers dominate South Carolina's terrain. Four major river systems drain the state: the Savannah, Edisto, Santee–Cooper, and Pee Dee.

The Savannah River Basin extends along a narrow strip paralleling the South Carolina–Georgia border for its entire length. Because the Ice Age never stretched into the state, it never gouged any large natural lakes here like those found farther north; all large lakes in the state are man-made, mostly for the creation of hydroelectric power. The Savannah River Basin contains five such lakes in South Carolina: Jocassee, Keowee, Hartwell, Russell, and Thurmond.

The Edisto River is famed as the longest undisturbed blackwater river in the world. The Edisto River Basin, which includes the Coosawhatchie, Salkehatchie, Combahee, Ashepoo, and Edisto Rivers, stretches from the Sandhills area between Aiken and Columbia southward to the renowned ACE (Ashepoo–Combahee–Edisto) Basin, a subdrainage at the southern end of the Edisto system watershed.

The upper reaches of the Santee–Cooper Basin comprise much of the north-central part of the state, from Sassafras Mountain in the west through Greenville and Spartanburg all the way to Rock Hill and Lancaster. Major feeders include the Upper, Middle, and Lower Saluda Rivers; the Broad River; the Catawba/Wateree River; and the Congaree River. The Santee–Cooper Basin narrows to a neck along the Congaree River south and east of Columbia before widening again below Lakes Marion and Moultrie and reaching the sea at Charleston via the Cooper River and below Georgetown via the Santee River. This mighty river system includes Lakes Greenwood, Murray, Wylie, Wateree, Marion, and Moultrie.

The final major drainage area, the Pee Dee River Basin, covers much of the eastern part of the state. This basin, encompassing a rich agricultural region centered on Florence, includes the Black, Lynches, Great Pee Dee, Little Pee Dee, Waccamaw, and Sampit Rivers, emptying into the Atlantic Ocean at Georgetown.

Trees and other plants are as diverse as the geography. The mountains are dominated by oak-hickory forest. Numerous varieties of oak are found in this habitat type noted for its huge diversity of plant species. Wetter areas are dominated by lovely mountain laurel and rhododendron, a special pleasure in the late spring when they bloom riotously.

The rest of the state is mostly covered by oak-pine forest, but exceptions are the rule. A few of our driving routes pass through coastal maritime forests, characterized by a mixture of vegetation resistant to the effects of salt spray and wind. Trees include live oaks, laurel oaks, Carolina palmettos (the state tree), and slash and loblolly pines. Other common vegetation includes hollies, redbays, dwarf palmettos, wax myrtles, and red cedars.

Coastal Plain wetlands are particularly appealing. Swamps feature tea-black water, Spanish moss, and bald cypress and tupelo trees. Another type of enticing wetland is coastal marshland reclaimed from the plantation rice culture of centuries past and managed today as habitat for migratory birds. Such areas are achingly beautiful, especially when wildflowers such as irises, yellow jessamine (the state flower), and spider lilies are blooming.

A Coastal Plain wetland type under serious threat is the Carolina bay. This is an unusual elliptical depression, often, but not always, filled with water. The word "bay" refers not to water, but to the bay trees that are usually the dominant vegetation. Carolina bays are found in their greatest numbers in the Coastal Plain areas of the Carolinas and Georgia. Most have been filled or drained for farming, roads, or development. Efforts to protect the remaining Carolina bays continue, particularly through the work of the Heritage Trust program of the South Carolina Department of Natural Resources.

Humans do not cause all the damage. Nature, too, can be capricious. South Carolina periodically suffers a population explosion of the southern pine beetle. Since 1995, the worst outbreak in state history has affected over half of South Carolina's counties, concentrated in the northwestern and southern parts of the state. Enough timber to build 50,000 houses was destroyed by the beetle.

Hurricane Hugo was another disaster for South Carolina and its ecosystems. On September 21, 1989, this killer storm slammed into the South Carolina coast just above Charleston and dramatically transformed the landscape in its path. The tidal surge washed completely over many barrier islands, including Bull Island and the Isle of Palms. The fishing village of McClellanville, just north of the spot where the center of the hurricane made landfall, was almost leveled. Furthermore, Hugo tracked rapidly inland, its extremely high winds causing severe damage far from the coast, through Camden all the way past Charlotte, North Carolina. The devastated woodlands of Cape Romain National Wildlife Refuge and Francis Marion National Forest will continue to display the scars of Hugo for decades to come.

Wildlife in the state is quite diverse. The mountains harbor species such as the raven and the endangered peregrine falcon, usually found much farther north. At the southern end of the state are found species common in Florida or other subtropical areas. In between are large populations of white-tailed deer (the state animal) and wild turkey (the state wild game bird). Black bears live secretively in the mountains and, surprisingly, in secluded Carolina bays within a few miles of the highly developed Grand Strand coastal resort area. Other well-represented mammals in the state include beavers, foxes, raccoons, bobcats, feral hogs, and river otters. Opossums, the only marsupials native to North America, are also quite common.

South Carolina is an underappreciated birding region, although sites such as Huntington Beach State Park and Savannah National Wildlife Refuge are becoming better-known to international bird enthusiasts. More than 350 species have been identified. Generally, wetlands along the coast are popular year-round host sites for wading birds such as herons and egrets. Ducks winter along the coast, and numerous bird species pass through the entire state during spring and autumn migration periods. Songbirds (look for Carolina wrens, the state bird) and woodpeckers fill the forests during all seasons, while various birds of prey prowl the skies.

South Carolina harbors many endangered or threatened species. The most prominent of these is our national symbol, the bald eagle. This great bird is making a strong comeback in South Carolina. The same is true for alligators, which are numerous in swamps and marshlands of the coastal plain. The red-cockaded woodpecker is badly threatened due to habitat loss, but South Carolina has some of the nation's largest remaining populations of this species, important as a bellwether of ecosystem quality.

South Carolina preservationists also work hard to protect nesting areas for loggerhead sea turtles (the state reptile) along the coast, and habitat for gopher tortoises in the sandy areas of the lower Savannah River Valley.

HISTORY

Human activity in South Carolina's **precolonial period** dates back almost 15,000 years, and there is much remaining evidence of Native American settlement along the coasts and rivers of the state. Ancient shell rings and mounds are particularly noteworthy, and access to such phenomena is available at a few spots along or near the designated scenic routes. Additionally, some of the back roads you will travel and cross were originally Native American trading trails.

Spaniards first explored the South Carolina coast in 1514, and in 1526 they attempted a settlement at Winyah Bay, near the site of present-day Georgetown. Weather, Indian attacks, and disease brought a quick end to this foray. Later, in 1540, Hernando de Soto crossed through the central part of the state in his explorations.

French Huguenots fleeing persecution tried to colonize Parris Island, near Beaufort, in 1562, but this attempt was also short-lived. The Spanish came to Parris Island in 1566 and established Santa Elena, which managed to survive until 1587, when the inhabitants withdrew southward to Saint Augustine. Native Americans had the South Carolina area entirely to themselves again, for almost another century.

However, in 1670, King Charles II established a settlement on the Ashley River, at a spot now protected as Charles Towne Landing State Historic Site, beginning South Carolina's **colonial period.** The settlers moved across the river to the Charleston peninsula in 1680, to the site of today's downtown Charleston Historic District.

The settled property was part of a large tract of land granted by the king in 1665 to eight lords proprietor, stretching from the southern Virginia border through northern Florida, and extending westward indefinitely. The territory of the Carolina proprietorship was whittled away over time, leaving South Carolina as a wedge between Georgia to the south and west and North Carolina to the north. North Carolina gradually separated from Charleston and the south simply because of geographic separation between Charleston and the area north of the Cape Fear River, and the fact that North Carolina in the early years was mainly settled by southern migration from Virginia, rather than by immigration through ports at Charleston, Georgetown, and Beaufort. The de facto separation became official in 1719.

In the coastal plain, South Carolina prospered during the colonial period, chiefly as a result of the involuntary but heroic efforts of African slaves who cleared swamps and forests to build great indigo, rice, and cotton plantations, generally owned by English and French Huguenot settlers, many of whom arrived by way of Barbados in the Caribbean. South Carolina in general and Charleston in particular were among the wealthiest of colonial locales.

Farther inland, settlement was somewhat less dependent on African slaves and more reliant on the work of immigrants from Scotland, Ireland, Wales, Germany, and Switzerland, although the use of slavery in that part of the state also took strong root over time, as cotton cultivation spread.

It could be said that the **American Revolution** began at Fort Charlotte in present-day McCormick County, where, on July 12, 1775, Patriot forces first used force to seize property belonging to the British. In any case, South Carolinians played a major role in the events leading up to the American Revolution, and South Carolina became a major battleground. This heritage indelibly marks the state to this day. Needless to say, the Daughters of the American Revolution are a big deal hereabouts. Prominent Revolutionary War landmarks are featured throughout the scenic drives in this book.

The period between 1783 and 1860 is the "glorious" **antebellum period** of fine mansions, prosperous plantations, and blooming magnolias. When the Old South is caricatured, this is the time that is brought to mind. Rhett Butler, of course, was from South Carolina, as were many real-life counterparts. Our scenic drives feature numerous homes, churches, and public buildings constructed in antebellum days.

The **Civil War** lasted only from 1861 until 1865, but, for some, this four-year period dominates our past. John C. Calhoun and other South Carolinians were among the staunchest defenders of the rights of states to allow slavery, and, in December 1860, South Carolina was the first state to secede from the Union, eventually joining ten other states in forming the Confederate States of America.

The first shots of the Civil War were fired in Charleston Harbor in April 1861, as Confederate troops on Morris and Sullivan's Islands bombarded Fort Sumter, still occupied by Federal forces. Naval and land skirmishes raged along the state's coast throughout the wartime period, and Union General Sherman brought the war tragically home to South Carolinians in the winter of 1865 with his burning and pillaging rampage through the middle of the state, climaxing with the torching of Columbia, the state's capital city.

A number of significant Civil War–era sites are included among our drives, and Confederate memorial monuments are located in virtually every county seat in the state. Like the DAR, the Sons of Confederate Veterans are quite in evidence, and the display of the Confederate flag continues to arouse extreme positive and negative emotions to this day.

Reconstruction, the period of Federal troop occupation from 1865 until 1877, was a period of equality and advancement for African Americans unmatched until the latter portion of the twentieth century. African Americans voted in large numbers, and African-American jurists, local officials, state legislators, and congressmen took office. Nevertheless, generations of South Carolina children later grew up being taught that this was a period of unmitigated horror ended only by the eventual disenfranchisement of African Americans, who made up the majority of the population of South Carolina until out-migration shifted the balance by the end of the 1930s.

It has taken South Carolina almost a century and a half to recover economically from the Civil War disaster. The state went from being very wealthy to extremely poor during the course of the war. The end of the slave labor economy, the shift in importance of industrial strength over agricultural strength, and the physical, human, educational, and political devastation caused by the war itself created a financial hole from which the state has only recently emerged.

In many ways, South Carolina's **post-Reconstruction period** lasted from 1878 until 1954, when the civil rights movement got under way in full force. Politics and economics became largely local. Small towns emerged as places for farmers to market their produce and buy their necessary wares from local merchants. Small banks arose in the towns, and artisans, lawyers, physicians, and others lived in settlements to provide their services to surrounding communities. Typically, the more important towns were located along railways and at significant cross-roads, as access to navigable rivers gradually became less important. In the hilly upper part of the state, industrialists built textile mills beside fast flowing rivers, and towns frequently grew up around the mills.

In the twenty years following withdrawal of Federal troops in 1879, white South Carolinians gradually eroded the political and economic power of African Americans, almost totally disenfranchising them by the turn of the century. Whites gained more prosperity than blacks, but lagged far behind the rest of the country. The Great Depression that hit the rest of the country in the 1930s ravaged the already poor, farm-based South Carolina economy beginning in the 1920s, when boll weevils ravaged cotton fields. Those at the bottom of the economic and political heap, African Americans, began heading north in large numbers, enough so that by the 1940s, whites outnumbered blacks in South Carolina for the first time in more than 200 years.

To some extent, the Old South that you see along our scenic drives is the South Carolina of this post-Reconstruction period. This is the South Carolina of small towns, small farms, small churches, small stores, large concentrations of blacks and whites living interspersed "out in the country," and unspoiled scenic beauty. It is a land of people living close to the land, of people whose parents, grandparents, and grandparents' grandparents chose to stay in communities where they grew up. It is not a land of huge wealth, but it is a land of considerable satisfaction with the way things are.

South Carolina's **civil rights movement era** was at its height from 1954, when a Clarendon County lawsuit resulted in the Supreme Court ruling to end school segregation, until 1972, when schools were finally fully integrated and blacks, empowered by the federal Voting Rights Act, began to make their impact at the polls felt, on behalf of both black and white candidates who were sympathetic to their aspirations. A little church where Clarendon County black parents met and organized in the early 1950s is featured on Scenic Drive 14.

The time frame since 1972 is the state's **New South period.** This has been a period of rapid economic growth, educational advancement, industrialization, and tourism development. Although here, as elsewhere, there is much yet to be done, race relations and the economic, social, and political status of African Americans have taken a quantum leap forward in the last half century.

Hopefully, development of South Carolina will continue to progress without diminution of the natural resources, historic character, and rural charm that make the Palmetto State such a special place.

PUBLIC LANDS

South Carolina's public lands are controlled by a variety of federal, state, and local entities, which have different rules for public access and use.

State parks are under the management of the South Carolina State Park Service, a division of the South Carolina Department of Parks, Recreation, and Tourism. Our drives take you to twenty-three parks, and close to several others. Many offer access at no charge, but there are small entrance fees for a few of the most popular, especially during summer at those that offer swimming. Annual passes, which provide unlimited admittance to all parks, are available.

Some parks that preserve important historic features are called State Historic Sites (for example, Oconee Station and Hampton Plantation). Parks with outstanding natural features are deemed State Natural Areas (Keowee-Toxaway and Woods Bay). A majority of facilities belonging to the State Park Service fall into three remaining categories: traditional parks (such as Table Rock), regional parks (Colleton), and outdoor recreation parks (Calhoun Falls).

Wildlife management areas (WMAs) and **heritage preserves** are under the jurisdiction of the South Carolina Department of Natural Resources. WMAs are managed for hunting, and WMA visitors are well advised to learn the hunting seasons, especially the periods for deer hunting in autumn. Hunting seasons vary significantly in different game zones throughout the state.

Heritage preserves are managed to preserve unique habitats, often protecting endangered plant or nongame animal species. However, hunting for game animals is allowed in some preserve areas. Both WMAs and heritage preserves are sometimes closed to public access in order to protect wildlife during sensitive seasons. There are no fees for admission to these properties.

South Carolina owns three **state forests,** managed for a variety of uses. Manchester State Forest (Scenic Drive 14) and Sand Hills State Forest (Scenic Drive 8) are featured in this volume. They charge no admission fees and offer miles of pleasant driving, hiking, and mountain biking.

National forests are managed by the U.S. Forest Service, a unit of the U.S. Department of Agriculture, for multipurpose use, including timber harvest and recreation of various types. In South Carolina, there are two national forests, Francis Marion (Scenic Drive 12) and Sumter. Sumter, located in the upper portion of the state, is composed of three diverse and geographically separate units: Long Cane Ranger District (Scenic Drives 4 and 5) and Enoree/Tyger Ranger District (Scenic Drive 7) in the piedmont, and Andrew Pickens Ranger District (Scenic Drive 1) in the mountains. There are no admission fees.

Although there are no large national parks in South Carolina, the state has six smaller units of the National Park system called **national monuments.** This book takes you to Congaree Swamp National Monument (Scenic Drive 15), Cowpens National Battlefield (Scenic Drive 3), Ninety-Six National Historic Site (Scenic Drive 5), Charles Pinckney National Historic Site (Scenic Drive 16), and Fort

Sumter National Monument (Scenic Drive 16), none of which charges an admission fee. These are managed by the U.S. National Park Service, a unit of the U.S. Department of the Interior.

National wildlife refuges, operated by the U.S. Fish and Wildlife Service of the Department of the Interior, are primarily managed as wildlife habitat, particularly for migratory birds. There are six national wildlife refuges in South Carolina; five of these—Carolina Sandhills (Scenic Drive 8), Santee (Scenic Drive 14), ACE Basin (Scenic Drive 19), Pinckney, and Savannah (both on Scenic Drive 21)—are included in our book. There are no charges for admission to the refuges, but access is sometimes restricted because of wildlife breeding seasons.

SEASONS AND WEATHER

The climate in South Carolina is ideal for sightseeing. Winters are mild, and spring and autumn are glorious. Some summer days can be uncomfortably warm, but that is why virtually all vehicles in the state have air-conditioning.

In summer, visitors often say, "It's not the heat, it's the humidity." Actually, it is both the heat *and* the humidity. However, frequent rains (often in the form of spectacular afternoon thunderstorms) cool things off and make summers pleasing for recreation. Summer temperatures range from average highs and lows of 84 degrees and 62 degrees Fahrenheit in the mountains to 91 degrees and 70 degrees Fahrenheit in the midlands. Because of invigorating sea breezes, the coast, with average highs and lows of 88 and 70 degrees, is slightly cooler than the midlands in the summer.

Apart from midsummer, South Carolina weather is very temperate. The long, delightful spring and autumn seasons make these times excellent for scenic driving.

High and low temperatures during the short winter period range from 51 and 28 degrees Fahrenheit in the mountains to 61 and 49 degrees along the seacoast, and many of the best sightseeing opportunities are in winter. In the mountains and other deciduous forest zones, scenic vistas are at their peak in winter, and winter along the mild-weather coast generally means no insect problems, no heat problems, low forest undergrowth, and high opportunity to view birds and other forms of wildlife. Winter, along with late fall and early spring, is the best time to travel the coastal plain.

The state's moderate rainfall (about 49 inches annually) is distributed fairly evenly geographically and seasonally.

HIGHWAY AND ROAD DESIGNATIONS

Highway and road designations are important and can sometimes be a little confusing. In this guide, our maps and directions indicate six basic types of roadways.

Interstate highways are written as I–26, I–95, and so on. The state is criss-crossed by five interstate highways: 20, 26, 77, 85, and 95. They are shown on our maps with the familiar interstate highway roadside shield symbol.

The older **United States highway** system is indicated on maps by the familiar roadside badge-shaped symbol in use on road signs across the country. These roads are identified as US 17, US 401, and so on. Sometimes, when the particular highway segment runs concurrently with a town or city street, or otherwise has a formal name, the name is shown behind a slash after the numeric designation.

South Carolina highways are state-maintained primary highways marked on roadways by signs displaying the highway number against a miniature outline of the state. In the maps in this book, however, these roads are indicated by a number inside a circle. These highways are identified with "SC" followed by the route number. As is the case with other highways, these roads are sometimes coidentified with slash-preceded names.

Secondary roads are nonfederal roads other than the primary highways in one of the above-indicated classifications. They usually have no roadside highway markers other than road signs at intersections. To find the number of a secondary road, look above any stop sign you encounter. A black horizontal sign should be there, emblazoned with a combination of white letters and numbers. For example, if you are traveling to Lower Whitewater Falls, you might find yourself on a road designated S-37-413, or SR-37-413. The 37 refers to the county (in this case, Oconee), and 413 is the road number. In our book, this road is designated as S-37-413, regardless of whether the prefix on the sign is S or SR.

As a result of the statewide 911 addressing effort, these roads now have written names as well, and these name signs, usually green, are often more prominent than the smaller black numeric signs. Secondary roads are indicated on our maps with unenclosed numbers. They are usually, but not always, paved.

Keep in mind that secondary road designations often change from county to county. For example, Key Bridge Road on Scenic Drive 4 changes numerical designation at Key Bridge, because Turkey Creek, which the bridge spans, is also the boundary between Edgefield and McCormick Counties. Key Bridge Road is S-33-227 north of the bridge and S-19-68 south of the bridge. Thus, do not be surprised at occasional sudden changes in secondary road nomenclature. Written names of roads may change without the numeric designations changing, and vice versa.

We generally stick with numeric designations in descriptions and maps because numeric designations have more consistency over distances, and are less likely to change from one intersection to the next, except when roads cross county lines. Additionally, map atlases that you may use to supplement our information usually show only road numbers. As is the case with United States and South Carolina highways, however, we sometimes indicate both the numeric and written names in the text.

USDA Forest Service roads in national forests are identified by "FR" followed by the road number. Typically improved gravel, but sometimes paved roads, they are shown on our maps with unenclosed numbers.

Town and city streets that do not have numerical designations are indicated with names only.

SCENIC DRIVE DESCRIPTIONS AND RELATED INFORMATION

Each drive description contains a standard set of information about the scenic drive.

General Description: A brief description of the drive and its highlights.

Special Attractions: Noteworthy places you will see along the way. Telephone numbers and other contact information are provided in Appendix A.

Location: A short description of where in South Carolina the drive route is located. This description complements the locator map on page vi.

Drive Route Numbers: A listing of roads you will be traveling. Both numbers and names are listed when both are available.

Travel Season: In South Carolina, every route can be enjoyed in every season. However, we try to provide an inkling of the seasons that might be most appealing.

Services: This item provides information on area towns in which travelers may find conventional hotels and motels, restaurants, grocery stores, automobile care, medical facilities, and other goods and services they may need.

The heart of each Scenic Drive presentation is a narrative description of what you can expect to see along the way and background information on areas and places, along with photographs and a detailed route map.

At the end of the book is the appendix section including: For More Information, packed full of addresses, telephone numbers, and Web sites for places mentioned in the various chapters; Helpful Organizations, with contact listings for public and private organizations that can provide additional information; and Bibliography and Further Reading, our annotated bibliography of reading materials.

ENJOY

South Carolina is a great place to visit and a great place to live. We hope you have as much fun using this book to explore the nooks and crannies of the Palmetto State's highways and byways as we did in compiling the information contained herein.

Blue Ridge Mountains

WALHALLA TO WHITEWATER FALLS

GENERAL DESCRIPTION: A spectacular 75-mile drive through forests, around and over mountains, and across rivers and gorges, offering majestic vistas and cool, idyllic resting spots. There are several opportunities to stretch your legs and visit waterfalls or follow mountain streams.

SPECIAL ATTRACTIONS: Walhalla, St. John's Evangelical Lutheran Church, Stumphouse Tunnel Park, Issaqueena Falls, Chattooga National Wild and Scenic River, Foothills Trail, Bad Creek Reservoir, Whitewater Falls, Lake Jocassee, Jocassee Gorges, Wiggington Scenic Byway, Walhalla State Fish Hatchery, Oconee State Park.

LOCATION: Northwest corner of the state.

DRIVE ROUTE NUMBERS: SC 28, S-37-226, Burrells Ford Road, SC 107, FR 710, Cherokee Lake Road, Cheohee Valley Road, S-37-534, S-37-57, SC 130, Bad Creek Road, S-37-413, S-37-325.

TRAVEL SEASON: All year. The upstate is especially beautiful in the spring when it is covered in wildflowers and in the fall when the trees are aflame in yellow, orange, and red foliage. Winter is good for distant vistas, and summers are shady and, for South Carolina, pleasantly mild.

SERVICES: Walhalla and Seneca have limited accommodations and services. A full range of motels, restaurants, and other services is available in Clemson.

See For More Information in the appendix for addresses and phone numbers of Attractions, Camping, Neat Places to Stay, Restaurants, Shops, Tours, and Nature-Based Services.

THE DRIVE

You begin in charming, historic Walhalla and then step back in time as you climb past apple orchards and ramshackle buildings into the forests of the southernmost Blue Ridge Mountains, at the bottom of the Appalachian Mountain chain. At Stumphouse Tunnel Park, you see Issaqueena Falls, where a lovely Indian woman successfully faked her demise. You cross the National Wild and Scenic Chattooga River into Georgia and quickly double back into South Carolina by recrossing the stream at Burrells Ford, hub of some of the state's most attractive hiking opportunities and site of two nearby gorgeous waterfalls.

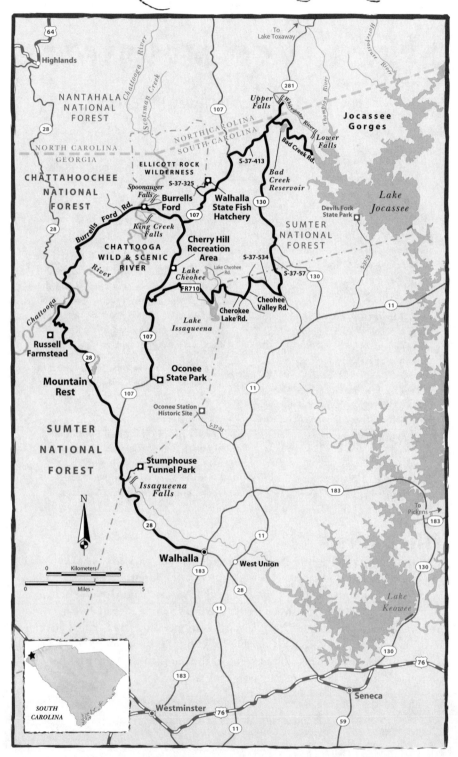

From Burrells Ford, you twist and turn through miles of forests and streams before emerging at Lake Issaqueena and heading northward and upward to Bad Creek Reservoir, the Whitewater River and Lower Whitewater Falls, Coon Creek Branch Natural Area, Jocassee Gorges, and Lake Jocassee. You then step into North Carolina to view the spectacular Upper Whitewater Falls, before heading back south along winding scenic Wigington Scenic Byway, stopping at the Walhalla Fish Hatchery before finishing at Oconee State Park, a place for many tastes.

WALHALLA TO STUMPHOUSE MOUNTAIN

Begin on SC 28/Main Street in downtown **Walhalla**, an attractive little town settled in 1850 by the German Colonization Society from Charleston. Nestled at the foot of the Blue Ridge Mountains, its name derives from a Norse mythology term meaning "Garden of the Gods," a place for fallen warriors to spend eternity as reward for their valor.

In mid-October, Walhalla holds Oktoberfest to celebrate its German heritage with a carnival and German food and music. In the spring, the community hosts the Oconee County Cultural Festival, celebrating Scottish, Native American and other heritages, in addition to German.

Walhalla features a traditional mid-twentieth-century main street lined with interesting shops, monuments, nineteenth-century churches, and stately old homes with wraparound porches. The small downtown shopping district is rich in antiques and crafts and hosts pleasant eateries.

Head northwest from the downtown shopping area on SC 28/Main Street. The tree-shaded median resumes as you pass the modern Oconee County Courthouse building on your left, with a war memorial out front.

At the intersection of Main and Church Street, on your left is **St. John's Evangelical Lutheran Church**, begun in 1859 and dedicated in 1861. The town clock is located in the steeple of this attractive, white wooden church with vaulted ceilings. An obelisk dedicated to the original German settler leaders rises in the median across from the church. Five blocks farther up the road, at Main and Poplar Streets, is a Confederate monument.

As you head north out of town, you pass Confederate flags, good ol' boy hangouts, kudzu, and junk vehicles that help remind you that you are entering *Deliverance* country as you begin a long, winding uphill drive. In the fall, you will spy numerous roadside stands selling apples and apple cider, as well boiled peanuts here and there. As you climb into the hills, enjoy distant vistas to the east and west.

After about 5 miles, you enter the Andrew Pickens Ranger District of Sumter National Forest. (General Andrew Pickens was a Revolutionary War hero in South Carolina's upcountry; General Thomas Sumter led Patriot troops in the Midlands.)

The entrance to **Stumphouse Tunnel Park** is about a half mile farther, on your right (east), immediately after the Yellow Branch Picnic Area on your left (west). Turn into the park on S-37-226 and ease your way down about a half mile around hairpin curves into a gully, along a roadway framed with dark, over-hanging mountain laurel and dogwoods. Turn right into the **Issaqueena Falls** parking area.

Issaqueena Falls

If you so desire, you can explore the beautiful 100-foot cascade by hiking about 0.2 mile down a pathway to the foot of the falls. Legend says that Issaqueena, a Cherokee woman married to an Englishman and subsequently captured by her countrymen, escaped and, in her flight, leapt over a precipice near the top of the falls. She fell only a short distance and eluded capture by hiding under an overhang now visible from the trail. The 6.5-mile **Blue Ridge Railroad Historical Trail** starts just above Issaqueena Falls, on the other side of a footbridge across Cane Creek.

The Enron-like Blue Ridge Railroad ended in this area. It was a grand dream of South Carolina statesman John C. Calhoun, who was a member of the original surveying team. The idea was to link the port of Charleston with the farms and burgeoning cities of the Midwest. The Civil War intervened, and the railroad was never completed. Its greatest monument, **Stumphouse Mountain Tunnel** (which wasn't completed either), can be explored if you are not afraid of the dark. Although the railroad was never built, the trail along the railroad bed endures, and offers fine hiking year-round.

To enjoy the rest of the park, walk or drive a few hundred feet past the picnic and recreation area to the entrance to Stumphouse Mountain Tunnel. This area has great natural variety. Trees include oak (mainly chestnut and chinquapin), maple, pignut hickory, tulip poplar, sassafras, pine, black walnut, locust, rhododendron, mountain laurel, dogwood, and sourwood. Trailing arbutus, elderberries, asters, wild hydrangea, Indian pink, honeysuckle, nettles, and snakeroot are under the trees; in the trees and undergrowth are red-eyed vireos, downy and pileated woodpeckers, rufous-sided towhees, cardinals, quail, and chickadees.

STUMPHOUSE MOUNTAIN TO BURRELLS FORD

Exit Stumphouse Tunnel Park and turn right (north) on SC 28. After 2.6 miles, you reach an intersection where SC 107 forks right (northeast). You should bear left (northwest) toward Mountain Rest and Highlands. Continue to climb past wooded hills and ravines. About 2.5 miles farther, you pass through Mountain Rest, a tiny community on the shores of Lake Leroy. On the north side of town, the ascent is steeper as you wind up a ridge before beginning a slow descent into the Chattooga River basin about 4 miles along.

Look for the marker about **Russell Farmstead** on your left (northwest) about 5 miles from Mountain Rest. The main house, once used as an inn for mountain wayfarers in the late 1800s and early 1900s, is long gone, but there is evidence of its remains. Some outbuildings are still about, including a cool, enchanting springhouse on a gurgling creek, which, in effect, served as the refrigerator for the old complex. This is a great place to stroll through quiet fields and woods, relax, and perhaps enjoy a snack.

A mile farther up the road is the Russell Bridge, which connects South Carolina and Georgia over the **National Wild and Scenic Chattooga River**. A parking lot on your right (east) just before the bridge offers an access point for fly fishers looking for mountain trout, as well as the Chattooga Trail, which heads northward on the South Carolina side of the river for 15 miles. On the Georgia side of the stream, the trail continues downriver for 20 more miles.

The Chattooga is a white-water river containing a large number of Class 3, 4, and 5 rapids that are extremely popular with rafters and kayakers from the Russell Bridge southward. Boats are banned upstream from the bridge. Much of the movie *Deliverance*, based on South Carolinian James Dickey's novel of the same name, was filmed on the portion of the river below the Russell Bridge.

Cross over the bridge into Rabun County, Georgia, and the Chattahoochee National Forest. A turnout with good views is just on the Georgia side, on your right. Immediately (0.3 mile) beyond the turnout, look for the second dirt and gravel roadway, Burrells Ford Road/Forest Road 646. Turn right (northeast).

Follow this road for 7 miles to a rustic bridge that takes you over the Chattooga River at Burrells Ford, back into South Carolina and the Sumter National Forest. This route takes you through thickly forested hillsides and ravines, past Carrol Mountain on your left and Mose, Oakey Top, and Rand Mountains on your right. At Persimmon Gap, you join Reed Creek and then Hedden Creek as you continue north for another mile before arriving at a junction at Carey Gap. Bear right (east) here to remain on your way to Burrells Ford, a mile away. Bee Bait Mountain rises to your left.

Cross the bridge eastward into South Carolina and the **Burrells Ford Recreation Area**. The river usually is rather peaceful on the stretch passing under the modest span. You may park on the roadside and look around.

The **Chattooga Trail** runs north and south from this point, and this is the best place to access it. A wild, rushing river, crashing waterfalls, coves lush with mountain laurel, and brilliant wildflowers make the Chattooga Trail a favorite of hikers who, because boating and rafting are banned along this stretch, share their delights only with other hikers and occasional fly casters. The trail follows the edge of the Chattooga River, a pristine and federally designated National Wild and Scenic River, often along the banks of the river and sometimes high up on bluffs. The mountains and cliffs of the Georgia side of the river form a scenic backdrop. Hikers ascend and descend frequently as they cross numerous small streams and wind around and through a seemingly endless series of coves and ravines and along mountain ridges. Locations for taking a cool dip abound.

The northward route is indicated by three large boulders and a small sign on the left indicating the way to Ellicott Rock Wilderness Area. If you head northward on the Chattooga Trail, you will have opportunities to connect with other beautiful pathways, including the Foothills Trail, East Fork Trail, and Fork Mountain Trail. However, you need only walk about 0.2 mile north to reach a sign indicating that **Spoonauger Falls** is on a spur 200 yards to the right (east). Take this spur. The trail follows switchbacks up a cascading series of small falls along Spoonauger Creek until it reaches the base of Spoonauger Falls, a spectacular crashing cascade also known, for self-evident reasons, as Rock Cliff Falls.

Continue east on Burrells Ford Road/FR 708 for 0.4 mile. You will see a large parking area on your right. This is an access point for the **Foothills Trail**, which crosses Burrells Ford Road just east of the parking area, as well as connections to the Chattooga Trail. The Foothills Trail stretches for more than 100 miles south and east from here, and is the premier backpacking experience in South Carolina. A primitive campground is a few hundred yards south, and modest rest room facilities are available at the parking area.

A great short-term experience is to hike southward along the Foothills Trail about a mile, taking a left on a short spur to visit roaring **King Creek Falls**, which makes a spectacular 70-foot tumble down a steep granite face into a lush gorge smothered in mountain laurel and rhododendron.

Fly fishing in Chattooga River

BURRELLS FORD TO WHITEWATER FALLS

From the parking lot, drive east uphill on Burrells Ford Road/FR 708 for 2.8 miles past King Creek and Mill and Ridley Mountains to your right to regain pavement and reach SC 107. Turn right (south) on SC 107/State Park Road. After 1.3 miles, you will see a pullover on your right for Moody Springs Picnic Area. It offers two stone picnic tables and grills, a modest rest room, and artesian well water flowing through a pipe jutting from the side of a hill. Moody was an early settler in the area, and Moody Springs became a favorite stopping point in the 1800s for travelers heading northward to High Hampton in North Carolina.

Continue southward. On your left just 0.1 mile farther is **Cherry Hill Recreation Area** and the northwestern trailhead for Winding Stairs Trail, a pleasant, easy

3.5-mile jaunt. On your right is the trailhead for Big Bend Trail, which takes hikers 3.2 miles to crashing Big Bend Falls on the Chattooga River, as well as connections with the Chattooga and Foothills Trails.

Drive south 2.6 more weaving miles, passing more little picnic areas, old homes, beautiful wildflowers, mixed forest, and Crane and Morton Mountains before turning left (east) onto FR 710/Winding Stairs Road (also known as Cheohee Road). The Foothills Trail crosses the highway here, leading from the Chattooga River on the west past Dodge Mountain southward to Oconee State Park. FR 710 is paved for only a short distance before giving way to dirt and gravel.

This lovely drive winds almost as much as the Winding Stairs Trail on an old roadbed to the north. You head downward through rich vegetation of mountain laurel and rhododendron thickets, dogwoods, hardwoods, ferns, and wildflowers. You pass around, over, and through numerous gulches, ravines, and ridges. In the winter, you have great vistas and can see for many miles. Autumn offers wonderful color, and spring and summer serve up lush flora.

The road follows and crosses Wash Branch down a long gulch as you slow down for hairpin turns while enjoying the shade of trees extending their long branches over the road. At about 3.4 miles, you cross a small brook and reach the southern trailhead of **Winding Stairs Trail**, on your left. You immediately cross the **West Fork of Townes Creek** and see on your right some large boulders and a series of primitive camping areas.

Head uphill for a mile through more scenic forest to cross Jumping Branch Road and continue on what has become Cheohee Road.

Circle southeast, then north, and merge right (northeast) on Jumping Branch Road to ride along a curving road around the northern top of **Lake Issaqueena** with neat waterfront homes on your right and green mountains to your left. Cross Cranes Creek after a mile and proceed east another half mile before turning left (north) onto Cherokee Lake Road. Head north on Cherokee Lake Road to the intersection where Lake Cheohee Road heads north, to your left. You bear right (east) to stay on Cherokee Lake Road.

For a pretty detour, follow Lake Cheohee Road northward beside Cranes Creek for a little over a mile to see the private, romantic Moody Cove community surrounding a sterling, placid body of water.

Continuing eastward on Cherokee Lake Road, cross Cheohee Creek after 1.4 miles, then turn left (north) on Cheohee Valley Road. Drive 1 mile and turn right (east) on S-37-534/Easy Street. Go 1.8 miles on Easy Street. Turn left (north) on S-37-57/North Little River Road to pass charming, steepled Little River Baptist Church, established in 1845, and go downhill across Mill Creek and then uphill through white pines and other fir trees to reach SC 130/Whitewater Falls Road, 2.2 miles from Easy Street.

Turn left (north) on SC 130 and climb steeply through forestland with attractive vistas here and there. After 5 miles, you pass S-37-413 to your left and continue another 0.7 mile to a right (east) turn for Duke Energy's **Bad Creek Reservoir**, with signs pointing toward the Foothills Trail and Whitewater River.

Turn right onto Bad Creek Road and travel 0.4 mile. Observe on your right Bad Creek Reservoir, a 1,200-foot-high rock-lined bowl of water. At night, when electricity demand is low and cheap nuclear power is in maximum supply, water is pumped from Lake Jocassee below to Bad Creek Reservoir above. At peak demand times during daytime hours, the reservoir water is released by Duke Energy through hydroelectric turbines to produce electricity when it is most needed and most valuable.

After 1.8 miles more, you come to a left (north), where signs point to Muster Ground Road and an access point for the Foothills Trail. A parking lot with small rest rooms and a couple of pay phones is a few yards down Muster Ground Road. From here, you can walk 0.6 mile over a ridge to the **Whitewater River** and several hiking options. Two bridges offer a good view of the Whitewater, an unusually clear and pristine stream with native populations of rainbow and brown trout, unusual for South Carolina streams, which normally rely on stocking with hatchery-reared fish.

One hiking option is to follow the 1-mile trail to the **Coon Branch Natural Area**. The path moves through a thick forest across a series of five bridges over tributaries, as towering hemlocks, aging hardwoods, and emerald rhododendrons highlight the way. At the end of the pathway is the Coon Branch Natural Area, a twenty-acre grove that's a treasure of never-felled timber, a glimpse of what this area looked like centuries ago, before the arrival of Europeans. The largest Fraser magnolia in the state grows here, 6 feet around and 86 feet tall. Giant tulip poplars, hemlocks, and chestnut oaks abound.

Another option is to follow the Foothills Trail and then a spur to reach an observation deck overlooking the beautiful **Lower Whitewater Falls**, crashing 400 feet to the backwaters of Lake Jocassee. With the Whitewater River descending over six cascades during its 800-foot tumble to the lake, the Upper and Lower Whitewater Falls together form the highest series of falls in eastern North America.

From the Whitewater River bridges, you can also hike northward, and uphill, to the Upper Whitewater Falls, or eastward to the Thompson River, 3 miles away. For the most hardy, the Foothills Trail continues eastward through the **Jocassee Gorges** for about 30 miles, and then onward to Table Rock and Mountain Bridge Natural Area.

Continue east on Bad Creek Road for another 1.5 miles, enjoying enticing views of mountains and valleys. Pull into Visitors Outlook and stroll under shade trees in the viewing area surrounding the parking lot. To your east and north is a deep, blue-green arm of **Lake Jocassee**, and a peninsula jutting from the Jocassee Gorges area. On clear days, there's a distant view of Lower Whitewater Falls. To the south is the larger body of Lake Jocassee.

Return to SC 130, turn right, and continue north for a half mile, crossing the North Carolina state line and immediately turning right (east) into the parking lot for **Upper Whitewater Falls**. The parking area has picnic areas, rest rooms, and water fountains. Park and walk several hundred feet to a spectacular overlook of the 400-foot Upper Falls, pausing along the way to look south to Lake Jocassee in the distance. The walkway is paved and handicapped accessible. Steps allow you to go downward for vistas that are even more dramatic. If you continue farther downward, you will reach the Foothills Trail, leading southward and across a suspension bridge to the Bad Creek area, and westward toward the Chattooga River.

WHITEWATER FALLS
TO OCONEE STATE PARK

Exit the parking area, turn left (south), pass a spot where the Foothills Trail crosses the highway, and head downhill back into South Carolina. After a mile, turn right (west) onto S-37-413, and begin your enjoyment of the **Wigington Scenic Byway**, which stretches from this point to Oconee State Park, 15 miles away and 1,300 feet lower.

Along this 2.3-mile segment of S-37-413, enjoy views of mountains and forestlands, and, to the south, great distant vistas of lakes and lowlands. You may want to stop at one of the turnoffs on your left.

When you reach the stop sign at SC 107, consider turning right (north) to drive 0.2 mile to stop at Sloan Bridge Picnic Area. This is the site of the northeastern trailhead for the Fork Mountain Trail, as well as another access point for the Foothills Trail, which heads both east and south from here.

From the intersection of S-37-413 and SC 107, turn left (south) toward Walhalla. Drive 2.3 scenic miles downhill, and turn right (west) onto S-37-325/Fish Hatchery Road. Drive 2 curving, downward miles to the parking lot of the **Walhalla Fish Hatchery**. Formerly a federal facility built by the Works Progress Administration and Civilian Conservation Corps in the 1930s, it is now operated by the South Carolina Department of Natural Resources and is open to the public from 8:00 A.M. to 4:00 P.M. daily, including weekends. Rainbow, brown, and brook trout are raised here and released into streams in the upper part of the state. More than 250,000 trout are raised and released annually. In addition to the large outdoor tanks where the growing fish can be seen, visitors can view an interpretive display.

The picnic area offers many spots for relaxing in the shade of giant hemlocks and white pines and to play in the shallows of the East Fork of the Chattooga River. Offering handicapped access for fishing in the stream, the area is a great spot for bird-watching. Broad-winged hawks, pileated woodpeckers, great crested flycatchers, eastern woodpewees, wood thrushes, red-eyed vireos, warblers, blue

Walhalla State Fish Hatchery

jays, bluebirds, cardinals, and Carolina chickadees are among the numerous feathered friends seen here.

The fish hatchery is also the northeastern trailhead for the East Fork Trail, which leads 2.5 miles to the banks of the Chattooga River through a lush, fertile gorge filled with unusually large white pines, along with hemlocks, mountain laurels, winterberries, and sweet pepperbushes. The trail is often smothered in rhododendrons and also features maples, oaks, hickories, tulip poplars, yellow birches, Fraser magnolias, hollies, and dogwoods. The East Fork is a large, swift, rocky stream that dances over rocks and around boulders along the south side of the pathway throughout the length of the trail.

Except for short distances at the two ends of the trail, the entire length of the East Fork Trail lies within the southernmost region of **Ellicott Rock Wilderness Area**, a pristine 9,012-acre preserve on national forest lands closed to logging, vehicles, and activities that disturb the natural state of the area.

Exit Fish Hatchery Road and turn right to resume your trip southward on beautiful SC 107. There are scenic outlooks and picnic areas, along with a few rustic structures and a deer viewing area, as you wind your way downward, passing Burrells Ford, Moody Springs, Cherry Hill Recreation Area, and Winding Stairs Road before arriving at the rhododendron-framed entrance to Oconee State Park, 9.6 miles south of Fish Hatchery Road.

Turn left (east) into the park to complete your drive. **Oconee State Park** was created in the 1930s, and its rustic facilities bear the stamp of the Civilian Conservation Corps (CCC), President Franklin Roosevelt's Depression-era army of public works builders. At 1,165 acres, the park encloses two mountain lakes. Although the park landscape is not conspicuously mountainous, its lovely rolling terrain makes for surprisingly challenging hiking, and if you don't want to walk around, you can still enjoy circling through the park's interlacing roadways. In addition to hiking, the facility also features lake swimming, paddle and pedal boat rentals, and an archery range.

Hiking is delightful, as Oconee State Park offers five trail opportunities, each with its own special attractions. Oconee and Old Waterwheel Trails are about 2.5 miles each and entirely contained within the park, while Tamassee Knob Trail and Hidden Falls Trail are each 2 miles one-way and extend beyond the park's boundaries. Finally, Oconee State Park is the western terminus for the Foothills Trail, which extends more than 100 miles to Table Rock and Caesars Head.

Oconee State Park charges a small admission fee and is open 7:00 A.M. to 7:00 P.M. during cold weather months, and until 9:00 P.M. during daylight savings time.

2

Mountain Bridge Natural Area

JONES GAP TO KEOWEE-TOXAWAY

GENERAL DESCRIPTION: This 80-mile drive takes travelers through the Mountain Bridge Natural Area and up and down the Blue Ridge Escarpment. A long precipice at the southern edge of the Blue Ridge Mountains, the escarpment was aptly named "The Blue Wall" by the Cherokee Indians. Along the way are spectacular views, mountain lakes, and the highest mountain peak in South Carolina.

SPECIAL ATTRACTIONS: Middle Saluda River, Caesars Head Overlook, Symmes Chapel at Pretty Place, Table Rock Mountain, Lakes Oolenoy and Pinnacle, Sassafras Mountain, Jocassee Gorges, Eastatoe Creek, Reedy Cove Falls, Lake Keowee.

LOCATION: Northwest corner of the state.

DRIVE ROUTE NUMBERS: S-23-97/Jones Gap and River Falls Road, SC 11, US 276, S-23-15/Solomon Jones Road, SC 8, S-39-25/East Ellison Road, US 178, S-39-199/F. Van Clayton Memorial Highway, S-39-237, S-39-100, S-39-92, Water Falls Road, S-39-143, SC 133, S-39-347/Museum Circle, S-39-74/Cabin Road.

TRAVEL SEASON: All year. The upstate is especially beautiful in the spring when it is covered in wildflowers and in the fall when the trees are aflame in yellow, orange, and red foliage.

SERVICES: Motels, restaurants, and other services are available in nearby Pickens, Easley, and Greenville.

See For More Information in the appendix for addresses and phone numbers of Attractions, Camping, Neat Places to Stay, Restaurants, Shops, Tours, and Nature-Based Services.

THE DRIVE

This ride takes you through the forested peaks and valleys of one of the most varied ecosystems in the eastern United States. You will be amazed and delighted with the variety of flora, fauna, and diverse wildlife, as well as the striking views at Caesars Head Lookout and Pretty Place, and the 360 degree panorama atop Sassafras Mountain. This area is home to two of the four National Wild and Scenic Rivers in the southeastern United States, Chattooga and Horsepasture, as well as more than fifty white-water waterfalls, some of which are the most

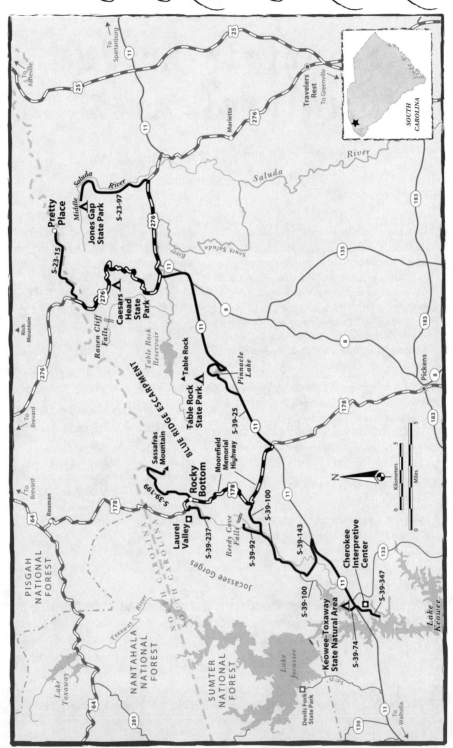

spectacular in this part of the country, including Whitewater Falls, Laurel Creek Falls, Reedy Cove Falls, Toxaway Falls, Raven Cliff Falls, and Rainbow Falls.

You begin on the Middle Saluda River at Jones Gap State Park and ride up US 276 to Caesars Head State Park, which combines with Jones Gap State Park to form the bulk of the 10,000-acre Mountain Bridge Natural Area. After meandering along the North Carolina state line to Symmes Chapel at Pretty Place, head back down the mountain and travel over rolling hills to see spectacular views of bald Table Rock and Pinnacle Mountains. Next you drive up a curving roadway to reach the top of Sassafras Mountain, the highest peak in South Carolina, before descending into Laurel Valley and Eastatoe Valley on your way to the Keowee-Toxaway State Natural Area.

Much of this upstate area has been carefully preserved through state, federal, and private initiatives, so future generations may continue to enjoy its pristine state. In addition to state parks and several heritage preserves, the state is also the proud owner of 32,000 acres of the Jocassee Gorges, an area of mountains, gorges, rivers, and lakes connecting Sumter National Forest on the Georgia–South Carolina border on its west side with the Mountain Bridge Natural Area on its east flank.

JONES GAP TO PRETTY PLACE

This drive begins at **Jones Gap State Park**, 5.5 miles off US 276/SC 11 on S-23-97/Jones Gap Road. (S-23-97 is called River Falls Road for the first 1.5 miles from the intersection with US 276/SC 11, and Jones Gap Road for the last 4 miles into the park.) The park's visitor center and office are a short walk through the woods off the dark, wooded parking area on the Middle Saluda River, the first river in South Carolina to be designated a State Scenic River. The Middle Saluda and its Cold Spring Branch tributary are part of the local beauty. The visitor center houses an interpretive environmental learning center with nature exhibits. The park is open seven days a week year-round from 9:00 A.M. to 6:00 P.M.; hours are extended to 9:00 P.M. daily from Memorial Day to Labor Day.

Between 1840 and 1848, Solomon Jones, for whom the area is named, built a 5.5-mile road across Caesars Head to Cedar Mountain, North Carolina. Originally, Jones Gap Road was a toll road, but it was abandoned in 1910. Now it is Jones Gap Trail, a pleasant walkway that allows hikers to meander along and across the Middle Saluda River and to the Caesars Head area. The trail wanders through a pristine valley, home to more than 400 species of plants, many rare and endangered.

Three much more difficult trails also interconnect here: Rim of the Gap (5.2 miles), Pinnacle Pass (13 miles), and Falls Creek–Hospital Rock (6.1 miles).

Leave Jones Gap State Park and take a slow, winding ride along S-23-97/Jones Gap Road for 1.5 miles and S-23-97/River Falls Road for 4 miles, to the intersection where SC 11 and US 276 occupy the same roadway. The road hugs mountains and fields of corn, beans, tomatoes, and kudzu. Pines, oaks, magnolias, and cedars form a canopy over the road in places, giving the passage a cathedral-like mystery—dark, cool, and serene. Old barns, grazing horses, and mountain bungalows are tucked behind trees or atop steep hills lavished with wildflower gardens.

At the intersection of S-23-97/River Falls Road and SC 11/US 276, turn right onto SC 11/US 276 and travel west toward Caesars Head. Along this stretch, you'll see a few exclusive residential developments, as well as cute bungalows, log cabins, and horses grazing in green pastures tucked on both sides of the road. Big J. Blythe Shoals Produce is on your right. Stop for peaches, okra, beans, cantaloupe, corn, and other seasonal produce.

About 4.1 miles from the intersection with River Falls Road, veer right, away from SC 11, and follow US 276 west toward Caesars Head. Caesars Head State Park is almost 8 miles from this turn. Here, US 276 is a narrow, curving road through thick forest. Making an extremely steep climb up the Blue Ridge Escarpment, you experience several hairpin turns while enjoying a mountain stream, bald rock faces, and small waterfalls. Sometimes it looks as if the road drops completely off the mountain. There are several pull-offs where you may stop to explore the dark and dense woods or just savor the view.

Once you see the Mountain House Restaurant on your left, you're almost at the **Caesars Head State Park** entrance. The park is open Monday through Sunday from 9:00 A.M. to 6:00 P.M.; during daylight saving time, hours are 9:00 A.M. to 9:00 P.M.

This park is one of the hot spots of the Upcountry because its elevation of 3,208 feet allows for unusually long-distance visibility. Barring fog and haze, you can see 50 miles on a clear day at Caesars Head Lookout. Table Rock and Pinnacle Mountains are in easy view, and, in the distance, the Blue Ridge mountain range and the skyline of Greenville can be discerned.

An on-site park naturalist conducts visitors' programs and workshops throughout the year, as well as bird walks, nature hikes, and overnight backpacking trips. Wildflowers bloom throughout the park, so you may encounter a diverse variety, such as grass-of-Parnassus, yellow fringed orchid, bluet, bird-foot violet, columbine, Indian pink, large whorled begonia, Indian pipe, bloodroot, cardinal flower, flame azalea, jack-in-the-pulpit, fire pink, wild geranium, mountain laurel, pussytoes, hepatica trillium, yellow lady's slipper, jewelweed, Indian paintbrush, and dwarf crested iris. The visitor center displays photographs of many of these spectacular blossoms.

A network of trails takes hikers across several mountains. Raven Cliff Falls near Caesars Head State Park is reached via a 2-mile trail to an overlook, or a 3.3-mile hike to a bridge below the falls. It is one of the highest waterfalls in the eastern United States, with a splendid 420-foot cascade. Bill Kimball–Coldspring Branch Loop (4.6 miles) and the Naturaland Trust Trail (9.5 miles), both quite strenuous,

Caesars Head Lookout

also connect near here, as do the western end of the Jones Gap Trail (5.5 miles) and the eastern end of the Gum Gap Segment of the Foothills Trail (12 miles).

Leaving Caesars Head, take a left out of the parking lot onto US 276. A mile north of Caesars Head, you will see the parking area for the moderately difficult trail to **Raven Cliff Falls**. The parking area is on your right and the trail is on your left. The awe-inspiring views of the Blue Ridge Escarpment and the falls make it well worth the effort to get there. The western trailhead for Jones Gap Trail is 1 mile farther, on the right.

On US 276, about 2.6 miles north of the Caesars Head parking lot, look on your right for a sign to Camp Greenville YMCA, immediately south of the North Carolina state line. Turn right (east) onto S-23-15/Solomon Jones Road. Mountain houses, brick bungalows, cornfields, and flower gardens filled with hollyhocks, zinnias, and wild daisies adorn this winding drive that crisscrosses the North and South Carolina border. After traveling 4.3 miles, you pass the camp office and a lake with a small stone waterfall on your left.

Take a right here and follow the signs toward Pretty Place and Symmes Chapel a mile away. Along this road, a few hundred feet past the office, two large marker stones indicate the entrance to the short but strenuous 1-mile trail to the bottom of **Rainbow Falls**, a beautiful setting where Cox Camp Creek plunges 100 feet and crashes onto rocks just in front of you. On sunny days, rainbow prisms glisten in the mist.

L. E. SMOOT MEMORIAL LIBRARY
9533 KINGS HIGHWAY
KING GEORGE, VA 22485

A stone wall and iron gates adorn the entrance to **Pretty Place**. Pass through the gates and see **Symmes Chapel** perched on the edge of the mountain overlooking the Middle Saluda Valley. Park and walk into the stone structure, where you will see a spectacular panoramic view of the valley and nearby mountains. When not reserved for weddings or other private use, the chapel, ringed by forty-nine inspirational plaques, is open to the public. It is quiet and peaceful, a great place for a breezy picnic or just a reflective break.

PRETTY PLACE TO SASSAFRAS MOUNTAIN

Head back on S-23-15/Solomon Jones Road and take a left on US 276, heading south and east and downward on the curving highway. For the first 6.5 miles after you pass the Caesars Head park headquarters until you reach the intersection of US 276 and SC 8, you might want to travel in a low gear. Veer right onto SC 8 toward Table Rock State Park. Travel on SC 8 for only 1.4 miles, and then, at a stop sign, take a right (west) onto SC 11. Table Rock State Park is 5.6 miles ahead.

On a tree-lined highway on the way to Table Rock State Park, Caesars Head, Table Rock, and other mountains sit to your right and in front of you. Aunt Sue's, an old-fashioned shopping area and restaurant that offers home-cooked meals, is on the right and offers a good place to eat and shop.

Table Rock State Park Headquarters and Cherokee Foothills Visitors Center are to the left of SC 11. The headquarters is a log cabin on the bank of Lake Oolenoy, named for the Cherokee Chief who sold the property to the state. The headquarters building offers a fantastic view of Table Rock's bald face. Cherokee Indians believed their ancestral chieftain god used the "Sah-ka-na-ga," the Great Blue Hills of God, as he chose. He dined by sitting on 2,600-foot Pinnacle Mountain, and used the 1.3-billion-year-old granite of Table Rock Mountain as his table.

To visit the park and its restaurant and camping area, cross SC 11 and enter a dark, forested area on S-39-25, a slender 3-mile loop that can be difficult to maneuver. The forest is thick, deep, and filled with rhododendrons.

Listed on the National Register of Historic Places, the park was established in 1935 in an effort to protect the beauty of the area. The Depression-era Civilian Conservation Corps (CCC) developed the park using rustic designs and locally available building materials. You can see evidence of this original construction in the lodge, restaurant, bathhouse, two picnic shelters, the lake spillway, and dozens of other log and stone structures.

Table Rock Mountain, reaching 3,200 feet, overlooks one of the state's oldest and most popular recreation areas. Camping, boating, fishing, swimming, nature trails, summit hikes, a restaurant, nature programs, and rental cabins are among the offerings. The park covers 3,000 acres of mostly oak and mixed pine/hardwood forests, home to such birds as peregrine falcons, ravens, and worm-eating warblers. A naturalist at the nature center schedules daily programs during the summer for visitors, and the thirty-six-acre Pinnacle Lake offers supervised swimming, rental canoes, and pedal boats. The park has a carpet golf course and playgrounds, picnic tables, and shelters. Fishing for bass and catfish is allowed in nonmotorized boats.

The park has a substantial trail system that is designated a National Recreation Trail. The short Carrick Creek Nature Trail begins behind the nature center and connects with two longer hiking segments. On the west side of the Carrick Creek Nature Trail loop is the Sassafras Mountain Segment of the Foothills Trail, leading to Pinnacle Mountain, 4 miles away, past Sassafras Mountain, 9 miles away, and on to Oconee State Park, 85 miles from Table Rock. On the east side of the nature trail, the hike to the top of Table Rock Mountain is a rugged 3.4 miles. From here, hikers can connect to Pinnacle Mountain and descend via Mill Creek Falls and Carrick Creek to complete a 10-mile loop.

Exit the park through the west entrance and turn right (west) onto SC 11. Travel west approximately 3 miles on SC 11, where you will see a stop sign and intersection with US 178. Take a right (north) at the stop sign onto US 178 West/Moorefield Memorial Highway, toward Rocky Bottom and Rosman, North Carolina.

Two miles after your turn onto US 178, you will see signs noting that you are entering the Jim Timmerman Wildlife Management Area and the Garvey Wildlife Management Area. Drive slowly on this sharply curving road. At one point there is a mirror attached to a tree adjacent to a hairpin curve that allows drivers to see oncoming traffic.

At 6.3 miles from SC 11, you reach the Rocky Bottom community. Look for the sign to Rocky Bottom Camp of the Blind and turn right onto S-39-199/F. Van Clayton Memorial Highway to the top of Sassafras Mountain. The drive to the top is almost 5 miles on a roughly paved road through a forest of oaks, white pines, maples, tulip poplars, locusts, black birches, witch hazels, mountain laurels, rhododendrons, and Fraser magnolias. About 1.4 miles along the way is a small parking area on the left with access to the boulder-strewn area of Chimneytop Gap, less than a mile away along the Foothills Trail.

From the parking area just below the mountain summit, step out of your car and stroll a few feet to the peak of Sassafras Mountain; at 3,554 feet above sea level, it's the highest point in South Carolina. Peer through the woods and you'll see a magnificent view of the mountains and valleys below, filled with oaks, hickories, and other hardwoods. On a clear day you can see four states at once.

This is a great birding area. You may spot or hear a plethora of warblers, such as black-throated blue, worm-eating, Blackburnian, Swainson's, and chestnut-sided varieties. Other often glimpsed birds in this area are ruffed grouse, ravens, dark-eyed juncos, Carolina chickadees, pileated woodpeckers, and solitary vireos.

The mountaintop provides access to three sections of the Foothills Trail. The Gum Gap Segment takes hikers to the Raven Cliff Falls area and US 278, 12 miles eastward. A trail segment leading southeast takes hikers to the Nature

Center at Table Rock State Park, 9.4 miles away, and a pathway heading southwest leads 4.7 miles downward to Laurel Valley.

SASSAFRAS MOUNTAIN TO KEOWEE-TOXAWAY STATE NATURAL RESOURCE AREA

Head back down S-39-199/F. Van Clayton Highway to the bottom of the mountain, turn right on US 178, and travel a mile north to visit another wildlife viewing area on Laurel Valley Road. As you cross the bridge over **Eastatoe Creek**, turn left into Laurel Valley, on the eastern edge of the **Jocassee Gorges**.

On your immediate left, S-39-237, a short paved road, parallels the trout-filled stream gurgling swiftly by Laurel Valley Lodge and an assortment of mountain cottages. Straight ahead, a dirt road takes you to a parking lot and trailheads for the Eastatoe Creek Trail (1.8 miles) in Eastatoe Creek Heritage Preserve, and the Jocassee Gorges Segment of the Foothills Trail (31 miles). At times, the dirt road past this point is barricaded. When it is not barricaded, a rough, rocky road provides access for high-suspension four-wheel-drive vehicles to travel 7 more miles to the camping and picnic area beside the top of the 80-foot straight drop of Laurel Creek Falls. The South Carolina Department of Natural Resources controls this area of the Jocassee Gorges and can be contacted for further information about access.

Drive along S-39-237 to a small bridge that crosses eastward over the creek. Turn around, return to US 178, and travel 5 miles south to the intersection with S-39-100. A rustic beer joint sits at the edge of this intersection, along with a sign that directs visitors to turn right (south) to reach McKinney Chapel.

Take a right on S-39-100 and enjoy the wildflowers, grazing horses, farms, and mountain views that cover the quiet Eastatoe Creek valley. After 2 miles, cross a bridge over Eastatoe Creek and turn right (north) on S-39-92. Travel 0.9 mile and turn right (east) onto Water Falls Road, a dirt road with a sign pointing toward Reedy Cove Falls. Travel 0.4 mile until you reach a parking lot at the end of the road. From here, a quarter-mile path northward along Eastatoe Creek leads to the spectacular twin cascades of **Reedy Cove Falls**.

Exit the dirt road the way you entered, turn left (south) on S-39-92 and merge right (southwest) onto S-39-100 to continue along the west bank of Eastatoe Creek. Old tin-roofed mountain houses, forests, cabins, horses grazing in green fields, and rolling hills accompany you through this idyllic valley.

After 3 more miles, S-39-100 forks to the right, but you should turn left (southwest) and go a few yards to a stop sign. Turn left (south) again, and drive 2.3 miles on S-39-143, crossing Eastatoe Creek, to another stop sign. Turn right (southwest) on SC 11.

As you head west, Cedar Creek Mountain is on your left and other mountains are directly in front of you on your way to Keowee-Toxaway State Natural

Eastatoe Creek Valley

Area, 4 miles away. The entrances to the park are right after you pass SC 133 on your left and just before the highway crosses the bridge over the top edge of Lake Keowee.

A quarter mile past SC 133, turn left (south) onto S-39-347/Museum Circle to enter Keowee-Toxaway State Natural Area and its Cherokee Interpretive Center. The interpretive center tells the story of the Cherokee Indians who once roamed this area and the Cherokee Nation capital, Keowee, once beside the Toxaway River and now under lake waters. In the Cherokee language, keowee means "place of the mulberry groves," and toxaway means "land of no tomahawks."

Exit the south section of the park, cross SC 11, and enter the north section of the park on S-39-74/Cabin Road. This side of the 1,000-acre park provides the park's campgrounds, lake access, and hiking trails. Campers may fish in Lake Keowee and picnic in the shelters. Head down to the shore of Lake Keowee and enjoy spectacular views of beautiful rock outcroppings and the Blue Ridge Mountains.

Rhododendrons, mountain laurel and other lush mountain vegetation can be found along the streams and trails in the park, which offers the moderate 1.1-mile Natural Bridge Nature Trail and the strenuous 4.2-mile Raven Rock Hiking Trail featuring great overlooks of Lake Keowee.

The park is open daily from 9:00 A.M. to 9:00 P.M. during daylight saving time, 9:00 A.M. to 6:00 P.M. daily (until 8:00 P.M. Friday) during standard time.

cherokee foothills scenic highway

LAKE HARTWELL TO COWPENS

GENERAL DESCRIPTION: Passing by state parks, fruit orchards, and small villages, the 110-mile Cherokee Scenic Highway (SC 11) follows an ancient Cherokee pathway in the looming shadow of the southern edge of the Blue Ridge Mountains known to the Cherokee as the "The Great Blue Hills of God." It ends at Cowpens National Battlefield Park, site of a pivotal battle in the American Revolution.

SPECIAL ATTRACTIONS: Lake Hartwell, Oconee Station State Historic Site, Station Cove Falls, Lake Jocassee, Lake Keowee, Table Rock Mountain, Jones Gap, Campbell's Covered Bridge, and Cowpens National Battlefield.

LOCATION: Northwest corner of the state.

DRIVE ROUTE NUMBERS: SC 11, S-37-95/Oconee Station Road, S-37-25/Jocassee Lake Road, S-23-97/River Falls Road and Jones Gap Road, S-23-976/Tugalo Road, S-23-175/North Campbell Road, SC 414, S-23-114/Pleasant Hill Road, Campbell's Covered Bridge Road.

TRAVEL SEASON: All year. Spring and summer are especially beautiful, with blooming flowers and orchards. Autumn, however, guarantees a spectacularly colorful show.

SERVICES: Conventional accommodations and services are plentiful in Clemson, Anderson, Easley, Greenville, Spartanburg, and Gaffney. Limited services are available in Walhalla, Pickens, Landrum, and Chesnee.

See For More Information in the appendix for addresses and phone numbers of Attractions, Camping, Neat Places to Stay, Restaurants, Shops, Tours, and Nature-Based Services.

THE DRIVE

Along the Cherokee Foothills Scenic Drive, you enjoy magnificent views of foliage, lakes, and apple and peach orchards as you drive the ancient foothills of the Blue Ridge Mountains, one of the oldest mountain ranges on earth. The roadway follows an ancient Cherokee pathway, often right at the foot of the mountains. Beginning on the banks of Lake Hartwell, you travel north, past Westminster and

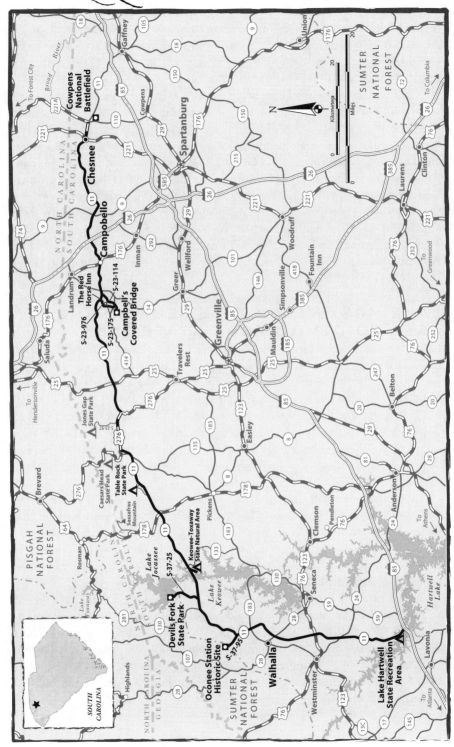

Walhalla to Oconee Station State Historic Site, and then to Devils Fork State Park on the banks of Lake Jocassee. You continue past Keowee-Toxaway State Natural Area, on the shore of Lake Keowee, past Table Rock and Jones Gap State Parks, and through fruit orchard country all the way to Campbell's Covered Bridge, north of Greer, and Cowpens National Battlefield.

The Cherokee Foothills Drive begins in Lake Hartwell State Recreation Area in one of South Carolina's most scenic and stimulating places, Oconee County. Oconee, meaning "water eyes of the hills," is situated in the extreme northwestern corner of the state, almost surrounded by the waters of the Chattooga River and Lakes Jocassee, Keowee, and Hartwell. The area was home to several Native American tribes, including the Creek and the Cherokee, but they gave up their lands in treaties signed in 1777 and 1785. After the American Revolution, settlers from other parts of the state began moving in, including Germans from Charleston, who founded the town of Walhalla in 1850. Several Revolutionary War heroes moved to present-day Oconee County after the war, including Andrew Pickens (1739–1817), Robert Anderson (1741–1813), and Benjamin Cleveland (1738–1806).

LAKE HARTWELL STATE RECREATION AREA TO DEVILS FORK STATE PARK

Lake Hartwell State Recreation Area offers boating and 14 miles of thickly wooded shoreline that provides ideal camping, hiking, swimming, and picnicking areas. The park is open between 7:00 A.M. and 9:00 P.M. during spring and summer months, and until 6:00 P.M. the rest of the year.

Exit the park and turn left (northeast) onto SC 11, a road that rolls up and down through lush fields and forests. While the rural landscape is scattered with some industrial development, old junkyards, and mobile homes, the overall feel of the ride is of rolling hills sluicing through idyllic farm country on the edge of a mountain range.

At 9.3 miles from Lake Hartwell State Recreation Area, the Cherokee Scenic Highway crosses SC 24. You may want to exit here and visit **Westminster**, a rustic mountain village 4 miles to the north. The South Carolina Apple Festival in Westminister begins on Labor Day and runs through the following weekend to celebrate the beginning of apple harvest season in Oconee County, the largest apple-producing area in the state.

About 10 miles farther, you cross SC 28, where a 1-mile northward detour will take you to the attractive shops and historic buildings of **Walhalla**, a quaint town settled by German immigrants in 1850. It has a traditional main street lined with interesting shops, monuments, a number of early nineteenth-century churches, and stately old homes with wraparound porches. In mid–October, Walhalla holds Oktoberfest to celebrate its German heritage, with a carnival and German food and music.

As you cross SC 28, you pass through West Union, an old town that has been overrun with sprawl. Some old buildings, such as a fire department housed in an old school, and fresh produce stands line the outskirts of town, along with well-manicured yards of ranch-style homes.

Turn left (northwest) at S-37-95/Oconee Station Road, 7 miles past SC 28. At 0.2 mile, the road forks, and you should veer left (west), passing a cinder block house and Pleasant Ridge Baptist Church on your left. The dappled and woodsy road is shady and punctuated with old trailers as it winds through farm-land, hilly fields, and tall pines. On the right, 2 miles from SC 11, is Oconee Station State Historic Site, a militia outpost and Indian trading place dating from the late eighteenth-century.

The 210-acre park has two historic structures, **Oconee Station** and the **William Richards House**. Oconee Station is the oldest extant structure in Oconee County, built in 1792 as part of a series of blockhouses along the South Carolina frontier. It was constructed at a frontier militia fort during a tense period between settlers and the Creek Indians. The last western militia outpost to be decommissioned in the upstate, the fieldstone blockhouse was garrisoned with troops until 1799, when they were removed. The site was later turned into an Indian trading post, operated by William Richards until his death in 1809.

The William Richards House, constructed in 1805 and believed to be the first brick house in northwestern South Carolina, is adjacent. Richards, an Irish im-

Oconee Station and William Richards House

migrant, established a successful trading post at Oconee Station. It declined when he died, but the home remained in the family through the twentieth century and is now on the National Register of Historic Places. The home was privately owned until the state purchased it in the mid-1970s. The two-story brick house is open for free tours. The park is open Wednesday through Sunday from 9:00 A.M. to 6:00 P.M., and also features a 1.5-mile hike to **Station Cove Falls**.

When leaving Oconee Station, take a left (southeast) back onto S-37-95/Oconee Station Road and retrace your route to SC 11. Turn left (northeast) and drive through rolling hills for 6 miles (2 miles past the intersection of SC 11 and SC 130) to a left (north) turn on S-37-25/Jocassee Lake Road for **Devils Fork State Park**, 4 miles away.

The ride to Devils Fork is serene. Mountains, gardens, wildflowers, and mobile homes adorn this road. Hoyett's Grocery and Tackle is a great shop to visit on the way into the park. It is a gas station and small store where you can purchase guided fishing trips, rent pontoons, and buy hunting and fishing licenses, bait and tackle, and drinks and food. Hoyett's also offers ferry service to the Foothills Trail on the north side of the lake.

The park's central feature is **Lake Jocassee**, named after an Indian princess whose name means "the place of the lost one." The lake is 1,000 feet above sea level, deep and icy cold, and surrounded by forested mountains. Its waters teem with brown trout, rainbow trout, white bass, smallmouth bass, largemouth bass, bluegill, and black crappie. The park has a tackle shop and boat ramps.

A 3.5-mile walking trail and 1.5-mile nature trail offer opportunities to view bloodroots, trout lilies, violets, jack-in-the-pulpits, and rare oconee-bells as you walk through forest inhabited by wild turkeys, white-tailed deer, raccoons, and grey foxes. In the trees are a variety of songbirds, including red-eyed vireos, scarlet tanagers, and many species of wood warblers. Peregrine falcons soar above.

In addition to a gift shop and eighty-four campsites, the 622-acre park offers twenty mountain villas that overlook the lake, complete with screened porches and fireplaces.

The park is open 7:00 A.M. to 9:00 P.M. during spring and summer, 7:00 A.M. to 7:00 P.M. the rest of the year.

DEVILS FORK STATE PARK TO CAMPBELL'S COVERED BRIDGE

Leave Devils Fork and head back out S-37-25/Jocassee Lake Road to SC 11. Take a left on SC 11 and travel northeast, crossing **Lake Keowee** after 3 miles and passing through **Keowee-Toxaway State Natural Area** (described in Scenic Drive 2). Stop and enjoy the interpretive center and walking paths.

When you cross Lake Keowee, you enter Pickens County, established in 1826. It had been Cherokee territory until the American Revolutionary War, when the Cherokee sided with the British and suffered defeat.

Forests and mountains lead the way down SC 11 for 9 miles to the intersection with US 178. A detour to the left (north) here will take you to Sassafras Mountain and Eastatoe Creek Heritage Preserve (see Scenic Drive 2).

As you continue past this intersection, look for majestic **Table Rock Mountain** on your left. Table Rock State Park and the Cherokee Foothills Visitor Center (described in Scenic Drive 2) are 4 miles past the intersection.

Aunt Sue's Restaurant is 2 miles past Table Rock State Park. After 5 more miles, SC 11 joins US 276 at the Greenville County line. The drive takes you through pastoral northern Greenville County, an area unexplored by many who are familiar with the textile mills and numerous international industries of the southern part of the county. Founded in 1786, Greenville County has the largest population in South Carolina.

Caesars Head (see Scenic Drive 2) is to the left (northwest) on US 276; US 276 and SC 11 run concurrently to the right (southeast). Turn right and travel 4 miles to S-23-97/River Falls Road, where a left (north) turn will take you 5.5 miles to **Jones Gap State Park** (described in Scenic Drive 2).

Continue on US 276/SC 11. Christmas tree farms, grazing horses, and huge old trees line the highway. Mountain cottages and bungalows are dispersed throughout the hills and valleys. Once you cross over the Middle Saluda River in the Cleveland community and drive a mile farther, take a left (east) to continue on SC 11. (US 276 heads south to Travelers Rest and Greenville.)

Mountains and forests still predominate as you travel 5 miles to the intersection with US 25, which connects Greenville with Hendersonville, North Carolina. Continue on SC 11 past horse pastures framed by mountains. About 4.5 miles after the entrance to Glassy Mountain Golf Course, look for S-23-976/Tugaloo Road on your right. Turn here and travel southeast for 1 mile. At the intersection with S-23-175/North Campbell Road, take a left (south) and drive through a picturesque agricultural valley with seasoned farm homes and scattered barns.

After about 0.7 mile, you'll see the **Red Horse Inn** on your left. This attractive bed-and-breakfast, situated on 190 acres in the midst of equestrian fox hunting lands, is a great place for a restful visit or romantic getaway. Rooms in the main inn and in outlying tin-roofed Victorian cottages offer breathtaking mountain views.

To drive on to Campbell's Covered Bridge, continue past the Red Horse Inn to the intersection with SC 414. Turn left (east) on SC 414 and drive slowly to a right-hand turn onto S-23-114/Pleasant Hill Road. Mountains puncture the horizon to the north as horses, goats, and bulls graze in vibrant green fields among abandoned farm buildings.

Drive slowly along Pleasant Hill Road for about a half mile; the turn to **Campbell's Covered Bridge** is not obvious. Look carefully for Campbell's Covered Bridge Road, and turn right (west). The bright red wooden bridge is less than a quarter mile down this residential road. Wooden slats compose the floor of the only remaining covered bridge in South Carolina. Constructed in 1909, it was restored in 1964 and then again in 1990.

CAMPBELL'S COVERED BRIDGE TO COWPENS NATIONAL BATTLEFIELD

Turn around at the bridge and backtrack to S-23-114. Turn left and head north across SC 414 for 2.8 miles to SC 11. Just after crossing Lister Road, the road turns to gravel, and you'll see the Greenville County Hounds Kennels on your left, where fox hunting equestrians hunt in the fall and winter months. If you're lucky, you may have to stop for a delightful view of red-coated horsemen parading their hounds across the road. You'll pass over the Middle Tyger River on a drive that takes you along a single-lane road through overhanging trees and past pastures and barns. Once you cross Smith Road, Pleasant Hill Road is flanked by two hunter-jumper barns.

At the intersection with SC 11, turn right (east) toward Campobello. *For an interesting detour, when you reach SC 14, go left (north) for 5 miles to the charming, restored village of* **Landrum***. Now filled with antiques, book stores, gift shops, and fine dining, Landrum was almost a ghost town prior to 1990. Pretty* **Lake Lanier** *is just west of town.*

Continuing on SC 11, cross into northern Spartanburg County, the name of which is derived from the Spartan Rifles, a local militia that played a major role in the Battle of Cowpens during the American Revolution. In spring, this highway is ablaze in pinks and yellows. In autumn, red and orange foliage leads you past rolling hills to the peach country of Spartanburg County.

Like Greenville County, Spartanburg County is heavily industrialized in its southern portion, in stark contrast to the pastoral northern section. Spartanburg County bills itself as "the fresh peach capital of the South," and for good reason. This one county produces more peaches than the entire state of Georgia.

As you enter peach country, you leave the mountains. In the village of Campobello, 4 miles from the junction with SC 14, you reach a traffic light at the intersection of SC 11 and US 176. Remain on SC 11 by turning left and driving through Campobello on Pine Extension.

Fragrant peach trees line the highway as you leave Campobello. With the mountains at your back, you traverse rolling hills past cultivated row crops, towering pecan trees, spicy fruit orchards, green pine forests, and fecund horse and cow pastures.

After crossing Interstate 26, 3.3 miles from Campobello, continue on SC 11 through New Prospect and Fingerville, past attractive houses, well-manicured yards, grazing cows, peach orchards, country homes, and old barns. Insistent signs beckon travelers to the numerous peach orchards on both sides of the road.

Enter Chesnee 16 miles past I–26. Here, SC 11 becomes West Cherokee Street, lined with two-story homes adorned by huge porches decorated with swings and rocking chairs. Verdant yards and lively flower gardens enhance the attractiveness of this small town. The Carolina Foothills Artisans Center in downtown Chesnee is a neat place to visit. The 3,200-square-foot facility, on your left just before the intersection of SC 11 and US 221, features juried art from throughout the state.

SC 11 is East Cherokee Road as you leave Chesnee and drive to **Cowpens National Battlefield Park**, 2.7 miles east. Turn right into the park.

A frontier pasture, Cowpens was the scene of one of the decisive battles of American history. On January 17, 1781, the British sustained one of the worst disasters of their Southern Campaign. American General David Morgan, surprised to learn of British Colonel Tarleton's approach, led his army to victory, achieving a vital link in the chain of British disasters in the South that led to a final defeat of the British at Yorktown, Virginia.

Originally called Cow Pens, the locale was a natural grazing area for cattle. Many streams, natural pea vines, and plentiful bamboo in the

Cowpens Battlefield Monument

area made ample forage for cattle. Cow Pens was well known to the ragtag militia who Morgan hoped to assimilate with his Continentals to help win this battle. The previous October, some of the same men had camped here on their way to the Battle of Kings Mountain. When Morgan sent out the word to meet him at Cow Pens, his men knew where to come.

Cowpens National Battlefield Park is operated by the National Park Service, and the visitor center and its museum are on your left shortly after you drive through the park entrance. Follow the Auto Tour Road along a 3-mile loop to complete your scenic drive.

The center presents a battle reenactment movie, *Day Break at Cowpens,* a narrated slide presentation, and a self-guided fiber optic map presentation. The park also offers a walking tour of the battlefield and a 1.25-mile nature trail that begins in the picnic area. The pleasant pathway takes walkers across streams and past beautiful ferns and wild ginger, an endangered species.

Pets are welcome as long as they remain on leash. The park is open from 9:00 A.M. to 5:00 P.M. daily. The Auto Tour Road closes at 4:30 P.M., and the walking tour closes at 4:15 P.M.

4

upper savannah river valley

LAKES HARTWELL, RUSSELL, AND THURMOND

GENERAL DESCRIPTION: Beginning on Lake Hartwell, this 110-mile drive past farmland, rural towns, lakes, and forests along the Savannah River National Scenic Highway takes visitors through the Upper Savannah River Valley along the state's western border with Georgia, an area sometimes called South Carolina's Freshwater Coast.

SPECIAL ATTRACTIONS: Lakes Hartwell, Russell, and Thurmond, Long Cane District of Sumter National Forest, John de la Howe Barn and Interpretive Forestry Trail, Mc-Cormick, Price's Mill, Key Bridge at Turkey Creek, Stevens Creek Heritage Preserve, and Sadlers Creek, Calhoun Falls, Hickory Knob, and Baker Creek State Parks.

LOCATION: Western border of South Carolina.

DRIVE ROUTE NUMBERS: SC 187, S-4-745/Sadlers Creek Road, SC 412/ Rainey Road, SC 81, S-33-7, Huguenot

Road, S-33-421, US 378, S-33-467, Gold Street/US 378, Main Street/S-33-31, Augusta Street, Oak Street, SC 28, US 221, S-33-138/ Price's Mill Road, S-33-227/Key Road, S-19-68/Key Road, S-19-118/Cold Springs Road, SC 23, S-19-139/Red Oak Grove Road, S-19-143/Garrett Road, S-33-88/ Garrett Road, S-19-345.

TRAVEL SEASON: All year. Spring displays wildflowers and blossoming trees, and fall is full of autumn color, especially throughout the Sumter National Forest.

SERVICES: Full services are available in Anderson and North Augusta, and most services are available in Abbeville, McCormick, and Edgefield.

See For More Information in the appendix for addresses and phone numbers of Attractions, Camping, Neat Places to Stay, Restaurants, Shops, Tours, and Nature-Based Services.

THE DRIVE

This ride winds past Lakes Hartwell, Russell, and Thurmond, through some of the most sought-out recreational areas in the state. In the eighteenth century, this area was South Carolina's western frontier, teeming with soldiers, frontiersmen, and Native Americans. The Cherokee owned Anderson County, the starting point of this ride, until the Patriots defeated them in 1776.

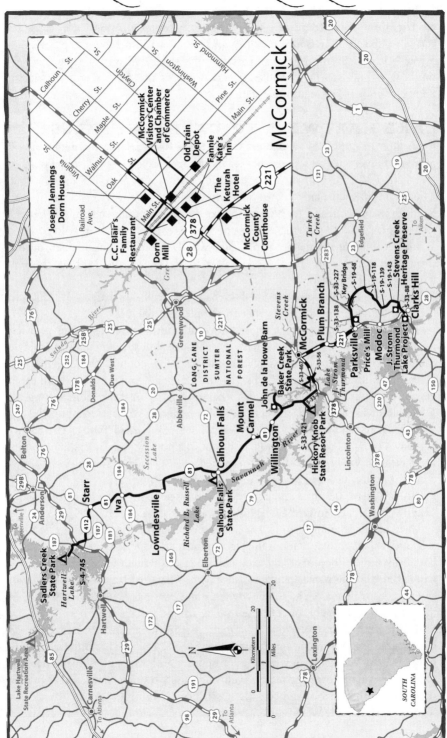

Built and operated by the U.S. Army Corps of Engineers to generate hydro-electricity, the three lakes total 153,000 acres of water, surrounded by 128,000 acres of public land in South Carolina and Georgia. Visitors along the Savannah River National Scenic Highway pass through sleepy villages and pastoral settings, in addition to the woodlands and water of the Long Cane District of Sumter National Forest and five state parks.

LAKE HARTWELL TO CALHOUN FALLS

Begin just off of SC 187 at **Sadlers Creek State Recreation Area**, which covers more than 395 acres on a peninsula extending into Lake Hartwell, a 56,000-acre lake with 1,000 miles of shoreline touching both South Carolina and Georgia. This beautiful man-made lake offers vast areas for sailing, waterskiing, fishing, boating, swimming, and Jet Skiing; the park offers camping and hiking on the lake's shore. Wildlife viewing is also popular here. Look for deer, wild turkeys, and other wildlife within the park's dark woods. Sadlers Creek is open during spring and summer months from 6:00 A.M. to 10:00 P.M., and 7:00 A.M. to 6:00 P.M. the rest of the year.

Turn west into the park on S-4-745/Sadlers Creek Road; travel 1.2 miles to the park entrance and a mile farther to the picnic pavilion.

Backtrack to SC 187, turn right, and head south. Travel 1.7 miles to a left (east) turn on SC 412/Rainey Road toward Starr, almost 6 miles ahead. Enjoy a rolling, curving drive through picturesque farming country dotted with hay fields, pecan orchards and old barns and farmhouses. If you're lucky, you'll catch glimpses of farmers tilling the fields or harvesting hay in this bucolic setting.

Small towns dot the road every few miles, remnants of water stops for the Savannah Valley rail system in bygone eras. Formerly named Twiggs, the town's name was changed to Starr Station, in honor of a popular railway engineer, when the Savannah Valley railroad was completed in 1884. Once home to an abundance of cotton farmers, **Starr** is now a sleepy rural outpost.

In Starr, drive 0.3 mile and continue on the scenic highway by turning right (south) onto SC 81 toward Iva, 5 miles away.

Originally a shipping station, **Iva** also went through a name change. The town was once called Cook's Station, for Dr. Augustus "Gus" Cook, a prominent local physician and businessman, and the post office was named for his daughter, Iva Cook Bryson. The name Cook was dropped in favor of Iva for both the town and the post office after it was discovered there was another Cook's Station in the state. Iva is the only town in the upstate named for a woman.

In the 1800s, Dr. Cook owned a general store near the Seaboard Railroad that faced the town square on what is now SC 81. The newly renovated square now includes a thriving downtown community and a mock public water well on the site of the original public well once used by merchants and shoppers shortly after the turn of the twentieth century. Old homes and an abandoned school adorn SC 81/West Front Street.

Ride 0.8 mile into Iva and veer left to continue south on SC 81. Cross into Abbeville County and enter Lowndesville, 6.5 miles from Iva. Drive 0.5 mile through Lowndesville and turn left to stay on SC 81 toward Calhoun Falls. After crossing the W. D. Nixon Bridge over a branch of Lake Thurmond 1.2 miles east of Lowndesville, take the right fork to continue on SC 81 for 9 miles to the town of Calhoun Falls, another old railroad community.

Calhoun Falls State Recreation Area is on the north side of town. Turn right (west) to enter a 438-acre park on the shores of **Richard B. Russell Lake**, one of South Carolina's (and Georgia's) most popular fishing lakes. The 26,650-acre lake is home to largemouth bass, bluegill, crappie, and catfish. Sailing, waterskiing, and boating are also popular at the Calhoun Falls park. Camping and hiking through the mixed pine-hardwood forest afford glimpses of a variety of birds, including loons, hermit thrushes, brown-headed nuthatches, and red-eyed vireos. Drive all the way to the park office and boat ramp, where you'll have a terrific view of Lake Russell with its pine-lined shore. During spring and summer months, the park is open from 6:00 A.M. to 9:00 P.M., and from 6:00 A.M. to 6:00 P.M. the rest of the year.

CALHOUN FALLS TO HICKORY KNOB STATE PARK

Exit the park onto SC 81 and travel 1.2 miles south to the junction with SC 72, where a left turn would take you east to Abbeville. Continue straight south on SC 81 and cross into McCormick County, largely engulfed by the Long Cane District of Sumter National Forest.

Slow down as you enter **Mt. Carmel**, 8 miles from Calhoun Falls, and take in this almost abandoned town. Old wooden homes topped with tin roofs look as if they have stories to tell as they sit silent, covered in overgrown ivy and wisteria. An old whitewashed church decorated with closed green shudders sits at the fork in the road on the edge of town. Deer even venture into this quiet and peaceful yard.

There is no mountain here. Mt. Carmel's name, decided upon by French Huguenot refugee families picnicking in the area, is derived from a town in France. Mt. Carmel originally served the surrounding farmers as a small trading center, and it boomed in the 1880s; a post office was established in 1885 and the Savannah Valley Railroad ran through the town in 1886. Mt. Carmel thrived until a boll weevil infestation wiped out the cotton farms in the 1920s, followed by the Great Depression in the 1930s.

Fort Charlotte, built west of the town between 1765 and 1767 to protect the French, British, and German settlements near Long Cane, was the site of the first overt act of the American Revolution in South Carolina. The site is now under Lake Thurmond.

McAllister and Sons is the oldest business in the county. Listed on the National Register of Historic Places, it is the only visible commerce here. Established in

Church in Mt. Carmel

1888 and now run by the fourth generation of the family, this old store sitting right on the highway at 100 Main Street once housed a bank, a drugstore, and a hardware store. Now the establishment sells furniture, appliances, and hardware. Some antiques remain on display.

Leaving Mt. Carmel on SC 81, travel 3.5 miles south to the abandoned town of **Willington**. This small town sits in the heart of the South Carolina National Heritage Corridor, which runs along our state's western border. Apart from the Mims Community Center, which serves as a cultural center for the arts in the area, the abandoned downtown is made up of only a single strip of brick buildings that look like empty carcasses completely open to the elements. The Willington community is currently embarking on a renovation project, "Willington on the Way," in an effort to revitalize the community by building an African-American cultural center and an information center for the Heritage Corridor.

The town of Willington was settled by Huguenots in the 1760s. It gained prominence when Willington Academy was founded in 1804 by Reverend Moses Waddell, one of the greatest educators of his day. The academy attracted some of the brightest and best students from 1804 to 1819, some of whom became among the South's most notable men, including John C. Calhoun, a U.S. senator and U.S. vice president, and James Petigru, a lawyer and the only South

Carolina statesman to stand against secession from the Union. Dr. Waddel later became president of the University of Georgia.

Continue past Willington for 3.5 miles on SC 81 to visit the John de la Howe Barn and Interpretive Trail. Once you cross the bridge over Little River, slow down. You'll see the **John de la Howe Barn** on your left. A boat access to Little River is on the right.

The **John de la Howe School**, a school for children since its creation in 1797 through the will of Dr. John de la Howe, a French Huguenot, is located along the upper shores of the Lake Thurmond and Little River. The school, which began educating twelve boys and twelve girls in the manual arts of farming, cooking, and cleaning to enable the students to become successful adults, sits in the midst of forest and farmlands and has been operated by the state since 1918. Today more than 200 students reside here and are educated at the school.

This rustic granite barn, built by the Works Progress Administration in 1931, was a working dairy that served the campus and the surrounding community until 1980. In 1992, the building was renovated and now houses a country market of plants and crafts made by students at the school and senior citizens of McCormick County. The barn serves as the focal point of Howe-To Industries, which helps youth develop small-business skills. The store is only open on Saturday, so you may want to plan accordingly. Around the barn are wildflower gardens and gravel paths that lead you to a vegetable garden dripping with beans and tomatoes.

Behind the barn is the **John de la Howe Interpretive Trail**, a 1.9-mile trial that takes about an hour to complete as it winds through a pine and hardwood forest. The area contains 120 acres of virgin southern piedmont forest and includes some of the state's oldest trees. Oaks, hickories, bottomland hardwoods, and shortleaf and loblolly pines offer homes to songbirds, upland birds, and waterfowl, including migrant thrushes, wood thrushes, summer tanagers, and red-shouldered hawks. The site is recognized as a National Park Service Registered Landmark and a South Carolina Heritage Trust Site.

After visiting the John de La Howe Barn and Trail, you can head directly to McCormick, an 8-mile drive on SC 81 and SC 28, by turning left (south) out of the parking lot. This drive is quite pretty, taking you over rolling hills of pastures and through the Sumter National Forest.

To visit the Hickory Knob State Resort Park and Baker Creek State Park, take a right out of the barn's parking lot onto SC 81 and backtrack northwest to S-33-7, 0.7 mile ahead.

Turn left (southeast) on S-33-7. Huguenot Road, 3.4 miles down this road on the left, is where **New Bordeaux**, the last of seven South Carolina French Huguenot colonies, was founded in 1764. The British Crown granted Protestants who were fleeing religious persecution in France 28,000 acres in the Hillsborough Township.

Almost 200 hundred French Huguenots landed in Charleston and began settling at New Bordeaux. Others followed a few years later. The colony produced silk and wine on a modest scale. The only sign that remains of this once thriving railroad stop is a large granite Huguenot cross, which marks the spot of the first worship place of the Huguenot settlers.

Continuing on S-33-7 for almost 3 miles past Huguenot Road, you reach 1,091-acre **Hickory Knob State Resort Park**, on the shores of Lake Thurmond. Turn right into the park and drive along S-33-421, lined with a verdant, rolling eighteen-hole championship golf course along the lake on the left and thick woods to the right. Ride to park headquarters and a good view of Lake Thurmond. The park offers hiking, walking, and biking trails, as well as archery and skeet shooting ranges and tennis courts. A motel, cabins, restaurant, lodge, and meeting facility are also available.

About 3.5 miles from your turn into the park is the **Guillebeau House** (circa mid-1770s), just off of the main road. A green sign denotes the turn to right, and the cabin is easily visible from the road. Turn right onto the gravel road to see the former home of Revolutionary War veteran Andre Guillebeau, now listed on the National Register of Historic Places.

The cabin was moved to Hickory Knob from New Bordeaux and is the only remaining documented structure of the French Huguenot settlement in South Carolina's upcountry. The house is restored and available for overnight accommodations. Visitors can stay in the square-logged cabin with a new back porch. An outhouse sits behind the cabin; a picnic table and grill are in the woodsy area.

HICKORY KNOB STATE PARK TO McCORMICK

To visit **Baker Creek State Park**, exit right (south) from Hickory Knob onto S-33-7 and travel 1.5 miles to US 378. Turn left (east) onto US 378, travel 2 miles to cross the bridge over Little River. Brown signs indicate the left turn onto S-33-467 to visit Baker Creek State Park, tucked in the heart of Long Cane District of the Sumter National Forest. The Dorn Fishing Facility at S-33-56 will be on your right.

Turn left (north) onto S-33-467 and travel 1.3 miles to a left (south) into the park at the green Baker Creek State Park sign. The heavily wooded road takes you through the rolling terrain of the park. Take the time to drive all the way to the Lake Pavilion (3.2 miles), where you can enjoy a panoramic waterfront view of the Little River Branch of Lake Thurmond while picnicking. The park is open during daylight saving time from 6:00 A.M. to 9:00 P.M. and from 6:00 A.M. to 6:00 P.M. during standard time.

Exit the park with a right (east) turn onto S-33-467, and then turn left (east) on US 378 to head toward McCormick, 3 miles ahead.

Just outside of McCormick are the Hawe Creek Campground and Rubbies Barbecue on the right. Continue past commercial and residential areas scattered along US 378 toward **McCormick**, a town with numerous historic structures that have been restored to their early 1900s appearance and remain in use today. Shops are built over old gold mine tunnels that date as far back as the mid-1800s. The town of McCormick was named for Cyrus McCormick, the inventor of the reaper, founder of International Harvester, and owner of the land where a large portion of the town was eventually built.

As you enter McCormick on US 378/Gold Street, go through the first stop-light, at SC 28. C.C. Blair's Family Restaurant at 108 Gold Street will be on your left as you ascend the hill toward downtown. Stop here for a buffet-style home-cooked meal prepared by the Blair family. Named for Deacon Blair Sr., C.C. Blair's continues to thrive today and pay homage to its gospel-singing founder.

As you top Gold Street/US 378 where it intersects with Main Street, look to your right to see the **Keturah Hotel** at 115 South Main Street, a vintage two-and-a-half-story structure (circa 1910) named after the builder's wife. The hotel features Doric columns and an enormous brick facade. Once a boardinghouse and an inn, the hotel is now listed on the National Register of Historic Places and serves as the home of the McCormick Arts Council, which offers monthly exhibits and a gallery shop.

Next to the hotel is **Fannie Kate's Inn, Restaurant, and Pub**, a restored hotel (circa 1884) open for hungry and weary travelers. You can relax on the porch and rock away the afternoon watching passersby after enjoying a meal in the pub.

Turn left (north) on Main Street/S-33-31. Railroad tracks run parallel with Main Street and are still in use, so look carefully when driving through downtown. On the far side of the railroad tracks are the brick shops of downtown McCormick.

When you reach a stop sign, the **Dorn Mill** will be facing you, on the corner of North Main and Virginia Streets. The mill was saved from demolition in the 1970s and added to the National Register of Historic Places in 1976. The steam-operated mill, built beside the railroad track in 1898, originally processed cottonseed oil. In the 1920s, however, the facility was converted into a flour and gristmill. It was the only steam-powered mill of its type in South Carolina, and one of only two in existence anywhere. The structure contains the original steam engines and milling equipment.

Turn right (east) over the railroad tracks. Follow the Heritage Corridor Nature Route signs, and take another right (south) onto Main Street. Now the railroad tracks will be to your right and McCormick's antique shops, hardware store, and pharmacy will be on your left.

Continue on Main Street, and cross over Gold Street. To your left on the corner of Gold and North Main Streets is the **McCormick Visitors Center** and

Chamber of Commerce, in a building that was once the town's first service station (circa 1920). Also to your left are more antique stores and the *McCormick Messenger*, a weekly newspaper established in 1902. To your right is the **Old Train Depot**, now home to two antique stores.

At the next intersection, turn left (east) onto Augusta Street, just before the Old Train Depot. Drive two blocks and turn left onto Oak Street. The Joseph Jennings Dorn House, circa 1917, will be directly in front of you. Take a left onto East Gold Street and continue on Gold Street to the traffic light at the intersection of US 378 and SC 28/US 221. Turn left (south) onto SC 28/US 221, also South Mine Street, toward Plum Branch and Augusta, Georgia.

Once you make this turn, you will see the **McCormick County Courthouse**, also listed on the National Register of Historic Places, on your right. The county courthouse was built in neoclassical style with a large Doric portico in 1923. There is extensive brickwork on its exterior, and a pressed metal ceiling inside.

McCORMICK TO J. STROM THURMOND DAM

Plum Branch, named for a nearby stream framed with plum bushes, is 5 miles south of McCormick on SC 28/US 221. Brecknell's, a local store, was built in 1902 and once was the largest merchandise house between Augusta and Greenville. The store closed in the 1980s, but it is now home to Brecknell's Farm House Restaurant. The railroad runs parallel to the highway on your left.

Continue through Plum Branch on SC 28/US 221 south toward Parksville, 5 miles ahead, past colorful forests and rolling hills filled with horses and grazing cattle. Parksville, the only town located on the shore of Lake Thurmond, is quite small. Quaint wooden houses with tin roofs and small porches line the highway on your way into town. Tiny Parksville Post Office to the right of the highway only has room for one or two customers, but it's still in use today. You can purchase hunting and fishing licenses, cold drinks, and snacks at Houston's Bait and Tackle. Three miles south of town, Hamilton Branch State Park sits on a peninsula reaching into Lake Thurmond.

In Parksville, drive slowly and look for the left turn (northeast) off SC 28/US 221 onto S-33-138/Price's Mill Road, where you will cross over railroad tracks that run through the middle of town.

Price's Mill, a tall two-story wooden mill on the banks of Stevens Creek, is 1.5 miles down the road. One of only two water-powered gristmills that operated in South Carolina, the mill is now closed and is on the National Register of Historic Places. The structure was built to replace the original mill, which was washed away in a flood. It began operation in 1890 and remained in production until recently. You can see the cement grists on the mill's porch and in the front of the yard of the Price family home on the hill to your right.

Continue east on S-33-138/Price's Mill Road for 3.5 miles through robust pine and hardwood forests. At the stop sign, turn right (southeast) onto S-33-227/

Key Road and travel 2.3 miles to **Key Bridge**, spanning a ravine to across dark **Turkey Creek**.

Stop at this isolated setting and enjoy the river as it lumbers below you on its way to join Stevens Creek 5 miles south. Massive oaks and tall bald cypresses mingle with oaks, maples, and pines along the riverbanks, where a large beaver population builds slippery paths to the water. On the west side of the river, the 12.5-mile Turkey Creek Trail leads both north and south along the banks of the stream, providing a great spot to explore a quiet section of Sumter National Forest.

Once you cross the bridge, you leave McCormick County and enter Edgefield County, so the road numbers change. S-33-227/Key Road becomes S-19-68/Key Road. Continue on Key Road for 3 miles and turn right (southwest) on S-19-118/Cold Springs Road.

Drive 3.1 miles on S-19-118/Cold Springs Road until it ends at a stop sign. Turn right (west) onto SC 23. Go 1.4 miles and turn left (southeast) on S-19-139/Red Oak Grove Road. This road takes you past pastures full of grazing horses and miniature ponies, as well as guineas, roosters, chickens, and turkeys that wander in the road, so drive slowly. When you reach a stop sign, after 2.4 miles, turn right (southwest) onto S-19-143/Garrett Road toward Stevens Creek Heritage Preserve.

Ride 0.9 mile to the bridge over Stevens Creek. As you enter Stevens Creek Heritage Preserve and cross the bridge, moving from Edgefield County back into McCormick County, the number of Garrett Road changes from S-19-143 to S-33-88.

The parking area for **Stevens Creek Heritage Preserve**, a National Natural Landmark, is on your right a mile past the bridge. You may want to stretch your legs here and enjoy a stroll along the nature trail.

Owned and managed by the South Carolina Department of Natural Resources, this 138-acre preserve provides habitat for a vigorous population of rare plants, including the Florida gooseberry, a federally listed endangered plant; the only other occurrence of this species is near Lake Miccosukee, Florida. The preserve is also home to a rare animal, the Webster's salamander. During springtime, the area's display of unusual wildflowers is unsurpassed.

This jewel in the heart of a national forest is home to a variety of forest types, including cove, oak-hickory, mixed pine/hardwoods, bottomland hardwoods, and shortleaf and loblolly pine. Remnant of an ancient glacial period, the area hosts plants native to the coastal plain, piedmont, and mountains. American ash, white oak, northern red oak, beech, sugar maple, bitternut hickory, bald cypress, and red cedar are among the tree species.

Streams and bluffs are located throughout the preserve, where upland and songbirds such as American woodcocks, Louisiana water thrushes, prothonotary warblers, red-eyed vireos, and pileated woodpeckers all find sanctuary.

J. Strom Thurmond Lake

As you leave the preserve, continue southwest on S-33-88 for 1.2 miles toward the village of Clark's Hill. Turn right (west) on S-33-345 and drive a few yards across the railroad tracks. Make another right (north) on SC 28, and then travel 0.2 mile to US 221. Turn left (west) to visit the **Savannah River** and the **J. Strom Thurmond Dam and Lake**, a mile away.

J. Strom Thurmond Lake, one of the largest inland bodies of water in the South, surrounds more than a hundred islands just above the lake's surface and hosts a diversity of plants and animals.

The dam, completed in 1954 as a Corps of Engineers hydroelectric project, impounds a lake that stretches 40 miles northward up the Savannah River and 26 miles up the Little River. On the south side of the dam, the Savannah River heads toward Augusta, Savannah, and the Atlantic Ocean.

When the dam and lake were completed in the 1950s, they were known as Clark's Hill Dam and Lake, after the nearby South Carolina community. At the venerable senator's urging in the 1980s, Congress changed the name to J. Strom Thurmond Dam and Lake to honor one of its own. This did not sit well with Georgians, who still call the facility Clark's Hill.

The J. Strom Thurmond Dam and Visitors Center offers a superb view of the dam and lake. Offering interpretive materials and programs, it's open from 8:00 A.M. to 4:30 P.M. every day except Thanksgiving, Christmas, and New Year's.

This is a good spot for nature walks and bird-watching. Wild turkeys, Bonaparte's gulls, loons, and double-crested cormorants make their homes here, along with a wide variety of other waterfowl and songbirds.

5

Long Cane Forest and the Eighteenth-century Frontier

PARSON'S MOUNTAIN TO LICK FORK LAKE

GENERAL DESCRIPTION: This 82-mile drive through the Long Cane District of Sumter National Forest includes Parson's Mountain and Lick Fork Lake Recreation Areas, the Revolutionary War–era Ninety Six National Historic Site, and the history-laden towns of Abbeville and Edgefield.

SPECIAL ATTRACTIONS: Long Cane District of Sumter National Forest, Parson's Mountain, Lick Fork Lake, Ninety Six National Historic Site, Edgefield and Abbeville town squares, Abbeville's Opera House, Belmont Inn, Burt-Stark House and Trinity Episcopal Church, Old Edgefield Pottery, Edgefield County Courthouse, National Wild Turkey Federation Center and Museum, Magnolia Dale, Tompkins Mem-orial Library, and Oakley Park Museum.

LOCATION: Western part of the state, between Aiken and Greenville.

DRIVE ROUTE NUMBERS: FR 514, S-01-251, SC 28, SC 72, SC 20, Trinity Street, Church Street, Pickens Street, SC 185, SC 246, SC 248, US 178, S-24-44, US 25, SC 23, SC 230, S-19-263, S-24-392.

TRAVEL SEASON: All year.

SERVICES: Conventional accommodations and services are plentiful in Greenwood, while many services are available in Abbeville, Edgefield, and Ninety Six.

See For More Information in the appendix for addresses and phone numbers of Attractions, Camping, Neat Places to Stay, Restaurants, Shops, Tours, and Nature-Based Services.

THE DRIVE

This ride starts and ends in the Long Cane District of Sumter National Forest. However, between Parson's Mountain Recreation Area in the north and Lick Fork Recreation Area in the south, visitors journey into charming, historic Abbeville and through rolling fields and green pastures to the colonial-era Ninety Six National Historic Site, before passing through more farmland and forests and touring the fascinating pottery center of Edgefield, a community alive with the past and known as South Carolina's Cradle of Governors.

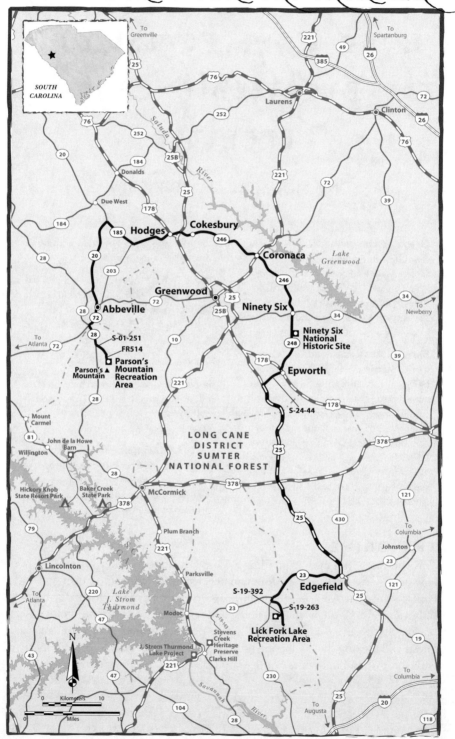

PARSON'S MOUNTAIN RECREATION AREA TO ABBEVILLE

Begin in Abbeville County at **Parson's Mountain Recreation Area**, in the midst of the Long Cane District of the Sumter National Forest. This district covers about 120,000 acres in Abbeville, Edgefield, Greenwood, McCormick, and Saluda Counties, and has an array of recreational opportunities to offer.

A 4-mile loop hiking trail begins at Parson's Mountain Lake and climbs up Parson's Mountain, past an abandoned gold mine to an observation tower. The surrounding oak-hickory and mixed pine forest is a terrific place to spot a number of interesting birds, such as wild turkeys, Bachman's sparrows, Kentucky warblers, and a variety of woodpeckers. The crest of the mountain offers especially picturesque views in the fall. Although the granite outcropping peak is only 800 feet high, the relatively flat surrounding land allows you to see for miles in all directions.

Swimming, fishing, and boating are allowed at the lake for nominal fees from April to December. The 22-mile Long Cane Trail loop also passes through the recreation area.

Begin your journey from the parking area beside the lake, where Mountain Creek flows into the lake and great blue herons and other wading birds are frequently seen. Drive along the lakeshore and through the recreation area on FR 514.

Exit the recreation area onto S-01-251/Parson's Mountain Road, turn left (west), and travel 1.5 miles to the intersection with SC 28. Turn right on SC 28, travel 1 mile to merge right (east) onto SC 72, and travel 2.1 miles to Abbeville.

Parson's Mountain Lake

At the intersection with SC 72 and SC 20/South Main Street, turn left on Main Street to tour the **Abbeville Town Square**. You will feel as if you're stepping back in time when you enter the square lined with vibrantly colored storefronts restored to their nineteenth-century style and see the ancient oaks and flower gardens that decorate the center of the square. Abbeville exudes southern charm and takes great pride in its history.

French Huguenot and Scotch-Irish farmers settled the area in 1755 on land that once belonged to the family of Andrew Pickens, a Revolutionary War leader. Since its establishment, important political figures have helped shape this quaint town. Patrick Calhoun, father of John C. Calhoun, helped found the county. John C. Calhoun, born in Abbeville, practiced law on this square from 1807 until 1817, and here he launched his career in public service that led to his becoming the Vice President, Secretary of War, Secretary of State, and Senator. Post–Civil War President Andrew Johnson had a tailor shop just off the square, and Robert Mills, the architect who designed the Washington Monument, lived in Abbeville for a time. Mills designed the county jail, built in 1854, which now houses the Abbeville County Museum.

In the Town Square to your immediate right, on Pickens Street, is the refurbished **Belmont Inn**, formerly known as the Eureka Hotel. Built in 1902, the inn was a popular stopping point for travelers who came to the area by rail on their way from Atlanta and New York, especially with the opening of the Abbeville Opera House opposite the hotel. This lovely hotel, bedecked with an enormous front porch (complete with rocking chairs and fans spinning overhead), antique-filled rooms, and the inn's original wood floor, invites visitors to enjoy fine dining in its restaurant or an ale from the pub downstairs.

Also to your right is the **Abbeville Opera House**, built in 1908. Fully restored to its turn-of-the-twentieth-century condition, it stages live theatre throughout the year, making it an entertainment hub of the Abbeville community. This 260-seat Opera House, listed on the National Register of Historic Places, flourished between 1908 and 1913, offering a variety of shows, from Shakespeare's plays to operas. Later, motion pictures were shown here. The Opera House is open for visitors Monday through Friday, from 10:00 A.M. to 5:00 P.M.

Beside the Opera House are the Abbeville County Courthouse, retail stores, real estate and law offices, and a pool hall, Rough House, which remains very much as it was when it opened in 1936. Decorated with old seats from the Abbeville Opera House, nostalgia-producing vintage posters, and old-fashioned pocket pool tables, this is a great place to stop in for a cold beer and a hot dog.

Continue to the top of the square and turn left onto Trinity Street. The **Trinity Episcopal Church**, a Gothic Revival pink stone church that's home to a small but devoted congregation is directly in front of you. Its rounded doors, wooden pews, and creaking floors take you back to the early nineteenth century. Stained-glass windows break the sunlight and keep the chapel dimly lit and cozy. Trinity

Episcopal was established in 1842; its present building was completed in 1860, the same year the Tracker organ was assembled and installed by John Baker of Charleston. The church also touts a chancel window imported from England and slipped through the blockade in Charleston Harbor in 1863. The church is open from 9:00 A.M. to 5:00 P.M. daily, and you are welcome to stroll through Trinity's cemetery to the rear of the church, with graves dating to the 1850s.

Take a left (south) on Church Street and another left (east) on West Pickens Street. You will pass the *Press and Banner*, Abbeville's community newspaper since 1844. To your left on the Town Square is Abbeville Chamber of Commerce and Visitors Center, located in a building constructed in 1860, where you can find guided tours. Also found along this side of the square are restaurants and more antique shops, all worth a step in to look around.

The center of downtown Abbeville is decorated with a garden area, a Confederate monument erected in 1906, a watering trough at the south end that has been converted into a fountain, and a monument erected in memory of a World War II hero.

Head back around the square toward the north end and continue north on Main Street/SC 20 to visit the **Burt-Stark Home** (circa 1830) that sits directly in front of you, hidden behind crepe myrtles. This National Historic Landmark is significant not only for its architecture and the preservation of the home, its contents, and lifestyle of the early nineteenth century, but also for two historic Confederate meetings took place here. On November 22, 1860, a meeting that launched South Carolina's secession from the Union was held here; one month later, South Carolina became the first state to secede. Then on May 2, 1865, Jefferson Davis held the last Confederate Council of War meeting at the Burt-Stark home, agreeing to give up the fight and dissolve the government. The home is open to the public on Friday and Saturday from 1:00 to 5:00 P.M. and by appointment. While here, you may wish to linger in the adjacent **Jefferson Davis Park**, a lovely place to relax.

Across from the Burt-Stark Home and the park is the **Smith-Visanska House** (circa 1822). This restored Steamboat-Gothic-style home is now a bed-and-breakfast that's listed on the National Register of Historic Places.

ABBEVILLE TO NINETY SIX NATIONAL HISTORIC SITE

When you have completed your tour of downtown Abbeville, continue north on Main Street/SC 20, past columned mansions and quaint cottages and then over rolling hills with peaceful pastures, farm houses, and woodlands.

Alternatively, to bypass some rural roads and visit the city of Greenwood, travel south on Main Street/SC 20. At the light, turn left (east) onto SC 72 toward Greenwood, 10 miles ahead along a four-lane highway.

As you approach Greenwood, you may wish to visit Park Seed. If you do, continue east on SC 72 for 2 more miles past SC Business 72. This 132-year-old global company is a showcase of color, especially from May through July, with more than 1,000 varieties of annuals, perennials, herbs, and vegetable plants arranged along trails in the nine-acre garden.

To visit the town of Greenwood, turn right onto SC Business 72. The Heritage Corridor Nature Discovery Trail signs show you the way. Turn right (south) on Greenwood's famous Main Street, one of the widest main streets in the United States, which offers a regional library, a community theater, and upscale shopping and dining.

Drive through Greenwood on Main Street/US Business 25/US Business 178. Outside of Greenwood, approximately 1.5 miles past town, take a left (east) on SC 34 toward Ninety Six, 9 miles away.

About 9.5 miles north of Abbeville, SC 20 merges into SC 185. *If you wish to visit the charming town of Due West (home of Erskine College, established in 1839), turn left at this junction and travel 2.5 miles west.* Otherwise, turn right (east) onto SC 185 and travel 4 miles over rolling hills and past the pecan fields that line the highway to the junction with SC 203. Take a left here to remain on SC 185 and travel 4 more miles to the crossroads community of **Hodges**, home to a number of antique stores and a quaint buffet eatery called Somebody's House, found just as you turn left (east) onto SC 246 in Hodges. Drive 1.5 miles, cross over US 25, and enter **Cokesbury**, a quaint village built around the long-defunct Cokesbury College, established in 1854. Cross over SC 254 and travel 0.8 mile to the college. Look for the brown sign on your right directing you to turn on Asbury Road for a closer look, or catch a glimpse of the college and its gardens from the highway.

From Cokesbury, continue southeast on SC 246 for 8 miles to Coronaca, and 7 more miles to Ninety Six, passing through more of the green hills and forests that inspired Greenwood County's name.

Drive into **Ninety Six** on SC 246/Cambridge Street. At the stoplight in town, the visitor center, housed in a miniature building beside the old stone fountain, sits to your left. On your right is a refurbished train station, and along the main street are a variety of shops worth a peek. To continue your drive, cross over West Main Street and remain on Cambridge Street, which becomes SC 248.

Travel 2 miles southward on SC 248/Cambridge Street to visit the Ninety Six National Historic Site and its Starr Fort, on your left (east).

The **Ninety Six National Historic Site** was a frontier outpost chosen for its convenient campground along the Cherokee trail that traversed the state. It was 96 miles southeast of the Cherokee village of Keowee. Hunters, cattle drovers, and traders passed this way on the path, and by 1753, Robert Gouedy had built a trading post that rivaled some Charleston merchants in terms of volume of trade.

The site was used as a blockade during the war with the Cherokee in 1760. The most famous action that took place here was the Siege of 1781 during the American Revolution. You can relive this battle by following a 1-mile paved interpretive walking tour through dark woods and green fields. A cannon used in

Battle of Starr Fort in June 1781 sits at the trailhead. The trail winds by remains of siege works, siege trenches, forts, and village sites. Adjacent to the parking lot is a museum that offers a ten-minute film on the Historic Site.

NINETY SIX NATIONAL HISTORIC SITE TO LICK FORK LAKE RECREATION AREA

Exit the Ninety Six National Historic Site by turning left (south) onto SC 248. Travel 4.4 miles until the highway ends at US 178. Turn left (southeast) on US 178 toward the Epworth Camp Meeting Grounds. Drive slowly, because you're going to turn right (southwest) after 0.2 mile onto S 24-44/East Epworth Camp Road. Old houses and green forests decorate the winding, roughly paved road.

S-24-44 intersects with US 25 after 2.5 miles. Turn left (south) onto US 25 toward Edgefield. The drive to Edgefield is a 23-mile stretch of rural homes, pecan groves, peach orchards, and horse pastures. You can easily envision carriages bumping along this route through hills adorned with white cotton fields in the autumns of the early nineteenth century.

English, German, Irish, Dutch, and French traders and farmers settled in the **Edgefield** area in the middle of the eighteenth century. The founders built a politically active community, supported by cotton and other agricultural crops on the fertile lands of the area. These lands also seemed to nurture public leaders. The entire community took part in an ugly civil war between Patriots and Tories during the American Revolution. Later, Jim Bonham, a hero of the Alamo, was born here, as were ten South Carolina governors, five lieutenant governors, and several U.S. senators and representatives, including Strom Thurmond, who began his political career here by running for county superintendent of education.

The entire town of Edgefield is listed on the National Register of Historic Places, so it has numerous eighteenth- and nineteenth-century churches, homes, farms, and plantations that tell the story of the Old Ninety Six district. Roadside vegetable and fruit stands, blooming peach orchards in the spring, and fields white with cotton in the fall decorate the outskirts of the picturesque town of Edgefield.

Continue south on US 25 to **Courthouse Square**, in the center of town, surrounded by a number of historic buildings still in use today. To your immediate right is the **Edgefield County Courthouse**, established in 1785 but rebuilt in 1839. Designed by Robert Mills, the courthouse is still in use and also houses the Old Edgefield District Archives, a haven for genealogists and area historians. A statue of a young Strom Thurmond is in a garden area across the street.

To your left is the Terry Ferrell Museum, an antique and curiosity shop. Mr. Ferrell is the father of the potter at Old Edgefield Pottery. Follow the lazy cats down Potters Alley to visit **Old Edgefield Pottery**, open Tuesday through Saturday from 10:00 A.M. to 6:00 P.M. The combination studio and museum displays nineteenth-century pottery and features a potter demonstrating the craft at the wheel. Pottery is important to the area; it was named Edgefield Pottery by Dr. Abner Landrum, who developed the local style of pottery. He shaped vessels from local clay and applied an alkaline glaze to give it a distinctive green or brown tone. Local potters produced practical and decorative stone pieces such as wine jugs, butter churns, mixing bowls, Toby mugs, and containers of all sizes. The most famous Edgefield potter was a slave named Dave who worked for Dr. Landrum. Dave's pottery is easily recognizable by the original verses he inscribed on his pieces. His work and the work of others is a unique folk art form exhibited in many major museum collections.

Also on the left-hand side of the square is the Edgefield Welcome Center, housed in the **Tompkins Memorial Library**, a repository of hundreds of volumes, microfilm, and loose files on the families and histories of Old Edgefield District. You can step into the courtesy center here and pick up brochures on the area, as well as ask for directions. The folks here are very helpful and will direct you to any number of homes, churches, and cemeteries in the area that are worth your while to visit.

At the eastern end of the square is the Ten Governors Café, where you can step in for a bite to eat.

Circle around the square and head east toward Johnston on US 25 for 0.3 mile. At the junction of SC 23 and US 25 is the **Oakley Park Museum**, sometimes referred to as the Oakley Park Red Shirt Shrine, an antebellum home. Built in 1835, it is the former estate of Confederate General Martin Witherspoon Gary who, with General M. C. Butler, guided the "Red Shirt" Movement to win a successful campaign to elect Wade Hampton as South Carolina governor in 1876 and effectively end the state's Reconstruction period. The house is operated by the United Daughters of the Confederacy as a museum. It's open to the public on Thursday, Friday, and Saturday from 10:00 A.M. to 4:00 P.M., or by appointment; a small fee is charged. Even if you don't want to tour the home, drive forward onto S-19-300 and take a ride around the home's circular drive that will take you back to the nineteenth century.

To see more peach country, take a right out of the driveway onto SC 23 and head east toward Johnston. Pass through the quaint towns of Ward, Ridge Spring, Monetta, and Hibernia and continue on to Batesburg-Leesville. This is an especially lovely drive during the spring and summer when the peach trees are a lush green or in full bloom.

If you'd like to visit a lovely nearby natural area, backtrack on US 25 to Courthouse Square, and drive west on SC 23/Jeter Street. On your right just past the square is the Village Blacksmith at 206 Jeter Street. In the early part of the twentieth century, this was a blacksmith shop operated by an African-American craftsman, McKinley Oliphant. Today, a working artistic blacksmith can be found here Tuesday through Saturday from 9:00 A.M. to 5:00 P.M.

Continue 8 miles west on SC 23 and then veer left (south) onto SC 230. Drive only 0.4 mile before reaching S-19-263/Lick Fork Lake Road on your

Oakley Park Museum

left (east). The area is identified with the brown wildlife viewing area signs. Take a left onto Lick Fork Lake Road and travel 2 miles before turning right (west) onto S-19-392 to enter **Lick Fork Lake Recreation Area.**

Open April through mid-December, the facility boasts a twelve-acre lake nestled in the southeastern portion of the Long Cane Ranger District, offering fishing for catfish, bream, and bass, as well as boating and swimming. Mountain biking and hiking in the heavily wooded park are also available. Two hiking trails are maintained, as well as a handicapped accessible fishing pier, picnic areas with tables, grills, and a shelter. There is a small fee for parking, if you decide to get out and look around.

A major attraction is two interlocking loop trails. The 1.7-mile Lick Fork Lake Trail, beginning at the north parking lot, offers a variety of wildflowers, including pink spiderwort. Other plant life on the pathway around the lake includes Christmas fern, beech, white oak, northern red oak, dogwood, sourwood, hickory, Virginia creeper, holly, and honeysuckle.

The Horn Creek Trail, a bike/hike trail of 5.4 miles, is accessible from the southwestern side of Lick Fork Lake Trail, or from the south parking lot. Visitors journey along creeks and through forest and wetlands full of pine, ironwood, maple, sweet gum, sycamore, swamp chestnut oak, water oak, river birch, Jessamine, and blackberries. You might spot a red-cockaded woodpecker or a Bachman's sparrow here. More common residents include other woodpeckers, pine warblers, brown-headed nuthatches, chickadees, turtles, frogs, squirrels, and deer.

6

Thoroughbred country

AIKEN TO BARNWELL

GENERAL DESCRIPTION: Begin in elegant Aiken and travel 75 miles through horse pasture countryside, past the dark waters of the South Edisto River, and into old railroad towns that time has passed by, before finishing in charming, historic Barnwell.

SPECIAL ATTRACTIONS: Hopeland Gardens, Thoroughbred Racing Hall of Fame, Aiken County Historical Museum, Willcox Inn, Aiken Center for the Arts, Aiken State Natural Area, South Edisto River, Wagener, Salley, Springfield, Williston, Blackville, Barnwell State Park, Historic Barnwell.

LOCATION: Western part of the state, in the middle portion of the Savannah River Valley.

DRIVE ROUTE NUMBERS: Dupree Place, SC 19, Easy Street, Newberry Street, Boundary Avenue, Colleton Street, Park Avenue, Laurens Street, US 78, SC 302,

S-2-576, S-2-1669, S-2-53, SC 39, S-2-59, Main Street, Pine Street, Brown Street, Magnolia Street, Walker Street, SC 3, L'Artigue Street, Boundary Street, Hagood Avenue, Jefferson Street, Academy Street, Franklin Street, Washington Street, Burr Street, Main Street, Wall Street, Gilmore Street, Bryan Street/S-6-43.

TRAVEL SEASON: All year.

SERVICES: Hotels and motels are plentiful in Aiken and along I–20. Aiken offers full services, and accommodations and many services are available in Barnwell. Blackville, Williston, and Wagener offer limited services.

See For More Information in the appendix for addresses and phone numbers of Attractions, Camping, Neat Places to Stay, Restaurants, Shops, Tours, and Nature-Based Services.

THE DRIVE

You begin in elegant, sophisticated Aiken, amid the lush beauty of Hopeland Gardens. You pass through the town originally made wealthy by early twentieth-century winter resort residents, through lovely residential areas and an attractive downtown. Then things change. You head into the countryside, which presents contrasts of affluent horse farms and good ol' boy country dwellings, stores, forests, and fields. You visit the quiet enchantment of Aiken State Natural Area beside the dark, foreboding South Edisto River before beginning a tour of several quaint railroad towns whose heydays were in the early part of the twentieth century. You conclude in beautiful Barnwell, full of history, grace, and Spanish moss.

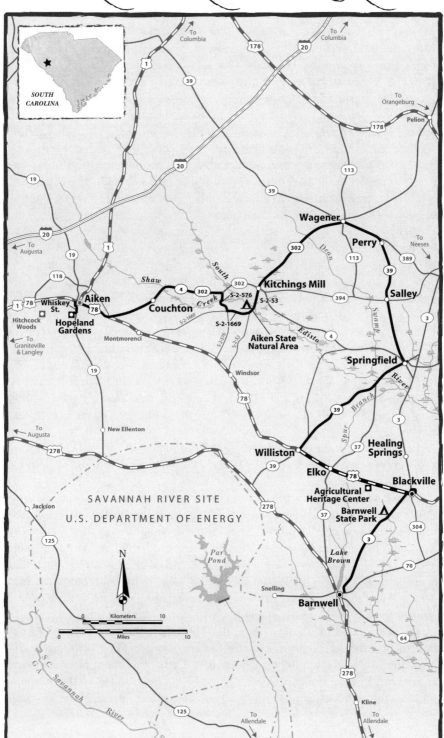

AIKEN

Aiken is a place of both old and new money. The old money began in the 1830s, when the mild climate and new railway made Aiken a favorite of moneyed South Carolina planters. The Civil War was the planters' demise. In the late 1800s, however, trains from the North began bringing in throngs of wealthy Yankees seeking respite from cold winters, and these visitors brought with them their love of polo and horse racing and breeding. The horse industry remains to this day a staple of the Aiken economy, as well as the area's most notable pastime.

West of Aiken, near the Savannah River, are a series of textile mills and company towns that brought jobs to thousands of South Carolinians and Georgians in the early part of the twentieth century. Although many mills have closed and mechanization has eliminated numerous other jobs, the textile industry continues to be a mainstay of the local economy.

New money came in the 1950s with the construction by the old U.S. Atomic Energy Commission of the huge nuclear weapons complex straddling Aiken and Barnwell Counties. This 300-square-mile facility employed 38,000 workers at its peak, and employment today ranges from 12,000 to 20,000, depending on assigned missions from the U.S. Department of Energy. Included among these employees, most of whom work for the civilian Westinghouse contractor, are a plethora of scientists, engineers, and other topflight technicians and executives who often choose to make Aiken County their permanent home.

Aiken County is also the site of Redcliffe Plantation, one-time home of former U.S. Congressman, U.S. Senator, and South Carolina Governor James Henry Hammond. A staunch defender of both slavery and male supremacy, Hammond is most famous for his "Cotton is king" speech on the floor of the U.S. Senate in 1858.

Begin in Hopeland Gardens, site of the Thoroughbred Racing Hall of Fame, at the corner of Whiskey Road/SC 19 and Dupree Place. Admission to both facilities is free.

Hopeland Gardens is a lush fourteen-acre park that was once the estate of Oliver and Hope Iselin, who donated the property to the city. Winding pathways take visitors through the shade of sprawling, moss-hung live oaks and past creeks and ponds to enjoy an immense variety of flowers and other vegetation. Camellias, azaleas, and dogwoods are prominent. A special feature is the Touch and Scent Trail with Braille signage for the visually impaired. Connected to the gardens is Rye Patch, an elegant residence now owned by the city, with a memorial rose garden and the Carriage House Museum on its grounds.

On the grounds of the gardens is the **Thoroughbred Racing Hall of Fame**, housed in a former carriage house of the Iselin estate. The Aiken area is the breeding ground for a number of Kentucky Derby, Preakness, Hambletonian, and other flat racing and harness champions. The museum, open most afternoons October through May, is a tribute to Aiken's heritage of thoroughbred breeding and training and honors horses bred or trained in the Aiken area since 1942. Aiken hosts polo matches almost year-round, and flat, steeplechase, and harness races in spring and fall.

From Hopeland Gardens, head north on Whiskey Road past lovely homes and gardens. To your right (east) is the Aiken Equestrian District, filled with polo fields, training farms, thoroughbred racetracks, and horses and their trainers.

After three blocks, you are at the delightfully named intersection of Whiskey Road and Easy Street. This may be a good place to retire. For now, however, turn left (northwest) on Easy Street, go two blocks, and turn right (northeast) on Newberry Street. The **Aiken County Historical Museum** is one block farther, at 433 Newberry Street, on your left. Located in a 1930s winter resort home called Banksia, the museum offers more than thirty rooms of exhibits, plus other items of interest outdoors, including a log

Hopeland Gardens

cabin built around 1808 and a one-room schoolhouse built around 1890. The grounds also feature a nature trail and an arboretum.

Ride one more block and turn right (southeast) on oak-canopied Boundary Avenue and, after one block, take a left (northeast) on Chesterfield Street/SC 19. Go one block, past the county library located in an old schoolhouse, and turn left (northwest) on Colleton Street to enjoy a sweeping view of the elegant front facade of the lovely **Willcox Inn**. Built in 1898 as a winter resort hotel for northern clientele escaping brutal weather, it remains to this day a splendid restaurant and inn, with four-poster beds and decorative fireplaces. At minimum, you should step into the gracious lobby with its huge stone fireplace, usually stoked with a roaring fire, where Franklin Roosevelt and Winston Churchill conspired and sipped toddies during World War II. Peek at the old-club-style Pheasant Room, which serves continental cuisine and traditional Southern specialties.

Travel Colleton Street for the one-block length of the hotel grounds and then turn right (northeast) on Newberry. Cross the railroad tracks and proceed one more block to Park Avenue. Turn left (northwest) and go one block on Park before turning right (northeast) onto Laurens Street, Aiken's vibrant, inviting downtown center. Antiques, artworks, and unique dining abound here. Be sure to stop in at the **Aiken Center for the Arts** at 122 Laurens Street SW, featuring exhibits by local and regional artists.

AIKEN TO WAGENER

After one block, turn right on Richland Street/US 78, a pretty street with a grass- and tree-filled median, and head southeast. Drive past lovely homes, commercial establishments, and churches for a few blocks before entering a more modest neighborhood. After 3 miles, veer left (northeast) onto SC 302/SC 4 toward Wagener.

You next pass a large, modern manufacturing facility and then travel through a folksy area of neat lawns, modest homes, pastured cattle, woodland patches, and pecan trees. After 4 miles, you reach the settlement of Couchton, a spread-out, good ol' boy community of rambling homes and small convenience stores. If you have killed a deer, you can get it processed here. You cross the swampy wetlands of Shaw Creek a mile on the other side of Couchton.

You now enter rolling horse country. Pastures, stables, and horse training facilities dot the attractive countryside, punctuated with farmhouses, pecan trees, and hayfields.

Slow down after 4.8 miles past the bridge over Shaw Creek, and turn right (south) on S-2-576/Mackey Scott Road. This narrow country lane takes you once again over Shaw Creek and through mixed hardwood/pine forest. Take the first paved left (east) past the bridge, onto S-2-1669/Old Tory Trail, 1.6 miles from SC 302/SC 4. Travel about 1.7 miles through more forest and past Uncle Herb's Blueberries on the left before turning left (north) into **Aiken State Natural Area**.

Centered beside the **South Edisto River** and four spring-fed lakes, the park is a combination of river swamp, bottomland hardwood forest, and dry sandhill forest. The sandhills of this area are remnants of an ancient era when the ocean reached this far inland. Built in the 1930s as a Civilian Conservation Corps project, the 1,067-acre park teems with wildlife. It is a birder's delight. Woodpeckers are everywhere, and many varieties of warblers populate the woodlands. Butterflies are plentiful, and near the water you may see wood ducks, hooded mergansers, pied-billed grebes, and wading birds. The water and moist forestlands provide excellent habitat for amphibians and reptiles.

The park offers fishing and a 3-mile nature trail, as well as a segment of the Edisto River Canoe Trail. The park is open 9:00 A.M. to 9:00 P.M. during warm weather months and 9:00 A.M. to 6:00 P.M. at other times. Bear right in the park and follow a 2-mile loop road counterclockwise along a shady, heavily forested road. After about a mile, turn into the parking area for the canoe trail and enjoy views of cypresses and tulip poplars protruding from the dark waters. Continue along the tree-canopied lane past the fishing lake, a picnic area, recreation fields, and a camping area before exiting Aiken State Natural Area back onto S-2-1669/Old Tory Trail.

Turn left (east), drive a few yards, and then turn left (northeast) onto S-2-53/State Park Road. You cross the black, foreboding South Edisto River after a half mile and continue 1.6 miles to the Kitchings Mill crossroad settlement, where you merge into SC 302 to continue northeast toward Wagener, 8.9 miles away.

Pass by a catfish farm and wetlands before entering more undulating countryside, featuring horse pastures, hay and cotton fields, farmhouses, ponds, and a variety of trees, including pines, oaks, sycamores, magnolias, dogwoods, and pecans. Horse training facilities are scattered here and there.

Enter downtown **Wagener** by merging left (northeast) onto SC 302/SC 113/Main Street and traveling 2 blocks to the intersection with SC 39/Railroad Avenue. A quiet town, Wagener's downtown faces a green median, once a railroad bed that brought commerce to the community when cotton was king. The old tracks are long gone, but in their place is an attractive four-block-long park, the centerpiece for the Wagons to Wagener festival held here each spring.

Take a left (northwest) on Railroad Avenue and drive two blocks past old storefronts on your left and green space on your right. Turn right (southeast) on S-2-59/ Park Street, which parallels Railroad Avenue. Ride two blocks to the intersection with Main Street and continue on Park Street, past interesting homes on the left and, on the right, the **Wagon House** with a conestoga wagon, a pavilion, and shade trees in the park. Storefronts line the other side of Railroad Avenue.

WAGENER TO BARNWELL

Continue three blocks on S-2-59/Park Street until it merges right (southeast) into SC 39 toward Salley, 8 miles away. Pass the Wok and Roll Asian restaurant and the Young Farmers Mud Run course, continuing 3 miles to tiny Perry. Bear right (southeast) to stay on SC 39 toward Salley.

Salley is another interesting little community with a greenspace through the middle of town occupying the old rail bed that the downtown once faced. The town's current claim to local fame is its annual fall Chitlin Strut, a festival during which several tons of hog intestines are boiled, fried, and consumed. The town is dubiously proud of its claim to be the "Chitlin Capital of the World." The community was burned during Sherman's burn and pillage march through South Carolina near the end of the Civil War. (It's not known if the destruction was a reaction to the smell of boiling chitlins.)

The **Hemrick House** (circa 1870) at 124 Pine Street was the first building constructed after the fire. To see this early Victorian with stained glass windows, turn right (west) on Pine and drive 2 blocks to the home, on your right. Then go left (south) on Brown Street for one block and left (east) on Magnolia Street for 2 blocks in order to resume your trip through Salley toward Springfield by turning right (south) on SC 39.

Drive 5 miles beside an old rail bed to cross into Orangeburg County and reach another railroad town, **Springfield**. You are riding on Festival Trail Road, which, in fact, is the site of yet another festival. This one is the fall Springfield Frog Jump, the winner of which gets to fly to Calaveras County, California, accompanied by his or her frog as the state's official entrant in the National Jump-Off. Springfield's pretty railway median is decorated with an old caboose, and the little community is dotted with nice shade trees, comfortable old homes, and some downtown storefronts that have seen better days.

In downtown Springfield, turn right (southwest), away from the old railway, to stay on SC 39 toward Williston, 10 miles away. This is a pretty stretch, as you first dip into the verdant South Edisto River wetlands and cross a bridge over the serenely flowing blackwater stream, emerging in Barnwell County. You pass several miles of mixed hardwood and pine forests, farmhouses, cotton fields, vegetable plots, and pastures.

Williston is next on your tour of old railroad villages. You might think you're in the movie *Groundhog Day* as you drive into yet another small town fronting yet another abandoned train track converted into a nicely appointed greenway park. This downtown area, however, is healthier than many, with several active shops and some former store space converted into attractive downtown apartments.

From SC 39, turn right (northwest) and travel three blocks on West Main Street. As you turn left (southwest) to cross the old rail bed, notice the stately, columned **John Ashley House** at 312 West Main, on your right. This home, built in the 1820s, was used as quarters by Sherman's troops and thus avoided being burned to the ground. It continued to be used by Union soldiers during the first four years of Reconstruction, until 1869.

Go one block back toward downtown, merging left (southeast) on US 78. Proceed through the shopping district, and follow the rail bed to the tiny crossroads town of Elko, 3 miles away. Continue through Elko to Blackville, 6 miles away, traveling beside a rail bed and past farms, pleasant homes decorated with magnolias and pecan trees, and crop fields and pastures. About halfway between Elko and Blackville, pull into the **Agricultural Heritage Center** on your right. A South Carolina Heritage Corridor visitor information center and hands-on learning facility, it explains the historical and cultural influences of agriculture in the area. In the fall, the Blackville area hosts the Old Time Horse Farmers Gathering, featuring draft horses and mules, as well as sweet potato digging, cane squeezing, and syrup cooking.

As you enter **Blackville** on US 78/Dexter Street, you pass the Confederate

Manor Bed and Breakfast on your right and the Floyd Manor, at 3614 Dexter Street, on your left. This charming home was once the manor house of an 8,000-acre plantation. The Masonic Gothic pillars that frame the front of the house were shipped from England in 1886.

Turn left (north) on Walker Street and then go right (east) to pass by old storefronts on Main Street facing the railroad tracks. In the median is a historic marker noting that in the early 1800s, Blackville was a major stop on the Charleston-Hamburg Railway, the first commercial rail line in America, which was once the longest commercial line in the world.

After one block, turn left (north) on SC 3/Solomon Blatt Avenue. (Blackville is the hometown of Solomon Blatt Sr., a former Speaker of the South Carolina House of Representatives who, with Barnwell Senator Edgar Brown, pretty much ran the state of South Carolina during the middle part of the twentieth century.) After one block, pull into the parking area of the **Old Depot Library**, housed in a red-shingled, green trimmed, Victorian-style former train depot that was moved one block to this location on the grounds of the old Blackville High School.

*For a detour, to **Healing Springs**, continue 3 miles north on SC 3 and turn right. Native Americans were the first to believe in the artesian water's healing powers, and they brought wounded Revolutionary War soldiers here to drink. In 1944, Luke Boylston*

Old Depot Library

deeded the property to God. Every month, thousands of visitors come here to wash, drink, and carry home the elixir's ailment-curing properties in plastic containers. You may drink directly from any of the well's twelve naturally flowing spouts.

Turn around at the library, head one block south, pass the railroad median, and turn left (east) on Main Street. On your right, at 322 Main Street, stop in at the renowned **Miller's Bread Basket**, offering home-style Mennonite cooking. Next door is a shop featuring antiques and handmade Mennonite crafts and quilts.

Turn right (south) on L'Artigue Street and take note of the **James Hammond Museum**, on your right, open by appointment only. This 1800s building contains memorabilia from the Civil War (Sherman swept through here also), along with artifacts that tell the history of Blackville. At various times, this building has served as the town hall, a private school, a jailhouse, and a movie theater.

L'Artigue House

Continue one block south past pretty Blackville United Methodist Church and then take a right (west) on Boundary Street. After one block, note the **L'Artigue House** (circa 1832) at the corner of Boundary Street and Solomon Blatt Avenue. Featuring a two-story portico and gracious columns, it housed Sherman's officers during their march and is the oldest structure in Blackville.

Turn left (southwest) on SC 3/ Solomon Blatt Avenue and head toward Barnwell. **Barnwell State Park** is about 2.5 miles down the road. Turn right (west) to enter the modest 307-acre park constructed by the Civilian Conservation Corps in the 1930s.

The park has two small lakes and an interpretive nature trail winding around them through pine and hardwood forest. The woods are full of woodpeckers and warblers; pied-billed grebes and ospreys inhabit the lake environs. The picnic and playground area is adorned with dogwoods, oaks, pines, poplars, hollies, and lots of magnolias. You may fish for bass, bream, and catfish off a dock or along the lake shoreline. Rest rooms are available. The park is open 9:00 A.M. to 9:00 P.M. during daylight saving time and 9:00 A.M. to 6:00 P.M. the rest of the year.

Exit the park by turning right and heading southwest toward your final destination, the town of Barnwell, 7 miles away along SC 3. You pass woodlands, small churches, and modest farms and homes before entering historic, picturesque Barnwell on SC 3/Marlboro Avenue. Ride several blocks south to the intersection of Marlboro and Hagood Avenues, where you may want to stop in at the **Barnwell County Museum** before traveling back in time to enter the heart of Spanish-moss-hung, live-oak-shaded Barnwell, one of the prettiest small towns in the state.

Turn right (west) on Hagood and travel five blocks to the **Episcopal Church of the Holy Apostles** at 1706 Hagood Avenue. This beautiful Gothic-design cypress wood church was completed in 1857. Church members hid the stained glass windows from Union troops in 1865, when they quartered cavalry horses in the building. You may want to stroll in the lovely old cemetery in back of the church, which holds the remains of a number of well-known statesmen and other notables.

Get back on Hagood Avenue heading west and take an immediate right (north) on Jefferson Street. Take the next right (east) on Academy Street, and travel one block to cross Madison Street. Here, on your right, is the quaint **St. Andrews Roman Catholic Church**. Built in 1831, it's the oldest church structure in town.

Continue to the intersection with Franklin Street. As you turn left (north), the **Old Barnwell Presbyterian Church** building is on your right. Now home to the Circle Theatre and the Barnwell Performing and Cultural Arts Center, it was built in 1848 in the Georgian Revival style. After Union troops burned the county courthouse, the church was used as a temporary courthouse for a time.

Go one block on Franklin, and then turn left (west) on Washington Street. Travel one block, turn right (north) on Burr, and ride one block to the quaint Barnwell town square. This is a great 1950s-style downtown area with thriving shops and eateries.

On the northern side of the square is the sprawling **Barnwell County Courthouse**, rebuilt in 1879. In front of the courthouse is a vertical sundial, erected in 1858 and said to keep perfect time. Nearby are statues of children at play.

At the intersection of Burr and Main Streets on the north side of the town square, go left (west) on Main Street for a half block, turn right (north) on Wall Street, and travel two blocks to view **Bethlehem Baptist Church** on your left. The original structure on this site was built in 1829 and donated to black Baptists in 1860. This is one of only a handful of pre–Civil War churches in the South organized by and for people of color. It was rebuilt in 1889 using some of the original materials from the first church.

Complete your journey by taking a left (west) on Gilmore Street and driving a couple of blocks to Bryan Street/S-6-43. Turn right (north) to ride a few yards to a dam that shores up restful **Lake Edgar Brown**, bordered by greenery, a paved walking trail, and some of the town's fashionable homes.

Midlands Forest and Rivers

NEWBERRY LOOP

GENERAL DESCRIPTION: A 110-mile loop drive highlighted by charming little towns, delightful old churches, and the rivers and woodlands of the Enoree/Tyger District of Sumter National Forest.

SPECIAL ATTRACTIONS: Little Mountain, Prosperity, Newberry Opera House, Newberry College, Old Newberry County Courthouse, Enoree/Tyger District of Sumter National Forest, Whitmire, Rose Hill State Historic Site, Broad River, Monticello Reservoir, Peak, Pomaria.

LOCATION: North central part of the state, northwest of Columbia.

DRIVE ROUTE NUMBERS: SC 202, Boundary Street, Mountain Street, Church Street, US 76, S-36-457, S-36-42, SC 395, SC 34, Cemetery Street, Luther Street, Evans Street, Lindsay Street, S-36-44, FR 387, US 176, S-36-81, S-36-481, S-36-32, FR 356, SC 66, FR 358, Railroad Avenue, SC 72, Church Street, S-44-18, S-44-16, S-44-163, S-44-45, S-36-45, S-36-55, S-36-28, S-20-99, SC 215, S-20-11, SC 213, S-36-28, Nelums Street, S-36-170, Hollaway Street.

TRAVEL SEASON: All year.

SERVICES: Newberry and Union offer full services and accommodations; Whitmire offers limited services. The western edge of the Columbia metropolitan area is a few miles to the east.

See For More Information in the appendix for addresses and phone numbers of Attractions, Camping, Neat Places to Stay, Restaurants, Shops, Tours, and Nature-Based Services.

THE DRIVE

Rivers, forestlands, and charming little towns highlight this 110-mile loop drive. You start out in the communities of Little Mountain and Prosperity before visiting restored downtown Newberry and its splendid old opera house. From here, you head into the Enoree/Tyger District of Sumter National Forest, passing by the recreation areas of Molly's Rock and Brickhouse Campground before touring the old Whitmire mill town. Next, you crisscross the Enoree and Tyger Rivers to enjoy more of the forest and take in the beauty of Rose Hill Plantation State Historic Site. Finally, you pass over the Broad River a couple of times to visit idyllic Monticello Reservoir and old country churches before winding through the remote, peaceful villages of Peak and Pomaria.

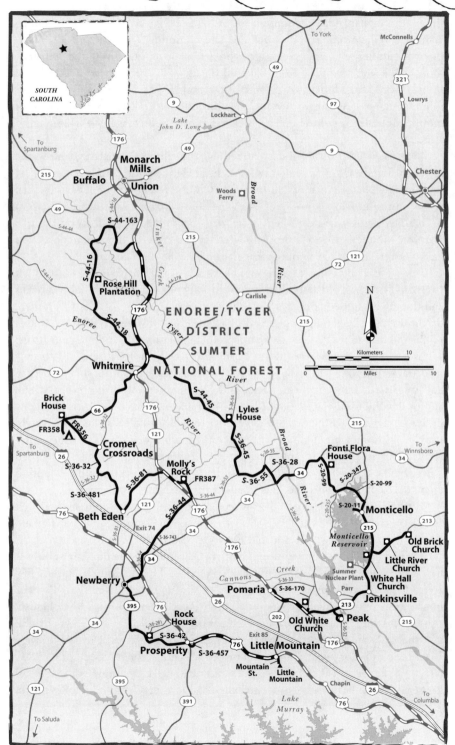

LITTLE MOUNTAIN TO NEWBERRY

Enter the town of **Little Mountain** on SC 202/Pomaria Street, driving southward, 1.8 miles from exit 85 on I–26. The community was settled by Swiss-German immigrants 250 years ago, and its name comes from the 200-foot monadnock you see rising from flat land on the south side of town, directly in front of you. Monadnocks are granite outcroppings that are remnants of ancient mountain ranges. As climatic events of eons took their toll, the softer elements of mountains wore away, leaving hard rock prominences such as Little Mountain to stand alone.

Take a left (east) on Boundary Street and ride along this narrow lane to the old Holy Trinity Church cemetery. Next, head right (south) on Mountain Street for one block before turning left (west) on Church Street. After a few yards, turn right (south) on Mountain Street, cross the railroad tracks, and turn right (west) on US 76/Main Street. Go a few more yards before taking a left to ride southward on Mountain Street a short distance up the slope of the mountain as you ease past interesting old homes, some dating back about a century.

Turn around after about a mile and backtrack to US 76/Main Street. Turn left (west) and ride past old-fashioned storefronts on your left, with the railroad tracks and the town's Little Mountain Park on your right. Journey 7 miles to Prosperity through gently rolling countryside, past meadows, timberland, Mid-Carolina High School, and residences with yards featuring pecan, oak, and magnolia trees.

As you enter **Prosperity** (motto: "Sanctuary for Senior Citizens") with railroad tracks on your left, look for S-36-457/Elm Street, also on your left. Turn left (southwest) here, cross the tracks, and continue westward into town, where author Erskine Caldwell (*Tobacco Road, God's Little Acre*) once lived with his family. His father was pastor of the local Associate Reformed Presbyterian Church. Lovely old homes highlighted with spacious porches decorate the street. After about a half mile, you arrive at the town square, adorned with a gazebo and lined with inviting little shops and commercial buildings. Get out and walk around to enjoy the flavor of 1940s and '50s small-town America.

Turn right (northwest) on Main Street and go one block before taking a left (west) on S-36-42/Brown Road. Cross more railroad tracks and pass the old Prosperity schoolhouse and neat old houses as you head toward Newberry.

Travel through red dirt country, past soybean and hay fields. After about 3 miles, on your left is the ancient cemetery of St. Luke's Church, with a few above-ground vaults, unusual for this part of the state; bear right here. Pass the intersection with S-36-281/Colony Church Road after 0.4 mile. **Rock House**, constructed with fieldstones around 1758, sits in the middle of a field to your right, 0.4 mile past the intersection. Next you cross Kinards Creek and pass a lovely farmhouse and silos jutting from a hill before arriving at the intersection with SC 395, 0.9 mile west of Rock House. Turn right and drive by an old white schoolhouse and more farmland before entering into Newberry, about 2.5 miles north.

The **Newberry** area was settled in the mid-1700s; the town was established in 1789. A community of delightful old homes and tree-lined streets that has become something of a middle-class retirement mecca in recent years, the town's German settler heritage remains strong.

Ride about 1.5 miles into town on SC 395/Nance Street. Turn right (east) on Main Street. Enjoy the beauty of the beautiful Gothic-style **Newberry Opera House** on the town green on your left. Built in 1882 and splendidly restored in the 1990s, this redbrick structure, with a steeple that houses the town clock, hosts an impressive array of big-name performances throughout the year.

You are now in Newberry's charming town center. A World War I monument adds to the ambience of the delightful shops, office buildings, and eateries that adorn Main and adjoining side streets.

Next on your left is the **Old Newberry County Courthouse**, built in 1852. Take note of the bas-relief on the front gable of the building. It was added in 1876, at the end of the state's post–Civil War Reconstruction period. It shows an American eagle with the scales of justice in its beak beside an overturned palmetto tree, representing South Carolina. On the eagle's scales are South Carolina's feisty gamecock on one side and a dove of peace, holding an olive branch, on the opposite side.

Continue east on Main Street two more blocks to US 76/College Street and take a left (north) to pass the Newberry County Courthouse and Newberry City Hall before visiting **Newberry College**, about a half mile north, on your right. Newberry College was established by Lutherans in 1856, and it retains its close church ties to this day. After driving by the main entrance and the college's oldest buildings, continue past the football stadium and turn right (east) on Cemetery Street, which separates a large burial ground on your left from the football stadium on your right. (We don't know whether or not the juxtaposition of the two facilities is simply a coincidence.)

After one block, take a right (south) on Luther Street, drive two blocks, and turn right (west) on Evans Street. Go one block and then take a left (south) on Lindsay Street to exit the campus. Four blocks down the street is picturesque **Wells Japanese Gardens**, created in 1930 by the H. G. Wells family as a private garden with exotic plants set among ponds. It's open 7:00 A.M. to 9:00 P.M. daily, free of charge.

NEWBERRY TO WHITMIRE

Continue south on Lindsay Street back to SC 34/Main Street, and turn left (east) to head out of town. After a little more than a mile, at the point where SC 219/Main Street heads right (northeast), veer left on SC 34/Winnsboro Road. About 0.4 mile farther, bear left again, this time onto S-36-44/Mt. Bethel Garmany Road.

You cross I-26 after 2 more miles and enter the **Enoree/Tyger District of Sumter National Forest**. The Enoree and Tyger Rivers flow west to east through this 168,000-acre land of forests and streams, emptying into the Broad River on the border between Newberry and Fairfield Counties. Opportunities for hiking, mountain biking, fishing, hunting, birding, camping, canoeing, and kayaking abound in this wildlife-rich area, where the proximity of dry upland forest to swampy river bottomland provides an appealing mix of habitats. Always be on the lookout for the forest's numerous deer as they bound across roads.

As is the case with South Carolina's other national forest tracts, the Enoree/Tyger property was mostly acquired from economically distressed landowners in the 1930s, and federal property is interspersed serendipitously with private holdings throughout northern Newberry County, southern Union County, and western portions of Chester and Fairfield Counties.

Proceed 7 miles northward through rolling countryside on S-36-44/Mt. Bethel Garmany Road, past an old two-room schoolhouse, the wood-frame Lebanon United Methodist Church, and an attractive mixture of proud and modest country homes, farmland, hayfields, horse pastures, and woodland.

At the Brown's Crossroads intersection with US 176, cross over and bear left (northwest) onto FR 387, a one-lane unpaved road that takes you 1.4 miles through pleasant woodlands to **Molly's Rock Picnic Area**, which you reach by turning right (north) when you arrive at a paved road section. This scenic little area that was once a homestead offers a fishing pond, a short nature trail, picnic shelters, grills, rest room facilities, drinking water, and a nice grassy field.

Follow FR 387 another half mile to US 176, and turn right (northwest). Cross Means Branch and Kings Creek and, after 1.4 miles, turn left (southwest) at Baker's Crossroads onto S-36-81/Old Whitmire Highway. Cross over SC 121 after a half mile and ride 4.3 miles through verdant countryside of forests, cattle pastures, silos, and farmhouses.

At S-36-481/Beth Eden Road, take a hard right (northwest) and continue for 4.2 miles past farms and forest. Little Beth Eden Lutheran Church, with its neat old cemetery, is perched on a red dirt hill just a few yards up the road, on your right. After crossing Gilders Creek, look on your right for a monument in memory of fourteen members of the U.S. Army Air Corps who lost their lives in a training crash near this spot in 1943.

Under overhanging trees, turn right (north) on S-36-32/Jalapa Road and ride 2.2 miles, across Indian Creek to Cromer's Crossroads, where you take a left (northwest) onto unpaved FR 356/Cromer Road. Ease along this shady road for 3.5 miles past ravines and through thick stands of pines and hardwoods. Hiking/biking/equestrian trails cross the road here and there, and you might want to explore some of the intersecting Forest Service roads punctuating this route.

When you reach SC 66 at Brickhouse Crossroads, turn left (west). On your right is the privately owned **Brick House**, an important stagecoach inn on the

Buncombe Road to Asheville during the nineteenth century. Turn immediately left (south) onto FR 358/Brickhouse Road in order to visit **Brickhouse Campground**. This road takes you a half mile into the facility, to the trailhead for the hiking/biking/equestrian Buncombe Trail, as well as a stopping point along the way for the Palmetto Trail, which will eventually take hikers and bikers all the way from the mountains to the sea. Camping, picnicking, grills, drinking water, and toilet facilities are also available.

This is a great place to stretch your legs and see some of the forest's natural attractions up close. The **Buncombe Trail** offers about 40 miles of hiking options through mixed forest along a long double loop trail. The inner loop is a little over 9 miles; the outer loop, which can be accessed from a number of unpaved roads, is 32 miles. The terrain is pleasantly hilly, with a number of small streams to add interest, along with myriad wildlife viewing opportunities.

Apart from ever present pines, the forest includes dogwoods, tulip poplars, cedars, maples, oaks, and bald cypresses. Some of the wildflowers present are Queen Anne's lace, elephant's foot, wild mint, nettles, coreopsis, mimosa, buffalo clover, mullein, honeysuckle, and butterfly pea. Christmas fern is among the many ferns found in low-lying areas, and blackberries are common in spots receiving large amounts of sunshine.

Deer and wild turkeys are abundant, and their tracks are frequently seen along the trails. Otters inhabit the wetlands. Cold-blooded residents include Carolina anoles, salamanders, and numerous frogs. Songbirds dart among the trees, trying to avoid a variety of high-flying birds of prey. Some insects and arachnids frequently seen are tiger swallowtails, red-spotted purples (butterflies), large beetles, velvet ants, millipedes, and orb weaver and funnel web spiders.

Exit Brickhouse Campground, turn right, and drive 6.7 miles northeast on SC 66 through pine forest. Cross Duncan Creek to enter the out-of-the-way, hilly, kudzu-laden textile mill town of **Whitmire**. As you drive in, notice the houses, almost all of which were built by the mill owners in the first half of the twentieth century. It is not difficult to distinguish those provided for management from those built for workers. Mill owners owned the houses and rented them to employees, thus providing, along with the company store, a means to keep the workers closely rooted to their jobs. In the last half of the century, houses were sold off, as mechanization and foreign competition greatly reduced the needed workforces.

Follow SC 66 into town; it coincides first with Central Avenue and then with Park Street as it jags left (northwest) in front of a huge redbrick textile plant. Pass old Park Street School and turn right (northeast) with SC 66 onto Glenn Street. Go one block and turn left (northwest) off SC 66 and onto Main Street. Decades ago, this was a thriving downtown area. Now it would make a good potential movie set for yesteryear. A highlight is the folksy little cafe named, appropriately, Cafe.

Go two blocks and turn right (northeast) on Railroad Avenue that (surprise!) parallels railroad tracks. Travel one block and turn right (southeast) on SC 72/Church Street. After four blocks, SC 72 veers left in front of the Whitmire Methodist Church, but you should continue southeast on Church Street for three more blocks, passing quaint workers' cottages, many decorated with porch flags. Confederate, Clemson Tiger Paw, and NASCAR banners seem to be the favorites.

WHITMIRE TO POMARIA

At the intersection with US 176/Colonial Drive, turn left (north) and head out of town, crossing the beautiful **Enoree River** and entering Union County a half mile north of Whitmire. The county and its seat of government were named in 1785 for Union Church, an amalgam of Episcopalians, Presbyterians, and Quakers.

Bear left to continue on US 176 at the point where SC 72/SC 121 forks right, and then turn left (west) 2 miles north of the Enoree, onto S-44-18/Sedalia Road. Journey 4.8 miles through lush forest lands, passing on your left numerous unpaved roads that lead southward to the banks of the Enoree.

Take a right on S-44-16/Sardis Road toward **Rose Hill Plantation State Historic Site**, 2.3 miles to the north. This beautifully situated forty-four-acre park in the heart of the national forest centers on the old home place of South Carolina's "Succession Governor," William H. Gist.

Made wealthy by cotton, Gist finished this Federal-style mansion in 1832. It served as both his private home and as the governor's mansion between 1858 and 1860, when the fiery secessionist worked ceaselessly to bring about South Carolina's withdrawal from the United States of America. He achieved his goal at the end of his term in December 1860, and four months later Confederate troops in Charleston fired the first shots of the Civil War.

Furnishings and clothing belonging to the Gist family adorn the inside of the white stuccoed brick mansion, fronted with a four-columned double porch facade. The attractive grounds, bordered by a healthy stand of hardwoods, are laced with ornamental plants and the heirloom rose gardens that gave the plantation its name. A number of original plantation outbuildings complement the main house. A delightful 1.5-mile nature trail leads from the picnic area through the oak/hickory forest down to the banks of the enchanting **Tyger River**.

Admission to the park grounds is free, but there is a small charge for tours of the mansion. The park is open year-round from 9:00 A.M. to 6:00 P.M. Thursday through Monday. Clean, modern rest rooms are located in an old log cabin with a tin roof and large brick fireplace.

Exit the park and turn right (north) on S-44-16. Cross a narrow bridge high above the Tyger River about 0.4 mile along the way. The bridge and the Rose Hill Landing on the south side of the river offer great vantage points for viewing this lovely waterway.

From the bridge, ride northward on S-44-16 for 4.7 miles through thick forest, crossing Fair Forest Creek and turning right (southeast) on S-44-163/Deepwater Road. *If you enjoy seeing old mill villages, continue north on S-44-16 for a few miles to* **Union**, *with its nicely restored town center, and visit the old* **Buffalo** *mill village, a couple of miles west on SC 215. Another concentration of old mill buildings and employee housing is in the Monarch Mills community, on the east side of Union.* **Lake John Long**, *about 5 miles east of Union in a pretty sylvan setting, is the site of the infamous Susan Smith drowning of her two sons and another tragic vehicle drowning situation a while later. Two memorials pay tribute to the young boys.*

Drive southwest past horse pastures, a little creek, and forest for 3.4 hilly miles on S-44-163. At a stop sign, take a right (south) on US 176. Cruise along for 4.3 miles, up and down more hills, to the historic marker for Otterson's Fort, at the intersection with S-44-278. Near here stood a colonial stockade to protect settlers during the Cherokee War of 1760–1761. Make another crossing of the scenic Tyger River a half mile farther.

Continue south another 4.8 miles and then go left (east) on SC 72/SC 121 for 1.2 miles. Turn right onto S-44-45/Maybinton Road, and head southeast through a long succession of undulating twists and turns. This road becomes S-36-45 after 5.5 miles, as you cross from Union County back into Newberry County. Look for the **Lyles House** 2.5 miles farther down the road, at the intersection with S-36-54. The dwelling was constructed prior to 1776 by members of the Lyles family, who operated a ferry across the Broad River and fought on the Patriot side in the American Revolution. Unfortunately, it is now in a state of disrepair and is in danger of being lost to neglect.

You pass over the Enoree River after 2.5 more miles and, 2.2 miles farther, S-36-45 ends at S-36-55. Turn left (east), following S-36-55 for 2.5 miles past farms and hayfields until it merges southward into S-36-28. Continue for 1.2 miles and take a left onto SC 34.

The **Broad River**, dark brown and, well, broad, is 1.2 miles along the way. Ride over the bridge and enter Fairfield County, settled by Scotch-Irish Presbyterians in the 1740s. According to local lore, it was named by Lord Cornwallis, who, while encamped here for several months during the American Revolution, admired the area's "fair fields."

Broad River

Keep going for another 3.2 miles and then turn right (south) on S-20-99. Look for the **Fonti Flora** house about a mile down the road, on your left. This gracious home, built between 1815 and 1825, sports a two-story portico buttressed with six large wooden columns.

Drive another 2 miles, passing meadows, crossing Terrible Creek, and exiting Sumter National Forest. Turn left (east) on Ladd Road at the intersection with S-20-257 in order to remain on S-20-99. **Monticello Reservoir** and an intersection with S-20-347 are just 0.7 mile farther. Public access areas are located on both the north and south sides of S-20-99. Both areas have picnic facilities, boat ramps, and rest rooms; the north area also offers swimming and fishing.

Continue 2 more miles on S-20-99 as it veers southeastward, traversing a causeway over the northern end of the lake. Look to your right for great views. A lakeside parking area is on the east side of the causeway.

Take a right (south) onto SC 215 and ease into the tiny, charming community of **Monticello**, 0.8 mile from the intersection. Turn right (west) onto the half-mile S-20-11/Monticello Street spur for an additional taste of Monticello. You pass abandoned country stores, farmhouses, and some fields before the road dead-ends at a spot where sunshine sparkles off the lake in the distance.

Backtrack to SC 215 and turn right (south). On your right are beautiful Monticello Methodist Church and its old cemetery, set on a hillside gently slopes down to the east bank of the lake. Stop in the shade of oak trees in the parking area and wander behind the church for an absolutely idyllic vantage point. Cows graze in verdant pastureland and wade into the water, as Canada geese laze around the lake. A comfortable old barn rests to one side. A few yards farther down SC 215 is the oak-lined entrance to Plainview Farm.

Monticello East Boat Landing is 2 miles farther on SC 215, and the intersection with SC 213 is only 1 more mile along the way. Turn left (east) here, and ride 0.6 mile to **Little River Baptist Church**, organized in 1768. The present one-story, four-columned structure was completed in 1845 and features a great stained glass window of Jesus with a flock of sheep. An old cemetery surrounded by granite walls and an attractive picnic area with granite tables frame the sanctuary.

The **Old Brick Church**, built in 1788 by a congregation dating from colonial days, is 1.1 miles up the road, on your right. The Associate Reformed Presbyterian Church of the Carolinas got its beginning here in 1803, and this facility was used until 1920. Another great cemetery with old tombstones adjoins this high-ceilinged, one-story piece of history.

Return to SC 215 and take a left (south) on what is now SC 215/SC 213. **White Hall African Methodist Episcopal Church** is 0.4 mile down the road, on the right, with its pleasant cemetery across the street. Built in 1867 as the first African-American church in Fairfield County, White Hall offers another shady parking area with a nice view of the lake.

In the Jenkinsville community, 1.2 miles farther south, veer right on SC 213,

The Old White Church

toward the Broad River, 2.7 miles away. Cross over the river just south of the Parr Shoals Dam as you head back into Newberry County.

After 0.7 mile, turn left (east) onto S-36-28/Broad River Road, and ease 1 mile down a winding road, under a railroad trestle and into delightful, sleepy, tiny **Peak**. The town's little stores, old schoolhouse, homes, and churches are set on a hillside around a hairpin turn that converts S-36-28 from Broad River Road into Stoudenmayer Road. As you climb back up the hill, turn right (northwest) on Nelums Street. Ride about 0.2 mile and take a left (southwest) back onto S-36-28/Broad River Road.

Return to SC 213 and turn left (west). After 2.1 miles, turn right (northwest) onto US 176. Drive 0.2 mile to S-36-170 and turn right (north) to go 0.4 mile to the **Old White Church**, built as St. John's Lutheran Church between 1800 and 1810. Organized by Swiss-German settlers, the church has solid wood shutters and arched panels above the doors and windows.

Return to US 176, turn right (northwest), and head into **Pomaria**, 2.5 miles away, just past Crims Creek. The John Summer House, built around 1825, is at the eastern edge this tranquil little village decorated with old homes and store-fronts. Turn right on Hollaway Street to ride to the rustic town center, passing the Solomon-Suber House (circa 1857) and the Hollaway House (circa 1811). Life here is slow, as perhaps life should be.

cotton and sand hills

WOODS BAY TO CHERAW

GENERAL DESCRIPTION: A 115-mile jaunt through cotton fields, peach orchards, and forested sand hills, beginning at a boggy "Carolina bay" and ending in the pretty and historic town of Cheraw, on the banks of the Great Pee Dee River.

SPECIAL ATTRACTIONS: Woods Bay State Natural Area, Lynchburg, Mayesville, Lynches River, Lee State Natural Area, Carolina Sandhills National Wildlife Refuge, Sand Hills State Forest, Sugarloaf Mountain, Cheraw State Fish Hatchery, Historic Cheraw, Great Pee Dee River.

LOCATION: Northeast part of the state, a little west of Florence.

DRIVE ROUTE NUMBERS: S-43-48, S-43-597, S-43-61, SC 341, S-31-661, S-31-671, US 76, S-31-53, S-31-327, SC 527, SC 154, US 401, S-16-27, S-31-39, S-31-22, Park Road, US 15, S-31-941, S-31-57, Dennis Avenue, SC 34, S-31-48, S-31-21, US 1, Wildlife Drive, SC 145, Winery Road, S-13-29, S-13-63, Bottom Road, Wire Road, Second Street, Kershaw Street, Greene Street, Boundary Street, Church Street.

TRAVEL SEASON: All year. Early summer to midautumn is best for observing crop fields in their full glory. Late fall, winter, and early spring are best for wildlife. Flowers peak in early spring.

SERVICES: Camden, Sumter, and Florence have full services. Bishopville, Hartsville, and Cheraw have accommodations and most basic services.

See For More Information in the appendix for addresses and phone numbers of Attractions, Camping, Neat Places to Stay, Restaurants, Shops, Tours, and Nature-Based Services.

THE DRIVE

Highlights of this drive are cotton fields, peach orchards, fascinating rural towns, several public nature preserves, beautiful lowland rivers and remnants of an ancient seashore known as the sand hills.

You begin in Woods Bay State Natural Area, which features a mysterious wetland depression area known as a "Carolina bay." From here you ride through lands where cotton was and is king, and folks live in small towns and villages or "out in the country." In spring, you are greeted by the glorious colors of azaleas, dogwoods, wisteria, and roses, along with the intoxicating scent of bee-attracting honeysuckle. In summer and early fall, crops are in the fields and greenery abounds. Late fall and winter are great for viewing wildlife, especially migratory waterfowl.

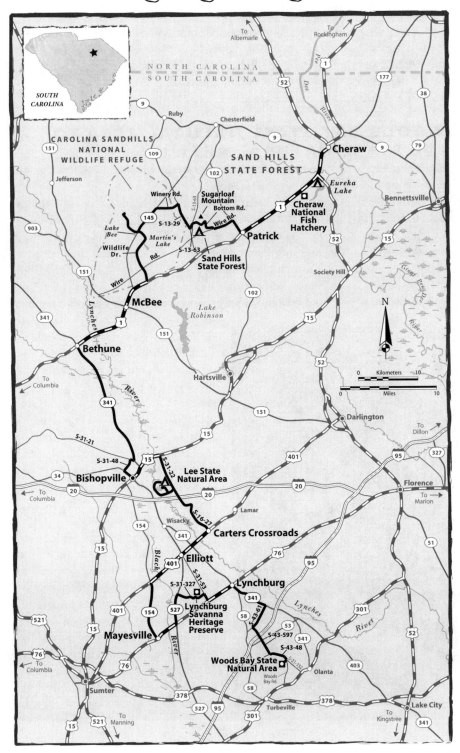

You ride through the quaint villages Lynchburg and Mayesville, whose glory days have come and gone, a state sanctuary for the imperiled longleaf pine savannah habitat, Lee State Natural Area, perky Bishopville, isolated Bethune, peach hub McBee, and the adjoining Sandhills National Wildlife Refuge and Sand Hills State Forest, before ending at the shinning jewel of historic Cheraw. Along the way are the Black, Lynches, and Great Pee Dee Rivers.

WOODS BAY STATE NATURAL AREA TO LEE STATE NATURAL AREA

Begin at 1541-acre **Woods Bay State Natural Area**, which can be reached via exit 136 or 141 off I–95 south of Florence.

Woods Bay is one of a series of natural wetland depressions known as Carolina bays, mainly concentrated in the coastal plains of South and North Carolina. South Carolina has 760 such phenomena. These shallow oval dents in the earth's surface are all oriented in the same northwest to southeast direction, and they range in size from a few acres to more than a thousand acres. Their origin is unknown, but meteor showers and ancient ocean currents are two possibilities. Typically, the bays collect rainwater and hold it slightly above normal water tables, thus giving rise to freshwater wetlands that support an abundance of plants and wildlife.

A 500-foot boardwalk allows visitors to walk out into Woods Bay and get a close-up view of the cypress-tupelo swamp filled with carnivorous bladderworts and pitcher plants. A short nature trail along the fringe of the bay and past an old gristmill pond provides additional sightseeing opportunities for sweet gums, maples, bay trees, water oaks, willows, loblolly, pines, and magnolias.

Chances of spotting wildlife are good. Alligators laze in the water, and river otters are active in winter and spring. Deer abound, carpenter frogs sound their peculiar nailing sound in spring, and turtles are plentiful. Birds include anhingas, herons, egrets, ospreys, wood thrushes, blue-gray gnatcatchers, red- and white-eyed vireos, orchard orioles, summer tanagers, and a variety of warblers.

Woods Bay State Natural Area

Woods Bay offers rest rooms, refreshments, and a small interpretive nature center. Canoes, perhaps the best means to view the sights, are available for rent. You can also rent fishing poles. The park is open 9:00 A.M. to 6:00 P.M. Thursday through Monday; admission is free.

Exit the park and turn left (west) on S-43-48 toward Shiloh. Drive 1.8 miles, passing S-43-412, and turn right (north) on S-43-597/Rush Street. Go 3.3 miles through fields and forestlands, and cross I–95 before coming to a stop sign and heading right (northeast) on S-43-61. This will take you 2.8 miles to SC 341/Lynches River Road.

As you turn left and head northwest, you leave Sumter County (named for Revolutionary War General Thomas Sumter, "The Gamecock") and enter Lee (as in Robert E.) County. Home of the South Carolina Cotton Museum and each October's Lee County Cotton Festival, Lee County is still a place where cotton is king.

Tanglewood Plantation and a small art gallery featuring the work of the current owners are just 0.8 mile up the road, on your left. This was once the home of "Cotton Ed" Smith, longtime U.S. senator, fierce segregationist, and occasional apologist for lynching.

Cruise 2.8 miles past more cotton and soybean fields, and then pass pretty **Lynchburg Presbyterian Church** on your right. Organized in 1855, it's the oldest church building in the area. Ease into the little town of **Lynchburg**, a once prosperous farm community whose best days seem to have come and gone. The town is an eclectic mixture of formerly grand old homes, numerous shanties, and a dilapidated downtown on the railroad tracks. Lynchburg has been passed over because of the deterioration of the family farm economy, the demise of passenger rail service, and modern highways. Patriot General Francis Marion, the "Swamp Fox," fought British troops here in 1781 under the cover of a grove of willow trees.

Cross US 76, travel one block, and cross the old railroad bed before turning left (southwest) on Main Street/S-31-661. After one block of old storefronts, turn left (southeast) on Griffin Street/S-31-671, cross the railbed again, go one block, and take a right (southwest) on US 76 to head past warehouses and out of town, in the direction of Mayesville.

Ride past a granary and cotton gin before arriving at Atkins, 3 miles down the road. Turn right (north) onto S-31-53, and ride 0.9 mile before turning left (west) onto S-31-327. **Lynchburg Savannah Heritage Preserve** is 1 mile along, on your right. This 291-acre tract of longleaf pine savannah habitat is an example of one of the most biologically diverse and imperiled ecosystems in North America. A haven for unusual and rare plants, it contains at least ten different carnivorous plant species and a plethora of wildflower types. Cricket frogs, wild turkeys, white-tailed deer, bobwhite quail, woodcocks, and red-cockaded woodpeckers are among the wildlife denizens, as well as a variety of sparrows, including Bachman's, Lincoln's, song, and field. Park your car and walk around a bit. If you are in a sports utility vehicle, you may be able explore the rough dirt roads on wheels. There is no admission charge.

Exit the preserve and continue 2 miles west on S-31-327 past pines and cotton fields. At the intersection with SC 527, turn left (south) and ride 3 miles back to US 76, at Rhodes Crossroads. Turn right (southwest) and ride 2.5 miles to Mayesville, crossing an upper portion of the mystical Black River.

The **Mayesville** community was settled in the early 1800s, and is decorated with beautiful old homes, small shanties, and a railroad track downtown area that seems to be from the Twilight Zone. It's famous as the childhood home of famed African-American educator Mary McLeod Bethune. Founder of both the National Council of Negro Women and Bethune-Cookman College in Daytona Beach, Florida, Dr. Bethune served as adviser to four U.S. presidents and was a U.S. delegate to the conference that drafted the United Nations Charter.

Pass the fork to the right, bearing left to go the intersection of US 76 and SC 154/Lafayette Street, where a historical marker about Dr. Bethune is located. Turn right (north) on SC 154/Lafayette Street. Old homes of the Mayes family are just up the way. They include the C. E. Mayes House, the Robert James Mayes House, and the Robert Peterson Mayes House, built between the mid-1800s and early 1900s.

Cross Main Street and the old railroad bed. To your right and straight ahead are the remnants of the once bustling downtown, including abandoned storefronts, an old two-story hotel, and cotton gins. You may want to explore the side streets. Those on the west (left) side of Lafayette include attractive, prosperous-looking homesteads; the east (right) side is lined with more modest homes of the majority of the population of the village.

Head north on SC 154 for 5.7 miles through pecan groves and cotton, corn, and soybean fields to the intersection with US 401. Turn right (northeast), cross the Black River again, and travel 4 miles to the crossroads village of **Elliott**. The quaint Elliott Post Office, a typical rural clapboard building with a front-gabled roof, is a few yards north, to your left.

Continue northeastward 2.5 miles to cross enchanting **Lynches River**. The section from Lee State Natural Area north of here to southern Florence County, where it eventually empties into the Great Pee Dee, has been designated a State Scenic River. From the bridge, ride 1.1 miles more to Carters Crossroads and turn left (north) on S-16-27/Lynches River Road. After a short sojourn in Darlington County, where you cross back into Lee County 3 miles up the road, S-16-27 becomes S-31-39.

Continue 0.4 mile, and then turn left (northwest) onto S-31-22. This road will carry you past I–20 and to the entrance to **Lee State Natural Area**, 2.7 miles away. Turn left (west) to enter the park and go to a stop about a half mile away. A left turn takes you to an artesian pond and park headquarters. Continue straight ahead to access the auto tour that loops 4.7 miles on a dirt road through forest and swamp, paralleling Lynches River on the back side.

Built in the 1930s by the Civilian Conservation Corps on the banks of Lynches River, the 2,839-acre park is a favorite launching area for canoes and kayaks heading down the pristine scenic river. The diverse habitat includes a hardwood floodplain forest, swampland, numerous artesian wells, a millpond, and dry sand hills.

This is a great place for wildlife viewing. The wetlands have river otters, beavers, muskrats, and rare spotted turtles, along with water moccasins and non-poisonous scarlet kingsnakes. On higher ground, look for white-tailed deer and wild turkeys.

Overhead and in the water, birdlife is plentiful. Seasonal and year-round residents include northern cardinals, Carolina chickadees, brown-headed and white-breasted nuthatches, blue-gray gnatcatchers, eastern wood pewees, summer tanagers, barred owls, red-shouldered hawks, belted kingfishers, wood ducks, and several varieties of woodpeckers, warblers, sparrows, vireos, and waterthrushes.

The river and ponds are popular for fishing, with bream, crappie, largemouth bass, catfish, and redbreast. Other amenities include campgrounds, picnic areas, rest rooms, a playground, an environmental education center, and nature trails, plus bridle paths and other facilities for equestrians.

Lee State Natural Area is open daily 9:00 A.M. to 9:00 P.M. during daylight saving time and 9:00 A.M. to 6:00 P.M. during standard time. Admission is free.

LEE STATE NATURAL AREA TO SUGARLOAF MOUNTAIN

Exit the park and take a left (north) on S-31-22. Go 3.7 miles and turn left (west) on US 15. At this intersection, a marker notes the site of South Carolina's last legal duel, in 1880, after which dueling was outlawed. Cross back over Lynches River and ride 3.5 miles to downtown **Bishopville**, the governmental and marketing center of Lee County. Settlement of this community of pretty homes, churches, and commercial buildings dates from late in the eighteenth century.

As you cruise into the middle of town, take a right (north) on Cedar Lane/ S-31-941 and stop at the **South Carolina Cotton Museum**, at 121 West Cedar Lane. Highlighting the economic, political, and social impact of cotton in the South, the facility has a array of displays ranging from the days of hand-picked cotton and mule-powered gins to today's machine-powered pickers and storage modules. A giant boll weevil model is a highlight, along with a crop-dusting Cessna Ag-Wagon hanging from the rafters. The museum has an excellent "Company Store."

Return along Cedar Street to US 15/Main Street, and turn right (west). On your left at the intersection of Main and Council Streets is the City-County Complex, originally constructed as the People's Bank around 1912.

As you cross Council Street, note the Opera House, where silent movies and traveling vaudeville performances were staged, but no operas. It now serves as a community center and hosts local performances and art shows. On this street, observe the workmanship of local artisans. Note the artistry of the brickwork and the cast iron and stamped tin building fronts. No two buildings display the same intricate geometric design and color or material.

Travel two blocks on US 15/Main Street to the Lee County Courthouse, with its Confederate soldier monument guarding against the North. Turn right (northwest) on Law Street/S-31-57, ride one block, and turn right (northeast) on Dennis Avenue. Go one block and turn left (northwest) to ease out of town on SC 34/Church Street, past tree-shaded homes and churches.

About a mile along, at the edge of town, turn right (northeast) on S-31-48. Travel 1.3 miles, turn right (southeast) on S-31-21, and then ride a half mile to the intersection with SC 341. Go left (north) toward Bethune, 13 miles into the **Sand Hills** (also spelled Sandhills), remnants of an ancient seacoast that now form a sandy belt stretching southwest to northeast across South Carolina's midriff, from North Augusta through Columbia and Camden all the way to Cheraw and into North Carolina. Along this lonely, rural road that parallels the west bank wetlands of Lynches River, you cross into Kershaw County and pass over Little Lynches River.

Bethune is a crossroads village nestled in the V of the junction of the wetlands of Lynches and Little Lynches Rivers. Railroad tracks and US 1 cross SC 341 in the middle of town. Take a right on US 1 and head northeast, crossing Lynches River for the last time after 1.8 miles. Here you enter Chesterfield County, settled by Welsh Baptists from Delaware in the mid-1700s and named for the Earl of Chesterfield, an English statesman of the time.

Proceed past forestlands and farm fields 5 miles to **McBee**, yet another railroad and crossroads village. The town once was the starting point for the Charlotte, Monroe and Columbia Railroad line, and a train depot built in 1915 now serves as a railroad museum and public library. McBee is also the center of a heavy concentration of peach growing in the surrounding area.

Cross SC 151 in the middle of town and continue 3.5 miles northeast past peach orchards and forest to the entrance for the **Carolina Sandhills National Wildlife Refuge**, on your left. Turn northward onto the delightful Wildlife Drive, a narrow, paved, winding roadway through the heart of the refuge.

There is no admission charge for Carolina Sandhills National Wildlife Refuge, which is open daily, sunrise to sunset. Hiking and mountain biking opportunities abound. Rest rooms and picnic facilities are located at the entrance off US 1 and at the Lake Bee Recreation Area off SC 145.

Carolina Sandhills National Wildlife Refuge was established in 1939 on 45,000 acres of land exhausted and eroded by farming. Through careful management, it has been restored to a rich, varied environment for many kinds of wildlife. Traversing the property is historic Wire Road, a route used by General Sherman's army on its rampaging Civil War march through South Carolina. The longleaf pine/wire grass ecosystem characteristic of the refuge's habitat once covered 90 million acres across the southeastern United States, from Virginia to Texas. Today, only scattered patches remain, mostly on public lands.

Rolling beds of deep sandy soils play host to an extensive longleaf pine forest, with an understory of scattered scrub oaks and a wire grass ground cover. Numerous small creeks and tributaries flow through the tract, providing corridors for hardwood species such as blackjack and black oaks, alder, bald cypress, southern red oak, dogwood, and sourwood, as well as dense stands of evergreen shrubs. The refuge also has thirty man-made ponds, numerous springs percolating through sandy soil, and 1,200 acres of fallow fields, forest openings, and cultivated fields, contributing to the land's richly diverse habitat.

At least 190 bird species, 42 mammal species, 41 kinds of reptiles, and 25 types of amphibians have been identified within the refuge's boundaries. The refuge is an important inland stopover for migratory waterfowl. Wood ducks, Canada geese and great blue herons are found here year-round, and great egrets and anhingas are usually in the ponds in spring and fall. Also, the refuge provides habitat for the endangered red-cockaded woodpecker. Trees housing nests of red-cockadeds are identified by white rings painted around the trunks. Red-tailed hawks, northern harriers, and American kestrels are common, and bald eagles and ospreys occasionally fly overhead.

Opossums, raccoons, fox squirrels, beavers, bobwhite quail, songbirds, wild turkeys, white-tailed deer, cottontail rabbits, foxes, yellow-bellied slider turtles, and buckeye and spicebush swallowtail butterflies are frequently spotted. Pine barrens tree frogs, listed by the state of South Carolina as "threatened," inhabit boggy areas.

Wildflowers go wild in the spring, and include trailing arbutus, orange milkwort, yellow jessamine, sweet pepperbush, wooly mullein, sensitive brier, lizard's tail, prickly pear, mountain laurel, and St.-John's-wort. Both the yellow and purple varieties of pitcher plants capture and devour insects.

One mile into the refuge is Pool A and the 1-mile Woodland Pond Trail loop around its edges. Ferns and wildflowers decorate the edges of the picturesque, stump-filled pond, and beavers are sometimes in evidence. Fishers are often seen dangling lines from the banks.

Continue uphill along Wildlife Drive, passing Wire Road, trees, more ponds, clearings, and lots of sand. A number of parking pullovers dot the way.

Martin's Lake Recreation Area requires a right turn 3 miles north of Pool A. The parking area is 0.8 mile from the turn. Beside the lake are both a photo blind and an observation tower. In winter, this is a special place for observing migratory waterfowl. Food plots are on the other side of the lake, creating additional opportunities for wildlife viewing. This is the southern trailhead for Tate's Trail, which runs northwest through sandy terrain for 2 miles, past Pool D and looping around Lake 12 to Lake Bee. The Martin's Lake end has lengthy boardwalks running through bald cypresses and briers.

Return to Wildlife Drive and continue northeastward. You cross between Pool D on your left and Martin's Lake 0.2 mile along, with great views of wetlands. At 0.6 mile past the wetlands, bear left (northwest) to stay on paved Wildlife Drive, rather than going right on the gravel road toward Mays Lake.

Pass Pool G on your right and, about 0.9 mile along, reach a left (south) turn toward Lake 12, where a kiosk provides a great deal of information about the refuge. Among many other interesting tidbits, you learn that beavers mate for life.

You reach SC 145 after another 0.1 mile. Go across the road and continue 0.2 mile to the Lake Bee Recreation Area on your left. For more delightful ponds, observation towers, forests, and meadows with great viewing opportunities, continue over gently rolling countryside for another 2 miles westward on Wildlife Drive. Pools H and J and Honkers and Oxpen Lakes provide great habitat, and side roads provide a number of sightseeing options.

CAROLINA SANDHILLS NATIONAL WILDLIFE REFUGE TO CHERAW

Return to SC 145 and turn left (northeast) toward Ruby. After 3 miles, just after you pass Refuge Road on your left and just before you reach the fire tower on your left, turn right (east) on unpaved Winery Road. Ride through forest for 2.6 miles before reaching S-13-29/Hartsville-Ruby Road. Turn right (southeast) and pass the former Tenner Brothers Winery (producers of such fine products Wild Irish Rose and Rock 'n Roll). Proceed 3 miles through hunting and logging lands and the Bay Springs community. As you enter **Sand Hills State Forest**, turn left (east) on unpaved S-13-63/Scotch Road, toward Sugar Loaf Mountain Recreation Area.

Sand Hills State Forest consists of 46,000 acres of infertile sand deposited by a prehistoric sea. The federal government purchased the land between 1935 and 1939 and turned it over to the state for management, before finally deeding it to South Carolina in 1991. Reforestation has been successful, and the once barren sand hills support productive stands of pines and a variety of wildlife and plant life. The state forest offers substantial mountain biking and equestrian opportunities, along with fishing, hunting, birding, and picnicking. It is open daily and is free of charge.

Quail, deer, wild turkeys, and mourning doves are among the favorites of hunters. The tract includes thirteen fishponds stocked with bass, bream, and catfish. Pine barrens tree frogs, red-cockaded woodpeckers, and Bachman's sparrows are among the more interesting species found here.

Follow Scotch Road 0.4 mile and then bear right on Bottom Road. A half mile along, you come to a small lake on the right, with a nature trail and picnic facilities. The road continues past large boulders and primitive camping areas before passing **Sugar Loaf Mountain** about 0.8 mile farther along, on your left.

Sugar Loaf Mountain is a monadnock, which is a granite outcropping remaining on flatter land that was worn away by climatic events eons ago. Sugar Loaf, covered with sand and once capped with ferrous sandstone, rises steeply about a hundred feet above surrounding terrain. An eight-to-twelve minute trek to the top is worth the effort. A viewing area allows visitors a 360 degree view of the surrounding forestlands. On the way up, notice the emerald mountain laurel and the diminutive pixie moss, which has a delicate pink bloom and fernlike appearance.

Continue 2.1 miles on Bottom Road and take a left (east) on Wire Road. Travel 2.2 miles to SC 102, where you turn right to head into **Patrick**, 1.7 miles south and surrounded by the Sand Hills Forest. Pass by modest homes, Patrick Baptist Church, and Patrick Depot, an old train station situated in the town park alongside the railroad tracks. The village, now reliant on timber trade, was once a distribution center for tar, resin, and turpentine. Cross the railroad tracks and turn left (northeast) immediately on US 1 to follow beside the tracks and past a mountain of wrecked cars to head toward Cheraw.

Cheraw National Fish Hatchery and Aquarium is 7 miles along the way, on your right. You can get out and walk around to observe specimens raised and exhibited here.

Continue 2.7 miles to a major intersection where US 1 and US 52 run concurrently northward, while US 52 winds southward alone. To visit 7,500-acre Cheraw State Park, turn right and travel 0.8 mile to the park entrance. South Carolina's oldest state park, it has a golf course, a swimming and boating lake with bathhouse facilities, equestrian stables and trails, picnic areas, and Turkey Oak Trail, a nature trail with 4.5-mile and 1.5-mile loop options. The pathway offers opportunities to see the rare red-cockaded woodpecker close at hand, as well as the lovely headwaters of the park lake, shaded by abundant bald cypress trees.

Return to the intersection of US 1 and US 52 and head north, crossing a causeway over the wetlands of Thompson Creek. Bear right (east) 2.4 miles along the way, where SC 9/Market Street joins US 1/US 52, and continue into **Cheraw**, which bills itself as "The Prettiest Town in Dixie."

Settled in 1740 as the site of a small trading post and water mill, the town was laid out with wide streets and a town green that are the nucleus of a 218-acre historic district. Rich with gardens, parks and the architectural legacy of more than two centuries, the area has a multitude of antebellum and Victorian structures.

The town was once the head of navigation for the Great Pee Dee River, which was used by steamboats in the nineteenth century to carry merchandise to Georgetown and the Atlantic Ocean. Local products sent downstream included cotton, indigo, tobacco, corn, rice, and cattle products. This commerce made Cheraw relatively wealthy, and the community once boasted the largest bank in South Carolina outside of Charleston. Its more recent claim to fame is as the hometown of Dizzy Gillespie, whose legacy is bebop, the fast, intense form of jazz he helped create.

Continue two blocks and notice on your left, at 700 Market, a classic Queen Anne house built in 1825. Across the street on the opposite corner is 617 Market, built about 1850. St. Peter's Catholic Church (circa 1840) is at 602 Market, and the houses at 504 and 505 Market were built around 1850. The "new" St. David's Episcopal Church, built in Gothic style in 1916, is at the corner of Market and Huger Streets. The homes at 320 and 317 Market Street were both built around 1822.

On the next block are the Merchant's Bank Building (circa 1835) and the **Town Green**, which hosts the Greek Revival Inglis-McIver Office (circa 1820), Town Hall (circa 1858), steepled Market Hall (circa 1837), and the Lyceum Museum (circa 1825), where Cheraw's history is depicted. At the intersection of Market and Second Street, a pretty little downtown shopping area is straight ahead. It includes the original B. C. Moore and Sons department store, cornerstone of what was once a major retail chain throughout small towns in the Carolinas.

Turn left (north) on Second Street and left (west) again to travel two blocks on Kershaw Street. The house at 212 Kershaw was built around 1830, and the house at 310 Kershaw was built about 1826. A 1902 neoclassic frame Victorian house is at 314 Kershaw.

As you take a right (north) on Greene Street, notice on your left, at 223 Greene, the Green-Prince House (circa 1824). At 307 Greene is Wesley United Methodist Church, which Dizzy Gillespie attended in his youth in the early 1900s. The late Queen Anne house at 323 Greene was built in 1895, and the home at 327 Greene was constructed around 1860. Across the street at 328 Greene is an old farmhouse. Built around 1815, it's said to be haunted by ghosts. In the next block are antebellum houses at 406 Greene (circa 1800) and 416 Greene (circa 1855).

Turn right (east) on Boundary Street and right (south) again on Third Street. Pass by a 1905 house at 427 Third and a nineteenth-century store at 407 Third. Across the street at 412 Third is a house built prior to 1850 and at 404 Third, a home built around 1837. On corners at the next block are a Dutch Colonial Revival house erected in 1901 and a brick neoclassic structure built in 1919. Houses built in 1820 and 1850 are next, at 321 and 313 Third Street. The Lafayette House (circa 1823), where the Marquis de Lafayette of American Revolution fame was entertained, is at 235 Third Street, and "The Teacherage," built prior to 1790 and the oldest house in town, is at 230 Third Street. A Charleston Box house (circa 1800) is at 226 Third Street, and the old Presbyterian Manse (circa 1836) is at 219 Third. The First United Methodist Church (circa 1851), built in Greek Revival style with four Doric columns, is on the next block.

Turn left (east) on Church Street. Go one block, cross Second Street, and bear left to cross the railroad tracks and arrive at Front Street. Turn right (south) on Front Street and go one block to return to Church Street.

Old St. David's Church, constructed around 1770 and the last Anglican "state church" built in South Carolina under King George, is to your right, on Church Street. It was used by both Patriot and British forces in the American Revolution, and by both Confederate and Union soldiers during the Civil War. Veterans from every American war are buried in the venerable cemetery. In front of the cemetery is the first Confederate monument in South Carolina, erected in 1867 while the state was still under occupation by Federal troops.

Old St. David's Church

Complete your tour by riding two more blocks east on Church Street to Riverside Park, on the banks of the majestic **Great Pee Dee River**. This is the site of the former steamboat landing and a covered bridge. The park offers a boat landing, trails, and picnicking.

The Great Pee Dee, which originates in the North Carolina mountains as the Yadkin River, is still passable by small boats for 175 winding miles downstream to Georgetown. Stephen Foster, inspired by a visit to South Carolina, originally called his famous song "Way Down upon the Pee Dee River," but he was somehow later persuaded that "Suwannee" sounded more melodious. South of Cheraw, the river, teeming with catfish, bream, and redbreast, flows through lowland swamps.

9

Tobacco Road

WILLIAMSBURG COUNTY

GENERAL DESCRIPTION: Visitors enjoy a 95-mile loop in the heart of South Carolina's coastal plain farm country, starting in live-oak-laden Kingstree beside the enchanting Black River, and crisscrossing the river several times as they travel past tobacco fields and green pastures, country stores and churches, tin-roofed homesteads and shanties, pine forests and hardwood swamps, and ancient barns and old settlements while glimpsing the rural South of yesteryear.

SPECIAL ATTRACTIONS: Kingstree, Williamsburg County Courthouse, Black River, Cooper's Country Store, Indiantown Presbyterian Church, Springbank Center.

LOCATION: Eastern part of the state, halfway between Georgetown and Florence.

DRIVE ROUTE NUMBERS: SC 527, SC 261, US 52, S-45-197, S-45-146, S-45-19, US 521, SC 377, S-45-142, S-45-285, S-45-30, S-45-254, S-45-218, S-45-24, S-45-121, SC 512, S-45-28, S-45-47, S-45-114, S-45-35, S-45-643.

TRAVEL SEASON: All year.

SERVICES: Kingstree, Lake City, and Hemingway have restaurants, accommodations, and most basic services. For a full array of options, go to Florence or Georgetown.

See For More Information in the appendix for addresses and phone numbers of Attractions, Camping, Neat Places to Stay, Restaurants, Shops, Tours, and Nature-Based Services.

THE DRIVE

This drive begins in Kingstree, settled in 1732 by Scotch-Irish immigrants. Some would say that little has changed since that time. You pass by live oaks, old homes surrounded by Spanish-moss-laden trees, and a courthouse designed by Robert Mills, and you cross the dark, mystical Black River. You then travel through rich farmland filled with tobacco, cotton, corn, and soybeans and past pastures full of hay, cows, and horses. You ride by pine forests and hardwood bottomlands and over creeks and swamps. You see country stores, numerous small churches, and farmhouses and shanties as you pass through one of the poorest, most agrarian, least industrialized counties in the state. The tiny communities of Salters, Millwood, Cedar Swamp, Nesmith, Indiantown, Cades, Hebron, and Mouzon await as you visit the true Old South, with its charm, beauty, and poverty.

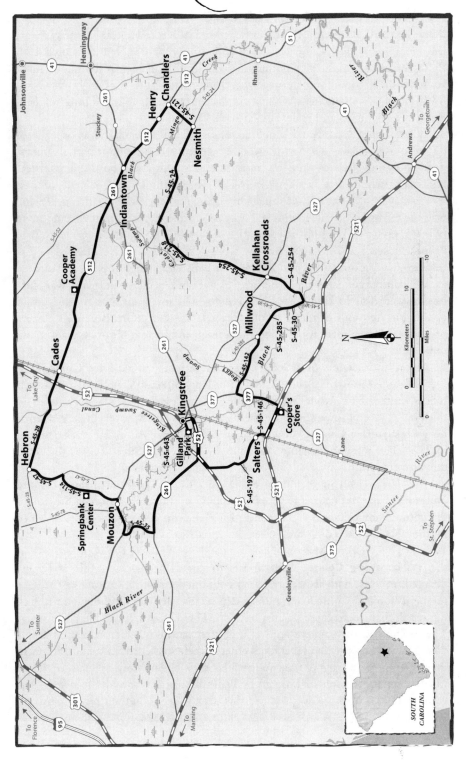

KINGSTREE TO SALTERS

Begin in quaint **Kingstree**, the county seat and largest town in the heavily agrarian county of Williamsburg. The town and county were settled by Scotch-Irish Presbyterians from Ulster beginning in 1732, and the names in the phone book attest to their continuing heritage. McBrides, McClams, McClarys, McCreas, McCulloughs, McCutchens, McElveens, McFaddens, McGills, McIntoshes, Mc-Kenzies, McKnights and many similar names abound.

Williamsburg County remained largely rural and agricultural as other areas began to industrialize during the twentieth century. For the most part, its inhabitants like things just as they are, away from the hustle and bustle of interstate highways and industrial smokestacks. When citizens think of the benefits of their locale, they think of hunting, fishing, and eating the world's best barbecue. By the way, the term "barbecue" here refers only to vinegar-based pork barbecue (none of that mustard or ketchup-based stuff), and certainly not to cattle products. Barbecue chicken is also popular, but the word "chicken" is always attached to distinguish that product from good ol' regular barbecue, which is pork, of course.

Williamsburgers also think heritage. A number of Revolutionary War skirmishes were fought throughout the county, and many citizens remain proud of the contributions of locals to the Confederate war effort. Because so many original families remain rooted here, genealogy and church history are also quite important.

At the intersection of US 52/Longstreet Street (named after Confederate General James Longstreet) and SC 527/Academy Street in Kingstree, travel seven blocks southeast on Academy Street. Notice the lovely homes and churches in this quiet, graceful town decked with live oak trees and Spanish moss. **Williamsburg Presbyterian Church**, on your right at 411 North Academy, was organized in 1736. The present structure was built in 1890. Mill Street begins the small downtown section.

Turn left on Mill Street and drive one block to visit the **Williamsburg County Museum**, in the old Carnegie Library building on the corner of Mill Street and Hampton Avenue. Take a right (south) on Hampton and go one block to once bustling but now serene Main Street, which is also SC 261.

Go right (west) on Main, and ride one and a half blocks. On your left, take in the **Williamsburg County Courthouse**, designed by Robert Mills and constructed in 1823, with its stately raised columned entrance. On the east side of the courthouse, a Confederate monument stands tall, with a soldier on top facing north to forever guard against invaders. There is a slight problem, however. The insignia on the soldier's apparel indicates that he is a Union man. It seems there was a mix-up when local folks ordered their statue from a manufacturer in Pennsylvania at the turn of the twentieth century. The mystery of what happened to the Confederate soldier ordered by Williamsburg was solved a few years ago when people in York, Maine, realized they had a Rebel on their monument.

The Confederate monument is nicely balanced on the west side of the courthouse, where a memorial to former U.S. Supreme Court Justice Thurgood Marshall and Dr. Martin Luther King Jr. has been erected. In 1954, Marshall represented parents in neighboring Clarendon County who won their lawsuit outlawing school segregation. King visited here in 1966 to launch eventually successful voting rights efforts in South Carolina.

Also on the courthouse grounds are markers honoring Revolutionary War, World War I, and World War II veterans, as well as a Liberty Bell recovered from the belfry of a demolished schoolhouse.

Proceed west on Main Street past the Greater Bethel African Methodist Episcopal church on your right. *You may wish to detour left (southeast) on Nelson Boulevard for 1.5 miles to visit* **Thorntree**, *a restored house originally built in 1749 and open to the public.*

At the end of the third block, one block after joining US 52 heading southwest, a small granite monument near the edge of the flowered median marks the spot where the original **King's Tree** was located. A young white pine stands behind the marker. When Scotch-Irish Presbyterians sailed up the Black River from Georgetown in 1732 looking for a place to disembark, they noticed a tall white pine, rare in this area, towering above a low bluff. At the time, white pines were reserved for use as masts on the king's ship. The settlers landed and settled the area around the King's Tree, which eventually became the seat of government for the new county of Williamsburg, named after William of Orange, hero to the Ulstermen.

Continue a few yards and cross the bridge over the beautiful, serene **Black River**, now protected as a State Scenic River. The river's color derives from tannic-rich decaying matter and the water's placid flow from its multiple spring headwaters in dark swamps to the north. The winding river is navigable for canoes and fishing boats many miles northward, and boaters can travel southward all the way to Winyah Bay and Georgetown.

Head southwest across the Lamar Nathaniel Johnson Bridge in the direction of Charleston. Drive along a causeway above the ponds and wetlands that border the Black River. After 2.3 miles past the Black River crossing, pass by a road sign indicating SC 261 and Manning to the right as you continue left (southwest) to stay on US 52.

A little more than a mile farther, you will see on your left the Tri County Gin and Cotton Company on your left. Just beyond the large cotton processing facility, take the next left (southeast) on S-45-197/Old Gapway Road to head toward Salters, 4.4 miles away. This road takes you past tiny churches, modest rural homes, farm fields and pastures, and a patch of wetlands.

When you pass by large, charming white dwellings on your right and reach the quaint railroad village of **Salters**, turn right (southwest) on S-45-146/Depot Street, split from the east side of town by a still heavily used double railroad track.

Salters is a throwback to early twentieth-century rural South Carolina. Mostly African-American folks live in the modest cottages on the east side of the tracks, and mostly white folks live in the homes on the west side. In the case of both races, most inhabitants are descendants of families that have lived in the area for a century or more.

Bright flowers adorn the attractively manicured railroad median as you ease your way down Railroad Avenue. Stately moss-hung oaks canopy the roads on both sides of the train tracks, and pecan trees shade the yards. You pass comfortable old country homes, including a rambling Victorian house on your right at the end of the street.

Pass long-abandoned stores, the old **Salters Depot Railroad Station**, and a small volunteer fire department as you turn left (east) onto Glad Street/S-45-19, and cross the railroad tracks.

SALTERS TO NESMITH

Merge into US 521/B. J. Gordon Highway after 0.3 mile and continue eastward, past kudzu and the wetlands of Thorntree Swamp toward Cooper's Country Store at the intersection of US 521 and SC 377, 2 miles away.

Cooper's Country Store is a delight. Famous for its smoked ham and fresh barbecue, it also sells boiled peanuts, Exxon gasoline, hunting and fishing licenses, pit and English bulldogs, guns and ammo, fishing canes, lawn mowers, kitchenware, men's underwear and ladies' "quality" lingerie, plumbing fixtures, tools, oil burning lamps, laundry scrub boards, and a variety of snacks and groceries, including twenty-pound sacks of Blue Ribbon Long Grain Rice.

This is a great place to take a break. Enjoy a cold, tangy Blenheim Ginger Ale along with a Moon Pie or a pack of Nabs while relaxing at the adjacent picnic table under the shade of old pecan trees. Clean rest rooms are attached to the exterior of the building. Behind the main building is a screened-in structure where cured hams hang.

Several generations of the Burrows and Cooper families have operated this significant cultural and architectural example of an early twentieth-century country store. It started with the motto "We Serve the Needs of the Neighborhood." Originally, the owners lived on the second story, above the white wooden store with red trim. The home's enclosed front porch stretches over the gasoline pumps. A sign on the front door warns: FREE RIDE IN A SHERIFF'S CAR IF YOU SHOPLIFT FROM THIS STORE.

Leave the store and head east a few yards to a stop sign. On your right is a historical marker noting the Battle of Lower Bridge during the American Revolution, where Patriot General Francis Marion and his irregulars defeated the British in 1781 and thwarted their attempt to cross the Black River and invade the heart of Williamsburg County.

Cooper's Country Store

Turn left on SC 377 and head north in the direction of Kingstree. You again cross the beautiful, winding Black River, with attractive views east and west. Three more bridges carry you over sprawling wetlands as you travel 2.9 miles to S-45-142/Millwood Road; turn right (east). A sign pointing toward S. A. Guerry and Sons General Merchandise marks the turn.

Drive 4 miles, passing Boggy Swamp and fields of tobacco to reach the heart of the old **Millwood** community and S. A. Guerry and Sons, another traditional, still-functioning country store with all kinds of items for sale. You can buy a hot dog for a dollar, and pick up some kerosene, but not gasoline. A comfortable old farmhouse and Millwood Methodist Church complete "downtown" Millwood.

Bear right (southeast) on S-45-285, which merges into S-45-30 after 2.5 miles. Tobacco, corn, soybeans, and pine trees are plentiful, and this route includes a few old-timey tobacco curing barns, rickety buildings about two stories high, topped by tin roofs, with their sides often wrapped in green roofing material. A sign on one reads, THERE'S ONE WAY TO HEAVEN—TRUST JESUS. Advertising on these back roads is scarce, and the few signs you see are often suggestions for saving your soul or directions to nearby churches.

About a mile and a half farther along S-45-30, you cross the Black River again, this time along one of its most scenic stretches. There are small boat landings on both sides of the river, and you can often see locals lolling in small boats, practicing the official pastime of Williamsburg: goin' fishin'. Bass, redbreast, crappie, catfish, and bream await baited hooks. Moss-laden trees overhang the stream, and lily pads decorate the shallows. Tupelos, cypresses, and live oaks frame the bucolic scene, while birds of prey circle lazily above, searching for victims in the dense wetlands below.

After you reach the far (west) side of the river, turn around and cross the bridge, heading east. Just beyond the east side of the river, turn right (northeast) on S-45-254/Kellahan Road toward Kellahan Crossroads, 3 miles away: the first mile is unpaved. When you reach Kellahan Crossroads, cross over SC 527 and continue north toward the **Cedar Swamp** community on S-45-254/Sam Brown Road.

This rich crop and pasture land is amid some of the earliest land cleared and settled by Scotch-Irish colonials in the first half of the eighteenth century. Horses, hogs, tobacco, and soybeans reign here, and the community still hosts an annual lancing tournament, in which riders use jousting lances not to attack each other, but to spear small rings dangling from cross-arms.

After 4.7 miles, turn left (northwest) onto S-45-218/Big Woods Road to cross through the middle of the Cedar Swamp community. Continue northeast 3.8 miles and turn right (southeast) on S-45-24 toward the Nesmith community, 6.7 miles away. After passing wetlands and more rich farmland, you enter **Nesmith**, which boasts a few ramshackle homes, an old post office, abandoned buildings, and one small store. A railroad track splits the settlement. Cross the tracks and turn left (northeast) on S-45-121/Old Mingo Road, toward Henry.

NESMITH TO HEBRON

Cross Black Mingo Creek, and, 2.2 miles from Nesmith, you reach an intersection with SC 512/Henry Road. A sprawling nineteenth-century farmhouse sits to the right, surrounded by tobacco fields. Take a left (northwest) toward Indiantown, about 5 miles away. Pass over the railroad tracks in Henry after a half mile and continue through countryside full of modest farmhouses, cotton, tobacco, corn, and soybeans. As you approach Indiantown, the farmhouses become more impressive.

Pass over wetlands to an intersection with SC 261, on the east side of the Indiantown community. Across the road, the Indiantown Market sells shrimp, crabs, oysters, and other fresh seafood, as well as watermelons and a variety of produce. Turn left (west) on SC 512/SC 261. A sign points toward Kingstree.

Travel only about 0.2 mile and pull into the parking lot of lovely **Indiantown Presbyterian Church** on your left. This congregation was organized in 1757, and its first building was destroyed by British troops in 1780. The present structure, the third on this site, was completed in 1830. The old cemetery behind the building is especially appealing, and includes the grave of Major John James, a hero of the Revolutionary War.

Leave Indiantown Presbyterian Church and continue west through farmland on SC 512/SC 261, past the old Indiantown School, the community school for whites during the first two-thirds of the twentieth century, and Battery Park School, once the community school for African-Americans. After 2 miles, bear to the right (northwest) on SC 512 toward Cades, as SC 261 veers southwest in the direction of Kingstree.

This 12-mile stretch to Cades is an exceptionally pretty roadway. After crossing more swamp wetlands, you pass through gently rolling, verdant pastures, forests, and crop fields. Horses and cows graze in the shade of hardwoods and drink from scattered creeks and ponds. Cowbirds, whose ancestors migrated from Africa on slave ships, stand watch over the cattle for bugs. Attractive farm dwellings can be spotted among the trees. About halfway along, look for the old **Cooper Academy** on your right, just before you pass the modern Bethesda Methodist Church building. The academy, which looks like a dilapidated two-story country store, was built in 1905 and operated until 1926. Continue eastward past the old, white frame Bethesda Methodist Church building, tin-roofed farm homes, and more tobacco and cotton fields until you reach the village of **Cades**, left behind when the railroad stopped bringing passengers and US 52 blossomed a half mile away.

Cross the railroad tracks and continue past the junction with US 52, heading westward on S-45-28 toward the **Hebron** community, 6 miles away. Pass by more attractive farm structures, cotton and tobacco fields, pastures, and woodlands. At the crossroads settlement of Hebron, you'll see the old Hebron School on your left, now a small garment-finishing facility. A ramshackle country store and a few homes dot the area, along with the steepled white frame Hebron United Methodist Church.

HEBRON TO KINGSTREE

Turn left (south) on S-45-47. After 2.5 miles, take a right onto S-45-114/Springbank Road. This is a pleasant lane through magnolias, dogwoods, oaks, and pines. You begin a long stretch past the walls of Springfield Plantation on your left as the **Springbank Center for Eco-Spirituality and the Arts** unfolds on your right. Formerly a plantation and then a quail-hunting reserve, Springbank became a monastery in 1955, known for its social outreach programs. In the 1980s, it was deeded in trust to an ecumenical board of directors. Today it is a retreat facility that offers seminars, workshops, and other healing and renewal experiences. You may stop at the lovely white-columned mansion headquarters, with its magnolia-lined front drive, and enjoy the natural beauty of the lush grounds.

The landscape features live oaks and flowering camellias, as well as a swamp wilderness filled with stately gums.

After 4.1 miles, Springbank Road ends at SC 527/Sumter Highway. Turn right (west) here and take a ride through the **Mouzon** community, past old homes, Mouzon Presbyterian Church, and Pudding Swamp. After crossing the swamp, look for a two-story wooden house on your left, known to some as Johnny's Doom. Turn left (south) just beyond the house, 2.3 miles from Springbank Road, onto S-45-35/Mt. Vernon Road.

S-45-35 carries you over a bridge that spans the Black River and seven more bridges over its extensive wetlands. On the other side of the wetlands, you pass pretty horse pastures and Mt. Vernon United Methodist, which is a redbrick instead of white wood frame structure, unusual for an older Methodist Church out in the country.

You reach SC 261 about 2.3 miles after the turnoff from SC 527. Turn left (east) here, at Parrott's Grocery, and head toward Kingstree, 8.3 miles away. As you approach the intersection, a JESUS SAVES sign is on the left and a sign on the right reiterates, ONLY ONE WAY TO HEAVEN . . . JESUS. Drive about a mile and a half, and take note of Way Antiques, housed in a former country store and featuring old farm implements and other relics of early twentieth-century rural life. Drive about 4.4 miles farther, passing more modest farmhouses, woodland tracts, hay and cotton fields, and grazing horses before turning left onto US 52, heading northeast into Kingstree.

South of Kingstree

Drive 2.4 miles, passing another JESUS SAVES sign and crossing the wetlands causeway and a bridge over Black River. Continue one block past the King's Tree marker on your left to the traffic light where US 52 turns left (north) onto Longstreet Street, toward Lake City. Follow US 52/Longstreet north for five blocks and turn left onto S-45-643/Singleton Street.

Singleton Street passes through swampland and crosses a small canal before emptying into **Gilland Memorial Park**, a municipal recreation area on the Black River a half mile from US 52. The park has a boat ramp, a picnic area with grills, rest rooms, and a swimming area with a hanging rope swing on the opposite bank. The snowy white, sandy beach area contrasts beautifully with the black, mysterious river. For many years before the park was established, this area was known as the Scout Cabin, and generations of Kingstree area young folks learned to swim here during the day and make whoopee during the evening. You are free to do either.

10

Waccamaw Neck

MURRELLS INLET TO PAWLEYS ISLAND

GENERAL DESCRIPTION: This 20-mile coastal drive begins in the restaurant-laden fishing village of Murrells Inlet and takes travelers to exquisite Brookgreen Gardens, salty Huntington Beach State Park, and the Waccamaw River before ending at the beaches of rustic Pawleys Island.

SPECIAL ATTRACTIONS: Brookgreen Gardens, Huntington Beach State Park, Waccamaw River, Atalaya, Litchfield Beach, Pawleys Island.

LOCATION: Northern coast.

DRIVE ROUTE NUMBERS: US Business 17, US 17, S-22-362/Sandy Island Road, S-22-46/Myrtle Avenue, Pritchard Street.

TRAVEL SEASON: All year. Several festivals in this area during the summer might be fun to attend: Atalaya Arts and Crafts Festival, Tidelands Birding Festival, and the Blessing of the Inlet. Brookgreen Gardens is especially beautiful in the spring when the azaleas are in bloom.

SERVICES: Accommodations are plentiful, especially in Myrtle Beach, but also in Litchfield Beach, Pawleys Island, and Georgetown.

See For More Information in the appendix for addresses and phone numbers of Attractions, Camping, Neat Places to Stay, Restaurants, Shops, Tours, and Nature-Based Services.

THE DRIVE

This trip begins in the midst of the lush tidal, salt marsh creeks of the fishing village Murrells Inlet, and takes you past the numerous and eclectic seafood restaurants that make Murrells Inlet the seafood capital of South Carolina. Next, you pass by stately oaks to visit Huntington Beach with its rolling sandy dunes and Moorish old seaside mansion, before stopping at Brookgreen Gardens, home to the world's largest outdoor collection of American figurative sculpture, set in exquisite botanical gardens. You glimpse isolated Sandy Island, the largest undeveloped tract remaining in the Waccamaw Neck area, continue past touristy Litchfield Beach, and wind up at rustic Pawleys Island, once a resort island for wealthy South Carolina plantation owners and now "arrogantly shabby."

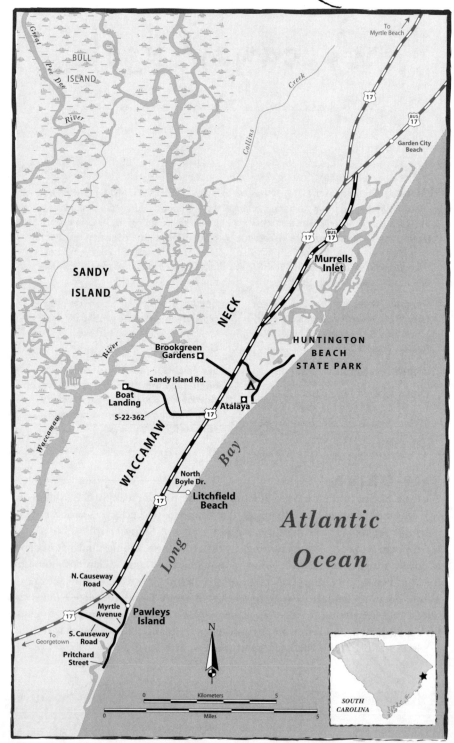

MURRELLS INLET

Begin this ride at the northern intersection of US 17 and US Business 17 at the northern edge of **Murrells Inlet**, South Carolina's Seafood Capital. The Myrtle Beach Chamber of Commerce's Visitor Information Center is at 3401 US Business 17 South. Here you can pick up brochures on Murrells Inlet and nearby Myrtle Beach restaurants, hotels, motels, rental units, and nature-based services, before heading south on US Business 17.

Founded in the late eighteenth century by Captain Morrall, Murrells Inlet, built on tidal and salt marsh creeks, has supplied the Waccamaw Neck with fresh seafood for more than 200 years. This quaint fishing village remains a port for commercial fishing boats and home to many deep-sea fishing charter vessels even today.

Part of the intrigue of Murrells Inlet is its interesting folklore. Drunken Jack Island, off of the coast of Murrells Inlet, is said to have been the site where an old pirate, Jack, was accidentally marooned with no provisions save his shipmates' rum supply. When the ship returned to the island months later to retrieve the rum cargo, the crew found case after case of empty rum bottles all along the shore, as well as the bones of Jack. This same island is believed to be where Blackbeard's treasure is buried, and it's the first recorded site of the Hot Fish Club clubhouse. Formed before 1816 by the planters of All Saints Parish dedicated to epicurean pursuits, this social club most likely dissolved before the Civil War. A nearby restaurant now has this name.

Murrells Inlet is also home to the ghost of Alice Flagg. The legend, which began in 1849, tells the story of Alice, who fell in love with a man of a different social class. Because he did not meet with her parents' approval, he and Alice became secretly engaged. When Mrs. Flagg discovered the engagement ring, Alice was sent to a school in Charleston to separate the engaged pair. Alice became ill in Charleston, so her brother was sent to retrieve her. On their journey home to Murrells Inlet, Alice died and was buried in the All Saints Church Waccamaw Episcopal cemetery, but without her engagement ring. It is said that Alice is still sighted today in that cemetery, searching for her ring.

If the ghosts of Murrells Inlet don't tickle your fancy, then perhaps the dozens of restaurants found here, most of which are arranged along US Business 17, will delight you and your taste buds. You can't go wrong at any of the village's eating establishments. Oliver's Lodge offers delicious seafood, fantastic hush puppies, and a great view of the inlet. Other longtime establishments, which antedate the village's current boom, include Lee's Inlet Kitchen and the Wayside. Flo's Place, a Murrells Inlet landmark, serves spicy Cajun dishes in a lively atmosphere with more than 3,000 hats hanging from the ceiling; the Divine Fish House, an elegant modern restaurant with a stunning view of Murrells Inlet, serves Lowcountry dishes. Not all of the delightful restaurants can be listed here, but stop in at any of them as you wander down US Business 17.

As you drive south, the beach and marsh are mostly on your left. Homes, some belonging to writers and other mild celebrities, are tucked behind old oaks, amid the numerous restaurants and pubs. The drive down "restaurant row" to the stop sign at US 17 South is only 4.5 miles.

When you arrive at the end of US Business 17, cross over US 17 North and merge onto US 17 South toward Huntington Beach State Park.

HUNTINGTON BEACH STATE PARK

Huntington Beach State Park is on your left (east), approximately 1.1 miles from US Business 17. The turn into the park is clearly marked, so you can't miss it. There is a small admission fee. The park is open daily from 6:00 A.M. to 10:00 P.M. during daylight saving hours, and from 6:00 A.M. to 6:00 P.M. the rest of the year.

Huntington Beach is in an area known as Waccamaw Neck, bounded by the Waccamaw River and the Atlantic Ocean, where rice plantations flourished in the eighteenth and nineteenth centuries. The park's 2,500 acres are remarkable for their range of habitats, including sandy ocean beach, freshwater and saltwater marsh, dunes, shrub thickets, freshwater lagoons, maritime forest, rock jetties, and inlets, not to mention the Atlantic Ocean. Saltwater marsh is considered the most productive habitat in the world, so this park is an exceptional example of a natural beach-dune-estuary system. More than 250 bird species are found here. Huntington Beach is probably best known for its public bird-watching, perhaps the best not only in South Carolina but on the East Coast.

Follow the main park road, which is lined with tall, thick vegetation. The stand of hardwoods near the park entrance is home to various warblers year-round. Seasonal visitors to this area include chickadees, titmice, nuthatches, sapsuckers, solitary vireos, brown creepers, northern parulas, and eastern screech owls.

Cross over a causeway where oyster beds bulge from the saltwater mud on your left and alligators bask in the sun to your right. Egrets wade in the marsh near the wooden walkways that stretch deep into the marsh. The causeway divides freshwater marsh from saltwater marsh. Turn right at the stop sign, a half mile from the entrance. The causeway parking lot is on your left. Stop here and walk to the long dock that extends into the freshwater lagoon. Living in the freshwater area are ducks (ruddy, teal, widgeon, pintail, canvasback), tundra swans, coots, common moorhens, pied-billed grebes, anhingas, bald eagles, sedge wrens, yellowthroat warblers, sora rails, scaup (greater and lesser), mergansers (hooded and red-breasted), buffleheads, least bitterns, and black-crowned night herons. In summer, least terns and white ibis are found here. Rare avian species found in this part of the park include old-squaw and surf scooter. Alligators in large numbers and pond sliders represent the reptiles here, swimming with bass and bream.

Follow the road to the right; a large parking area is clearly identified on your left. Here the park offers picnic areas with shelters, boardwalks, surf fishing, crabbing, and bird-watching, as well as a visitor center and gift shop. Two camping areas offer 127 campsites. The beach is accessible from this parking area, where rest rooms, shower facilities, and picnic grounds are also located.

Atalaya is off to the right (south) side of the parking lot on this end of the park, and you are welcome to stroll through the complex. Called "The Castle" by locals, Atalaya is the Moorish-style former vacation home and studio of philanthropists Archer and Anna Hyatt Huntington, the creators of nearby Brookgreen Gardens.

Leave the parking area and drive north. Just past the causeway, stop at the education center and marsh boardwalk on the left and enjoy the salt marsh. Across the road from the small parking lot is the south entrance to the Sandpiper Pond Nature Trail.

The salt marsh is dominated by cordgrass (spartina). Birds in the marsh area include herons (tricolored and great blue), egrets (snowy and great), willet, American oystercatchers, plovers (black-bellied and semipalmated), sandpipers, clapper rails, boat-tailed grackles, seaside sparrows (sharp-tailed sparrows in winter), and marsh wrens. Diamondback terrapins, fiddler crabs, periwinkle snails, and shrimp are also present, sometimes in astonishing numbers.

As you drive to the north end parking area, 1.5 miles from the south end, you are surrounded by a shrub thicket with pines, live oaks, wax myrtle, red cedar,

Atalaya

tamarisk, groundsel, yaupon holly, yellow jassamine, smilax, Virginia creeper, black needle rush, and saltmarsh aster. Birds found here include common ground dove, prairie warbler (spring and summer), gray catbird, rufous-sided towhee, Carolina wren, yellow-rumped warbler, cedar waxwing, robin, sparrows (white-throated and fox), hawks (sharp-shinned and Cooper's), and painted bunting (in spring and early summer). Bobcats are around, but you are likely to see only their tracks.

At the north end of the park is a large paved parking area where picnic areas, vending machines, and a large grass meadow are available for your use. Two nature trails are accessible here.

Both birds and birders flock on and near the jetties, a 2-mile walk northward from the parking area. Some birds seen here include ruddy turnstone, purple sandpiper, double-crested cormorant, horned grebe, and scooter. Rare birds found are old-squaw, eider and harlequin duck, greater cormorant, greater black-backed gull, and brant. Red drum, spotted sea trout, and flounder swim in the ocean and inlet. Offshore are gannets, common loons, and black skimmers.

On the lagoon and in the dunes live gulls, terns, snow buntings, longspurs, short-eared owls, ground doves, marsh wrens, and, in winter, sedge wrens. Sparrows that make their home here include seaside, rare Savannah, Le Conte's sharp-tailed, and Ipswich varieties.

If you happen to visit the park late into the evening, you may get a glimpse of the ghost of Theodosia Burr Alston, daughter of American Founding Father Aaron Burr. Theodosia, who was unhappy in South Carolina and wanted to visit her father in New York, disappeared after boarding the *Patriot* in Georgetown on December 30, 1812. After the ship left Georgetown, it was never seen again. On foggy nights, Theodosia is sometimes sighted suspended above the waves of the Atlantic Ocean.

Backtrack for 2.9 miles to exit Huntington Beach State Park, and take an immediate left onto US 17 South.

BROOKGREEN GARDENS

Brookgreen Gardens is 0.3 mile down the highway on your right (west). You can't miss Anna Hyatt Huntington's statue of two fighting horses at the entrance.

Brookgreen Gardens touts botanical gardens, a wildlife park, creek and rice field pontoon cruises, and a new *Southern Living* home. This sanctuary was developed in the 1930s by Anna Hyatt Huntington on the site of four colonial rice and indigo plantations covering more than 9,000 acres of savannah, marshes, and beaches. It displays more than 550 nineteenth- and twentieth-century sculptures and 2,000 species of plants.

Visitors are treated to magnificent live oaks, formal gardens, sculpture gardens, and botanical gardens, as well as a wildlife park with foxes, deer, turkeys, raccoons, squirrels, snakes, otters, and alligators, a bird sanctuary and raptor aviary, and a serpentine boardwalk around a half-acre cypress swamp. In the cypress swamp, an impressive aviary features herons, egrets, ibis, bald eagles, owls, and red-tailed hawks. In addition, a herd of about forty deer roam a twenty-acre enclosed savannah. The nature trail passes a native plant garden, which features insect-eating Venus's-flytraps and pitcher plants, as well as other plant life. A furnished *Southern Living* model house/house, a 2,200- square-foot cottage on Jessamine Pond surrounded by pines and a backyard garden, is open to visitors.

A place of great natural beauty, Brookgreen Gardens also has the largest outdoor collection of American figurative sculpture in existence. Developed first as a showplace for the works of Anna Hyatt Huntington, the gardens are laid out like separate rooms. They showcase daylily, rose of Sharon, dwarf box, barberry, laurel, American holly,

Brookgreen Gardens

trifoliate orange, glossy abelia, pineapple guava, loblolly bay, camellia, Irish ivy, and coral bean. The 250-year-old Live Oak Allee, which leads from the former site of the Brookgreen Plantation mansion, is a particular attraction.

The gardens are a good bird-watching area, especially in autumn and winter. The birds move in mixed flocks, comprising red-bellied and downy woodpeckers, yellow-bellied sapsuckers, eastern phoebes, Carolina chickadees, tufted titmice, white-breasted nuthatches, Carolina wrens, golden-crowned and ruby-crowned kinglets, blue-gray gnat-catchers, eastern bluebirds, hermit thrushes, American robins, brown thrashers, solitary vireos, and warblers of many varieties, including the orange-crowned, yellow-rumped, pin, palm, black-and-white, and common yellowthroat. Sparrows found here in winter include chipping, field, song, swamp, and white-throated. Lincoln's sparrow might be seen, but it is elusive.

Birds of prey in the neighborhood include American kestrel and sharp-shinned, red-tailed, red-bellied, and Cooper's hawks, as well as turkey vultures, ospreys (common in spring), bald eagles, Northern harriers, and the rare peregrine falcon and merlin. Great horned owls can sometimes be heard or glimpsed at closing time.

The best bird viewing at Brookgreen Gardens is along the Waccamaw River and Brookgreen Creek, at the back of the park. The latter has an observation deck. One might find rails (sora, Virginia, and king), which are more readily heard than seen, marsh wrens, least and American bitterns, common moorhens, wood ducks, American wigeons, American black ducks, Canada geese, and bald eagles.

The Garden, which charges moderate admission fees, is open daily year-round from 9:30 A.M. to 5:30 P.M. Tours and programs are offered every day except Christmas. Brookgreen is handicapped accessible.

BROOKGREEN TO PAWLEYS ISLAND

Exit Brookgreen and turn right (south) onto US 17. Ride a mile through maritime forest, then turn right (west) onto S-22-362/Sandy Island Road. A boat landing on the Waccamaw River is at the end of the road, 2.3 miles west. Across the water is forested **Sandy Island**, a pristine piece of property between the Waccamaw and Pee Dee Rivers.

The island is the largest undeveloped tract remaining in the Waccamaw Neck, and the largest freshwater island in the east. Four miles wide and six miles long, the property is an unusual treat and contrast to the highly developed communities to the north of Pawleys Island. No bridge spans the waters of the Pee Dee or Waccamaw River to reach the island, and, happily, none ever will, thanks to the one hundred or so residents of the Gullah community of Sandy Island, most of whom are descendants of freed slaves in the area. If you want to visit, you need to bring your own boat or make arrangements with Captain Sandy's Tours or Cap'n Rod's Lowcountry Plantation Tours.

Residents work and attend school on the mainland, but at the end of the day, they retreat by boat to a serene existence on the island. They came together in the early 1990s, when their way of life was threatened by possible development and construction of a bridge from the mainland. The community united and, with assistance from public agencies, local environmental groups, and elements of the business community, they determined how to preserve their island's sensitive ecosystem and protect their community from future development.

The South Carolina Department of Transportation purchased a majority of the 12,000-acre island with the financial assistance of the Nature Conservancy, which now holds that land in trust. More than 9,000 acres of longleaf pines, cypress trees, marine forests, endangered wildlife, and wetlands are being protected in perpetuity for the benefit of not only the local residents, but also for visitors like you. Hiking trails and sandy roads lace the property.

Along the Waccamaw River on the eastern side of Sandy Island are 1,100 acres of wetlands filled with bald cypresses, tupelos, and swamp pocosins, and freshwater swamps, which supported rice plantations during the 1800s. Along the Pee Dee River that abuts the western portion of the island are approximately

3,000 acres of bottomland hardwood forests. Some of the longleaf pines are more than a century old. The island's forests protect a number of endangered species, including the red-cockaded woodpecker. You may be lucky to spot one as you walk through the forest.

In addition to natural attractions, visitors are often delighted by New Bethel Baptist Church, a picturesque white stucco structure sitting atop a high sandy ridge, shaded by longleaf pines and symbolizing the strength and integrity of this community. Built in 1818, the church serves as the social and spiritual center of the island. The edifice presents six arched blue windows to adorn the two main walls of the church. They make an alluring reflection on the interior of the church, which is decorated with a red carpet that leads to the sanctuary's altar.

Backtrack to US 17 and turn right (south). **Litchfield Beach** is about a half mile down the road. To drive through the oceanfront part of Litchfield Beach, turn left on North Boyle Drive. Private houses line the road on the beachfront, and there are a few public beach access areas.

Take North Boyle Drive back and continue south to US 17 past the Hanser House Restaurant, the Litchfield Beach and Golf Resort, and then the Litchfield Beach Fish House. You'll enter the mainland portion of the Pawleys Island community 3.5 miles from North Boyle Drive. You'll see on your left the Shops at Oak Lea, featuring Eleanor Pitts Fine Gifts and Jewelry and Pawleys Pedalar Shoes. Another 0.2 mile brings you to the Hammock Shops, which offer unique shopping in quaint cottages and fine dining at the Fish Camp Bar and Louis's at Pawleys Restaurant. Next is Pawleys Town Square Shops, where you'll find Magnolia Cafe, ice cream, antiques, gifts, and sporting goods as well as the chamber of commerce's visitor center tucked in an old-fashioned blue home right off of US 17. At the Island Shops to the right, you'll find Pawleys Island Tavern, Island Cafe and Deli, and the Hook Restaurant and Bar.

Just past the Island Shops, be sure to get in the left-hand lane to make the left (east) turn that takes you to **Pawleys Island** proper. No road sign is visible, but you can trust the green sign to the right of US 17, directing you to turn onto North Causeway Road.

Cross a bridge over the marsh, and the barrier island is directly in front of you. Turn right onto S-22-46/Myrtle Avenue to visit the historic district of Pawleys Island. This narrow road is lined with historic homes, sand dunes, and lovely trees on your left and the marsh on your right. Travel at a leisurely pace; the drive to the end of the island is only about a mile.

Pawleys Island, once a refuge for rice planters who sought to escape the malaria epidemic, is one of the oldest beach resorts in the state. The island was originally developed as a summer retreat for rice and indigo planters during the eighteenth and nineteenth centuries, and its heyday was during the 1930s and '40s. Pawleys describes itself as "arrogantly shabby," which sums up the situation nicely. Its longest-staying visitor is a famous ghost, "the Gray Man." Legend has it that the Gray Man first appeared on the beach at Pawleys Island before the great hurricane of 1822. He is said to have given warnings of severe storms ever since.

As you approach the marshlands, you'll see on your right a small white cottagelike church. Three tenths of a mile farther on your left is the beginning of the historic district. The first home you will see in the historic area is the **Joseph Blythe Allston Pawley House**. This house stands on land owned by Robert Frances Withers Allston (1801–1864), which was granted to him in 1846. Allston served as governor of South Carolina from 1856 to 1858. Allston was a prominent property and slave owner, and a successful rice planter in the area. His nephew Joseph Blythe Allston obtained the land in 1866, and it is thought that he then moved this circa 1800 house onto this property. After Hurricane Hugo hit Pawleys Island in 1989, the house was extensively altered and placed on a higher foundation. Mortise-and-tenon joints with pegs can still be seen under the house.

Just past the Joseph Blythe Allston Pawley House is the South Causeway (site of the raucous Pawleys Pavilion of 1950s and '60s fame, long since burned but still mourned by old-timers). Robert Frances Withers Allston is also responsible for building the causeway between 1845 and 1856, connecting the island to the mainland. The causeway and contiguous property remained in the family until 1901.

P. C. J. Weston, who served as lieutenant governor of South Carolina from 1862 to 1864, owned the Pelican Inn, formerly the PCJ Weston House. Weston obtained land here in 1844; by 1858 he had built this beach residence. In 1864 the Weston family sold the property to William St. Julian Mazyck, who sold the house to Atlantic Coast Lumber Company in 1901. The company permitted its employees to vacation here, and after ownership changed some years later, the house was named the Pelican Inn.

Farther along is the All Saints Summer Parsonage, at 516 Myrtle Avenue. Built by 1848, it served as the summer parsonage for All Saints Episcopal Church for many years. Summer evening services were held by the congregation, which included a number of rice plantation owners who spent summers at Pawleys Island. The congregation sold the parsonage rectory to a private owner in 1960.

The Ward House, or Liberty Lodge, at 520 Myrtle Avenue, one of the oldest buildings on Pawleys Island, was reportedly moved here around 1858. It stands on land once owned by area rice planter Joshua J. Ward (1800–1853), who was lieutenant governor of South Carolina from 1850 to 1852. The house has hand-hewn sills and joists and mortise-and-tenon joints. It remained in the Ward family until 1912 when Cornelius C. Ehrich purchased it and named it Liberty Lodge. Ownership is still in this family.

The LaBruce family, successful rice planters in All Saints Parish, owned the LaBruce Lemon House at 546 Myrtle Avenue, built around 1858 on ten acres of

Pawleys Island

beach land. According to local tradition, two small dwellings on the property were slave cabins. The residence was purchased by Calhoun Lemon of Barnwell in 1952 and still remains in his family. Although additions have been made to the house over the years, the slave quarters can be seen from the street.

The Nesbitt/Norburn House at 560 Myrtle Avenue, constructed in 1842, was owned by Robert Nesbitt (1799–1848). A native of Scotland and a rice planter in this area, he also owned nearby Caledonia Plantation. The house on Pawleys Island remained in the Nesbitt family until after the death of Ralph Nesbitt in 1938. The house is hidden behind thick vegetation.

Pawleys Island Historic All Saints Academy Summer House at 566 Myrtle Avenue was built between 1838 and 1848 as summer lodging for the academy's headmaster, Robert F. W. Allston. Governor of South Carolina from 1856 to 1858, Allston actively participated in the leadership of the school. After some years, the academy's dwelling passed into private ownership. It was extensively damaged by Hurricane Hugo in 1989, but it has been meticulously restored.

At the end of Myrtle Avenue, turn left onto Pritchard Street/S-22-265. Drive to a small beach at the end of the island less than a half mile away, where you can take a relaxing walk on this quiet, secluded seashore.

11

Winyah Bay and Santee River Delta

GEORGETOWN TO McCLELLANVILLE

GENERAL DESCRIPTION: Beginning in the heart of historic Georgetown, this 45-mile tour takes visitors through plantation-dotted coastal marshland and the northern edge of Francis Marion National Forest before ending in the quaint fishing village of McClellanville.

SPECIAL ATTRACTIONS: Prince George Winyah Episcopal Church, Rice Museum, Kaminski House Museum, Tom Yawkey Wildlife Center, Hopesewee Plantation, Santee Delta Wildlife Management Area, St. James Santee Church, Hampton Plantation State Historic Park.

LOCATION: Northern coast.

DRIVE ROUTE NUMBERS: US 17, High Market Street, St. James Street, Prince Street, Screven Street, Front Street, S-22-

18/South Island Road, S-22-30/Estherville Drive, S-10-857/South Rutledge Road, FR 211/Millbranch, SC 45, South Pinckney Road, Oak Street, Church Street.

TRAVEL SEASON: All year. In early spring, flowers and foliage are especially attractive. Winter is best for viewing waterfowl.

SERVICES: Conventional accommodations and other services are abundant in Georgetown, Pawleys Island, and Litchfield. Limited services are available in McClellanville.

See For More Information in the appendix for addresses and phone numbers of Attractions, Camping, Neat Places to Stay, Restaurants, Shops, and Tours and Nature-Based Services.

THE DRIVE

The Carolina Coastal Plain area around Georgetown sits astride Winyah Bay, where the Waccamaw, Great Pee Dee, Black, and Sampit Rivers empty into the Atlantic to form one of the finest natural harbors in the United States. A few miles south of Winyah Bay are the wetlands of the sprawling Santee River delta, home to several important wildlife reserves because of its great ecological significance, especially for ducks and other shorebirds. This drive takes visitors through the lands surrounding these great outlets to the Atlantic Ocean.

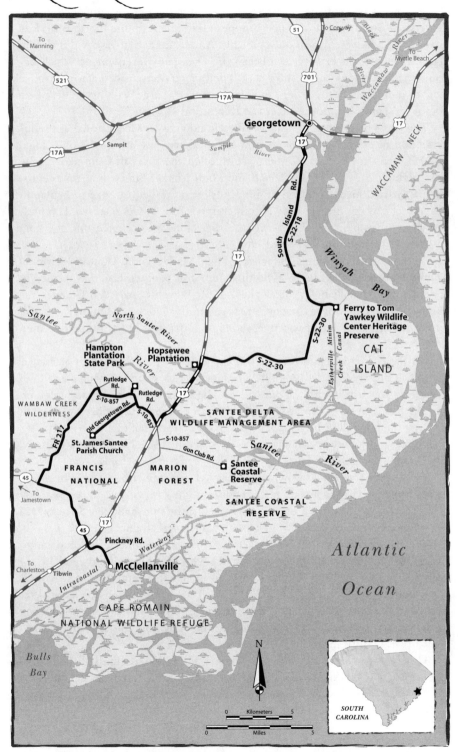

HISTORIC GEORGETOWN

Here in 1526, almost two centuries before Georgetown was occupied by British settlers, the Spanish made the first European settlement on the North American mainland. They were driven out by Native Americans and disease within a year. The British arrived in 1705 and began the Georgetown settlement, which became the third oldest town in the state. The French Marquis de Lafayette landed here to join the fight for American independence. George Washington slept here too, as did James Monroe, Martin van Buren, and Grover Cleveland.

The drive begins in the heart of historic downtown Georgetown at the intersection of High Market Street and US 17. Turn east off US 17 onto High Market Street for a short 2-mile drive through the heart of Georgetown. On your right at the corner of Cleland and High Market Streets (0.2 mile) is the **First Baptist Church**, founded in 1794. Originally called the Anitpedo Baptist Church, it was the first separate Baptist congregation in Georgetown. The present church was built in 1997, but two earlier churches occupied this site, from 1915 to 1949 and from 1949 to 1996.

At the corner of Orange Street and High Market is the **Duncan Memorial United Methodist Church**. In 1785 the Methodist congregation was formed in Georgetown by William Wayne, nephew of the Revolutionary War General Anthony Wayne. Cross over Orange Street to see the Duncan Memorial Chapel, site of an early cemetery, parsonage, and church that was in use from 1833 until 1903.

On the corner of High Market and Broad Streets, on your left, is St. Mary's Catholic Church, founded in 1899, a beautiful brick structure with a statute of the Virgin Mary at its front. Continue on High Market across Broad Street; on the left-hand corner is **Prince George's Winyah Episcopal Church**, established in 1721 by the Church of England. The parish church was built here between 1737 and 1750, and the tower and chancel were added in 1824. Notice the weathered brick wall enclosing the church.

Continue a few blocks down High Market Street, turn right (south) on St. James Street, and then make an immediate right onto Prince Street. At 509 Prince Street (at the corner of Cannon Street) is the **Winyah Indigo Society Hall Free School**, completed in 1753. The society began as an informal club in 1740, but was incorporated in 1757 by an act of parliament to educate children and to ensure stronger financial support for the free school that it had founded. The society maintained a library and thrived as an intellectual center for the Georgetown community until the Civil War, when Federal troops occupied and later destroyed the library. Instruction began again in 1872, and the school merged with the state system in 1887. Now the original building houses Winyah Academy, a private institution.

Three houses down, at 515 Prince Street, is the Live Oak Inn Bed and Breakfast, named for the state champion live oak found on the premises. The tree, estimated to be more than 500 years old, measures 23 feet in circumference, 120 feet in height, and has a crown spread of 125 feet.

Cross over Queen Street. Across from Alexander's Inn Bed and Breakfast at 620 Prince Street is the **Baptist Church Cemetery** where William Screven, first pastor of the earliest Baptist Church in the South, is buried. Screven, a native of England, established a Baptist church in Kittery, Maine, in 1682. By 1698, he had led his congregation to Charleston, South Carolina. He later moved to Georgetown, where he continued to pastor until his death in 1713. If you wish to visit the small plot, park and walk the stone path to the left of the historical marker beside the white two-story house at 619 Prince Street. The cemetery is decorated with four rounded boxwoods enclosed within an iron and brick fence.

Continue one block to Screven Street, turn left (south), and on your right will be the Georgetown County Courthouse (circa 1824). Designed by South Carolina native Robert Mills, this structure replaced a courthouse that was damaged by two hurricanes. Mills called it a "great ornament to the town."

Directly in front of you is the **Old Market Building**, built in 1842. Inside is the **Rice Museum**, dedicated to the history of the cultivation of rice, the crop on which Georgetown's great wealth was based in the eighteenth and nineteenth centuries. Also here is the **Maritime Museum Gallery**, which presents the permanent exhibit of Browns Ferry Vessel. Built in the early 1700s, it sank in the Black River around 1730. This is the oldest vessel on exhibit in America.

Tiny LaFayette Park is adjacent to the museum, and behind it is the 1,000-foot Harbor Walk along the Sampit River docks. The Francis Marion Park is farther west down the Harbor Walk, in front of the historic River Room restaurant.

From the Rice Museum, turn right onto Front Street, where you will pass unique stores such as the Georgetown Art Gallery, Vienvenue Interiors, Pinckney's Exchange, the Osprey's Nest, and Pelican Pete's. If you're hungry, step into Syd and Luther's Chop House, the Big Tuna Restaurant and Bar, the Front Street Deli, or the River Room and Harvest Moon Ice Cream on the corner of the Harbor Walk. Be sure to park here and stroll down the boardwalk to catch a glimpse of shrimp boats and the bend in the Sampit River. You can also catch a ride on the Carolina Rover here. This cruiseline, complete with an onboard naturalist, takes you to the Georgetown lighthouse, on shelling excursions to a remote barrier island, and past historic plantations.

Continue west on Front Street. Just past King Street on your left is the Georgetown Visitors Center where you can step in and pick up brochures on the surrounding area as well as access Swamp Fox Tours that offer tours of historic homes in the downtown area. Behind the Visitors Center is the **Kaminski House Museum**. Built in the late 1700s, it's filled with antiques, including a Spanish wedding chest dating back to the fifteenth century. Guided tours are available for a small donation.

The **Robert Stewart House**, to the right of the Kaminski House, was built in the mid-1700s by Robert Stewart. This house is the only extant brick residence built before the American Revolution. When President George Washington arrived in Georgetown on April 30, 1791, during his southern tour, he spent the night here as the guest of a local merchant.

GEORGETOWN TO HOPSEWEE PLANTATION

As you approach the end of Front Street where it intersects with US 17, you'll pass Georgetown Steel Mill, which extends all the way to the Sampit River. Turn left onto US 17 South and cross the bridge over the Sampit River, where you will see the International Paper Mill and the marshy banks of the river on your right.

A half mile from the Sampit River, turn left onto S-22-18/South Island Road and into the Winyah Community. Three and a half miles down this rural residential road, you might want to make a short diversion a half mile down White-hall Avenue. At the famous Roycroft Daylily Farm, which ships daylilies worldwide, picnicking facilities and comfortable seating areas are available, as well as endless walks through the farm.

Continue 5 more miles south on South Island Road through a quiet, woodsy residential area lined with thick pine forests. The road ends at the South Island Ferry Public Boat Landing at the Estherville Minim Creek Canal. South Island Road runs directly into a parking lot on the water's edge. The canal that separates the mainland from Cat Island is only 20 or so feet across.

To visit Cat Island and the **Tom Yawkey Wildlife Center Heritage Preserve**, sometimes called the most valuable gift in public conservation's history, push the call button at the boat ramp and wait for the ferry to pick up you and your car. The ferry is on call from 7:00 A.M. to 10:00 P.M. daily. A gift from Yawkey to the state of South Carolina, the wildlife center is operated by the South Carolina Department of Natural Resources. Lying on either side of the mouth of Winyah Bay, the center's 17,700 acres are split among North, South, and Cat Islands.

Ecosystems range from ponds and barrier island beaches to maritime forest and pine flatwoods. Huge numbers of waterfowl and shorebirds visit, especially during spring migrations, and endangered loggerhead sea turtles nest on the 13 miles of undeveloped beach. Turkey, deer, and quail are permanent residents at the center. Sadly for visitors, but happily for the wildlife, access to the center is severely limited.

Bus tours of the center, which run each Tuesday from October through February and on Wednesday at other times, are often booked months in advance. Some people have luck arriving on tour days and taking the place of someone who has canceled a reservation.

Turn around in this parking lot and head north on South Island Road. After only 0.7 mile, turn left on S-22-30/South Estherville Drive. Continue down this curving, dark road for approximately 8 miles until you reach US 17 again. (After about 3 miles, you must make a sharp right; the road remains S-22-30 but is named North Santee River Road).

Although all of the plantations on S-22-30 are private, a drive down this canopied road of enormous oaks dripping with Spanish moss allows slight glimpses of the old homes, slave quarters, and farm buildings, and is well worth the quiet drive. Estherville, Pine Grove, Annandale, Millbrook, Wicklow Hall, Kinloch, Newland, Woodland, and Rice Hope are among the private plantations you will pass. The Retreat Rice Plantation is perhaps one of the most well known of these old home sites. Oak trees leading up to and around the house give one the sense of the old-style plantation. Wild turkeys can sometimes be glimpsed darting across roads and through the woods.

HOPSEWEE PLANTATION TO McCLELLANVILLE

Where S-22-30 runs into US 17, turn left (south) and enjoy wildlife and historic treasures on both sides of the highway. Less than a half mile down US 17 on your right is **Hopsewee Plantation**. Built around 1740, it is the birthplace of Thomas Lynch Jr., a signer of the Declaration of Independence. This plantation is privately owned but open to the public for tours Tuesday through Friday, and Saturday by appointment. The cost is $8.00 for adults and $5.00 for children.

Directly across the highway from Hopsewee Plantation is the Poleyard Public Boat Landing, affording access to the North Santee River. The landing is the southern terminus of the Santee River Canoe Trail, which flows 65 miles from Lake Marion to its estuary south of Georgetown.

Continue south on US 17 across the North Santee River, a beautiful, wide, smooth-flowing brown river that is a key part of the **Santee Delta Wildlife Management Area**. The main dike of the wildlife management area runs south from the bridge over the North Santee. Its parking lot is on the left (east) side of the highway, and it can be walked as a trail. However, much of the area is closed during duck hunting season, December 1 through January 20.

The Santee Delta, formed by silt deposits that divide the Santee River, is the largest river delta on the Atlantic Coast. Extensive rice plantations were established around the Santee Delta in the pre–Civil War era, and many still exist. These wetlands have been developed as vital wildlife habitats since the demise of rice culture. This wildlife area offers scenic vistas, good bird viewing, and plenty of alligators. Rare bird species include American swallow-tailed kits, bald eagles, and sandhill cranes. Access roads to the eastern and western portions of the Santee Delta Wildlife Management Area are easily visible and accessible on both sides of US 17.

About 1 mile south of the North Santee bridge, the Santee Swamp, a great area for wildlife viewing, envelops both sides of the highway. White egrets, hawks, and ducks are plentiful in the marsh and easily visible on a clear day.

As you cross the bridge over the South Santee River, you leave Georgetown County and enter Charleston County. At the intersection of US 17 and S-10-857, 1 mile south of the bridge, turn right onto Rutledge Road. (S-10-857 on the right is Rutledge Road; on the left, it is South Santee Road.)

You may want to detour to the **Santee Coastal Reserve.** *Managed by the South Carolina Department of Natural Resources, it's one of the prettiest places on the East Coast. To visit the reserve, proceed 1.5 miles on South Santee Road/S-10-857 and turn left just before the South Santee Community Center onto unpaved Santee Gun Club Road that is the entrance to the reserve. The reserve is open daily from February through October. February hours are 1:00 to 5:00 P.M. daily; from March through October, hours are 8:00 A.M. to 5:00 P.M. Monday through Saturday and 1:00 to 5:00 P.M. Sunday.*

The reserve is among the most important breeding grounds for wading birds in the eastern United States. The Nature Conservancy maintains possession of a 1,040-acre cypress and tupelo swamp, Washo Reserve, within the boundaries of the Santee Coastal Reserve. Totaling 23,024 acres, the Santee Coastal Reserve is primarily marsh, but the property also has fourteen Carolina bays. It is said that every Atlantic species of shorebird is found in the reserve. Moreover, twelve species of orchids and five types of lilies are present here.

There are foot trails here, as well as a canoe trail. Another 0.9 mile down the road is the entrance to the Hike-Bike Trail, the Marshland Trail, and the Washo Reserve Boardwalk, almost 10 miles of interconnecting pathways. The Hike-Bike Trail runs mostly along old rice plantation dikes beside the Intracoastal Waterway and the South Santee River. A 4.25-mile canoe trail winds its way through an impoundment area. If you visit the reserve, backtrack and cross US 17 to S-10-857/Rutledge Road.

Drive 1.5 miles on S-10-857 into the **Francis Marion National Forest** until you reach Old Georgetown Road on your left. Take a left (southwest) onto this heavily packed dirt road, and continue 2.3 miles to St. James Santee Parish Church, a National Historic Landmark that was the center of one of the earliest settlements in South Carolina. St. James Santee Parish was a major agricultural area, containing a number of large rice plantations. In 1787, at nearby Peachtree Plantation, Jonathan Lucas introduced a watermill for beating rice, which gave impetus to the rice culture in this area.

St. James Santee Parish Church, erected in 1787, combines elements of Georgian and classical architectural styles and reflects a late eighteenth-century trend toward a more sophisticated design for parish churches. This particular church is the fourth to serve the St. James Santee Parish. The parish was founded in 1706 at the request of French Huguenot settlers and is the second oldest in South Carolina. The church has a square brick floor and wooden pews that are enclosed with benches completely wrapped around all sides. You may open the doors into the pews and sit inside the worn brown wood enclosure. Visitors are also welcome to wander through the small cemetery on the grounds.

To reach your next stop, turn around and head back the way you came, north on Old Georgetown Road. When you reach Rutledge Road again, turn left and travel less than a half mile to visit **Hampton Plantation State Historic Site**, on the banks of Wambaw Creek. Turn right (east) into the park. A bumpy dirt road amid thick pines opens up to the majestic plantation house surrounded by lush vegetation and slightly hidden behind the famous Washington Oak.

Hampton Plantation, on the National Register of Historic Places and a National Historic Landmark, is an example of eighteenth- and nineteenth-century working rice plantations. The Lowcountry rice culture and plantation system shaped the lives of the residents of this area. The mansion, open for tours, is built in the Georgian style, circa 1750, and is an architectural monument to the skills of enslaved African-Americans. Inside, cutaway sections of walls and ceilings detail eighteenth-century building techniques. While here, ask about John Henry's ghost.

Hampton Plantation State Historic Site's 322 acres are centered on the plantation mansion that has been home to much history and to longtime state Poet Laureate Archibald Rutledge, who donated the property to the state. The grounds feature huge live oaks draped with Spanish moss. One of these, the Washington Oak, was left standing on the advice of President Washington during his visit in 1791. Giant camellias abound, and sundew, pitcher plants, rare orchids, and unusual spider lilies and irises may be found. The park also encom-

Hampton Plantation

passes cypress swamps, abandoned rice fields, and pine and hardwood forests. Wild turkeys, towhees, deer, hawks, woodcocks, whippoorwills, eagles, ospreys, squirrels, owls, warblers, pileated woodpeckers, and Mississippi and swallow-tailed kites can be encountered here, as well as the endangered Rafinesque's big-eared bat. In the dark waters of Witch's Pond and Wambaw Creek are alligators, otters, snakes, and tortoises.

Picnic tables, rest rooms, and vending machines are available, making this a perfect spot to stop for a snack or lunch under the ancient trees and feel the history of the quiet land. You can explore the mansion and walk the grounds, where a 3-mile nature trail is easily accessible. The plantation is a noted wildlife viewing area, and you may be fortunate enough to see a rare red-cockaded woodpecker.

When you exit the park, turn right (northwest) on S-10-857/Rutledge Road in order to see more of the Francis Marion National Forest. You'll reach a gravel road about 1.5 miles from the park. Once you come upon the gravel road, look for FR 211/Millbranch on your left, about a half mile after the pavement ends. Turn left (south) onto FR 211/Millbranch to enjoy a leisurely loop through the forest.

You will soon reach a stop sign. Turn left and continue down FR 211 for a slow 5.5-mile ride. Elmwood Hunt Club is to your right. FR 211 runs directly into SC 45, a paved two-lane road. Take a left (east) onto SC 45 to explore McClellanville, 4 miles away on roadway lined by lush green trees and absolutely no development. During the summer, blueberry picking is available at a local farm on your right before you reach US 17.

McCLELLANVILLE

Where SC 45 intersects with US 17, cross US 17 onto South Pinckney Road, which takes travelers into the sleepy fishing village of **McClellanville** on the banks of Jeremy Creek. Bulls Bay Supply and General Store is on your right.

McClellanville was established in the late 1850s and early 1860s when local plantation owners A. J. McClellan and R. T. Morrison sold lots to planters of the Santee Delta seeking relief from summer fever. The first store opened soon after the Civil War, and the village became the social and economic center for a wide area that produced timber, rice, cotton, naval stores, and seafood. Incorporated in 1926 and encircled by the Francis Marion National Forest and Cape Romain National Wildlife Refuge, McClellanville is best known for its shrimp fleets and seafood industry. Beautiful churches and old homes hide behind ancient oaks, including the summer home and birthplace of Archibald Rutledge (1883–1973).

You'll reach downtown McClellanville a little more than a mile down South Pinckney Street. On your right is Elizabeth Bronson's Artist Studio, housed in a small yellow shack at 829 South Pinckney Street. Across the street is the town dentist's office. Drive slowly because dogs wander across the street at their leisure. At 824 South Pinckney is the Nature Conservancy's headquarters. The Lighthouse Shop, on your right, sells handcrafted lighthouses and yard birds at 825 South Pinckney.

Next on your left is the unique Sassafras Clothes Store, and T.W. Graham and Company General Merchandise, which has sold groceries, produce, and meat since 1894.

A tenth of a mile farther on your left is Mercantile Road, which takes you to the Village Bed and Breakfast. At the corner of Cassena Street and South Pinckney are the McClellanville Arts Center and Pinckney Street Gallery, offering arts, books, and crafts.

Ramble on down South Pinckney past the McClellanville Public School to the corner of Scotia Street, where you'll see the lovely Wappetaw Presbyterian Church, a white wooden structure with a columned facade. The church was founded in 1872.

At the next block, turn right on Oak Street. On your left is an open space and the namesake of the street. An enormous oak tree hangs over the road and the park; a tire swing dangles from one of its limbs. The park has a picnic table, in case you want to stop and take a rest.

Continue on Oak Street to Church Street. On your left you will see **St. James Santee Episcopal Chapel of Ease**, established in 1706. It is constructed of wood that has weathered through the years, but is very attractive with its

St. James Santee Episcopal Chapel of Ease

South Santee River

gingerbread filigree. Chapels of ease were usually built for parishioners who were unable to attend their main church services regularly. This must have been the case with the vacationing rice planters in McClellanville. To the left of the church on a dirt road are some authentic McClellanville homes.

Continue on Oak Street past neat bungalows and stately homes to the docks at the end of the street. Here you're afforded a great view of the fleet of local shrimp boats.

After turning around at the dock, head north on Oak Street and take a right (south) on Pinckney Street. **Little Hampton**, the Rutledge Home, is 0.3 mile down Pinckney Street on your right. The first Little Hampton was built by Henry Rutledge, the father of the late Archibald Rutledge, poet laureate of South Carolina. The original log structure was destroyed by Hurricane Hugo in 1989, but the house was rebuilt with unpainted wood and a tin roof, and a screened-in porch that faces Jeremy Creek. Rutledge is best known for *Home by the River* (1941), describing the people, wildlife, and landscape of this area.

Continue on South Pinckney Road for another block to the Village Museum and the Robert E. Ashley Landing. Your ride ends with a beautiful view of the Intracoastal Waterway.

Francis Marion National Forest

AWENDAW TO BIGGIN CHURCH RUINS

GENERAL DESCRIPTION: A 48-mile cruise in the Coastal Plain through nature, history, and rural culture, past beautiful forests, marshlands, and streams, punctuated with historic sites and sprinkled with flavor buds of South Carolina backwoods living.

SPECIAL ATTRACTIONS: Francis Marion National Forest, Sewee Visitor and Environmental Education Center, I'on Swamp, Wando River, St. Thomas Church, Cainhoy, Quinby Bridge, Huger Recreation Area, Childsbury and Strawberry Chapel, Mepkin Abbey, Wadboo Creek, Biggin Church ruins and cemetery.

LOCATION: Lower Coastal Plain, northeast of Charleston.

DRIVE ROUTE NUMBERS: US 17, FR 228, S-8-98, S-8-100, SC 41, S-8-33, S-8-98, SC 402, S-8-376, S-8-44, S-8-1054, SC 402.

TRAVEL SEASON: All year. Summer is a bit warm, but late fall, winter, and early spring are great.

SERVICES: Charleston and Mount Pleasant have numerous restaurants and full accommodations and other services. Moncks Corner has accommodations and most services. McClellanville has eateries and limited services.

See For More Information in the appendix for addresses and phone numbers of Attractions, Camping, Neat Places to Stay, Restaurants, Shops, Tours, and Nature-Based Services.

THE DRIVE

Nature, old history, and modern rural culture describe this drive. Beginning at a great interpretive center in the Francis Marion Swamp, visitors ride to the wildlife sanctuary of I'on Swamp, then drive through forestlands and marshlands to make two scenic but widely differing crossings of the Wando River. Next, you travel through the highly rural Cainhoy community, whose well-rooted, socially cohesive inhabitants largely descend from antebellum plantation slaves who worked the fields in this same area a century and a half ago. Old and new churches and dark streams punctuate the ride.

Next, you pass through the isolated Huger community inside the national forest and experience a lovely river setting at Huger Recreation Area. From here,

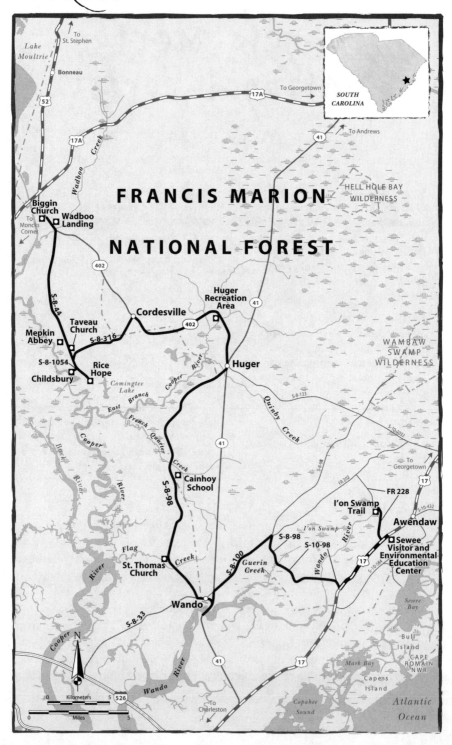

you continue through the faded village of Cordesville, and then head to the now pastoral site of colonial Childsbury and a church dating back to 1725. The neighboring hidden community around Rice Hope Plantation, on the east bank of the Cooper River, seems almost idyllic. Finally, you visit Mepkin Abbey, Wadboo Creek, and the ruins of Biggin Church to complete your ride.

SEWEE CENTER TO THE WANDO RIVER

Begin at the **Sewee Visitor and Environmental Education Center**, located on the southeast side of US 17 about 15 miles northeast of Charleston in the Awendaw community. The Sewee Center is located near the southeastern edge of 250,000-acre Francis Marion National Forest, just west of 64,000-acre Cape Romain National Wildlife Refuge, composed mostly of coastal habitat islands. A joint effort by the U.S. Forest Service and the U.S. Fish and Wildlife Service to provide information the two sprawling federal properties, this excellent facility includes trails and boardwalks, an orientation film, numerous informational materials, an interactive map, educational programs, rest rooms and canteen facilities, and an extremely helpful staff. A special feature is a red wolf enclosure and educational area.

Francis Marion National Forest is named for General Francis Marion, a local Revolutionary War hero who was a genius at guerilla warfare. He continually harassed and caused losses to British forces as they attempted to extend their control from their strongholds at Charleston and Georgetown. Evading counterattack and capture by continually fading into the myriad swamps throughout the South Carolina coastal plain, Marion became known by friend and foe alike as the "Swamp Fox." *The Patriot,* a movie filmed in South Carolina, is loosely based on his exploits.

The forest is composed of farm, plantation, and lumber company holdings acquired by the federal government in the 1930s. Much of the land was played out and in poor shape, and authorities found most owners willing to sell during the hard times of the Great Depression. However, some landowners hung on to their land, or at least parts of their properties, which explains the frequent interspersion of private homes, churches, and other inholdings throughout the forest.

With a variety of hardwoods interspersing a largely longleaf pine forest, Francis Marion National Forest offers attractive fall foliage, good views of wintering birds, and a beautiful array of springtime wildflowers. Flowers and other attractive foliage and wildlife are also present throughout the summer months.

Most of the pine forest is relatively young. The eye of Hurricane Hugo came ashore at Awendaw, and the storm passed through this area in full fury. Remnants of pines snapped by roaring winds at a height of 15 to 20 feet are prevalent throughout the area, as is the aftermath of large-scale clear-cutting in scattered segments throughout the forest.

The loblolly and longleaf pine stands alternate throughout the forest flatlands with stretches of mixed pine and hardwoods. The species mix that occupies a specific site is heavily dependent on the history of land use and natural disturbances. Fire, grazing, winds, storms, disease and past agricultural use all influence forest structure. Thus, parcels of similar terrain will host quite diverse vegetation.

The low-lying bottomlands, most of which escaped the worst effects of Hugo, are composed almost entirely of hardwood species, including beech, dogwood, sweet gum, hickory, cypress, maple, tulip poplar, and a variety of oaks, often draped with gray Spanish moss.

The lush understory abounds with holly, wax myrtle, sweet bay, red bay, and sassafras shrubs. Christmas ferns and grapevines are plentiful. Visitors encounter cattail, switch cane, orange milkwort, yellow jessamine, honeysuckle, purple aster, wisteria, blackberry, wild ginger, beautyberry, bladderwort, water hyacinth, wild azaleas, wild roses, Carolina sundrop, partridge peas, pinewoods lilies, and insect-devouring trumpet pitcher plants. A special treat is the frequency of blue flag irises sprouting from ditches and depressions alongside the road.

White-tailed deer and wild turkeys are plentiful. Squirrels, raccoons, and opossums are common, and frogs, turtles, and snakes may be seen in ponds and creeks, along with a large number of alligators. Attracted by the bountiful flowers, multitudes of butterflies perform airborne dances here and there. The most common wildlife species are, of course, the birds. Bobwhites inhabit the grasslands, and overhead are Carolina chickadees, eastern kingbirds, swallow-tailed kites, American kestrels, warblers, sparrows, brown-headed nuthatches, and varieties of woodpeckers, including the endangered red-cockaded. Egrets, herons, ibis, ospreys, wood ducks, and bald eagles are among the wetlands inhabitants.

Just north of the Sewee Center are two vastly different trails. About 6 miles north is the short but sweet **Sewee Shell Mound Trail**, *a 1-mile loop that carries walkers to the edge of a saltwater marsh and creek and the Sewee Shell Ring, created by Native Americans 4,000 years ago.*

Paralleling this scenic drive, approximately 5 to 15 miles to the northeast, is the 49-mile **Swamp Fox Passage of the Palmetto Trail**, *which takes hikers and bikers through coastal pine forest and across creeks and swampy wetlands of the Francis Marion National Forest. The southeastern trailhead is on US 17 at Buck Hall Recreation Area on the north side of Awendaw, and the northwestern trailhead is at Canal Recreation Area on US 52, near the shore of Lake Moultrie. This is the southernmost segment of the Palmetto Trail, which, when finished, will stretch all the way from the sea to the mountains in the northwest corner of the state. Currently, you can hike continuously northward for 150 miles, to Manchester State Forest on the banks of the Wateree River.*

From the Sewee Center, head southwest on US 17 for about 0.2 mile, then turn right on unpaved FR 228/I'on Swamp Road. Drive 2 miles through mixed pine/hardwood forest and turn left (west) into the parking lot for **I'on Swamp Trail**. Although this gorgeous trail through old rice fields rich with wildlife and plant life is 2 miles long, mostly in the form of a loop, a short walk of a few hundred yards down the pathway takes you past alligator-laden backwaters to an old dike at the edge of Witheywood Canal, with a wonderful view of moss-hung bald cypresses and oaks, as well as other flora and fauna.

From the parking area, you enter a tangle of young trees, heavy vines, and thick brush. A short boardwalk takes you across water-soaked ground to an old roadbed, which gives way to a footpath along the top of an earthen dike, the only high ground in sight as you move through the quiet and still wetlands. To your right is a piped wellhead of a natural artesian well, splashing sparkling clear water in the black swamp. On the left is open water; in season, it's home to impressive alligators and water lilies.

I'on Swamp is famous among birders for the wide variety of species present, particularly during fall and spring migration seasons. It is a great spot for warblers; the popular prothonotary warbler is often seen. The most elusive bird in North America, Bachman's warbler, has been sighted here, although not in recent years. Deer are common in the swamp, and turtles are sufficiently plentiful to help keep the abundant alligators well fed.

If you have sufficient time and energy, hike the full loop. I'on Swamp Trail runs along a gridwork dike system of what was once part of Witheywood Plantation, a rice-growing estate. It provides a fascinating glimpse of the heart of South Carolina's Coastal Plain wetlands.

From I'on Swamp, backtrack 2 miles on FR 228/I'on Swamp Road, and turn right (southwest) on US 17, toward Charleston. Drive 3.2 miles past forestland and a couple of small country churches, and turn right (northwest) on S-10-98/Guerin Bridge Road. Pass through pastureland for 1.2 miles, then cross Ward Bridge over the **Wando River**, the headwaters of which arise from springs in I'on Swamp. This is a good spot to view marshland and waterfowl.

Wind 2.7 miles through forest and beautiful wetlands, crossing a small white wooden bridge before traversing a third bridge, over **Guerin Creek**, which takes you from Charleston County into Berkeley County. Continue through thick, grapevine-laden forest for 3 miles to the intersection with S-8-100.

Take a left (southwest) on S-8-100 and ride 4 tree-lined miles to the intersection with SC 41, in the community of Wando. Turn left (south) and travel 1.4 mile to cross an ancient bridge over a much wider stretch of the Wando River, with neat views east and west, including marshland and an interesting cluster of ship repair facilities on the southwest side.

WANDO RIVER TO BIGGIN CHURCH RUINS

On the south side of the river, turn around, drive 0.5 mile north, and bear left (northwest) onto S-8-33. Drive 1 mile, turn right at the intersection with S-8-98, and head northward into the church-filled old community of **Cainhoy**, a densely populated, mostly African-American community of residents whose freed slave ancestors continued to make this area their home after their emancipation in 1865. The main highway through the community is an old road that parallels the east side of the Cooper River, 3 or 4 miles away. Look for side roads with names such as Toomer, Napoleon, Jing Jing, Nat, and Jak.

Drive 2.5 miles, crossing Flag Creek wetlands and arriving at the Greek Revival–style **St. Thomas Church**, established in 1706 for worship in French by Huguenot settlers. The present white stucco structure was erected in 1819. Bullet holes from the 1876 "Cainhoy Massacre" race riot are said to have scarred the church's small vestry building.

Continue northward, crossing the East Cooper and Berkeley Railroad tracks after a mile. Head into the heart of the Cainhoy community, with recreational facilities, churches, homes, little stores, Libby's Family Restaurant, and, 3.3 miles past the tracks, Cainhoy School on the right. You cross French Quarter Creek 0.6 mile north of the school.

After another mile, the road reenters forestland. Here and there on your left, long driveways lead to private estates on the Cooper River and its tributaries.

About 4 miles past French Quarter Creek is the entrance to **Pompion Hill Chapel**, on your left. Pretty wildflowers dot the long driveway. Established in 1703 as a Chapel of Ease for St. Thomas and St. Denis Parish, this was the first Church of England structure located outside of Charleston. The original bald cypress wood structure, overlooking the East Branch of the Cooper River, fell into disrepair, and the present Georgian brick chapel was built in 1763.

Quinby Bridge is 2 miles farther northeast. In July 1781, British troops retreating from Moncks Corner burned the bridge over Quinby Creek. Somehow, they held off pursuing troops under the legendary Patriot triumvirate of General Thomas "the Gamecock" Sumter, General Francis "the Swamp Fox" Marion, and General Henry "Lighthorse Harry" Lee. (In South Carolina during the American Revolution, if you didn't have a nickname, you weren't worth diddly-squat.) The wildflower-edged boat landing on the north side of the creek, with its small pier, is a great place to enjoy views of the serene, dark waterway.

After another 0.2 mile, turn left (north) onto SC 41 and ease into "downtown" **Huger**, a tiny settlement anchored by the P and C Grocery and Gas, on your right, where you can buy refreshments. You can also buy worms here, but a sign warns that you should check them before leaving, because you're not allowed to return dead worms.

After 0.1 mile on SC 41, bear left (due north) on SC 402, as SC 41 goes northeast toward Jamestown. On your left after a mile is the entrance to Silk Hope Plantation, founded by Sir Nathaniel Green, who settled this area in 1683. A half mile farther, on your left, is a tiny old cemetery that once adjoined a small chapel of ease.

Turn right at FR 251/Irish Town Road for a short, pleasant nature trail loop, 0.4 mile past the cemetery. After rejoining SC 402, you cross blackwater Huger

Creek about 0.3 mile farther north, and turn immediately left into **Huger Recreation Area**. Picnic tables are scattered among moss-laden live oak trees in a nicely landscaped loop venue. Drive down the roadway on the south side of the picnic area to reach the Huger Creek boat ramp. A constantly flowing artesian well makes quiet music as you enjoy views of the dark, foreboding waters.

Only 0.2 mile after you take a left out of the recreation area to continue on SC 402, the highway swings west, at an intersection where Copperhead Road extends right (northeast) toward Witherbee Ranger Station and a middle section trailhead of the Swamp Fox Passage, 3 miles away. Bear left to continue on SC 402, heading west toward Cordesville under a shady, moss–hung canopy of oaks.

Pass entrances to Girl Scout Plantation and Bonneau Ferry Conference Center on your left after 4 miles. At 4.7 miles past the Copperhead Road intersection, a railroad track crosses the highway as you enter **Cordesville**, once a thriving farm village, but now a quiet, pretty settlement of comfortable bungalows and deserted country stores. Drive 0.2 mile through the village, and then turn left (southwest) on S-8-376/Sawmill Road to ride 4 miles through forest before intersecting with S-8-44/Comingtee Road at a stop sign.

Turn left (south), go 0.2 mile, and turn right (southwest) on S-8-1054. At the end of this road, 0.2 mile from the turnoff, is gracious **Strawberry Chapel**. Built in 1725, it stands sentinel over the long-abandoned colonial village of **Childsbury** in a beautiful pastoral setting on a bluff of the east bank of the comfortably twisting, plantation-lined Cooper River. The site of this former town, founded in 1707, was recently saved by conservationists from destruction by developers and is now a South Carolina Heritage Trust Preserve property, under the protection of the state's Department of Natural Resources.

Return to S-8-44, and turn right (southeast) to continue a half mile to **Rice Hope Plantation Inn** and a charming surrounding cluster of Spanish-moss-draped live oaks shrouding country homes. Rice Hope Plantation was established in 1696 on the tidal banks of the Cooper River. The present house was erected in 1840, replacing the burned-out original. The formal gardens date from 1795 and feature camellias more than 200 years old.

Turn around and head back north on S-8-44. About 0.3 mile past the intersection with S-8-376, **Taveau Church** and its old cemetery are on your right. This Greek Revival–style structure was built in 1835 as a place of worship for Presbyterians, but it is now used by a Methodist congregation.

Mepkin Abbey, a Trappist monastery, is on your left, 0.6 mile north. The plantation was once the home of slave trader Henry Laurens, president of the Continental Congress in 1777–1778, and his grave site is on the premises. Henry and Clare Booth Luce owned the property in the early part of the twentieth century; they donated it to the Catholic Church, which turned it into a monastery in 1949. The gardens and chapel of Mepkin Abbey are open to the public from 9:00 A.M. to 4:30 P.M. daily, free of charge.

Ruins of Biggin Church

From Mepkin, continue northward 5.8 miles, past timberland, churches, pastures, homes, and Bubba Lane, until you reach SC 402. Turn left (northwest), and immediately cross a bridge over **Wadboo Creek**, a beautiful spot with coffee brown waters and high marsh grasses. The boat landing on the north side, decorated with more wildflowers, contains a historical marker. This spot was the southwest corner of Wadboo Barony, a 12,000-acre estate granted in 1683 to James Colleton, son of one of the original lords proprietor of Carolina.

Your scenic drive ends 1.4 miles farther northwest at the old cemetery and the lovely, haunting ruins of **Biggin Church**. First built in 1712, it burned three times, twice by forest fires and once by British forces during the American Revolution. Baseball existed by 1886, the date of the last fire, and local residents must have learned of the adage, "three strikes and you're out." The church was not rebuilt after that.

Lаkе моultrіе Loор

PINOPOLIS TO DIVERSION CANAL

GENERAL DESCRIPTION: A 70-mile trip around the edges of Lake Moultrie, full of canals, history, and natural beauty.

SPECIAL ATTRACTIONS: Pinopolis, Old Santee Canal Park, Tail Race Canal, Francis Marion Forest, Swamp Fox Trail, Lake Moultrie and Swamp Fox Passages of the Palmetto Trail, Bonneau Beach, St. Stephen Episcopal Church, Rediversion Canal, Sandy Beach Wildlife Management Area, General Francis Marion Burial Site, Diversion Canal.

LOCATION: Lower Coastal Plain, northeast of Charleston.

DRIVE ROUTE NUMBERS: S-8-5, S-8-315, Old Dike Road, SC 6, US 52 Bypass, Stony Point Landing Drive, US 52, S-8-35, S-8-42, S-8-41, S-8-351, S-8-40, SC 45, Main Street, Elm Street, S-8-18, S-8-204, Matilda Circle, Sandy Beach Road, S-8-132, S-8-1141.

TRAVEL SEASON: All year. Fall, winter and spring are great for waterfowl and other wildlife.

SERVICES: Charleston and Summerville have numerous restaurants and full accommodations and other services. Moncks Corner has accommodations and most services. St. Stephen has limited services.

See For More Information in the appendix for addresses and phone numbers of Attractions, Camping, Neat Places to Stay, Restaurants, Shops, Tours, and Nature-Based Services.

THE DRIVE

This semicircular drive around Lake Moultrie is a trip full of canals, natural beauty, and man-made wonders. You begin in the quaint peninsula community of Pinopolis with its charming homes and churches, and head through the town of Moncks Corner to languidly beautiful Old Santee Canal Park, a landmark of South Carolina's natural and commercial heritage.

Next, you proceed across the Tail Race Canal to the shores of Lake Moultrie, before heading through farmlands and forests to the little town of St. Stephen and its colonial-era parish church. After returning to Lake Moultrie, you cross the Rediversion Canal and ride through countryside to enter Sandy Beach Waterfowl Management Area, then visit the idyllic General Francis Marion Bur-

Lake Moultrie Loop   **133**

ial Site. You complete your trip by crossing two more canals, the northern remnant of Old Santee, along with the Diversion Canal connecting Lakes Marion and Moultrie.

PINOPOLIS TO OLD SANTEE CANAL PARK

Begin your journey at the tiny Post Office in the village of **Pinopolis**, a half mile from Somerset Point and Wampee Conference Center, at the end of what is now a peninsula jutting into Lake Moultrie. The community arose in the 1830s as a summer retreat for residents living on the great plantations in the hot, wet, muggy basin of the Santee River. Pinopolis was on a cool, shady ridge above the bottomlands and provided some relief to the denizens of the lower-lying areas.

Since the basin was flooded at the beginning of the 1940s to create Lakes Moultrie and Marion and provide much-needed hydroelectricity to rural South Carolina, Pinopolis has been on an out-of-the-way peninsula mostly surrounded by the popular recreational waters of Lake Moultrie.

A variety of houses have arisen over the 170 years of the existence of Pinopolis; amazingly, the assortment of older and newer houses blends seamlessly into the pines and moss-hung live oaks that keep the community cool and give it a homey, comfortable ambience.

From the post office, head south on S-8-5/Pinopolis Road 0.2 mile to the redbrick **Trinity Episcopal Church** on your right, which began as a small chapel of ease in 1845. Continue another 0.2 mile south past lovely homes to the wooden **Pinopolis Methodist Church**, constructed in 1900. The white church's open bell tower is highlighted by a pair of arched openings.

Drive 1.3 miles more on S-8-5/Pinopolis Road to a fork and bear right (southwest) onto S-8-315/Sugar Hill Road. Drive about 0.1 mile and turn left into the cemetery churchyard of **St. John's Baptist Church**. Simple yet full of character, the white wooden structure sports a tin roof and four long columns supporting its portico. The congregation was organized in 1851, and this little gem was built in 1881.

Circle through the old cemetery, and exit back onto S-8-315/Sugar Hill Road. Turn right (northeast), drive a few yards, and take a right (east) onto Old Dike Road. After a few more yards, turn right (southeast) again onto S-8-5 and ride a mile before merging into SC 6/Main Street and heading eastward another mile into Moncks Corner.

You travel past Berkeley High School, home of the Stags, and a number of churches before arriving at the intersection of US 17A. Cross US 17A and notice on your right the former **Berkeley Elementary School**, a unique design with two Spanish-fort-looking turrets standing sentinel beside the front entrance. (Berkeley is the name of the county you are in for this entire drive. It was named for Lord Berkeley, one of the eight original lords proprietor of the colony of Carolina.)

Cruise eastward along rustic Main Street, crossing railroad tracks after 0.6 mile. An old train depot is on your right; on your left is Howard's Restaurant, a favorite gathering place for locals that touts the "Best Food on the Corner Since 1960."

Another half mile brings you to US 52; cross it and travel 0.3 mile to turn left (north) onto US 52 Bypass/Rembert Dennis Drive. Stony Point Landing, the entrance drive for the Berkeley Museum and Old Santee Canal Park, is 0.7 mile up the road, on your right (east). Turn here and drive into the parking lot of the park and museum.

Berkeley Museum traces the county's history from Ice Age Native Americans 12,000 years ago to the Revolutionary War, antebellum plantation days, the Civil War, Reconstruction, and developments of the twentieth century. The exhibit hall is designed to reflect the county's historic architectural heritage. There is a small admission fee.

Old Santee Canal Park preserves remnants of the defunct canal's southern terminus, where it brought the waters of the Santee River into Biggin Creek, which flows into the Cooper River. The Santee River, a giant watershed for much of the state, empties into the Atlantic at a relatively unpopulated area between Charleston and Georgetown. The canal brought the commercial activity of this watershed to the much shorter Cooper River and the Port of Charleston. Under construction for seven years, the canal was completed in 1800, and for fifty years it carried goods between Charleston and the South Carolina Midlands, including Columbia.

At the time of its completion, it was America's first commercial canal and considered one of the foremost engineering achievements and economic development projects of its day. The canal's economic usefulness withered away in the 1840s when railway lines to Columbia and Camden were completed.

An exceptional historical and natural interpretive center stands at the entrance to the park, operated by Santee Cooper, the state-owned electric utility. The natural beauty of the Santee Canal's location is shown through displays of wildlife and a 30-foot replica of a live oak tree towering to the ceiling of the center. The center is styled after the locks of the original old canal, and it tells the story of the project in diorama.

Outside, 4 miles of trails wind and crisscross along Biggin Creek, Old Santee Canal, and the currently active Tail Race Canal, which carries water and boats from Lake Moultrie and the Santee Cooper hydroelectric facility to the Cooper River.

Trees in the park typify Lowcountry swampland. Giant bald cypress is king, but it is attended by quite a court, including sweet gum, laurel oak, live oak, red maple, dogwood, magnolia, red bay, slippery elm, basswood, sugar maple, redbud, mulberry, and black willow, many of which are draped with ever present gray Spanish moss.

Old Santee Canal Park

An abundance of plant life is found here. Among the numerous species are holly fern, little sweet Betsy, mullein (or flannel plant), evening primrose, false garlic, buttercup, resurrection fern, bear's foot, swamp rose, alligator weed, water-spider orchid, cardinal flower, climbing aster, pickerelweed, supplejack, cattail, poison ivy, royal fern, honeysuckle, hydrangea, geranium, vetch, woodbine, red buckeye, and tallow tree (popcorn tree).

An unusual feature is a steep bluff composed of limestone rock known as Cooper marl, formed from tiny ocean organisms left behind millions of years ago. High levels of calcium in the marl make the soils of the bluff alkaline, allowing plants that require high levels of calcium to flourish here.

The stars of the bird set are ospreys perched high in their nests, but they have plenty of company, including red-winged blackbirds, red-shouldered hawks, wood ducks, little and great blue herons, prothonotary warblers, pileated wood-peckers, vireos, Carolina wrens, and cardinals. Alligators lazily police the water-ways, in the company of a variety of frogs and turtles, and white-tailed deer and wild turkeys roam the woodlands.

A variety of piers, boardwalks, and camouflaged observation posts make this a great place for wildlife viewing. Canoes can be rented in order to explore the black waters.

Next door to the interpretive center is the Stony Landing Plantation House, built around 1840 on a bluff. A dock extends into the Cooper River.

Park hours are 9:00 A.M. to 6:00 P.M. Monday to Friday and 9:00 A.M. to 7:00 P.M. Saturday and Sunday from April to October; 9 A.M. to 5 P.M. daily from No-vember to March. There is a small admission fee.

OLD SANTEE CANAL PARK TO ST. STEPHEN

Exit Stony Landing Road and head right (north) back onto US 52 Bypass/ Rembert Dennis Drive. The tall buildings rising above the trees to your right 0.4 mile up the road are the headquarters of **Santee Cooper**, the state-owned util-ity established in the 1930s to manage the new hydroelectric project. Today it delivers wholesale and retail electricity to more than a third of South Carolina's citizens, making it the fourth largest public power company in the United States.

After 0.6 mile more, you merge into US 52/Alternate US 17 and head northeast a half mile to the **Tail Race Canal.** Just before you cross the bridge over the canal, a road to your right (east) runs downhill to the Dock Restaurant and its boat landing. Lake Moultrie sends water through generators and a huge lock into the 4-mile Tail Race Canal, which connects with the Cooper River to carry water and vessels 48 more miles to Charleston.

From the Tail Race Canal, continue 0.6 mile to the fork where Alternate US 17 goes right (northeast) to Jamestown; bear left (north) on US 52 toward St. Stephen and Florence, passing by more churches and entering the Santee Circle community.

After 1.5 miles, a detour to the left on S-8-20/Powerhouse Road leads 1.4 miles west to the Pinopolis Dam and Lock and the Jefferies Hydroelectric Generating Station. Al-though less than 4 percent of Santee Cooper's power output today derives from hydro, this was the heart and soul of the original operation. The giant lock, the largest single lock sys-tem in the world at the time it was built, raises and lowers boats 150 feet between Lake Moultrie and the Tail Race Canal, allowing them to travel all the way from Charleston to Columbia, although few head farther north than Lake Marion.

Ride north on US 52 through the McBeth community. On your left, 3.3 miles from the Tail Race Canal, you can view a miniature Statue of Liberty and one of the busiest and, uh, most interesting collection of lawn ornaments you will ever see.

Canal Recreation Area, in the easternmost tip of **Francis Marion National Forest**, is on your left, 3.5 miles along US 52 past the fork. The pine-shaded area offers picnic tables, grills, rest rooms, pump well drinking water, and benches where you can relax and enjoy the view of a brook spilling from nearby Lake Moultrie. The area's main significance is as the northern trailhead for the 50-mile **Swamp Fox Passage of the Palmetto Trail**, which heads southward through the forest all the way to the coastal marsh at Buck Hall Recreation Area in Awendaw, and the southern trailhead of the **Lake Moultrie Passage of the Palmetto Trail**, which circles the lake's eastern shore for 26 miles. A kiosk beside the brook offers brochure information on both trails.

To sample the Lake Moultrie trail and attain a great view of the big lake, take a half-mile walk west through a generously green stand of young pines, across a railroad track, and up a stairway made of rail ties to the top of the large earthen Pinopolis East Dike. The view of the lake from this point is spectacular, particularly at sunset. The sinking sun sets the western side forest on fire, and the drama is played out doubly over the expanse of the reflective lake.

From here, the hiking and biking trail first heads north 3.5 miles along the top of the dike to the community of Bonneau Beach, which you can see in the distance. You can also look south to see towers of fossil fuel power plants adjacent to the Pinopolis Dam. Although much of the Lake Moultrie Passage takes you over service roads on top of the lake's dike system, the scenery is quite varied. The trail winds 26 miles along the eastern edge of Lake Moultrie, passing through lush wetlands, regrowth forests, open loblolly pine savannas, and dense lowland forests. White-tailed deer, wild turkeys, red-tailed hawks, and hundreds of other species abound. Wildflowers bloom year-round.

From Canal Recreation Area, take a left out of the parking area and continue northward into the town of **Bonneau** (pronounced *BUN-oh*), bearing left (northwest) after 1.7 miles onto S-8-35/Murray's Ferry Road. Drive through this village of comfortable cottages about a half mile and turn left (west) over the railroad tracks to join S-8-42/Black Oak Road, heading toward Bonneau Beach.

Travel another half mile and pull into the **Dennis Wildlife Center** on your left. Operated by the South Carolina Department of Natural Resources as a research and development center for wildlife and fisheries, the center offers interpretive displays and, between March 20 and May 7, tours of the striped bass hatchery, the culture of which makes the Dennis Wildlife Center famous among fishing aficionados across the nation. Visits to the facility, open 8:30 A.M. to 5:00 P.M. daily, are free of charge.

Continue westward and watch the lake's dike rise on your left as you approach Bonneau Beach, 2 miles from the Dennis Wildlife Center. On your ride into town, look for hikers and bikers exiting the downward slope of the dike on your left, just as they emerge from a section of the trail bordering fragrant water lilies and floating hearts. Trail followers navigate the streets of Bonneau Beach before rejoining the dike on the north side of the settlement.

Bonneau Beach is a fishing village, as attested by the tackle and bait shops and small motel on the way in. S-8-42 ends at the Mac Flood Landing on **Lake Moultrie**, offering a great panoramic vista. Lake Moultrie was constructed between 1939 and 1941 as part of the Santee Cooper Hydroelectric and Navigation Project, a massive federal effort to provide electricity to rural South Carolina. The lake and dam system diverts water from the Santee River into the Cooper River, the major river feeding into Charleston Harbor.

The 60,000-acre bowl-like lake was carved out of swampland interspersed with farms and a few plantations. Along with Lake Marion to the north, Lake Moultrie is famous for catfish and striped bass fishing.

"True sportsmanship begins with safety on land and water," says the sign here. A marina beside the boat ramp offers fuel and supplies. If you are looking for other activities, adjacent establishments offer pool, karaoke, beer, big-screen football, oysters, and home-cooked meals.

Turn around and drive northward back to the town of Bonneau on S-8-42. After crossing the railroad tracks, turn left (north) immediately onto S-8-35. Go one block and follow S-8-35 as it takes you sharply left (west) to recross the railroad tracks. Here S-8-35 is unpaved and called Dennis Ridge Road. Follow it northward for 3 miles, past modest homes, patches of forest, wildflowers, and fields of tobacco, soybeans, corn, and okra.

At the stop sign and intersection with S-8-41/Mandella Road, turn left (west) and go 1.2 miles to reach a remote section of the Lake Moultrie dike. This is a great spot for enjoying the natural beauty of the Lake Moultrie outback. Get out of your vehicle to a walk a few yards in either direction. A water-pump-equipped campsite for the Lake Moultrie Passage is less than a half mile south of this spot, on the lake (west) side of the dike.

Along this and most sections, the dike is entirely earthen on both sides. The side toward the lake is filled with bays and backwaters, islands, marshy patches, and wading bald cypress trees. These quiet waters are home to pickerelweed, fragrant water lilies, floating hearts, and handsome cattails. On the land side are mixed tracts of pine and hardwoods, interspersed with cultivated fields in power line rights-of-way. The dike itself has a bounty of wildflowers, with common dandelions, strikingly beautiful passionflowers, daisies, and spike lobelias.

Turn around and head east on S-8-41. Pass the S-8-35 intersection, cross US 52 after another 0.8 mile, and cruise 1.5 miles more, passing Bo Cat Alley, Ike Road, small homes, garden plots, and Bethel Church before arriving at a stop sign where S-8-41 ends at the intersection with S-8-351/Mendel Rivers Road. Turn left (north) and ride through the hardwood bottomlands of Walker Swamp before emerging into countryside full of farmhouses, crop fields, pasturelands,

Tobacco field near Dennis Ridge Road

and woodlands. After 3.6 miles, you arrive at the intersection with S-8-40/Hood Street, with the sanctuary and cemetery of Allen African Methodist Episcopal Church on your left.

Turn left (northwest) onto S-8-40 and head into the little town of **St. Stephen**. About 0.7 mile along the way, you arrive at Elm Street, with the Disciples of Christ Church on your left. Cross Elm and pass by the white brick First Baptist Church on your left, fronted by a bell tower. Go three more blocks north on Hood Street and turn right (east) on SC 45/Church Street.

Travel 0.2 mile and turn right (south) onto Church Circle Road. This U-shaped one-way street provides excellent perspectives on your left of venerable **St. Stephen Episcopal Church** and its well-worn cemetery. The congregation of the parish church began worship on this spot in 1754, and the present Georgian-style brick edifice was completed in 1769. Windows and doors are topped by elliptical fanlights, underneath a gambrel roof. If you have time, get out and walk the grounds of this well-preserved reminder of South Carolina's rural colonial past.

Exit Church Circle Road and turn left (west) on SC 45/Church Street, toward downtown. About 0.3 mile along the way, you come to Main Street, paralleling railroad tracks and Depot Street, on the opposite side of the tracks. The old train depot and storefronts of this little downtown area take you back to the early decades of the twentieth century. There are still signs of activity in some of the old buildings, including the Temple of Prayer for All People in one of them.

Turn left (south) on Main and drive past old storefronts and homes four blocks back to Elm Street. Turn right (west) on Elm, cross the train tracks, and take a left (south) on US 52. Go two blocks and turn right (west) on S-8-18/Russellville Road.

ST. STEPHEN TO THE DIVERSION CANAL

Drive 3 miles through fairly densely populated rural lands to the crossroads community of Russellville. At the little convenience store here, you can buy ice cream and play pool. Cross over S-8-35 and continue west on S-8-204 for 1.3 miles. You'll cross a railroad track, pass a huge particleboard manufacturing facility, and travel through thick forest before the Lake Moultrie dike emerges into view on your left as you arrive at the Henderson G. Guerry Public Boat Landing.

This is a great scenic spot, where Lake Moultrie flows into the **Rediversion Canal**. To your south is the trail along the top of the dike and lovely views of the lagoons and backwaters of the lake. The large main body of Lake Moultrie stretches to the west, and the grassy shores of the Rediversion Canal are on the north side, offering attractive opportunities for sunbathing and fishing. There is also a swimming area here.

The Rediversion Canal was built in the 1980s when federal officials decided that waters rushing from Lake Moultrie through the Pinopolis hydro facility were responsible for carrying excessive amounts of silt down the Cooper River into Charleston Harbor, exacerbating the continual need for dredging in order to provide adequate clearance for large ships. Their solution was the Rediversion Canal, which reduces water flow into the Cooper River by channeling much of Lake Moultrie's water into the Santee River, about 8 miles downstream. A small hydro project south of here helps compensate for the reduction of hydroelectric output at the Pinopolis Dam.

Turn around here and head back along S-8-204 to the Russellville intersection with S-8-35. Turn left (northwest) and ride past extensive wood products manufacturing facilities before crossing the Joseph H. Jefferson Bridge over the Rediversion Canal after 1.2 miles. The bridge, which also provides passage over the canal for Lake Moultrie Passage hikers and bikers, offers neat views of the canal. To your left, you can see the Lake Moultrie Passage trail reaching along both sides of the canal toward the lake dike, a mile west.

Ride past little homes, vegetable fields, and Singapore and Mystic Lanes 1.1 miles to J. K. Gourdin Elementary School, at the intersection with SC 45. Turn left (west) and ride into the isolated Pineville community, squeezed between Lake Moultrie to the south and the sprawling Santee River swamps and wetlands to the north. Like Pinopolis, Pineville was once a high-ground haven for plantation inhabitants in the lowlands below. After 2.4 miles, turn left (south) on Matilda Circle. Tiny, quaintly beautiful antebellum Pineville Chapel is a few yards along, on your left.

Return to SC 45, turn left (west), and drive 2.3 miles past homes, churches, woodlands, and fields, until you reach the unpaved left (south) turn for Sandy Beach Road, across the highway from a forest fire lookout tower on your right.

Head down Sandy Beach Road, hemmed in on both sides by thick forest. After 2.2 miles, you arrive at a parking area beside the dike. Here you may want to stroll westward along the trail on top of the dike. The dike, decorated with fleabane, dandelion, and deep purple bull thistles, continues for 1.1 miles before ending in a quiet spot at the northern remnant of the Old Santee Canal. You can cross the canal on the railroad trestle, which offers a pleasing view of the dark waters below, and walk a short distance alongside the stream. In spots where the water is most calm, fragrant water lilies and white water buttercups are abundant, while bald cypress trees rise grandly from the dark surface.

Follow the dirt road south across the dike and continue to another parking area another 0.6 mile along. From here, you may walk into the **Sandy Beach Waterfowl Management Area**, except from November 16 until March 1, when it is closed to the public.

The trail passes through wetlands and past a broad, shallow pond where deer enjoy grazing. The best time to appreciate this field of fragrant water lilies is before noon, when the flowers are in full bloom. After midday, the large white flowers close and sink, allowing just the tips to be seen above the water.

The wetlands are habitat to numerous waterfowl and other bird species, as well as plentiful deer, raccoons, opossums, frogs, turtles, snakes, and alligators. Red-winged blackbirds, sparrows, and eastern kingbirds are visible, but the songs and voices of many other birds surround the hiker.

A few bald cypress trees shade the plentiful water lilies. In the shrubs that sometimes line the trail, brilliant red trumpet honeysuckle flowers bloom on long vines. In shallow pools and ditches, pickerelweed produces its lovely violet flower spikes. Along the road are daisylike mayweeds and white-topped sedges with their striking long, drooping bracts.

Sandy Beach lies about a mile from the parking area. It is a bald-cypress-framed area with primitive camping facilities, a sandy lake floor ideal for frolicking, a reasonably close-up view of a bald eagle nest, and a panoramic view of Lake Moultrie looking south.

Return northward on Sandy Beach Road to SC 45, and turn left (west). After 1.3 miles, turn right (north) into the entrance for the **General Francis Marion Burial Site**. The wood-lined drive takes you 1 mile to a pretty little cemetery holding the long-interred remains of Marion and a number of family members. A lovely array of trees and shrubs decorates the area, and the tombstone inscriptions are fascinating.

General Francis Marion, a local Revolutionary War hero who was a genius at guerilla warfare, continually harassed and caused losses to British forces as they attempted to extend their control from their strongholds at Charleston and Georgetown. Evading counterattack and capture by continually fading into the myriad swamps throughout the South Carolina coastal plain, Marion became known by friend and foe alike as the "Swamp Fox." *The Patriot*, a movie filmed in South Carolina, is loosely based on his exploits.

Drive southward back to SC 45 and take a right to continue west. After 2.2 miles, S-8-31 forks to the right. *For a pleasant side trip, take this fork and ride 4.1 miles through the Eadytown community and along the edge of the Diversion Canal to reach Santee Dam. Here, the Diversion Canal sends some of Lake Marion's water to Lake Moultrie. Another portion is released through a series of floodgates into the meandering Santee River, which snakes through wetlands all the way to the Atlantic Ocean, at a spot between Georgetown and Charleston.*

Continuing on SC 45 for an additional 3 miles, on your left (southwest) is unpaved Eadie Lane, which takes travelers a few yards to the northern trailhead of the Lake Moultrie Passage of the Palmetto Trail. As you ride by, note the long, high ridge of kudzu-covered dirt, a remnant of the dredging of the Diversion Canal, about 0.1 mile past the Eadie Lane turnoff.

The **Diversion Canal** connects Lakes Marion and Moultrie, South Carolina's two great fishing lakes, especially famed for striped bass and record-size catfish. It is a key component of the original hydroelectric project that enabled water to be diverted from the Santee River through power generators near Moncks Corner and into the Cooper River. The Diversion Canal also allows boats to travel all the way from Charleston to Columbia.

As you top the bridge over the canal, you will likely see a profusion of fishing and pleasure boats, along with an eclectic string of commercial fish camps on the west bank of the busy water thoroughfare.

Complete your tour by visiting Black's Fish Camp a few miles south. Turn left (south) onto S-8-132 just past the bridge, ride 2.1 miles, and turn left (east) on S-8-1141, which will take you 1.2 miles to a backwater lagoon of Lake Moultrie. Here, beside green duckweed, marsh grasses and water-swollen, moss-hung bald-cypress trees, you will find a boat landing, grassy campgrounds, a motel, an excellent seafood restaurant, and a rather peculiar statue of Revolutionary War General William Moultrie, who faces away from the water.

Wateree Basin

WATEREE RIVER TO SANTEE NATIONAL WILDLIFE REFUGE

GENERAL DESCRIPTION: This 95-mile drive through rural Coastal Plain South Carolina is a delightful blend of nature, history, agriculture, and southern culture in its most basic sense.

SPECIAL ATTRACTIONS: Wateree River, Boykin Mill, General Thomas Sumter Memorial Park, Stateburg, Manchester State Forest, Poinsett State Park, Sparkleberry Swamp, Rimini, Liberty Hill AME Church, Lake Marion, Santee National Wildlife Refuge, numerous historic churches.

LOCATION: Middle of the state, east of Columbia.

DRIVE ROUTE NUMBERS: Interstate 20, US 521, SC 261, S-28-2, S-43-488, S-43-400,

S-43-420, S-43-63, S-43-51, Sparkleberry Landing Road, S-14-76, S-14-373, US 301/US 15, S-14-803, S-14-127, S-14-559, S-14-260, Cuddo Unit Road.

TRAVEL SEASON: All year.

SERVICES: Columbia, Camden, and Sumter have full services. Santee, on Interstate 95, offers motels and outlet shopping. Summerton has eateries and limited services.

See For More Information in the appendix for addresses and phone numbers of Attractions, Camping, Neat Places to Stay, Restaurants, Shops, Tours, and Nature-Based Services.

THE DRIVE

This 95-mile ride through rural countryside on the east side of the Wateree River Basin and along the banks of the old bed of the Santee River mostly follows the route of the former King's Highway, which connected Camden with Charleston in the 1700s. This area was saturated with antebellum plantations. Today, most of the former plantation lands are small farms or hunting preserves. Change has come slowly, and the people who currently live here, both the black majority and the white minority, are descended from the area's black and white inhabitants prior to the Civil War.

The tour is rich in history, including Revolutionary War, Civil War, and Civil Rights. Religion is important here, and you pass numerous churches, many of which are historically significant. Much of what you see is representative of the poor South, as opposed to the New South. Nevertheless, social institutions are

Wateree Basin

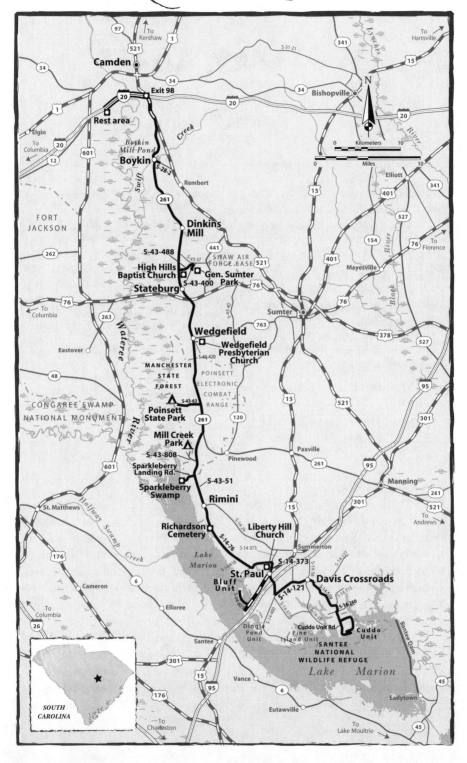

strong, and both races display a strong attachment to family, land, church, and nature.

You begin by crossing the Wateree River and its wetlands and proceeding through the quaint Boykin settlement. From there, you pass farmland and historic structures before visiting the tomb of General Thomas Sumter and Stateburg, the village he wanted to establish as South Carolina's capital. You continue to the Wedgefield community, to Manchester State Forest and Poinsett State Park, and then to Sparkleberry Swamp, Rimini, the Liberty Hill AME Church that played a major role in school desegregation, and Santee National Wildlife Refuge.

WATEREE RIVER TO STATEBURG

Begin at the rest stop on the eastbound section of I–20 south of Camden, between US 601 and US 521. Drive east toward Florence. On your left you see farm silos and pecan trees before you enter the wetland forest of mixed hardwoods and pines as you approach the Wateree. You enter a causeway through swampland and travel over a bridge above the **Wateree River** 2.3 miles from the rest stop. Crossing at a major bend in the waterway, you enjoy great views northward, where the river is flanked by low, wooded bluffs, and southeastward, where swampy wetlands begin to close in on the river.

The Wateree River is the easternmost major artery of the Santee-Cooper River Basin, the biggest river drainage system in South Carolina. The main water flow that is the Wateree River begins in the mountains of North Carolina as the Catawba River. The Catwaba flows through unimpounded stretches and through lakes, such as Norman and Wylie, for more than 200 miles. It courses past Charlotte and Rock Hill, and joins with Big Wateree Creek on the Fairfield/Kershaw County line to form Lake Wateree and the Wateree River. The Wateree River empties through Lake Wateree Dam and returns to its normal riverbed about 10 miles north of the I–20 bridge over the river. South of the bridge, the Wateree snakes through the massive Wateree Swamp all the way to its convergence with the Congaree River, where the two waterways form the Santee River just north of Lake Marion. The Santee River exits Lake Marion at the lake's southern end and flows through more wetlands to the Atlantic Ocean at a point south of Georgetown. However, much of the water in Lake Marion is diverted through a canal into Lake Moultrie and then into the Cooper River, the biggest stream that empties into Charleston Harbor.

After crossing the Wateree River, continue on a causeway and another bridge over wetlands for 2 miles until you reach Sumter/Camden exit 98, where US 521 crosses I–20. Exit here and turn right (southeast) toward Sumter.

You might want to consider turning left and heading into historic Camden, 3 miles north. This beautiful little city is chock-full of old homes, churches, and public buildings. During the American Revolution, British General Lord Cornwallis and his troops were headquartered here for a year in 1780–1781; a number of battles and skirmishes occurred in the area. The old British fortified area is now a historic park, with a number of interpretive exhibits and a full-size replica of the Revolutionary-era Kershaw-Cornwallis House.

Heading south on US 521, you are enter the flat, rural Coastal Plain area of South Carolina. You pass beautiful wetlands, a tree-filled pond, forestland, and white, wooden Wesley Chapel Methodist Church. Two miles south of I–20, veer right (south) on SC 261 toward Boykin, 4 miles away.

As you pass along this route, keep in mind that you are following the east side of the Wateree River, which winds and curves along on your right at distances of 2 to 5 miles from SC 261, with extensive swamplands extending eastward. Ride through cotton fields and woodlands, past redbrick Broom Hill Baptist Church, pecan groves, and an old home place on your right, with oak trees canopying the long driveway.

On the outskirts of the Boykin community, you cross Swift Creek and its wetlands, with pretty **Boykin Mill Pond** on your left. Turn left (east) on S-28-2, where a historical marker tells the story of South Carolina's last Civil War engagement, the Battle of Boykin Mill. Here, on April 18, 1865, Confederate regulars and home guardsmen fought a delaying action against Union troops from Georgetown who had marched north to destroy a railroad track connecting Camden and Sumter. Among those killed was the last Federal officer to die in a Civil War battle, as well as fifteen-year-old Burwell Boykin, son of Confederate Colonel Alexander Hamilton Boykin.

Boykin was settled in 1755 by William Boykin II and his sons. It became a regional focal point as the family, over time, built a water-powered flour and gristmill, a cotton gin, a sawmill, a church, and a tavern. Most of the property around here is still owned by descendents of William Boykin II, whose progeny also developed the Boykin spaniel breed for hunting. **Boykin Mill**, on the local pond, continues as it has for centuries to grind out freshly milled whole-grain grits and meal on hand-dressed millstones. Tours are sometimes available.

On your right on S-28-2 is Boykin Mill General Store, established in 1792 and adorned with Nehi soft drink, Gulf Oil, and other signs of the mid-twentieth century. Here you can shop for freshly ground grits and cornmeal from Boykin Mill, fresh farm products, plants, gifts, jellies and jams, candles, and general merchandise. Delicious soup, salad, and sandwich lunches are offered here, as well as barbecued pork, chicken, and ribs on weekends.

Also at this intersection are the Mill Pond Restaurant, offering fine regional cuisine in a series of connected old country store buildings, and the Broom Place, where the delightful owner uses century-old original equipment to make a variety of useful and decorative brooms and other crafts in a restored cabin dating from 1740. A few yards east on S-28-2 is **Swift Creek Baptist Church**, a gray and white two-story Greek Revival building constructed in 1827 and listed on

Boykin Mill

the National Register of Historic Places. A nice little picnic area sits between the church and the pond.

If you are around the last Sunday before Christmas, come over to see the Boykin Christmas Parade, filled with unconventional participants of many types. The parade is preceded by a roadkill cook-off and ends with a gospel concert at Swift Creek Baptist Church.

Return to the intersection of S-28-2 and SC 261 and turn left to continue southward along the eastern edge of the Wateree Swamp as you cross from Kershaw into Sumter County. Drive through pastoral settings of old farm homesteads, pecan groves, live oaks adorned with Spanish moss, barns, goats, horse pastures and pens, country stores and churches, woodlands, and fields of corn, cotton, soybeans, and hay.

After passing Wateree Correctional Institute, a minimum security prison farm, look on your right for the **Church of the Ascension Episcopal Church**, about 2.3 miles from Boykin. This delicate white Gothic-style building, constructed in 1895, sits beside a charming cemetery dating back to 1807.

Drive southward a half mile farther, past Oak Grove Plantation, to see **Dixie Hall Plantation Home**, a three-story clapboard home with a double piazza supported by four columns. It was built in 1818.

Continue south on SC 261 for 2.2 miles and pass the Rafting Creek community. On the left (east) side of the road a short distance farther south is the old Dinkins Mill, surrounded by pecan trees.

Continue south about 4.5 miles past farmland, country stores, and the Sanders Corner community before turning left (east) on S-43-488/Meeting House Road to see the General Thomas Sumter Tomb. On your right is **High Hills Baptist Church**, a white Greek Revival structure with four columns and green trim. This building was erected in 1803, and the congregation, which began in 1770, is the second oldest Baptist congregation in South Carolina. At the beginning of the nineteenth century, the Reverend John Roberts opened Roberts Academy, the state's first Baptist educational institution here, and went on to establish Furman University in 1826.

Drive east 1.3 miles, past High Hills African-Methodist-Episcopal Church and Pine Hills Baptist Church, to enter a residential neighborhood. Following brown signs for Sumter's tomb, turn right (northeast) on S-43-400/Acton Road and go 0.2 mile to arrive at the charming little cemetery known as **General Thomas Sumter Memorial Park**. General Sumter, nicknamed "The Gamecock" for his ferocious, tenacious fighting tactics in the South Carolina midlands during the American Revolution, lived in this area and led Patriot forces in a number of engagements against British and Loyalist troops. On the enclosed grounds are a memorial to Sumter, graves of the general and many members of his family, and a chapel surrounding the grave site of Sumter's French-born daughter-in-law, Nathalie Marie Louise Stephanie Beatrix de DeLage de Volude Sumter. This quiet, restful spot is a great place to relax, offering stone benches, magnolias, and shady hardwood trees.

Return westward 1.5 miles and turn left on SC 261 to resume your journey toward **Stateburg**, 2 miles south. Stateburg was laid out by General Sumter in 1783 and given its name in the hope that it would become the state capital when lawmakers moved their seat of government inland from Charleston. Alas, lawmakers chose a plot of land on the banks of the Congaree River and named it Columbia, leaving Stateburg an unincorporated village sleepier today than it was more than 300 years ago. Therein lies its charm.

As you enter the settlement, take note of several private mansions on your right, marked by white fences, shady yards, and PRIVATE signs. Among them is the **Miller/Ellison House**, built around 1800 for Governor Stephen Decatur Miller. It was purchased in 1836 by William Ellison, a wealthy freedman who owned a plantation and fifty slaves. Also on the right, across the street from a church, is the **Borough House**, built as a wood frame house in the 1750s and remodeled in 1821 with a colonnaded facade and two wings of *pisé de terre* (rammed earth). During the American Revolution, it served (at different times, of course) as headquarters for both British Lord Cornwallis and American General Nathaniel Greene.

On your left is the lovely **Cathedral of the Holy Cross Episcopal**, begun as a chapel of ease in 1770. The driveway is one-way, and you need to enter at the second turn into the parking area. The current Gothic Revival pisé de terre structure, designed by architect Edward C. Jones of Charleston, was built between 1850 and 1852. The east and west stained glass windows were made in Bavaria, and the nineteenth century organ inside was built by Henry Erben, the renowned organ maker from Newark. It was installed in 1851 and is one of the few Erben organs still in use. The charming cemetery holds the remains of a number of local notables, including war veterans, several Sumter family members, and Joel Poinsett, the noted botanist and statesman who brought the poinsettia plant to this country from Mexico, where he served as U.S. Ambassador. Poinsett died in the Borough House.

STATEBURG TO POINSETT STATE PARK

From the churchyard, turn left and drive south on SC 261 for 0.7 mile to the intersection with US 76/US 378.

You may choose to take a short detour here to enjoy the best available highway view of the Wateree River and Swamp. To do so, turn right (west) toward Columbia and drive 5 miles over swamp-surrounded causeways to the bridge over the river. Cross the river and drive 1.2 miles up the bluff, turn left at the intersection with SC 263, and return 6.2 miles on the eastbound lane of US 76/US 378.

Cross US 76/US 378 and continue southward toward Pinewood on SC 261/Charles Griffin Memorial Highway. Travel 4 miles past both elegant and modest homes surrounded by pines and hardwoods to the crossroads community of **Wedgefield**. After crossing the railroad tracks and passing SC 763, take a left on S-43-420 to see pretty Wedgefield Presbyterian Church, circa 1881, a wooden structure with forest green shutters and trim.

Return to SC 261 and resume your southward journey. After about 2 miles, SC 261 begins a long stretch as the border between a U.S. Air Force bombing range on the left (east) and **Manchester State Forest** on the right. On your left 4 miles from Wedgefield, at a fork in the road, is a historical marker noting that the town of Manchester once stood in this area. Manchester was a stagecoach relay station and a shipping center for cotton. A busy point on the Wilmington and Manchester Railroad, it also served as an entertainment center, with taverns, horse racing, ball games, and other contests. In 1840, it was listed as one of the ten largest towns in the state. The inhabitants were wealthy planters who owned plantations along the Wateree River. Manchester was burned by Union troops in 1865 and never rebuilt.

The state forest contains 23,500 acres of pines and hardwoods, which were severely damaged by Hurricane Hugo's onslaught in 1989. This public property was once the site of three former estates: Bellefield, Melrose, and Milford. Ridges, sand hills, hardwood bottoms, bays, ponds, and swampland are scattered throughout the property, and you will find pockets of mountain laurel, red cedars draped with Spanish moss, dogwoods, and live oaks, composing a rather unique plant mix for the state. Deer are plentiful, and birds include red-cockaded woodpeckers, songbirds, wading birds, and birds of prey. Separate trails are available for horses, mountain bikes, motorcycles, and hikers, and you are free to drive the dozens of dirt roads that crisscross throughout the park.

Bear left (southeast) to stay on SC 261 for an additional 2.5 miles before turning right (west) onto S-43-63/Poinsett Park Road. Follow this road 1.9 miles to the entrance gate of **Poinsett State Park**, in the midst of the state forest. The parking area is 0.3 mile farther. Poinsett, constructed by the Civilian Conservation Corps in the 1930s, offers 5 miles of hiking along three connecting trails through hilly and wonderfully diverse terrain, presenting an interesting juxtaposition of mountain and coastal plain flora.

The park is a unique and exciting place, a taste of the mountains in the coastal plain. The park features 1,000 acres of hilly terrain adjacent to Wateree Swamp, and it incorporates a small part of the swamp. These are the High Hills of Santee, an area famous for producing political and military leaders. The elevation changes create a fascinating environment and marvelous hiking, as well as providing a variety of natural habitats.

Surveys have identified 337 flowering plants in the park. Wildflowers put on an impressive show in the early spring. Naturalists have also identified sixty-five trees and shrubs in the park. Wildlife includes snakes, alligators, eastern fence lizards, bullfrogs, southern leopard frogs, squirrels, white-tailed deer, rabbits, raccoons, opossums, and bobcats, along with more than fifty bird species.

Old Levi Mill Pond, bordered by moss-draped bald cypresses and tupelo gums, is beside the park headquarters and is the trailhead for the interpretive Coquina Trail circling the pond. Coquina, a naturally cemented rock formation laced with seashells, is abundant in the park, reflecting the fact that this area was underneath the sea in prehistoric times. The lake was built as a freshwater reserve for flooding rice fields in the eighteenth century, and only later used as a millpond.

The Hilltop Trail forks away from the Coquina Trail, and then descends to intersect with Laurel Group Trail. Both require a fair amount of climbing and have a nice winding character over pleasantly rolling terrain. The mountains-to-the-sea Palmetto Trail also passes through here, running concurrently with park trails for a distance.

Poinsett State Park is open 9:00 A.M. to 9:00 P.M. during daylight saving time and 9:00 A.M. to 6:00 P.M. during standard time. A small admission fee is charged. Rest rooms are located adjacent to the park office. Paddleboat rentals are available, as are picnic tables. Mountain bike and equestrian trails are also offered.

POINSETT STATE PARK TO SANTEE NATIONAL WILDLIFE REFUGE

Head back out on S-43-63/Poinsett Park Road and take a right (south) on SC 261. Drive 2.4 miles through forest, then veer right (southwest) onto S-43-51 toward Rimini. About 1.7 miles farther, turn left into the grounds of **St. Mark's**

Episcopal Church, founded in 1757. The current structure was erected in 1855, made of brick baked from local clay. The church is coated with white stucco that contrasts nicely with the pretty red tile roof. Six governors and a number of other notables have attended St. Mark's. A pleasant, tree-shaded cemetery adjoins the church.

Turn left out of the churchyard and head south on S-43-51.

If you have time, you may want to detour by taking a right (northwest) on S-43-808, 1.4 miles from the church. Drive 0.8 mile, to where the pavement ends, and turn right (east) into Mill Creek County Park. Bear left after you enter the park and ride past the western side of dark Mill Creek Pond, filled with lily pads. You pass a lodge building and then enter a sprawling, shaded picnic area with campsites, rest rooms and showers. The clean ground cover is grass and pine straw. This is the southern trailhead for the High Hills of the Santee Passage of the Palmetto Trail, leading to Poinsett State Park, plus a horse trail. The park is open daylight to sunset, and admission is free.

At 2.7 miles from St. Mark's, turn right (east) off of S-43-51 onto unpaved Sparkleberry Landing Road. Drive downhill for 1.6 miles past fields and mixed forest to reach the boat landing for **Sparkleberry Swamp**. This is a great place to view the bald cypresses, tupelos, and huge amounts of aquatic plant life that populate the upper swampland reaches of Lake Marion. Fishing boats, canoes, and kayaks put in at this point to explore the far reaches of Sparkleberry Swamp. Grassy knolls and green trees make this an enjoyable picnic spot.

Backtrack to S-43-51 and turn right (south) to continue toward Rimini, 3 miles away, passing the Safety Kleen hazardous waste landfill site on your right. Ironically, the exterior of this extremely controversial facility is attractively landscaped.

You enter the impoverished community of **Rimini** just as you cross from Sumter County into Clarendon County. The intriguing village, located somewhat in geographic and cultural isolation, has a few small stores and churches and an assortment of modest homes.

Bear right onto S-14-76/Old River Road and head southeast. About a mile south of Rimini, you pass a marker indi-

Sparkleberry Swamp

cating the site of the Battle of Halfway Swamp, where, in 1780, Patriot forces and smallpox combined to defeat British forces heading north from Charleston.

Pass **Elliott's Pond**, a hauntingly beautiful cypress lagoon on your left. About a mile farther, you come to the **Richardson Cemetery**. Turn right (west) and drive about 300 yards to a remote fenced-in graveyard surrounded by crop fields. Among the notables buried in this bleak setting are Revolutionary War Brigadier General Richard Richardson, James Burtrell Richardson (governor of South Carolina from 1802 to 1804), and John Peters Richardson, who founded The Citadel to train militia to defend against slave revolts, and served as governor of South Carolina from 1840 to 1842.

Continue southeast on S-14-76, passing through an impoverished, somewhat densely populated area of farm fields and forestland punctuated with modest homes and a country church. After 5.5 miles, where a sign points to Billups Landing to the right, veer left (west) to stay on S-14-76. Drive 2.1 miles, crossing the wetlands of Big Branch before arriving at a stop sign at the intersection with S-14-373/Liberty Hill Road. Turn right (southwest) and turn right again after a few yards, into the parking lot of **Liberty Hill African Methodist Episcopal Church**, with its adjacent old cemetery.

Liberty Hill Church was established in 1867; the present redbrick building was completed in 1905. Meetings held here in the 1940s and 1950s led to local court cases that culminated in the landmark U.S. Supreme Court ruling of 1954 that segregated public schools are inherently unequal and thus unconstitutional.

The cases originated when local African-American parents were unable to persuade the all-white local school board even to provide bus transportation for their children to attend the dilapidated school buildings grudgingly provided for their use. Some parents and others attending meetings here were fired from their jobs and endured threats of bodily harm, but their courage paved the way for a series of legislative, executive, and judicial decisions that ultimately resulted in victory for the civil rights movement. Unfortunately, local white residents remained steadfast in their dedication to segregation, and Clarendon County School District One remains to this day de facto segregated, with black youths attending the public schools and white youths attending private schools or fleeing to neighboring school districts.

From Liberty Hill Church, continue southwest on S-14-373 for a mile, past St. Paul Holiness Church and St. Paul Primary School, to the intersection with US 301/US 15, location of the 301 Disco Club. Turn right (southwest) and drive through farmland and forest 3.2 miles to the causeway over Cantey Bay, a backwater of **Lake Marion**. Travel a half mile farther and turn right (northwest) on S-14-803 to enter the **Bluff Unit of Santee National Wildlife Refuge**. Admission is free.

Santee National Wildlife Refuge is a 15,000-acre tract on the northern side of Lake Marion, consisting of mixed hardwoods, mixed pine-hardwoods, pine plantations, marsh, croplands, old fields, ponds, impoundments, and open water.

It was created in 1941 as a way station for migrating waterfowl and is a winter stopover point for about 50,000 ducks and 8,000 geese and swans. There are thousands more year-round residents, including red-cockaded woodpeckers, bald eagles, hawks, killdeer, ospreys, alligators, white-tailed deer, raccoons, squirrels, and bobcats throughout the four separate units of the refuge.

Ride past moss-hung oaks and other hardwoods 0.3 mile to the visitor center on your left. Open 8:00 A.M. to 4:00 P.M., Tuesday through Sunday, this is a good place to view interpretive exhibits, obtain information about the refuge, and enjoy great views of **Lake Marion** from the center's wraparound porch. Look north across the cove to get your first glimpse of Santee Indian Mound.

Lake Marion's 110,000 acres were carved out of the swampy Santee River Basin in the late 1930s and early 1940s for a massive hydroelectric project to provide power to rural South Carolina and to provide jobs during the Great Depression. Because of the sudden wartime power needs of World War II, the basin was flooded in 1941, earlier than planned; one result was numerous trees left standing and fallen in the water. Those trees produce great fish habitat, and Lake Marion is one of the nation's premier freshwater fishing locales. More than 120 fish species flourish in Lake Marion, including ten varieties of catfish, longnose gar, Atlantic and shortnose sturgeon, striped mullet, and striped, white, and largemouth bass.

Proceed northward from the visitor center a half mile to **Fort Watson/Santee Indian Mound**. This spot was used as an Indian ceremonial mound around A.D. 1200–1400. During the Revolutionary War, the British established Fort Watson on top of the mound to command a strategic position on the Santee River, and its fall to General Francis Marion's Patriot forces in 1781 was an early part of a string of setbacks for the British that led to their final defeat two years later. This is another good spot for viewing Lake Marion.

A little farther north is a parking area for hiking trails and bike paths. Turn around here and head back to the entrance to the Bluff Unit of Santee National Wildlife Refuge.

You may choose to turn right (southwest) here and drive a mile out onto the old US 301 causeway and bridge over Lake Marion, now closed to vehicles, which must detour onto the I–95 bridge. At the point where US 301 forks left to join I–95, bear right on Old US 301. Both the northern and southern ends of the old bridge/causeway are now park areas, and you can fish here, walk or bike across the bridge, or simply enjoy pleasant views.

From the refuge entrance, turn left (northeast) on US 301/US 15, drive 3.7 miles back to the intersection with S-14-373, and turn right (southeast). Travel 2.2 miles, crossing I–95, and turn left (northeast) on S-14-127/Bill Davis Road. Drive 3.6 miles past forest and fields to Davis Crossroads. Go a half mile farther and turn right (southeast) on S-14-559/William Brunson Road toward Potato Creek. After 3.6 miles, you come to a stop sign. Turn right (south) on Rogers Road to stay on S-14-559 for another half mile. At the next stop sign, turn right

Pond in Cuddo Unit

(west) onto S-14-260/Old River Road (toward John C. Land Boat Ramp) and immediately left (south) onto an unpaved road to enter the **Cuddo Unit of the Santee National Wildlife Refuge**.

Drive a mile past open fields, shrub wetlands, and forest. On your left is the one-way exit for the loop you are entering. Continue straight south through dark hardwood forest with a sprinkling of dogwoods and then past more shrubs and wetlands. After another mile, you pass the exit for a second one-way road, on your left. Proceed straight ahead 0.3 mile more through fields and wildflowers. At a gate where the road goes left (east), you can park and walk westward along a pathway toward Black Bottom, a good place to find alligators.

Continue east on what has just become a one-way loop road through more fields. After a half mile, bald cypress and tupelo trees rise to your right, with Lake Marion on the other side. Clearer views of Lake Marion appear as you round a curve after another half mile and head back west. A half mile farther, you leave the fields on your left altogether and curve north and then back east through forests and beautiful, soggy marshland. You pass lovely lily ponds that are home to alligators, frogs, turtles, and snakes. After 0.8 mile, you reach the entrance to 1.4-mile Foot Trail One.

Turn left and drive north about 0.1 mile. Here you can walk to your right (east) to reach the beginning of Foot Trail Two, also 1.4 miles. Take a left (west), and you reach a fork after another 0.1 mile. The road straight ahead goes back to the main entrance road; turn right (north) and head 1.1 delightful miles past open fields, dark hardwood forest, and shrub wetlands. When you reach the next junction, turn left (straight ahead is a dead end), and proceed westward for a winding 1.2 miles through forest and fields.

Turn right (north) on the tree-canopied main entrance road to head north for 1 mile and complete your scenic drive by exiting the Cuddo Unit of Santee National Wildlife Refuge.

Congaree Basin and Lake Marion

HOPKINS TO SANTEE STATE PARK

GENERAL DESCRIPTION: This is a pretty 65-mile countryside ride to scenic natural areas and remote villages in South Carolina's upper coastal plain.

SPECIAL ATTRACTIONS: Congaree Swamp National Monument, Cedar Creek, Congaree River, Fort Motte, Lone Star, Upper Santee Swamp, Elloree, Santee State Park, Lake Marion.

LOCATION: Middle of the state, south of Columbia.

DRIVE ROUTE NUMBERS: S-40-37, SC 48, S-40-734, Entrance Drive, S-40-1288, US 601, S-9-80, SC 419, S-9-150, SC 267, S-9-11, S-9-54, S-9-402, S-9-326, S-9-129, S-9-286, SC 6, Cleveland Street, Railroad Avenue, Barkley Street, S-38-105, S-38-82.

TRAVEL SEASON: All year. Fall, winter, and spring are best for watching wildlife in Congaree Swamp National Monument, but summer is a great time to enjoy Santee State Park and the rich crops and pasturelands along the way.

SERVICES: Columbia has full accommodations and services. Santee, on Interstate 95, offers motels and outlet shopping. St. Matthews and Elloree have eateries and limited services.

See For More Information in the appendix for addresses and phone numbers of Attractions, Camping, Neat Places to Stay, Restaurants, Shops, Tours, and Nature-Based Services.

THE DRIVE

This drive begins in farm country on the outskirts of Columbia and takes riders through attractive countryside, forests, and wetlands typical of South Carolina's rich agrarian and natural heritage. You ride through densely populated rural areas in Richland County, visit the fabulous Congaree Swamp National Monument, enjoy scenic cotton fields of Calhoun County, wander through the almost ghost towns of Fort Motte and Lone Star, gaze at the Upper Santee Swamp from Low Falls Landing, amble into quaint little Elloree, and conclude at nature-filled Santee State Park, on the shores of huge Lake Marion. As is often the case when riding through rural South Carolina, you go by a passel of little churches along the way, and homes whose occupants descend from local families that have been in these specific locales since the 1800s or before.

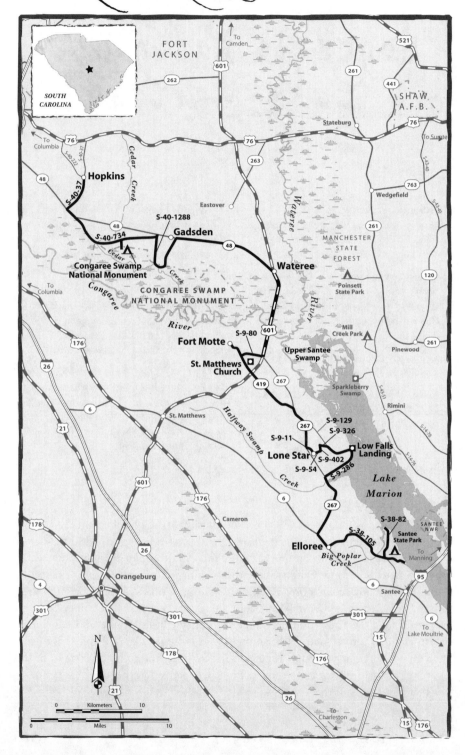

HOPKINS TO CONGAREE SWAMP NATIONAL MONUMENT

Begin southeast of Columbia, shaded by Spanish-moss-hung oaks in the sleepy Richland County village of **Hopkins**, at the intersection of S-40-37 and S-40-222, between US 76/US 378 and SC 48/Bluff Road. Hopkins dates from colonial times, and during the 1800s it was a hub for surrounding plantations. Head south on S-40-37, pass the post office on your right, and ride among picturesque horse and cattle pastures and country homes. Hopkins County Park is on your right after 1.5 miles, after which you pass denser, more modest houses before reaching SC 48/Bluff Road 1 mile farther down the road.

Turn left (southeast) on SC 48/Bluff Road and drive 0.7 mile to the intersection where S-40-734/Old Bluff Road forks to the right. Bear right (southeast) here and pass by a number of modest homes in an old African-American settlement before crossing a couple of bridges over the wetlands and the channel of Cedar Creek, which flows a twisting course into the Congaree Swamp and River. Next, you pass a pretty marsh pond on your left before arriving at the entrance to **Congaree Swamp National Monument** 4.5 miles after the turn onto S-40-734/Old Bluff Road.

Turn right (south) and wind 1.2 miles through coastal plain forest before reaching the Harry Hampton Visitors Center, which offers excellent interpretive displays, a free film about the swamp, brochures, maps, and guidance from park staff and volunteers. Rest rooms, water fountains, and vending machines are available.

Congaree Swamp National Monument, more than 22,000 acres in the heart of the Congaree River floodplain, represents the largest stand of old-growth river bottom hardwood forest in the United States. In 1983 it was named an International Biosphere Reserve.

Hit hard by Hurricane Hugo and other powerful windstorms in recent years, Congaree Swamp has lost many of its national record trees, but a host of huge, impressive specimens still remains, including three that are still the largest of their type in the country: a 42-foot possum haw, a 132-foot persimmon, and a 148-foot water hickory.

Congaree Swamp offers more than 20 miles of interlocking hiking trails, including a 2-mile handicapped-accessible boardwalk loop from the visitors center. This short loop carries you past towering loblolly pines, water-soaked floodplain, enchanting Weston Lake, fascinating bald cypress trees and knees, immensely diverse vegetation, and one of the highest forest canopies in the world. Other walkways include Weston Lake Trail, River Trail, Oak Ridge Trail, Kingsnake Trail, and Bluff Trail. Cedar Creek offers superb canoeing and kayaking options, and, along with Weston and Wise Lakes, good fishing.

In addition to those named above, the area's more than eighty tree and shrub species include beech, hornbeam, sycamore, pawpaw, red maple, red mulberry, sassafras, cottonwood, sweet gum, water tupelo, dwarf palmetto, tulip tree, five hickory varieties, mountain laurel, holly, black walnut, magnolia, dogwood, wax myrtle, three types of elm, and fourteen varieties of oak. Wild azaleas bloom around the Bluff Trail.

The plentiful wildlife-viewing opportunities include 170 bird species. Among them are herons, ducks, egrets, white ibis, ospreys, vultures, bald eagles, bobwhites, wild turkeys, doves, cuckoos, hummingbirds, wrens, flycatchers, bluebirds, robins, mockingbirds, red-winged blackbirds, orioles, blue jays, four owl species, four swallow species, five varieties of vireos, red-cockaded and six other types of woodpeckers, eight hawk varieties, ten swallow species, and twenty-six types of warblers.

Additionally, the park offers a native plant butterfly garden with forty-five varieties of butterflies, skippers, and moths. Eight types of bats inhabit the forest, but none are of the Transylvanian variety.

Furthermore, the park hosts five lizard species, seven types of turtles, eleven kinds of salamanders, eighteen snake varieties, and nineteen species of frogs and toads, in addition to white-tailed deer, feral hogs, bobcats, raccoons, opossums, gray foxes, river otters, marsh and cottontail rabbits, and gray, fox, and flying squirrels. The park is truly an ecological wonderland.

The park's gates are open daily from 8:30 A.M. to 5:30 P.M. Park in the lot just before the chained entrance area if you wish to enter or leave at other times.

Head back out to S-40-734/Old Bluff Road and turn right (east). Drive 2.6 miles past homes and fields to a stop sign. Take a right on S-40-1288/South Cedar Creek Road and drive 1.8 miles to the **Cedar Creek** parking area for Congaree Swamp National Monument. Park here and walk a few yards downhill to the eastern trailhead for Kingsnake Trail and a footbridge over mystical, meandering Cedar Creek. The lush vegetation and slow, foreboding stream provide a great locale for pictures, meditation, and relaxation.

CONGAREE SWAMP NATIONAL MONUMENT TO LOW FALLS LANDING

From the Cedar Creek parking area, take a right, head east on S-40-1288/South Cedar Creek Road, then curve northeastward past more fields, forest, and modest dwellings for 3 miles. Cross a railroad track to rejoin SC 48/Bluff Road in Gadsden, an old railroad village that has seen more prosperous days. Turn right and drive 7.8 miles on SC 48/Bluff Road through more densely populated countryside.

At the intersection with US 601 in the Wateree settlement, look to your left (northeast) to see the tall structures of SCANA's Wateree coal-fired power plant rising above the forest. Historic Kensington Mansion (circa 1854) is about 9 miles to your left (north) from here, located on property owned by International Paper Company and open to the public for tours for a moderate price.

Turn right and head south on US 601. This road provides a great perspective of the Congaree River and its wetlands. After about 0.6 mile, you come to the first of a series of causeways and bridges across vast river wetlands, with excellent views east and west of the dense bottomland forest and waters. About 4 miles along the elevated wetland roadway, you reach Bates Bridge Landing on your right, just before crossing the John M. Bates Bridge over the **Congaree River**. Turn right (southwest) and drive a few feet down into the landing area. Here you can get an up-close view of the mighty Congaree.

Go back up to US 601, turn right, and continue south, passing over the Congaree River with nice views on both sides of the winding central South Carolina water artery. On the south side of the river, you ascend quickly up a bluff to emerge into the farmlands of Calhoun County, named after antebellum firebrand statesman John C. Calhoun.

At 2 miles past the bridge, turn right (west) on S-9-80/Adams Road, toward Fort Motte. Drive past kudzu, cotton fields, and scattered farmhouses for 1.6 miles to a stop sign; turn right (northwest) onto SC 419/Fort Motte Road. This is prime hunting country, especially for pheasant, quail, and deer.

Ease downhill 1.1 miles to enter **Fort Motte**. As you cross Buck Head Creek and a railroad track, turn right (northeast) on S-9-150/Old Town Square. You may feel as though you have entered the Twilight Zone and arrived at a town untouched for a hundred years. Deserted storefronts facing the train tracks are now tangled in vines and canopied with moss-hung trees, emitting an unsettling eeriness.

The town is named for Revolutionary War heroine Rebecca Motte, who lived nearby and drove a British garrison from her home by setting it ablaze with fire-tipped arrows. Fort Motte was once a bustling cotton and timber shipment center, but twentieth-century highways passed the town by long ago. Now it is almost, but now quite, a ghost town.

Ride two blocks down S-9-150 and turn left (northwest) with the paved road, away from the tracks. Go past unpaved Wise Road until S-9-150 turns left again, this time southwest. Tin-roofed cottages with comfortable porches are tucked into the undergrowth here and there as you follow a 0.6-mile loop around the little village. Turn left (southeast) one more time to stay on S-9-150/Town Square Street and pass more dilapidated commercial buildings before arriving back at the railroad tracks after completing your loop.

Turn right (southwest), drive a few yards, and turn left (southeast) to exit Fort Motte the way you came in, passing over the railroad tracks and Buck Head Creek. This time, however, stay on SC 419 past S-9-80/Adams Road and continue another mile to **Saint Matthews Parish Episcopal Church**, on your left, established in 1765. The current Gothic-style structure was built in 1882, and the old church cemetery contains the remains of a number of local notables, including South Carolina writer and Pulitzer Prize winner Julia Peterkin.

Continue southeast another 0.4 mile to Wiles Crossroads. Cross US 601 to pass through countryside full of cotton fields, farmhouses, and churches until you reach SC 267 after 4 miles. Turn right (southeast) and drive 3 more pretty miles until S-9-11 forks left (southeast) toward Lone Star.

Follow S-9-11 for 0.7 mile into **Lone Star**, another farm/railroad town that time and highways passed by long ago. The train still comes through, but it's been decades since it stopped here. The old railroad depot is on your left as you enter town, having been moved from its original location. As you turn left (northeast) on S-9-54, picturesque old stores line up on your left, facing the tracks. On the opposite side of the tracks, the Last Stop Convenience Store on a dirt road still does neighborly business with African-American families nestled in cottages amid the trees.

Go 0.6 mile beside the tracks and turn left (north) on S-9-402. After 0.4 mile, turn right (east) on S-9-326, go 0.5 mile, and turn right (southeast) on S-9-129 to ride through cotton fields toward Low Falls Landing, 1.9 miles away.

Low Falls Landing is a beautiful spot to view the **Upper Santee Swamp** of Lake Marion, where Lake Marion pushes northward to blur the dividing line between the bottom end of the northern section of the Santee River and the beginning of the lake.

Swollen-based, moss-hung bald cypresses and water tupelos dot the waters. Floating mats of vegetation provide excellent habitat for numerous types of fish, including bass, catfish, and bream, plus waterfowl in winter and migrating songbirds in spring and fall. This swamp also hosts a huge nesting colony of blue herons, as well as other wading birds, alligators, and numerous snakes, frogs, and turtles. A pier provides good opportunity for fishing, wildlife viewing, and photography. Kayaks, canoes, and all manner of boats can put in here.

LOW FALLS LANDING TO
SANTEE STATE PARK

Backtrack on S-9-129 for 0.1 mile up a hill, then turn left (south) on S-9-286/ Stoudenmire Drive. This winding road carries you a pleasant 3.3 miles past lake cottages downhill to your left and cotton fields, forestland, and horse pastures on your right. When you reach SC 267, turn left (southeast) and cross a double bridge over Halfway Swamp Creek. Continue 4.5 miles to the intersection with SC 6, where you bear left and head on into Elloree, a half mile southeast.

Elloree is a pretty little town with an attractively maintained downtown area. Comfortable old homes line the road as you enter town on SC 6/Main Street. The Snider House at 550 Main was built by town founder William Snider in 1850. It has a double front porch and a garden behind a brick and wrought iron wall.

At the stoplight, turn right (southwest) on Cleveland Street to tour the quaint one-block downtown area, lined with antique shops, gift boutiques, an art gallery, arts and crafts, restaurants, and the Elloree Heritage Museum. The 100-

foot-wide street has brick crosswalks and is lined with flowering and hardwood trees.

Horse breeding and training are big in this area, and much of the artwork reflects this. Each March, the town features the Elloree Trials horse race for thoroughbreds and quarter horses.

Turn left (southeast) on Railroad Avenue, left (northeast) on Barkley Street, and left again on SC 6/Main Street to return to the intersection of Main and Cleveland. This time, head east (right) on S-38-105/Cleveland Street toward Santee State Park, 5 miles away. Horse pastures, hay fields, and forestland line the way.

Santee State Park is the only major public park on 110,000-acre **Lake Marion**. Its 2,500 acres offer hiking, fishing, boating, biking, swimming, and birding. Special features are the rare limestone sinkholes and caverns, which can be viewed from the Limestone Nature Trail and the Sinkhole Pond Trail. The park has a fact-filled interpretive center, and offers great views of Lake Marion from the fishing pier area on the west side and the swimming area on the east side, as well as from the 3.4-mile Bike Trail. The Oak-Pinolly Trail provides a walk through mixed forest and some marshland, and offers the best chance to see forest wildlife.

Downtown Elloree

Lake Marion Backwater

Birds frequently seen in the park include quail, eastern wood pewees, wild turkeys, brown thrashers, ospreys, bald eagles, mourning doves, owls (great horned, eastern screech, and barred), Carolina wrens, and all South Carolina woodpeckers, including the rare red-cockaded. Anoles scamper on the ground, while metalmark butterflies flit overhead. Deer, raccoons, opossums, and gray and fox squirrels are among the park's other wildlife. Rare southeastern myotis bats inhabit the limestone regions.

Trees in the park include loblolly and longleaf pines, swamp and turkey oaks, dogwoods, bald cypresses, sweet gums, red maples, and red bays. Dog-hobble, yucca, wax myrtle, wild ginger, pawpaw, trumpet creeper, and partridge pea are among the wildflower varieties at Santee.

When you arrive at the intersection of S-38-82/State Park Road and S-38-105/Cleveland Road at the park entrance, continue on Cleveland Road 1.5 miles to the swimming area, where you can rent paddleboats and enjoy expansive views of Lake Marion. Retrace your route back to the intersection and turn right on State Park Road. Travel 2.3 forested miles to the fishing pier and interpretive center to conclude your scenic drive.

Santee State Park is open 6:00 A.M. to 10:00 P.M. year-round. A nominal fee is charged for use of the swimming and picnic area.

Hístoríc charleston

DANIEL ISLAND TO JAMES ISLAND

GENERAL DESCRIPTION: This fascinating and diverse drive in metropolitan Charleston takes visitors across major waterways, through stunning saltwater marshlands, along inviting beaches, and past numerous beautiful homes, gardens, and historic sites.

SPECIAL ATTRACTIONS: Daniel Island, Palmetto Islands County Park, Charles Pinckney National Historic Site, Boone Hall Plantation and Gardens, Isle of Palms, Sullivan's Island, Fort Moultrie, Patriots Point, Historic Charleston and its homes and gardens, spectacular views of the Cooper, Wando, and Ashley Rivers.

LOCATION: Central coast.

DRIVE ROUTE NUMBERS: Interstate 526, Clements Ferry Road/S-10-33, St. Thomas Island Drive, Fairchild Street, Bellinger Street, Beresford Creek Street, Corn Planters Street, Brady Street, Daniel Island Drive, Seven Farms Drive, River Landing Drive, Long Point Road/S-10-97, Needlerush Parkway, US 17, SC 517, 14th Avenue, Ocean Boulevard, Third Avenue, Palm Boulevard/SC 703, Middle Street, Station 32, Marshall Avenue, Station 28,

Atlantic Boulevard, Station 23, Palmetto Street, Poe Avenue, Station 17, I'on Avenue, Station 22, SC 703, Center Street, Pitt Street, Middle Street, McCants Drive, Church Street, Hibben Street, Whilden Street, West Coleman Boulevard, Patriots Point Road, Meeting Street, South Battery, East Battery, Murray Boulevard, Ashley Avenue, Calhoun Street, St. Phillip Street, Wentworth Street, Glebe Street, George Street, Coming Street, King Street, Broad Street, Church Street, East Bay Street, State Street, Chalmers Street, South Market Street, North Market Street, Anson Street, Hasell Street, Beaufain Street, Lockwood Drive, SC 30.

TRAVEL SEASON: All year. Flowers and weather peak in March and April.

SERVICES: Motels, hotels, and all services are plentiful in Charleston, North Charleston, Mt. Pleasant, and Summerville.

See For More Information in the appendix for addresses and phone numbers of Attractions, Camping, Neat Places to Stay, Restaurants, Shops, Tours, and Nature-Based Services.

THE DRIVE

Beginning on Interstate 526 in North Charleston, this 45-mile drive takes sightseers over the bridges of the Mark Clark Highway with views of the Cooper and Wando Rivers, through neotraditional residential areas of Daniel Island, and across a high-rise span over the Intracoastal Waterway, providing a stunning over-

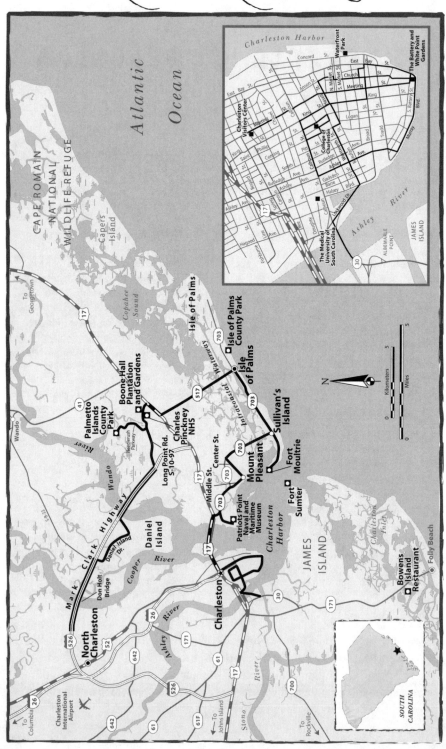

look of the waterway, adjacent salt marshes, and the barrier Isle of Palms. Next, visitors travel past Atlantic Ocean beaches to historic Sullivan's Island and on to the old-town neighborhood of Mt. Pleasant and fascinating Patriots Point. Finally, followers of this route cross the Cooper River Bridge into Charleston and go past numerous gardens and significant structures in the Historic District of the city, along the waterfront Battery, and to panoramic views at the top of a bridge over the Ashley River.

DANIEL ISLAND TO ISLE OF PALMS

Begin by traveling east on the **Don Holt Bridge**, on I–526/Mark Clark Highway, taking you from North Charleston to Daniel Island.

At the crest high above the **Cooper River**, look south, to your right, and enjoy captivating distant views of the two antiquated spans of the Cooper River Bridge between Mt. Pleasant and the elegant, beautiful Charleston city center, usually busy with large container ships. Straight ahead to the east, flocks of gulls and pelicans hover over dredge-material-filled marshlands that form Clouter Island, a small piece of land between the Cooper River and Clouter Creek. Looking north, you see the North Charleston Terminal of the State Ports Authority, riverside industrial facilities, marshland, and forest.

As you head down the east slope of the bridge and into Berkeley County, you view a scattering of docks extending like long, skinny fingers from unseen, tree-shrouded homes, past spartina grass and palmetto trees to meandering, dark marshland tidal streams.

Descend toward dry land on the east side of the bridge and exit right (south) on Clements Ferry Road/S-10-33, 2 miles from the crest of the Holt Bridge. At the stop sign, turn right (south) and drive 0.3 mile before turning left (east) on St. Thomas Island Drive. Travel 0.7 mile through a rustic, rural African-American community that was quite isolated prior to the construction of the bridges on the Mark Clark Highway a little more than a decade ago.

Cross a short, low bridge that spans the winding, tidal Berefords Creek. On the west side of the bridge, to your left (north), a small public dock provides an excellent location for fishing and relaxing. On the east side of the bridge, you are on **Daniel Island**, proceeding on Daniel Island Drive. Note Blackbaud Soccer Stadium, home of a local professional team, on your left (north), as you cross a second short bridge.

Continue 0.2 mile until you see Fairchild Street on your right (south). Turn right on Fairchild Street to get a taste of Daniel Island's residential community built in the new urbanism architecture. Homes here are built in the style of the 1930s and '40s and provide a real sense of community, with sidewalks, parks, and porches encouraging neighbors to visit in their front yards. You can't go wrong wandering on any of the streets through this neighborhood, but you might try traveling a half mile on Fairchild and then turning left (east) on Bellinger Street.

Travel one block and take a left (north) on Beresford Creek Street, then turn right (east) on Corn Planters Street and left (north) on Brady Street. At the next stop sign, turn right (east) back onto Daniel Island Drive.

Travel two blocks east to the intersection of Daniel Island Drive and Seven Farms Drive. Turn right (south) at the traffic light on Seven Farms Drive toward the great row of live oaks that lines the median. Bishop England High School, home of the Fighting Bishops, rises ahead. Follow Seven Farms Drive around the palmetto-tree-framed roundabout and head back out of the circle northward on Seven Farms Drive.

Continue on Seven Farms Drive over Daniel Island Drive and past Providence Baptist Church, on your left, a modern interpretation of traditional Lowcountry architecture amid patches of forest and wetlands. As you approach Daniel Island's small, new, mid-nineteenth-century-style commercial center, look ahead (north) to see, but not pass, the **Daniel Island Tennis Center**, home of the Women's Tour Family Circle Cup and accented by an impressive 8,000-seat center court stadium. At a traffic light, turn left (northwest) on River Landing Drive, following signs pointing toward Mt. Pleasant.

Follow the signs to return to I–526 and head southeast over the next bridge, 2 miles away. From the span's heights, you get a terrific view to your right (south) of the tennis complex and Daniel Island Town Center on the west side of the river, and the Wando State Ports Authority Terminal on the east side of the river. Cross over the wide **Wando River**, and, as you enter the city limits of Mt. Pleasant, take in another, closer perspective of the Cooper River Bridge and the Charleston skyline to your right, looking southwest.

On the far (west) side of the Wando, 2 miles past the river, exit onto Long Point Road/S-10-97. Ride east 1.9 miles to the left (north) turn for Needlerush Parkway, which takes you 1.2 miles to **Palmetto Islands County Park**. The park, which charges a nominal entrance fee, offers playgrounds, boating, bicycling, and walks through a wonderland of tidal marsh, maritime forest, and a multitude of palmetto trees.

Backtrack to Long Point Road and turn left (east). Ride a half mile past marshland and overhanging oaks to the entrance to **Boone Hall Plantation and Gardens**. The estate dates from 1681 on land granted by the lords proprietor to Major Hon Boone, a member of Charles Town's first fleet of settlers. It was primarily a cotton plantation. Today its ancient live oaks decorate a three-quarter-mile-long avenue to Boone Hall, a Georgian mansion constructed in 1935 on the site of the previous house. The original cotton gin house and slave row are standing, and visitors can tour the plantation seven days a week for a small fee.

The **Charles Pinckney National Historic Site**, 0.1 mile farther east, on the right (south) side of Long Point Road, touts archaeological remains of brick foundations and an unfurnished 1820s tidewater cottage. These are the last protected remnants of Snee Farm, the country estate of Charles Pinckney, a drafter and signer of the Constitution. The national park site offers interpretive exhibits that are open to the public daily, free of charge. The site is handicapped accessible.

Continue eastward on Long Point Road another 0.6 mile to the intersection with US 17. To your left, stands of sea island vegetables, fruit, and sweet grass baskets dot the highway. Sweet grass baskets, made of coiled native sweet grass and pine needles sewn together with strips of palmetto leaves, are unique to the Lowcountry, and represent one of the oldest West African art forms in America. Basket design and craftsmanship that originated from the rice culture in West Africa were brought to America by the slaves who made the cultivation of rice a success in South Carolina. These unique baskets, originally used on plantations in the production of rice, have been displayed for sale along the Charleston-Georgetown highway since the 1730s. The art of weaving the baskets has been handed down through African-American families since the 1700s and the earliest days of the colony.

Turn right (south) on US 17 and ride 1 mile to a stoplight and the entrance to SC 517/Clyde Moultrie Dangerfield Highway, leading to the Isle of Palms. Turn left (southeast). A little over a mile down the road, palmetto trees, spartina grass, and seabirds draw your eye to marshlands lining the **Intracoastal Waterway**. Ospreys fly overhead, and huge nests sit atop poles in wetlands and forests tucked close to the highway. Crossing the bridge over the Intracoastal Waterway, you have an expansive view of the waters surrounding the entire island dotted with vacation homes, the inland waterway and its boat traffic below you, and the majestic Atlantic Ocean on the far side of the Isle of Palms.

When you reach the end of the bridge, 3.8 miles from US 17, you're on the **Isle of Palms**, an incorporated city. For many years, visitors to the Isle of Palms arrived by water or a single railroad bridge from Sullivan's Island. Today this resort island is accessible by two highway bridges. It includes the gated golf course/beach/yachting community of Wild Dunes, as well as numerous residential and vacation homes and family beach areas where dolphins romp offshore. Although many people have made the Isle of Palms their permanent home, it remains a quiet, family-oriented vacation spot.

At the intersection at the base of the bridge, cross over Palm Boulevard/SC 703 onto 14th Avenue. The **Isle of Palms County Park** is on your left, and for a small fee you can enjoy the public beach here.

Follow 14th Avenue as it curves to the right and becomes **Ocean Boulevard**, leading you to the heart of the island's commercial and public beach areas. To the right (west) of Ocean Boulevard are a large public parking area and an ice-cream parlor, along with boutiques of swim gear and bike rentals and sandwich shops.

On your left (east), facing the ocean, is Windjammers Food and Spirits, a lively restaurant and bar that hosts local bands like the Blue Dogs at night and beach volleyball tournaments on the sandy court during the day. Stop in for the best cheeseburger on the island. Next door is the One Eyed Parrot, where you can eat fresh local seafood and enjoy a terrific view of the ocean on the restaurant's upper deck.

Travel down Ocean Boulevard to experience the residential area of the island. Newly built modern homes stand on the beachfront to your left (east), and older, more traditional beach homes line Ocean Boulevard on your right (west).

ISLE OF PALMS TO PATRIOTS POINT

Travel 1.2 miles south to the end of Ocean Boulevard, and turn right (west) on Third Avenue. Cross over two streets and, at the third stop sign, take a left (southwest) on Palm Boulevard/SC 703 to head south toward Sullivan's Island. The Intracoastal Waterway stretches on your right. Pass by a marina a half mile from Third Avenue and drive on Thompson Memorial Bridge across the treacherous tidal waters of Breach Inlet to enter aged, serene **Sullivan's Island**.

Charleston residents built summer homes here in the early nineteenth century. Edgar Allen Poe was a resident at one time, and based his tale of *The Gold Bug* on pirate treasure believed buried on the island. (Street names here include Poe and Goldbug Avenues, as well as Raven Drive.) Between 1700 and 1775 the island was a holding site where tens of thousands of Africans were brought to North America to be sold as slaves.

Shelling on the island is terrific. You're likely to find sand dollars, sea stars, angel wings, whelks, scallop shells, and ark shells if you stop at any of the numerous public access points and trek out to the glistening white sands of this extremely wide beach.

After you cross the bridge, bear left (southeast) on Middle Street. Take the next left (southeast) onto Station 32, travel two blocks alongside Breach Inlet, and then turn right (southwest) onto Marshall Avenue, lined with beachfront homes.

These impressive new structures on highly valuable property were built after their predecessors were destroyed during 1989's Hurricane Hugo. Many older homes, however, serve as restful reminders of the island's longtime role as summer quarters for Charleston's elite. Travel past villas protected by whitewashed picket fences covered with blue and purple dappled morning glories, and sandy yards dotted with palmettos and oleanders.

After four blocks on Marshall, turn right (northwest) on Station 28, drive two blocks, and turn left (southwest) on Atlantic Boulevard. Go five blocks to Station 23. Turn right (northwest) here, travel two blocks, and turn left (southwest) onto Middle Street.

You are now in the heart of tiny downtown Sullivan's Island, featuring good food and drink at such establishments as Dunleavy's Pub, Saltwater Grill, Gibson Cafe, Station 22 Restaurant, and Atlanticville Restaurant and Cafe.

Continue past quaint Victorian cottage architecture for 1.5 miles to **Fort Moultrie**, on your left (southeast). A unit of Fort Sumter National Monument,

Fort Moultrie overlooks the Atlantic Ocean and the city of Charleston to the south, guarding the entrance to Charleston Harbor along with Fort Sumter across the water.

Originally built of palmetto logs during the Revolutionary War, the fortification has since been rebuilt many times and testifies to the development of coastal defenses. This fort protected Charleston in every major war from the War of 1812 to World War II. It is most famous for its role in April 1861 when cannons from this location and others touched off the Civil War by bombarding Fort Sumter, where Union garrison forces from Fort Moultrie had retreated for safety. Fort Moultrie is open daily from 9:00 A.M. to 5:00 P.M., free to the public.

Walk or drive to the southeast side of Fort Moultrie, at the end of S-10-419, for a great view of **Fort Sumter**, on an island in the middle of the entrance to Charleston Harbor and accessible only by tour boats.

After driving past Fort Moultrie, turn around and head east on Middle Street for four blocks, then turn right (southeast) on Station 17/S-10-906. Drive two blocks and then turn left (northeast) on I'on Avenue to see some of the largest and oldest homes on Sullivan's Island, decorated with huge wraparound porches and stately colonial and Victorian facades. Sprawling live oaks, palmettos, and other lush greenery surround these beautiful structures. On your right (east) you will see the **Sullivan's Island Lighthouse** rising 161 feet above sea level, and pass the **Edgar Allen Poe County Library** and **Sullivan's Island Elementary School**, which were built in bunkers that served as military batteries during the first half of the twentieth century.

After about seven blocks, turn left (northwest) on Station 22. Drive one block, turn right (northeast) on Middle Street and then left on SC 703 as it heads northeast toward Mt. Pleasant. Travel about 1.8 miles on a causeway through aromatic tidal salt marsh bordering Charleston Harbor and the Intracoastal Waterway. The causeway is lined with pretty oleanders and palmettos, and often you can see locals fishing and crabbing in the ponds and creeks. Midway along, you cross the **Ben Sawyer Bridge**, a drawbridge over the Intracoastal Waterway that swings open several times a day.

On the north side of the marsh, you enter the city of **Mount Pleasant**, now a sprawling suburb but once a sleepy harborside village across the water from Charleston. To reach the heart of the old village, turn left (southwest) on Center Street, just after Simon's Seafood and just before Mama Brown's Barbecue, both on your left. Travel 1.2 miles on Center Street to the southern tip of Mount Pleasant, past new residential developments overlooking the marsh and older ranch-style homes on your right.

One block before Center Street ends, turn left (southwest) on Pitt Street and drive four blocks past enchanting cottages under moss-hung oaks to reach a short causeway leading into the marsh. The old roadbed, once the highway to

Sullivan's Island, is now Pickett Bridge Recreation Area. This is an excellent area to get out of your car and walk farther out on the abandoned road to enjoy salt air, fishermen, and crabbers, along with gulls and herons playing amid the spartina grass.

Backtrack to Center Street, go left (southeast) for one block, and then turn right (northeast) on Middle Street. Cozy bungalows fortified by short picket fences and ivy-covered two-story brick and wooden homes line the streets of this tranquil neighborhood. A children's park lies to the east side of Middle Street, and picturesque **Alhambra Hall**, a public facility, is on the west side of the road, surrounded by green space. This a good spot to walk to water's edge and view the Charleston's Battery waterfront across the way, as well as Fort Sumter to the south. Middle Street, like others in the neighborhood, stretches past and around old oaks, adding a special touch to the community.

After two long blocks on Middle Street, turn right (northeast) on McCants Drive, go one block, and take a left (northwest) on Pitt Street. St. Paul's Lutheran Church is on your right (east), established in 1884. Drive past **Patjen's Post Office** (circa 1880), **Town Hall** (circa 1884), and beautiful homes. After seven blocks, you arrive in the old village's tiny downtown area, where 101 Pitt Restaurant, Guilds Inn, and the old Pitt Rexall Drug Store are seen on your left.

Cross Venning Street and continue northwest, as Pitt Street ends and Church Street begins. Drive one block on Church Street past more lovely old dwellings. At the intersection with Hibben Street after one block, the **Mount Pleasant Presbyterian Church** is directly in front of you. This white, wooden, two-story structure, erected around 1854 and originally a Congregational Church, served as a Confederate hospital during the Civil War, and then briefly housed a school for freedmen during Reconstruction. The structure was renamed Mount Pleasant Presbyterian Church in 1870.

Go right (northeast) one block on Hibben and turn left (northwest) on Whilden Street. Travel one block, then bear left (northwest) at the traffic light to merge into Coleman Boulevard/SC 703.

Cross over **Shem Creek**, where a number of shrimp boats are sure to be docked and bobbing in the waters surrounding the local seafood restaurants that are all worth trying, including Shem Creek Restaurant, Ronnie's Seafood, the Trawler, and Vickery's.

Continue on Coleman Boulevard for 1.1 miles until you reach the intersection with Patriots Point Road. Turn left (southeast) on Patriots Point Road to visit **Patriots Point Naval and Maritime Museum**.

Even if you don't want to get out and explore the exhibits, it is worth the time to drive to water's edge for an up-close view of the museum's centerpiece, the retired aircraft carrier USS *Yorktown*. Its 41,000 tons and 888 feet of steel are permanently moored in the mud. Originally named *Bon Homme Richard*, the ship was renamed in 1942 to honor the previous *Yorktown* aircraft carrier that was lost

Boats docked along Shem Creek

at the World War II Battle of Midway. The present ship was the tenth aircraft carrier to be commissioned by the U.S. Navy. It saw extensive action in the Pacific during World War II, and played a key role in the Vietnam Conflict. The walking tour of the gigantic ship allows you to see fascinating maritime equipment and other historical material that tells the story of the importance of sea power.

Other ships at Patriots Point include the Coast Guard cutter *Comanche*, the submarine *Clamagore*, the destroyer *Laffey*, and the N.S. *Savannah*, our first and possibly last nuclear-powered commercial vessel. Other attractions at the site include the National Congressional Medal of Honor Museum, Missing in Action Prisoner of War Display, Battle of Midway Carrier Torpedo Squadrons Memorial, National Memorial to Carrier Aviation, Smokey Stover Memorial Theatre, Yorktown Carrier Aviation Hall of Fame, Carrier Aviation Test Pilot Hall of Honor, World War II Battleship Exhibit, Battle of Charleston Harbor Exhibit, Black American Military Exhibit, Women in the Military Exhibit, and the Maritime Legends Exhibit.

PATRIOTS POINT TO HISTORIC DOWNTOWN CHARLESTON

Backtrack to Coleman Boulevard, and turn left (west) at the traffic light. Travel 0.2 mile to the intersection with US 17. Veer to the left to join US 17 South and cross the **Cooper River Bridge** into the heart of old Charleston. You'll be crossing the Cooper River westward over a high, rickety, narrow, double-crested span that will soon be replaced. Be thankful it is now a one-way thoroughfare. Until a few decades ago, when the bridge to your left (south) was built, it was a two-way roadbed that was the only way to cross between Charleston and the east side of the Cooper River.

From the bridge, you'll see big ship terminals of the State Ports Authority to your left (south), and Daniel Island and the Mark Clark Highway in the distance to your right (north). Take the Meeting Street exit to your right and circle around, following the signs that direct you under the overpass and southward to Meeting Street. Bear left and head south on Meeting Street, following signs to the Visitors Center.

Charleston was settled in 1670, and by the mid-1700s it had become the richest and fourth largest city in Colonial America. Plantation owners flocked here during the summer to escape the malarial backcountry and to experience the theater, ballrooms, and other cultural and social events of the times. The city maintains its aristocratic, southern gentility established during the plantation era, and remains an eclectic and inviting locale to this day.

Traditionally based architecture rules here, but homes are set apart with colorful paints, one-of-a-kind wrought iron gates, and banisters and balconies. Enormous columned homes on the Battery and densely packed shanty homes make Charleston unlike any other city you will ever visit.

Although this is a driving tour, Charleston is best seen on foot. This drive will only whet your appetite for the narrow avenues and gardens tucked behind stately homes that you can only truly appreciate on foot. Walk on the cobblestone streets, speak with the Gullah basket weavers of the Market who make their sweet grass basket wares right before your eyes, and step into the numerous ice-cream parlors, sandwich shops, and fine-dining restaurants. You'll never have enough time to enjoy all there is to do in this exciting, historic city.

The **Charleston Visitors Center** is six blocks south of US 17, on your right (west) at the intersection of Mary and Meeting Streets. Turn right into the parking garage on the Visitors Center's north side. This facility provides a wealth of information on places to stay and eat and things to do. It offers maps with a variety of walking tour options. For a nominal fee, you can watch the excellent, twenty-one-projector, multi-image slide show *Forever Charleston*. You can also buy a day pass to ride on the DASH, a shuttle bus that circles around and through the historic area. The Visitors Center is open daily from 9:00 A.M. to 5:00 P.M.

Across the street at 360 Meeting Street is the **Charleston Museum**, collecting and preserving artifacts relating to the Lowcountry. Visitors are welcome Monday through Saturday from 9:00 A.M. to 5:00 P.M. and on Sunday from 1:00 to 5:00 P.M.

At 350 Meeting Street is the **Joseph Manigault House**, a National Historic Landmark. The worn brick wall that surrounds the home will catch your eye when you look to the left. Built in 1803, the Manigault home represents a first-class example of neoclassic architecture. The home is open to visitors Monday through Saturday from 10:00 A.M. to 5:00 P.M. and on Sunday from 1:00 to 5:00 P.M.

Continue south on **Meeting Street** and take in the pink Embassy Suites Hotel on your right (west), located in the original building (circa 1822) of the South Carolina Military College, The Citadel, on the corner of Hutson and Meeting Streets. The hotel looks like a fortressed castle at the top of **Marion Square Park**, a pedestrian greenspace decorated with azaleas, magnolias, crepe myrtles, and palmettos that offers a peaceful refuge in the midst of bustling downtown Charleston. Note the statute of John C. Calhoun in the middle of the park and the Holocaust Memorial that was recently erected at the corner of Calhoun and King Streets. As you pass Marion Square, you reach the intersection of Meeting and Calhoun Streets.

If you wish to detour in order to visit the **South Carolina Aquarium**, *take a left (east) here onto Calhoun, drive four blocks to East Bay, and continue on to the entrance for the aquarium, as well as departure docks for boat tours to* **Fort Sumter**. *You'll also pass Buist Academy on your right, a dark brown brick building that was originally an African-American high school attended by the noted ironworks artist Phillip Simons. It now serves as a Charleston County School for gifted and talented students.*

From Marion Square, drive south on Meeting Street across Calhoun Street. At the intersection with Market Street, about six blocks past Calhoun, is **Market Hall**, at 188 Meeting Street. This is the site of the first public market established after the Revolutionary War. The Greek Revival structure dates back to 1841. Look for the frieze of the sheep and bull's head, which indicated that meat was sold here. Today the market sells an array of handmade crafts and interesting items, and you're sure to see resident Gullah women weaving their sweet grass baskets and offering them for sale. The market is worth a walk through even if you're not looking to buy.

Continue southward on Meeting Street. After you pass Cumberland Street, you will see on your left the **Circular Congregational Church**, organized around 1681 as the Independent Church of Charles Town, at 150 Meeting Street. The first building for this church, made of white brick, was called the "The White Meeting House" and is believed to be the namesake of Meeting Street. The first circular church built in 1806 was destroyed by fire and earthquake. The present Romanesque Revival–style structure was built in 1891, using brick from the previous building. The church's cemetery is the oldest in the city, with graves dating as far back as 1695.

To your right at 135 Meeting Street is the **Gibbes Museum of Art**. Established in 1858, the present Beaux Arts building was constructed in 1905 and now serves as headquarters of the Carolina Art Association. Noted for its outstanding collection of South Carolina portraits and miniatures, the museum offers the Robert Marks collection of photography, a twentieth-century African-American art collection, a Japanese woodblock gallery, a miniature portrait gallery, and the Charleston Renaissance Gallery. It includes works of well-known Charleston artists who brought national attention to Charleston in the 1920s, such as Anna Heyward Taylor, Elizabeth O'Neil Verner, and Alice Ravenel Huger Smith. The Gibbes Museum is a delight, and is open to visitors for a small fee Monday through Saturday from 10:00 A.M. to 5:00 P.M. and Sunday from 1:00 to 5:00 P.M.

At 115 Meeting Street is the **Mills House Hotel**. The current Italian style building stands on the site of the original Mills House Hotel, circa 1853. It has incorporated the original iron balcony where, in 1861, General Robert E. Lee watched a great fire sweep through Charleston and destroy more than 500 buildings.

Next to the Mills House Hotel is historic **Hibernian Hall** at 105 Meeting Street. Built in 1840 by one of the oldest Irish fraternal societies in America, this enormous Greek Revival structure plays host to elegant wedding parties and the annual Hibernian Society's St. Patrick's Day party. The porch is decorated with stone brought from Ireland in 1851 and Irish harps above its door and iron gates.

To your left at 100 Meeting Street, at the corner of Chalmers Street, is the **South Carolina Historical Society**, housed in the "Fireproof Building." Designed by Robert Mills and constructed of brick (circa 1822–27), this stone and iron neoclassic building is the first fireproof structure built in the United States.

Next on your left is **Washington Park**. The monument in the center was erected by the Washington Light Infantry to honor its members who died in the Civil War. This small urban jewel is, surprisingly, a great setting for bird-watching.

The famous **Four Corners of Law** is at the intersection of Broad and Meeting Streets, so named because each corner represents a different branch of the law: city, county, federal, and religious.

To your immediate left (east), just past Washington Park, is Charleston's **City Hall**, designed by Gabriel Manigault and built in 1801. Several historic portraits hang here, including Trumbull's painting of George Washington in 1791, and visitors are welcome.

To your right is the **Charleston County Court House**, site of the original State House of South Carolina, built in 1752. The present building was completed in 1792, two years after Columbia became the state capital.

Across Broad Street on your right is the **U.S. Court House and Post Office**. Constructed in 1898, this Renaissance Revival structure was built after the Old Guard House was destroyed by the 1886 earthquake. A post office museum is inside and open to visitors. Sweet grass baskets and cut flowers are sold by local women on the sidewalk here, an old Charleston tradition.

On the far left corner of Meeting and Broad Streets is **St. Michael's Episcopal Church**, the oldest church building in the city, constructed in 1752–61. The clock bells were imported from England in 1764. The church's steeple served as the city's lookout and alarm tower for many years and was used by pilots at sea to find their bearings. During the Civil War, however, the steeple was painted black so the enemy could not spot the city so easily. The church welcomes visitors, and you might also wish to visit St. Michael's churchyard, where two signers of the U.S. Constitution are buried, as well as James L. Petigru, a noted antisecessionist.

Cross Broad Street and continue southward on Meeting Street. Just past St. Michael Alley at 72 Meeting Street, on your left is an Adamsesque building constructed in 1804 that is home to the **South Carolina Society**. The society was founded by French Huguenots in 1737 to help support a local tavern that was doing poorly. Today, the Society remains charitable by donating scholarships to the College of Charleston.

On your left at 64 Meeting Street is the **Andrew Hasell House**. Built in 1789, this house represents typical Charleston design with its deep, narrow lot. It is designed with gables facing the street, only one room wide and two rooms deep, with a porch on one side and a front door in the center of the porch. Charleston's piazzas are built on the southern or western portion of the house to protect from the hot afternoon sun and to provide cross-ventilation from the southwesterly breezes when the homes' windows and doors are open.

Opposite the Andrew Hasell House is the **Branford-Horry House** at 59 Meeting Street. Built in 1767, this Georgian structure is called a "double house," because it's two rooms wide and two rooms deep on each floor. A center hallway and stairwell divide the house. The parlor is found on the second floor.

After crossing Tradd Street, on your left at 57 Meeting Street is the **First (Scots) Presbyterian Church**, established when twelve Scottish families withdrew from the Independent Church in 1731 and formed the "Scots Kirk," or Scotch Meeting House. The building you see today, with the seal of Scotland above the window over the main entrance, was completed in 1814. Note that the church bell is missing. Its metal was given to the Confederacy in 1863, and it has never been replaced.

Beside the church is the **Nathaniel Russell House** at 51 Meeting Street. Built between 1808 and 1811 by Nathaniel Russell, who made his fortune as a Charleston merchant, this Adams-style home is decorated with oval rooms and a free-flying staircase that remains unsupported for three floors. The brick adorning the exterior of the home was made on local plantations, and if you look closely, you'll see Russell's initials in the front panel of the wrought iron balcony. The home is open to visitors for a small fee and is maintained by the Historic Charleston Foundation.

Continue southward on Meeting Street, past Prices Alley and Water, Ladson, and Atlantic Streets, all the way to South Battery. You'll pass a number of interesting homes, including the Otis Mills House, the Bull-Huger House, the Colonel Isaac Mottee House, the Major James Ladson House, the Thomas

Heyward House, the John Edwards House, the Calhoun Mansion, and the Tucker-Ladson House. Each home has a unique design and a quaint garden worth a peek.

Meeting Street ends at South Battery Street, with White Point Gardens across the way. To your left (east) on the corner of South Battery and Meeting Streets is the **Two Meeting Street Inn**. This magnificent Queen Anne–style mansion, circa 1892, was a wedding gift from a wealthy merchant banker to his daughter. The home has Tiffany windows, crafted and installed by Louis Tiffany himself.

Turn left onto South Battery Street. At 8 South Battery, on your left (north) is the Georgian-style **Colonel William Washington House**, built in 1768 and purchased by Colonel William Washington, cousin of George, in 1785.

At 4 South Battery is **Villa Marguerita**, circa 1892. This Italian Renaissance Revival–style home was built as a gift by a Charleston businessman for his bride. In 1905, the home was made into a luxury hotel that played host to Henry Ford, Alexander Graham Bell, and Teddy Roosevelt.

On your right (south) is **White Point Gardens**, named for the large mounds of white oyster shells that once blanketed the southern tip of the city and were used to cover the streets in earlier days. This southern portion of the city, also known as the **Battery**, is the meeting place of the Ashley and Cooper Rivers, where Charlestonians claim the Atlantic Ocean begins. The Battery is so-named because of fortifications that were placed along the seafront.

At the next corner, take a right (southeast) onto East Battery Street. On your left, paved walkways line the harbor's concrete seawalls. As East Battery curves around and heads northeast, look southward across the water to the island fortress of **Fort Sumter** in the distance. To the left of Fort Sumter is Fort Moultrie on Sullivan's Island. To its west is Fort Johnson on James Island.

Follow East Battery past White Point Gardens until the road becomes Murray Boulevard; continue northwest on Murray Boulevard for about a half mile past magnificent old homes that face the Ashley River.

Near the end of Murray, turn right (north) onto Ashley Avenue to enjoy a glimpse of an early twentieth-century residential section. Cross over Tradd and Broad Streets and enjoy lovely **Colonial Lake**, a saltwater pond on your right surrounded by blooming oleanders and lined with stately three-story homes.

Follow Ashley Avenue six blocks past Colonial Lake and turn right (east) on Calhoun Street. Pass through a portion of the Medical University of South Carolina (MUSC) campus on the north (left) side of Calhoun and continue to the delightful, historic **College of Charleston** campus, beginning four blocks ahead.

The College of Charleston was chartered in 1770, and today it is renowned as one of the premier public liberal arts institutions in America. After passing the new Addlestone Library and Coming Street, you will see on your right the fences and buildings encircling the college's pedestrian mall. Drive one more block and turn right (south) on St. Philip Street. Drive slowly to get a peek to

On the campus of the College of Charleston

your right (west) into the live oaks dripping with moss that decorate the oldest portion of the college's campus, the **Cistern** greenspace in front of **Randolph Hall** where students loll about. The college's unique, formal-dress spring graduations are held here every Mother's Day; the location has been used for scenes in several movie and television productions.

Follow St. Philip Street past George Street to Wentworth Street, and turn right (west). Travel one block and turn right (north) on **Glebe Street**, just before the lovely **Grace Episcopal Church** on the corner. At 6 Glebe Street on your right (east) is the college president's residence, built in 1770 as a church rectory. Travel Glebe Street's one short block past historic houses incorporated into the college campus. At the intersection of Glebe and George Streets, look ahead to your right to see the Roman Revival **Porter's Lodge**, with its elegant arched gateways, the Cistern courtyard, along with the front facade of Randolph Hall and other new and old college buildings.

Turn left (west) on George Street, drive one block, turn right (north) on Coming Street and drive another block. Take a right (east) on Calhoun and drive two blocks to King Street, where the early twentieth-century **Francis Marion Hotel** towers on your left, across King Street from Marion Square.

Turn right (south) onto **King Street** to experience the hustle and bustle of the historic district's retail shopping area, where antiques, unique gifts, clothes, and shoes abound, as well as some popular college eating and drinking spots tucked along the way.

Follow King Street for nine blocks, turn left (east) on **Broad Street**, travel two blocks to **Church Street**, and turn right (south). Cross St. Michael's Alley and on your left (east) are the homes of **"Cabbage Row,"** from 89 to 91 Church Street. These post-Revolutionary double tenements are called Cabbage Row because African-American tenants displayed cabbages and other vegetables for sale on their windowsills here. DuBose Heyward, who lived at 76 Church Street, used this area as a model for his novel *Porgy*, on which George Gershwin's opera *Porgy and Bess* was based. Heyward called the neighborhood "Catfish Row" and based the character Porgy on an actual resident, Goatcart Sammy.

Across the street at 94 Church Street is the **Thomas Bee House**, circa 1730, where Theodosia Alston, daughter of Aaron Burr, resided and where John C. Calhoun and his supporters drafted nullification papers in 1832.

On your left at 87 Church Street is the **Heyward-Washington House**, built in 1770 for Thomas Heyward, a signer of the Declaration of Independence. President George Washington rented the house during his visit to Charleston in 1791. Note the home's flat brick facade decorated with white shutters on the first floor, black shutters on the second floor windows, and closed shutters on the third floor. The home is furnished with Charleston-crafted furniture pieces, which are considered to be the finest examples of American-made furniture in existence today. A formal garden is found here too. Now owned and operated by the Charleston Museum, the home is open to visitors for a small fee from 10:00 A.M. to 5:00 P.M. Monday through Saturday and from 1:00 to 5 P.M. on Sunday.

Continue south on Church Street past a number of famous homes and structures, such as the Colonel Robert Brewton House at 71 Church, the First Baptist Church at 61 Church, the Thomas Rose House at 59 Church, the A. W. Todd House at 41 Church, the George Eveleigh House at 39 Church, the George Matthews House at 37 Church, and the Thomas Young House at 35 Church. Also on Church Street are a number of art galleries and rare-book stores.

Once you cross over Water Street, be sure to veer to right and then swing left to remain on Church Street, which becomes a brick road that takes you past elegant private residences. When Church Street ends at South Battery, turn left (east) and then take an immediate left (north) onto East Battery to see more historic waterfront homes on your left (west).

Dr. St. Julien Ravenel, inventor of the "Little David," a semisubmersible vessel used by the Confederate navy, once lived in the **John Ravenel House**, circa 1847–49, at 5 East Battery.

The **William Roper House** at 9 East Battery is a Greek Revival mansion built in 1838. A fragment of a Civil War cannon shell is embedded in the home's roof rafter. Look also for the ornate lions' heads decorating the earthquake bolts on the home.

At 13 East Battery is the **William Ravenel House**, circa 1845, and at 21 East Battery is the **Edmonston-Alston House**. The latter home was built from 1817 to 1828 by Charles Edmonston, a merchant and wharf owner. It was purchased and remodeled by Charles Alston, a wealthy rice planter, into the Greek Revival home you see today. Visitors are welcome Tuesday through Saturday from 10:00 A.M. to 5:00 P.M. and on Sunday and Monday from 1:30 to 5:00 P.M. for a moderate fee.

Continue northward on East Battery as it becomes East Bay Street. From 79 to 107 East Bay Street, on your left (west), you'll pass an oft-painted stretch of joined houses known as **Rainbow Row**. The colorful buildings constructed between 1740 and 1787 were originally merchants' homes, with shops on the first floors and living quarters on the second floors. During the colonial period, these homes were directly on the water, providing easy access to nearby ships.

*If you would like to stroll on the **Waterfront Park** pier or along its walkways beside the Cooper River, turn right (east) on Adger's Wharf, Boyce's Wharf, or Exchange Street, and drive one block.* Otherwise, continue northward on East Bay until it intersects with Broad Street, about four blocks ahead. You'll see the **Old Exchange and Provost Dungeon**, circa 1767–71, on your right (east), at 122 East Bay Street. The pirate Stede Bonnet was imprisoned here in 1718, and three signers of the Declaration of Independence were incarcerated here when the British occupied the city in 1780. The building is open to the public for a small fee.

In the nineteenth century, slaves were sold beside the Old Exchange Building, until a city ordinance was approved in 1856 forbidding such sales in the streets due to traffic congestion. The open-air market was known as the "Ellis Island of Black America" because more than a third of all slaves in the American colonies arrived here. This was once the commercial center of Charleston.

Turn left (west) onto Broad Street. To your left at 1 Broad Street is the Carolina First Bank Building, an Italian Renaissance Revival–style edifice, circa 1853, built with Connecticut brownstone. Turn immediately right (north) on State Street, and then take a quick left (west) onto cobblestoned **Chalmers Street**. These cobblestones are from European ships that traveled to Charleston. When the ships arrived from Europe, the stones were removed from their ballasts and used to cover the streets of Charleston. The ships were reloaded with such South Carolina goods as rice, cotton, and indigo before heading back to Europe.

At 6 Chalmers Street is the **Old Slave Market Museum**, located in a building that came into use in 1856 as a result of the new ordinance forbidding sales in the street. Since 1938, this facility has been a museum documenting African and African-American history and arts.

If you're in the market for some unique art, antique furniture, and paintings, you're in the right area to find it. Charleston's **French Quarter Galleries** are found tucked on Church, East Bay, Queen, and Meeting Streets. The Charleston Visitors Center has a complete list of the twenty-eight member shops.

Turn right (north) onto Church Street at the next intersection. At 135 Church Street, on your left, is the historic **Dock Street Theater**, built on the site of one of America's first playhouses, constructed in 1735. The present structure was built in 1809, and it is used extensively to this day.

To your right is the **French Huguenot Church** at 136 Church Street, organized by French Protestant refugees in 1681 and constructed in 1687. Services were held according to the tides because Huguenot planters would come to town via water.

Cross over Queen Street, and notice the **"Pirate House"** at 145 Church Street, built of Bermuda stone, circa 1740, by a Huguenot merchant. Pirates traded here until they began pillaging the merchant ships of Charles Town and were no longer welcome.

Across the street to your right is **St. Philip's Episcopal Church**, organized in 1680 and home of the oldest congregation in Charleston. This is the third church built for the congregation at this site; the other two were destroyed by fire. The steeple at this church was used as a guide for ships entering the port, and its bells were donated to the Confederacy for cannon material. The church is open to visitors daily.

St. Philip's churchyard is divided into eastern and western segments. Across from the church is the western graveyard, which was set aside in 1768 for burial of "strangers and other transient whites." Some of the men buried there are John C. Calhoun, fiery defender of Southern rights and vice president of the United States, Edward Rutledge, signer of the Declaration of Independence, and DuBose Heyward, author of *Porgy*.

Continue northward across Cumberland Street. Worth noting on your left (west) at 79 Cumberland is the **Old Powder Magazine**, the oldest public building in Charleston. Built in 1712, just inside the northern wall of the city, the structure's 32-inch brick walls and vaulted ceiling were designed to contain any potential explosion of its contents. The magazine is open daily to visitors for a small fee.

Follow Church Street three blocks ahead, passing Bocci's, Tommy Condon's, Garibaldi's, and other popular restaurants as you turn right (east) on South Market Street and enjoy the congested marketplace on your left. Travel one block and turn left (north) on State Street, and immediately left (west) on North Market Street. After one block, take a right (north) on Anson Street to enter **Ansonborough**, where you'll find a number of beautiful brick homes built after the Great Fire of 1838 that devastated much of this neighborhood.

Continue two blocks on Anson, crossing Pinckney Street before you turn left (west) on charming Hasell Street. Look for **St. Johannes Evangelical Lutheran Church** at 48 Hasell Street, a circa 1841 Tuscan-columned church designed by E. B. White. At 50 Hasell Street is the St. Johannes Rectory, built around 1846 by planter Joel Smith, which became the rectory for St. Johannes in 1920. Take in the **Colonel William Rhett House** at 54 Hasell Street, a gem built around 1713 and thought to be the oldest dwelling in the city. It was once the main house of a thirty-acre plantation owned by Colonel Rhett, who was responsible for the capture of Stede Bonnet and his pirate crew in 1718.

At 60 Hasell Street is the **George Reynolds House**, circa 1847, decorated with Egyptian-like pillars and an Italianate-style tower. A Greek Revival mansion built in 1843 by Charleston merchant Benjamin F. Smith is at 64 Hasell Street.

Continue west on Hasell across Meeting Street. At 90 Hasell Street is the **Kahoal Kadosh Beth Elohim Synagogue**, built in 1840–41 to replace the first synagogue, which was built in 1792. This Classic Revival structure is the country's second oldest synagogue and the oldest synagogue in continuous use in the United States. Visitors are welcome.

St. Mary's Roman Catholic Church is at 95 Hasell Street, on your left. The present structure was completed in 1839 and is the Mother Church for Catholics in the Carolinas and Georgia. Visitors are welcome to step in and experience this solemn place.

Turn left (south) on bustling King Street, go one block, and turn right (west) on Beaufain Street. Go two blocks on Beaufain, and take a right (north) on Coming. After one block, turn left (west) on Wentworth Street. Follow Wentworth through a pleasant turn-of-the-twentieth-century residential area for about a half mile.

At the end of Wentworth, take a right (north) on Lockwood Drive. The Ashley River and a large yacht marina will be on your left. Follow signs directing you to James Island and Folly Beach. Bear right and curve left to ascend the James Island Connector, a high, 2-mile-long bridge that takes SC 30 westward from the Charleston peninsula to James Island.

At the crest of the span, you'll have an expansive view of the **Ashley River**. Sailboats dot the waters to your left and right, and sunlight dances on the flashing dark water. The historic district of Charleston and its lovely, steepled skyline

St. Philip's Episcopal Church

fall behind as you approach the ever thickening marshlands on the western side of the Ashley. Ahead lies James Island, and beyond, rustic, quaint Folly Beach.

Wadmalaw, Johns, and Edisto Islands

ROCKVILLE TO EDISTO BEACH

GENERAL DESCRIPTION: This 75-mile trip across South Carolina's rural Sea Islands begins in the village of Rockville and ends at Edisto Beach on the Atlantic Ocean, crossing Wadmalaw Island, Johns Island, and Edisto Island, with views of the Edisto and Stono Rivers, sandy beachfront, the Intracoastal Waterway, and beautiful tidal marshlands.

SPECIAL ATTRACTIONS: Edisto and Stono Rivers, Angel Oak, ACE Basin National Wildlife Refuge, The Grove, Charleston Tea Plantation, Adams Run and Hollywood communities, Edisto Island, Edisto Beach State Park.

LOCATION: Midcoast, just below Charleston.

DRIVE ROUTE NUMBERS: SC 700/ Maybank Highway, Grace Chapel Road, Angel Oak Road, S-10-20/Bohicket Road, S-10-20/Main Road, US 17, SC 162, SC 165/Toogoodoo Road, S-10-390/Toogoodoo Road, SC 174/Edisto Road, S-10-55/ Willtown Road, S-10-346/Jehossee Island Road, Chisolm Plantation Road, Botany Bay Road, SC 174/Palmetto Boulevard.

TRAVEL SEASON: All year.

SERVICES: All services are plentiful in Charleston. Johns Island, Edisto Beach, and Jacksonboro offer limited services.

See For More Information in the appendix for addresses and phone numbers of Attractions, Camping, Neat Places to Stay, Restaurants, Shops, Tours, and Nature-Based Services.

THE DRIVE

This tour of the eastern edge of the great river watershed known as the ACE Basin (Ashepoo, Combahee, and Edisto Rivers) takes travelers from waterfront to waterfront, with great marshland, maritime forest, and other coastal area scenery in between. You begin in the village of Rockville, where the North Edisto River empties into the Atlantic Ocean. You visit a tea plantation, the gigantic Angel Oak, the enchanting ACE Basin National Wildlife Refuge headquarters at a plantation known as The Grove, and a state park that hosts an ancient Indian shell mound, some of the state's tallest palmetto trees, and a long stretch of sandy, white beach, before ending your drive in a quiet oceanfront community.

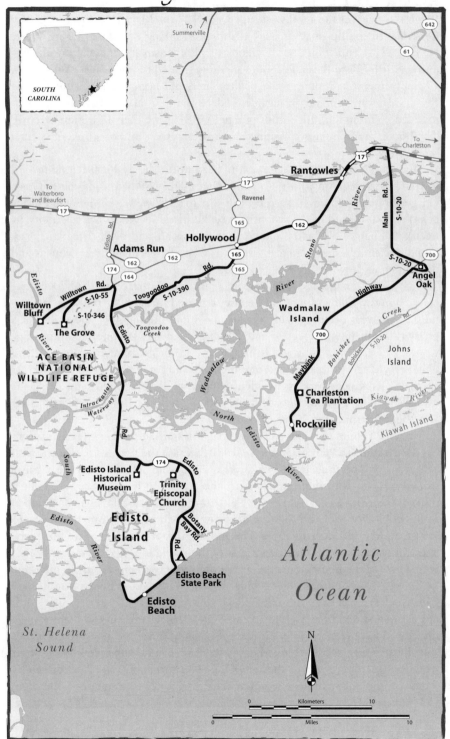

SOUTH
CAROLINA

To
Summerville

642

61

To
Charleston

17

Rantowles

17

To
Walterboro
and Beaufort

17

Ravenel

165

162

17

Stono River

Main Rd.

S-10-20

165

Hollywood

162

Edisto Rd.

Adams Run

162

162

165

S-10-20

700

Angel
Oak

174

164

165

River

Highway

S-10-20

Creek

Rd.

Willtown Rd.

S-10-55

Toogoodoo Rd.

S-10-390

Wadmalaw
Island

Bohicket

Johns
Island

Willtown
Bluff

S-10-346

Edisto River

The Grove

Toogoodoo
Creek

Edisto

700

Maybank

Bohicket Rd.

Kiawah River

ACE BASIN
NATIONAL
WILDLIFE REFUGE

Intracoastal
Waterway

Wadmalaw

North

Charleston
Tea Plantation

Rockville

Kiawah Island

Edisto
River

Edisto

Rd.

North Edisto River

174

Edisto Island
Historical
Museum

Edisto

Trinity
Episcopal
Church

River

Edisto
Island

Botany
Bay Rd.

Edisto River

Rd.

Atlantic

Ocean

Edisto Beach
State Park

Edisto
Beach

St. Helena
Sound

N

Kilometers
0   10

Miles
0   10

ROCKVILLE TO ANGEL OAK

Begin this drive at the southwestern end of SC 700/Maybank Highway, in tiny **Rockville** on the tip of Wadmalaw Island, overlooking the **North Edisto River**. Here at "land's end," you can see sailboats and other small watercraft on the glittering North Edisto River. Porpoises are often spotted romping in the tidal water.

Enormous oaks protect some of the stately old homes on the banks of the river. Green yards and colorful gardens adorn the rural mansions, bedecked with rounded columns and huge front porches raised above their Lowcountry yards. The homes are built close together and give one the sense of a tight-knit rural community.

With the North Edisto behind you, head north slowly for 0.1 mile toward town. The first road on your right (east), Grace Chapel Road, leads you to Grace Chapel Episcopal Church. Turn on this dirt road to view a simple white clapboard church tucked in the woods and backyards of its Rockville neighbors. Its steeple still has an old belfry and a tall, thin cross atop its peak. A flat lawn surrounds the church, and a circular dirt drive, Grace Chapel Lane, takes you around the church back to Grace Chapel Road.

Exit Grace Chapel Road by turning right (north) back onto SC 700/Maybank Highway. Old and new houses are dispersed throughout this area. Beautiful old oak trees dripping with Spanish moss line the highway and make for a pretty ride. Quaint cottages decorated with Confederate jasmine, blooming dogwoods, and vibrant azaleas add to the beauty in spring. Numerous tomato and strawberry farms sit astride this rural highway, and some invite you to "pick for yourself." Roadside markets, wooden cottages, and old churches dot the landscape here. Cherry Point Road, which offers access to Bohicket Creek, is on your right 0.3 mile from Grace Chapel.

About 1.5 miles up the road on your right is our nation's only tea plantation, the **Charleston Tea Plantation**. Drive slowly because the turn is not marked with a sign as you approach from this direction. On your left you will see a barn-shaped mailbox with the number 6615; the plantation is on your right. Follow the signs near the fence to enter the plantation, which is locally owned and open to the public for tours on the first Saturday of each month, from 10:00 A.M. to 1:30 P.M., May through October. The history and production of tea are highlighted on a walk in the fields with one of the plantation owners. The tour ends with a taste of the homegrown tea and an opportunity to browse in the gift shop.

Travel 9 miles farther on SC 700/Maybank Highway. When you cross over Church Creek and enter John's Island, go slowly because the turn to the right is not clearly marked. Turn right (east) off SC 700/Maybank Highway onto Angel Oak Road just before St. John's Episcopal Church. Travel 0.4 mile past cornfields and thick forests, and look for the left (east) turn into **Angel Oak Park**. Short wooden signs direct you to the tree. Once you turn, you can't miss the enormous oak to your right. Its circumference is 25½ feet, and it stands 65 feet high.

The tree's arms bend down to the ground and seem to rest from her weary weight. Angel Oak's largest limb's circumference is 11¼ feet and 89 feet in length. The shade provided by Angel Oak encompasses 17,000 square feet. The visual effect of this gigantic tree is stunning.

Angel Oak is a live oak (*Quercus virginiana*), a common tree found throughout the low country. No one is certain of Angel Oak's age, but it is speculated she might be as much as 1,400 years old.

The tree has been recognized and protected locally for centuries. Since 1991, Angel Oak and the surrounding property have been owned and maintained by the City of Charleston, but the tree was cared for by a number of private and public groups prior to that time. The first recorded landowner of the area is Abraham Waight, a prosperous planter who owned several plantations and was granted the land in 1717. The land remained in the Waight family as the property was passed from generation to generation, but the tree didn't receive its name until Martha Waight married Justis Angel in 1810.

A quaint, cabinlike gift shop beside the parking area has photographs of Angel Oak, birdhouses, and other interesting gifts. A number of wooden picnic tables on the Angel Oak grounds, shaded by much smaller oaks, offer a restful area to contemplate the beauty of the magnificent ancient specimen. The tree and its grounds can be visited free of charge Monday through Saturday from 9:00 A.M. to 5:00 P.M., Sunday from 1:00 to 5:00 P.M.

ANGEL OAK TO ACE BASIN NATIONAL WILDLIFE REFUGE

Leaving Angel Oak, turn left (east) onto Angel Oak Road. Travel 0.4 mile to S-10-20/Bohicket Road and turn left (northwest) toward Charleston; Kiawah and Seabrook Island are to your right. At the next major intersection (Fenwick Crossroads), continue west on S-10-20/Bohicket Road, crossing SC 700/Maybank Highway, where Bohicket Road becomes S-10-20/Main Road. Remain on this road for 7 miles, until you cross the drawbridge over the brackish **Stono River** and arrive at the intersection with US 17. Until the new bridge is completed, be prepared for a long wait if the drawbridge is turned and sailboats are passing through on the river. Take a left (southwest) on US 17 toward Savannah.

Drive 1.5 miles on US 17 and cross the Rantowles Creek wetlands. You're now in the town of Hollywood. A historic marker here tells of Colonel William A. Washington's grave nearby. Colonel Washington, a native Virginian, made his home in this area and led Patriot cavalry during the American Revolution. In 1791, Colonel Washington entertained his kinsman, President George Washington, during the president's tour of the South.

Travel 1 mile farther on US 17 and veer to the left (southeast) onto SC 162. Marshlands and small bungalows are tucked into the forestlands, and vegetable and wildflower gardens dot the highway.

Travel 7 miles through Hollywood, then turn left (south) on SC 165/Too-goodoo Road. *If you would like to do some window shopping in downtown Hollywood, continue for one block to Robert Sarco's Antique Market to the left of US 17. Then back-track to SC 165 and turn right.*

At 0.8 mile, SC 165 turns left. Continue straight on S-10-390/Toogoodoo Road. Enjoy 7 pleasantly winding miles though beautiful horse pastures, hay fields, and the marshlands of Toogoodoo Creek. A little more than 3.5 miles down Toogoodoo Road is the Toogoodoo Christmas Tree Plantation, where you can choose and cut your own Christmas tree.

When the road ends at SC 174/Edisto Road, take a right (north), drive 1.2 miles, and turn left (west) onto S-10-55/Willtown Road. A brown sign notes the left turn to the **ACE Basin National Wildlife Refuge**. Travel 2 miles and then take a left (south) on S-10-346/Jehossee Island Road to enter the wildlife refuge. The gravel and dirt road is bumpy, so you'll need to drive slowly. The surrounding woods are dark and dense, full of short palms and tall pines. This is a terrific place for wildlife viewing.

Two miles down this dirt road, you'll see the white brick gates of **The Grove**. Bird-watching pamphlets are available to the right of this entrance. The planta-tion house and its parking lot are a half mile directly ahead. The grounds are open from 7:30 A.M. to 4:00 P.M. Monday through Friday, except on holidays. The refuge is unstaffed on weekends, but the public may visit the property dur-ing daylight hours.

The two-story white home is spectacular. Its front circular drive is lined with shrubbery and flowers. This antebellum mansion is one of only three homes in the ACE Basin that survived the Civil War. The Grove was formerly a rice plan-tation home, built in 1828. It now serves as the office for the Edisto Unit of the refuge. Park to the left of the house, near the whitewashed former slave quarters that have been transformed into maintenance buildings. Behind the home are ancient oak trees strewn with Spanish moss. The lawn is a green terrain that stretches deep into the marshlands. Egrets glide over the tall grasses, and other small birds flit around the yard. The grass trails that wind throughout the prop-erty provide ideal bird-watching. The quiet and frequent breeze in this awesome yard is delightful. A picnic table sitting under the oaks is perfect for a picnic be-fore exploring the area.

This site is only a small portion of the 350,000 acres of marsh, swamp, and uplands that make up the ACE Basin, stretching across Beaufort, Colleton, Hampton, and Charleston Counties. Although much of the land in the ACE Basin is privately owned, most of it is under permanent protection from devel-opment, due to conservation arrangements between landowners and state and federal government agencies. Private and public conservation agencies own and manage the public properties. These public lands are the Donnelly Wildlife Man-agement Area (WMA), Bear Island WMA, ACE Basin National Estuarine Re-search Reserve, and ACE Basin National Wildlife Refuge.

The Grove

Protection of wildlife habitats in the ACE Basin, the watershed of the Ashepoo, Combahee, and Edisto Rivers that flow into St. Helena Sound, is the primary goal of the ACE Basin management areas. These areas contain upland habitats, freshwater and brackish impoundments, mixed pine/hardwoods, bottomland hardwoods, longleaf pine forests, shortleaf/loblolly pine forests, maritime forests, and saltwater marsh. Wildlife viewing is plentiful here. You'll encounter a wide variety of birds—waterfowl, birds of prey, wading birds, songbirds, shorebirds, including the white ibis, snowy egret, blue heron, wood stork, and Swainson's warbler—and other wildlife, such as alligators, deer, and wild turkeys. The ACE Basin is also home to the largest nesting population of bald eagles in the state.

This portion of the ACE Basin refuge adjacent to the Edisto River lies along the Atlantic Flyway, often referred to as the "highway in the sky." Here, numerous waterfowl, shorebirds, neotropical songbirds, and birds of prey migrate from their nesting grounds to find wintering areas throughout eastern North America.

Exit the refuge on the same dirt road, S-10-346/Jehossee Island Road. Backtrack north 2 miles and turn left (west) on S-10-55/Willtown Road. Drive 2.5 miles to the charming **Willtown Bluff** community at the end of the road, and take in the splendid view of the South Edisto River and its adjacent alligator-infested rice field marshlands. The pavement ends a mile from Jehossee Road. Continue for 1.5 miles to the site of the old town called Willtown, or New London, established in 1685, and to the South Edisto River.

ACE BASIN NATIONAL WILDLIFE REFUGE TO EDISTO BEACH

Turn around and drive 5 miles back (east) on S-10-55/Willtown Road to the intersection with SC 174/Edisto Road. Turn right (south) toward Edisto Island and Edisto Beach to enjoy maritime forest lands and saltwater marshes.

Cross the **McKinley Washington Bridge** after 6 miles to enter Edisto Island. Elevated for boat passage below, the bridge provides a panoramic view of the Atlantic Intracoastal Waterway and the surrounding marsh. The tufts of grass, wading egrets, and perched pelicans are breathtaking. Drive slowly and take in the Lowcountry's salty air and visual wonders.

Edisto Island, one of South Carolina's largest barrier islands, is a treasure. The North and South Edisto Rivers border two edges of the island, connected by the Atlantic Ocean and the Intracoastal Waterway. This island is home to unspoiled saltwater marshes, rich agricultural lands, and some of the tallest palmetto trees in the state. The beach is also one of the state's best shelling beaches and havens for prehistoric fossils such as sharks' teeth.

The Edistow Indians first inhabited Edisto Island 4,000 years ago. Spanish explorers arrived here during the 1500s but didn't settle; the English who arrived in the 1600s stayed. It is believed that the Earl of Shaftsbury, one of the original lords proprietor, purchased Edisto Island in 1674 from the Edistow Indians. Settlers tried their hand at rice and indigo crops, and then cotton. The cultivation of the popular Sea Island cotton in the 1790s is what established the prosperity of the island, as evidenced by some of the plantation homes that were built during the late eighteenth century. Some stand today and are listed on the National Register of Historic Places. Early Union occupation of the island during the Civil War made the area a home base for Union troops and thus helped prevent destruction by Sherman's army near the war's end.

The early prosperity of the island did not last. The Civil War and the boll weevil wiped out the cotton industry by the early 1900s, so islanders focused on Lowcountry seafood as a means of income. The area might have lost its wealth, but it never lost its charm. In the early twentieth century, Edisto Beach became a popular summer beach, and it remains so today. Edisto is a quiet, unspoiled island.

The road on the south side of the bridge passes through a wonderful variety of forests, fields, marshlands, tiny communities, and diverse homes. Five miles south of the bridge is the **Edisto Island Historical Museum**. If you wish to visit the museum, turn right (southwest) on Chisholm Plantation Road. The museum is on your left, just off the highway. The Edisto Island Historic Preservation Society manages the museum, which is open from 1:00 to 4:00 P.M. Tuesday, Thursday, and Saturday for a small admission fee. During June, July, and August, it's also open on Friday from 1:00 to 4:00 P.M. Here you can learn the history of the island and its people.

Exit the museum on Chisolm Plantation Road and continue south on SC 174/Edisto Road for 1.3 miles. Edisto Tours and Tings, which offers tours of the plantation homes on the island and an interesting gift shop, is to the left of the highway. You can also pick up Pon Pon River Tours and ACE Basin and birding tours here.

Trinity Episcopal Church, a church with a rich history and strong community ties even today, is 1.2 miles farther on your right. The church was first constructed in 1774, then replaced in 1841. This second structure was destroyed by fire in 1876. The present church, consecrated in 1881, remains standing and is in exceptional condition. The exterior of the church is simple, with whitewashed wooden slats, a modest porch, a tall triangular steeple, and crisp black shutters adorning the windows. The interior of the church, however, is decorated with a vibrant red carpet and an altar area constructed completely of beautiful cherry wood. Wooden pews fill the main church, making this an exceptionally attractive house of worship.

Another 0.7 mile brings you to some unique stores worth stopping in, such as With These Hands Gallery, which offers glass works, original art, and other collectibles. Beside the Gallery is the Old Post Office Restaurant, a definite treat for your palate. Store Creek Antiques and Collectibles is a block off of SC 174.

Cross over the marsh and stop at the Edisto Island Serpentarium to explore the island's wildlife. (The serpentarium is sometimes closed during winter months.)

Drive less than a mile farther on SC 174/Edisto Road to Botany Bay Road on your left (east). Turn left on this sandy road to step back into the days of rice and indigo plantations. The 1.5-mile dead-end road is completely canopied with huge, knarled oak tree limbs that interlock above your head. Spanish moss dangles from the trees, which are so closely grown that the end of the road is hardly visible through the black canopy overhead. This road is really a must-see. When you reach the end, turn around and return to SC 174/Edisto Road.

Across the street from **Botany Bay Road**, in the midst of a marsh, is a lighthearted tree, always decorated to celebrate the most current national holiday. Some locals in the community take particular pride in adorning this tree with Easter eggs, Christmas tinsel, and patriotic flags on the Fourth of July. It's a special treat to see how the tree is decorated each time you pass along this highway.

Almost 3 miles past Botany Bay Road is the Edisto Island Chamber of Commerce and Visitor Center on your left. Stop in here for brochures on the area, then continue a few tenths of a mile farther to the northern section of **Edisto Beach State Park**. State Cabin Road, a rough and bumpy dirt road on your right (west), takes visitors to the Live Oak Camping Area, as well as the trailhead for **Indian Mound Trail**. The trail is an easy 1.8-mile jaunt through maritime forest to an ancient mound of seashells called Spanish Mount, said to be more than 4,000 years old. Parts of the trail overlook the salt marsh expanses of Big Bay Creek and its tributaries, and visitors can often catch glimpses of such local denizens as the clapper rail, brown pelican, painted bunting, marsh wren, tern, gull, and heron.

Travel only a half mile farther on SC 174/Edisto Road to Edisto Beach. The Edisto Beach Welcome Center is on your right just off of Jungle Road. Step in here for information on area attractions, vacation coupons, free maps of the area, and rental information. A tenth of a mile farther is the main entrance of Edisto Beach State Park on your left (east).

Edisto Beach State Park, developed by the Civilian Conservation Corps in the 1930s, covers 1,255 acres. It is home to a dense maritime forest, an expansive salt marsh, and a 1.5-mile stretch of beach bordered by some of the state's tallest palmetto trees. Porpoises are frequently spotted frolicking in the surf.

Edisto Beach

Picnic areas, ocean fishing and swimming, and summer nature programs are available here. The park offers a number of free entertaining and educational programs at its nature center, including a forty-five-minute program about the Indian Shell Mound. The center conducts walks on the beach and to the saltwater marsh to discuss plant and animal habitats and threatened species such as the loggerhead turtle. It also teaches children how to crab, and about fossils that may be found in the area. A small admission fee is charged for entrance to the southern section of the park, open daily during daylight saving time from 6:00 A.M. to 10:00 P.M., and 8:00 A.M. to 6:00 P.M. during standard time.

To complete your drive, continue past the park and cruise southeast along the coast for 4.5 miles to the end of SC 174/Palmetto Boulevard. The Town of Edisto Beach is a wonderfully noncommercial coastal vacation and retirement community, composed mainly of single-family dwellings and great for bikers, joggers, and walkers.

Edisto and Ashley Rivers

CHARLESTON PLANTATIONS TO FRANCIS BEIDLER FOREST

GENERAL DESCRIPTION: Beginning on the west side of Charleston, this 70-mile drive passes Drayton Hall, Middleton Place, and Magnolia Plantations on the Ashley River, then travels through isolated rural areas to two state parks on the Edisto River before ending at an old-growth swamp sanctuary, the Francis Beidler Forest.

SPECIAL ATTRACTIONS: Ashley River, Drayton Hall, Middleton Place, Magnolia Plantation and Its Gardens, Edisto River, Givhans Ferry State Park, Colleton State Park, Francis Beidler Forest.

LOCATION: Coastal Plain northwest of Charleston, along the Ashley and Edisto Rivers.

DRIVE ROUTE NUMBERS: SC 61 West/Ashley River Road, Alternate US 17, S-18-30/Givhans Ferry Road, Augusta Highway, US 15, Wayside Lane, US 78, US 178, S-18-28/Beidler Forest Road, Sanctuary Road.

TRAVEL SEASON: All year. Spring and fall are prime times for wildlife viewing and to see the plantation gardens in full bloom.

SERVICES: Motels, hotels, and all services are plentiful in Charleston, North Charleston, Summerville, and Walterboro. Limited services are available in St. George.

See For More Information in the appendix for addresses and phone numbers of Attractions, Camping, Neat Places to Stay, Restaurants, Shops, Tours, and Nature-Based Services.

THE DRIVE

This tour is a study in contrasts. It begins on a State Scenic Highway that parallels the venerable Ashley River, taking visitors to the splendor of manicured antebellum plantation houses and gardens at Drayton Hall, Magnolia Gardens, and Middleton Place. Then drivers head north, first along the Ashley, then along the Edisto River, through lonely rural wetlands, forests, farms, and communities, stopping at the state parks of Givhans Ferry and Colleton, which hug the foreboding, black-water Edisto. After passing through the once thriving railroad town of St. George, the tour finishes at Beidler Forest, a splendidly preserved and presented old-growth wetland forest in the middle of Four Holes Swamp, where

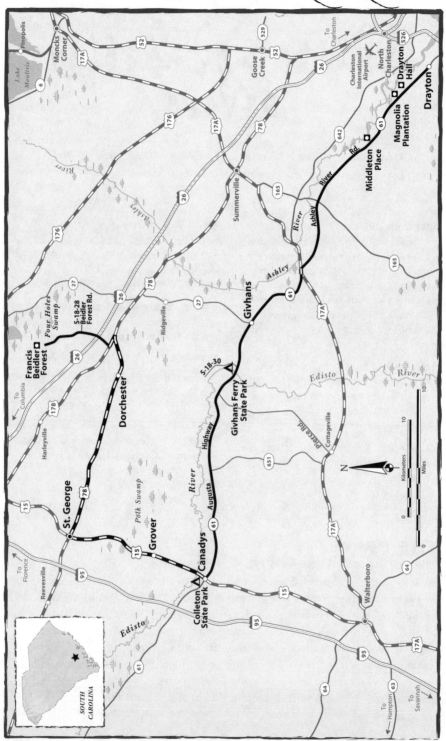

bald cypresses and tupelos grow to magnificent sizes amid a plethora of alligators, waterfowl, and other wildlife.

DRAYTON HALL

Begin your drive at **Drayton Hall** on SC 61/Ashley River Road, a State Scenic Highway and the Discovery Route of the Heritage Corridor, 4 miles north of the intersection of SC 61 and Interstate 526. Drayton Hall is a National Historic Landmark owned jointly by the State of South Carolina and the National Trust for Historic Preservation. An accredited museum, Drayton Hall remains the oldest preserved plantation house in America open to the public, one of the finest examples of Georgian Palladian architecture in America, and the only surviving colonial plantation house on the **Ashley River**. A stroke of good fortune and some ingenuity on the part of the Drayton family protected the mansion from Sherman's troops in 1865, unlike nearby plantations that were pillaged and burned to the ground. Today, Drayton Hall shares its beauty and history with visitors year-round.

Royal Judge John Drayton (1713–1779) failed to inherit his family's Magnolia Plantation, so in 1738 he acquired the land on which Drayton Hall sits and made it the center of his extensive indigo and rice planting ventures. In 1744 Drayton acquired next-door Magnolia Plantation from his nephew, William Drayton, who moved out of the state.

Construction on Drayton Hall, a two-story brick plantation home, was completed in 1742. With the assistance of European and enslaved African-American craftsmen, Drayton constructed first- and second-floor front porches centered between the home's extensive brick wings and two staircases, giving the home a commanding presence. Two chimneys over the left and right walls of the home create a balanced, symmetric, and classic design. Indoors, the absence of furniture in the home emphasizes the craftsmen's detailed wooden banisters and ornamented doorways and mantles.

Guided tours of Drayton Hall are offered on the hour, and visitors are encouraged to take a leisurely stroll along the scenic trails along the banks of the Ashley River or enjoy the picnic tables that sit under ancient oak trees. Throughout the year, special events and programs are offered at Drayton Hall, presenting exceptional intellectual programs such as the Seasonal Friends lecture series, candlelight and spiritual concerts, and plantation oyster roasts.

Drayton Hall's grounds, rest rooms, museum shop, marsh and river walks, and most of the plantation home are handicapped accessible. Hours of operation from March to October are 10:00 A.M. to 4:00 P.M., from November to February, the grounds are open from 10:00 A.M. to 3:00 P.M. There is a moderate fee for a house tour and a nominal fee for access to the grounds only.

Exit Drayton Hall to the right (northwest) onto SC 61 West/Ashley River Road. Drive 0.7 mile, and Magnolia Plantation and Its Gardens will be on your right (east).

MAGNOLIA PLANTATION AND ITS GARDENS

Magnolia Plantation and Its Gardens adjoin Drayton Hall Plantation and have remained in the Drayton family for nine generations, since the arrival of Thomas Drayton from Barbados in 1671. Both the original plantation home and the garden are National Historic Landmarks, but the garden can boast of being America's oldest.

Thomas and Anne Drayton, whose family played an important role in America's colonial revolution and independence history, completed the first residence at Magnolia Plantation in 1676. After this home burned, a second was built on the banks of the Ashley River with bricks salvaged from the first structure. The second dwelling, a three-story structure built mainly of cypress, burned in 1865 at the hands of Sherman's troops. Only the steps and the ground floor were saved. During the Civil War era, the Reverend John Grimke Drayton, rector of nearby St. Andrews Episcopal Church, inherited Magnolia Plantation. In order to rebuild, he sold his sea island plantation, his town house, and much of the property surrounding Magnolia Plantation.

Rev. Drayton owned a pre-Revolutionary summerhouse in nearby Summerville. He disassembled this home, loaded it on barges, and floated it 14 miles on the Ashley River to Magnolia Plantation, where he mounted it on the brick remainders of the second home. It has since been expanded, and the stucco that covers the house was made from the phosphate mined on the plantation and applied after the earthquake of 1886. Tours of the existing home highlight the Drayton family history, life on the plantation for the past three centuries, and the home's extensive collection of Early American furniture.

Magnolia Plantation and Its Gardens

One of the most notable aspects of Magnolia Plantation is its garden, the oldest in America. The most formal portion of the garden, "Flowerdale," was established the same year the plantation home was built, and it remains mostly unchanged even today. The gardens are planted for year-round blooms, and they include a Barbados tropical garden, an eighteenth-century herb garden, a Biblical garden, a topiary garden, the Audubon Swamp Garden, and a horticultural maze of camellia and holly bushes. Although spring offers a terrific array of the 250 varieties of azaleas, winter is equally beautiful, with 900 varieties of camellias in bloom.

The plantation offers a number of ways to enjoy its grounds. A nature train provides forty-five-minute narrated tram rides through Magnolia Plantation's historic wildlife areas and rice field reserve lakes that border the Ashley River. Guides interpret daily life on the plantation from the colonial period to the present, highlighting the flora and fauna here, such as the plantation's alligators, turtles, herons, egrets, and a variety of birds. The nature boat offers a forty-five-minute tour of the old 150-acre flooded rice field, now a wildlife refuge for many water-loving birds and aquatic creatures. Guides describe the role of the Ashley River and the plantation's wildlife. The Audubon Swamp Garden, a sixty-acre black-water cypress and tupelo swamp full of boardwalks, bridges, and dikes, lets you experience a variety of wildlife among native and exotic flowering plants.

Since 1975, the entire 500 acres of the plantation have been managed as a wildlife refuge. The diversity of the terrain lends itself to a variety of bird, animal, reptile, and plant life, and is an unusually productive bird-watching area that can be reached by walking and bike trails. Canoe rides offer an especially neat view of the rice fields, which are also open to freshwater fishing. A wildlife observation tower within 50 yards of the garden also provides an excellent view of waterbirds and small land birds. In the Audubon Swamp, blue herons, wood ducks, snowy egrets, and anhingas are commonly spotted among the water oaks, cypress trees and knobs, tupelos, duck weeds, exotic ferns, bulbs, and lilies, along with a variety of bog plants, ornamental grasses, and colorful wildflowers.

Magnolia Plantation and Its Gardens are open every day from 8:00 A.M. to 5:30 P.M. Moderate fees are charged for admission to the grounds and house.

MIDDLETON PLACE

Exit Magnolia Plantation and turn right (northwest) on SC 61/Ashley River Road, a shady, canopied highway of Spanish-moss-draped oaks. Even on a sunny day, this road feels dark and cozy. Continue for 3.5 miles, until you see Middleton Place on your right (east).

As you enter **Middleton Place**, the plantation's dark brick home is seen in the distance behind a green pasture of grazing livestock. This National Historic Landmark, home to America's oldest formal landscaped gardens (circa 1741) was also the home of one of South Carolina's most influential families. Not only did Henry Middleton once have some of the largest landholdings in America, it's been said that the Middletons "started high society" this side of the Atlantic. Henry Middleton, builder of the sixty-acre landscaped garden and accompanying plantation home, was president of the First Continental Congress. His son, Arthur Middleton, was a signer of the Declaration of Independence. Arthur's son, Henry, was governor of South Carolina and an American minister to Russia, and Williams, Henry's son, signed the Ordinance of Secession.

Built in 1755 on the banks of the Ashley River, Middleton Place continues to thrive today. Most of the gardens and the home were burned in 1865 by Sherman's army; only the gentleman's guest wing survived. After Union troops departed, this wing was refurbished and became the family residence. Middleton Place also survived the Charleston earthquake in 1886. Guided tours of the home interpret the Middleton family's role in South Carolina and American history and highlight the home's furniture, paintings by Benjamin West and Thomas Sully, rare books by Audubon, antique rice beds, the family's original silver and china, and other personal belongings.

Middleton Place's formal gardens are nationally recognized and definitely worth a tour. In 1941, The Garden Club of America awarded Middleton Place the Bulkley Medal "in commemoration of two hundred years of enduring beauty." Fifty years later, in 1991, the International Committee on Monuments and Sites named Middleton Place one of six United States gardens of international importance.

Stroll through the terraced gardens on the banks of the Ashley and wander through the intricate mazes that were influenced by English and French landscape design. A gardener was brought from England to design the terraced gardens above the butterfly lakes. Vast plantings of rare camellias, the first four ever grown in America, were planted here. All of the gardens are interesting in design and use of color. Kalmias, azaleas, crepe myrtles, orchids, roses, and magnolias are spectacular.

One unique feature of Middleton Place is its stable yards, featuring a resident blacksmith, potter, carpenter, and weaver who re-create activities of a self-sustaining Lowcountry plantation and sell their wares in the Middleton Place Museum Shop. Horses, mules, hogs, milking cows, sheep, goats, and guinea hens are still raised here and represent the life of the rice plantation home and era. A freedman's home, Eliza's House, presents the story of the African-American community.

The plantation offers kayak trips on the Ashley River and a black water cypress swamp, horseback riding, biking tours, and guided nature walks around the rice field banks and the Ashley River. Throughout the grounds and tidal estuaries, herons, egrets, bald eagles, otters, alligators, bobcats, and other creatures abound. A number of special events are scheduled throughout the year, highlighting particular gardens, nature walks, and plantation life at Middleton Place.

Middleton Place is open from 9:00 A.M. to 5:00 P.M. daily. Separate, moderate admissions are charged for the grounds and for the house tour.

MIDDLETON PLACE TO BEIDLER FOREST AT FOUR HOLES SWAMP

Exit Middleton Place and turn right (northwest) onto SC 61/Ashley River Road. Travel 10.3 miles to the intersection with Alternate US 17. Take a left (southwest) at the stop sign to travel on Alternate US 17/SC 61 a few yards, and then bear right (northwest) to continue on SC 61/Ashley River Road. At the fork in the road is 17A & 61 Bait and Tackle, where you can pick up minnows, crickets, worms, and sodas.

Travel 4.7 miles through forest and swampland and past some modest country dwellings to reach the isolated crossroads outpost of Givhans, then continue 3.5 miles on SC 61 to the turnoff for Givhans Ferry State Park, just before the bridge that spans the **Edisto River**. A brown sign notes the turn. Take a right (north) on S-18-30/Givhans Ferry Road and travel 0.1 mile to enter the state park, on your left (west).

Givhans Ferry was originally a ferry crossing in the eighteenth and nineteenth centuries, connecting Charleston with inland areas. **Givhans Ferry State Park**, a 988-acre park built on high bluffs along the scenic Edisto River, offers terrific views and access to the black-water river. President Roosevelt's Civilian Conservation Corps constructed the park in the 1930s, one of a series of similar work projects across the nation.

When you drive into the rustic but well-maintained park, on a dirt road that can be quite muddy on rainy days, past rental cabins and campsites to Overlook Picnic Shelter, you see the beautiful, meandering Edisto River. Picnic tables are scattered throughout the park, which also provides the 1.5-mile River Bluff

Givhans Ferry State Park

Nature Trail, fishing opportunities, and a meeting facility. The park is situated along the 56-mile Edisto River Canoe and Kayak Trail, a black-water river course that carries paddlers past scenic natural areas. Wildflowers bloom along the banks in both the spring and the fall, and giant live oaks, black willows, red swamp maples, cypresses, tupelos, gums, and tall stately pines decorate the edges of the river. Givhans Ferry Park is open during daylight saving time from 9:00 A.M. to 9:00 P.M. and from 9:00 A.M. to 6:00 P.M. the rest of the year.

Exit the park by turning right (south) onto S-18-30/Givhans Ferry Road, and turn right (northwest) again on SC 61/Augusta Highway. You'll immediately cross the Edisto River and travel through wetlands down a rural road that seems a bit rundown. Old farm houses and mobile homes dot the landscape of this country road.

You are in the heart of Bubba Country, where hunting and fishing reign. Watch out for deer and pickup trucks with gun racks. Homes and small farm fields are scattered throughout the forestland on both sides of the road. A mile down the road, a sign points left toward Pierce Road and Cottageville. Edisto Tackle and Tradin' Post, a mile farther on your right, offers minnows, crickets, worms, fishing and hunting licenses, beer, and a wild turkey check station.

Almost 3 miles from the turnoff to Cottageville is the right-hand turn onto Bittersweet Lane that takes you to Bee City Honeybee Farm and Petting Zoo (population 1,260,000), which offers homemade honey, pollen, beeswax, and candles.

Continue northwest on SC 61/Augusta Highway to Canadys, 14.5 miles from Givhans Ferry State Park. In Canadys, turn right (northeast) on US 15/North Jefferies Road. Drive 0.3 mile and turn left (west) into Colleton State Park on Wayside Lane.

Colleton State Park, a thirty-five-acre facility also built by the Civilian Conservation Corps in the 1930s, serves as the headquarters for the Edisto River Canoe and Kayak Trail. Formed more than twelve years ago as the first official canoe and kayak trail in the state, it covers 56 miles of the Edisto River, from Whetstone Crossroads near the intersection of US 21 and SC 61 to an area near Jacksonboro on US 17. The trail was developed to promote wise use of the river and to protect it as a valuable natural resource.

The Edisto forms the northern border of the ACE Basin, an important watershed and natural area in South Carolina. Black water indicates the peaceful rate of flow of the river and accurately describes the coloration of the tannin-rich spring water. It is reported to be the longest free-flowing black-water stream in America. The Edisto River is an ancient waterway that was important to Native Americans and to commerce in colonial times. Today it is a haven for several wildlife species, such as blue herons, turtles, alligators, egrets, and bald eagles.

Colleton State Park has a well-maintained interpreted foot trail (the Cypress Swamp Nature Trail) along the river bank. Fishing is encouraged, and bream, redbreast, and catfish are plentiful. River access for private boats is a quarter mile from the park. Picnic shelters are also available. The park is open from 9:00 A.M. to 9:00 P.M. during daylight saving time and from 9:00 A.M. to 6:00 P.M. during standard time.

Exit the park by turning left (northeast) onto US 15. Cross the Grady C. Murray Bridge over the Edisto River and pass through substantial wetlands. The first town is **Grover**, 3 miles ahead. If you don't slow down, you won't know that you have missed this quiet town, where horses and cows graze. You might spot rabbits hopping on the sides of the road and hawks overhead. Ranch-style homes line the highway, usually with small gardens or huge row crops of corn or soybeans. In the summertime, look for Gruber Farms, where you can pick your own strawberries. The only commerce in town is Johnnie's Bait and Tackle Shop on your right. Stop here for any mechanical services you might need, as well as worms, fishing bait, lines, hooks, ice, or a variety of picnicking provisions.

A half mile outside of Grover, you'll cross Polk Swamp. Continue 5 more miles to the farm market town of **St. George**, county seat of Dorchester County and home to the annual Grits Festival. Old wooden houses, abandoned stores, and some mobile homes line the road before the street opens up to more fields of corn, soybeans, and a number of churches. In town, a historical marker near the railroad tracks that cross US 15 explains the role of South Carolina's Canal and Rail Road Company. It began the first successful scheduled steam railroad service in America on December 25, 1830. By 1833, its 136 miles from Charleston through St. George and on to Hamburg made it the world's longest railroad.

At the second traffic light past the railroad tracks, turn right (southeast) on US 78, which becomes Memorial Boulevard, and drive 11 miles to the village of Dorchester. Continue 3 more miles and turn left (northwest) onto US 178, where there is a small, well-landscaped park with a gazebo and park benches situated around a historical marker and a cannon memorializing a battle at Four Holes Swamp. If you don't wish to stop here, continue on US 178 less than a half mile, then turn right (northeast) onto S-18-28/Beidler Forest Road, an old country road lined with thick vegetation and lovely open fields of grazing horses, goats, and cows.

Travel 4 miles until the pavement ends, and continue another mile down the dirt road. Turn right (east) on Sanctuary Road to enter the **Francis Beidler Forest**, home to the largest remaining virgin stand of bald cypress and tupelo trees in the world, some more than 1,000 years old. It encompasses 6,000 acres of riverine sanctuary and 1,800 acres of ancient trees that tower over black-water streams and clear pools. The swamp forest contains groves of giant bald cypress, tupelo gum, laurel oak, and water ash. It is home to forty-four species of mammals, 140 species of birds, thirty-nine species of fish, fifty species of reptiles, forty species of amphibians, and other creatures.

Four Holes Swamp, which begins as a narrow swamp-stream system in Calhoun County, is fed by springs and rainfall to widen and flow 62 miles through four Lowcountry counties before its waters join the Edisto River and the Atlantic Ocean. Because the swamp is largely dependent on rainfall, its water levels fluctuate with the seasons. During wet seasons (winter and spring) the swamp is a shallow river flowing through a 1.5-mile-wide floodplain. In the summer and fall, the swamp shrinks to a series of well-defined creeks connecting larger "lakes."

No one is sure of the origin of the Four Holes Swamp name, but it has been speculated that it refers to four lakes once fished by the Yemassee Indians. Patriot Generals Francis "The Swamp Fox" Marion and Nathanael Greene staged guerrilla actions here during the Revolutionary War.

Francis Beidler, a lumberman and conservationist, acquired this part of the Four Holes Swamp in the 1890s. When he was a young man, he had visited Yellowstone National Park and was amazed by the beauty of the natural geysers and mountains of that area. He left determined to preserve the land that he had inherited in South Carolina. Better appreciating its beauty and unique habitat, he resolved to leave most of the timber standing. Beidler died in 1924; thankfully, his family members continued to preserve the area well into the 1960s, when the National Audubon Society and the Nature Conservancy purchased the land. Today the Audubon Society manages Francis Beidler Forest as part of its national system of wildlife sanctuaries.

The National Audubon Society's Francis Beidler Forest at Four Holes Swamp is full of rich habitats. Birds are easily spotted during winter and spring. On the elevated and winding boardwalk, you can catch glimpses of turtles and alligators. The loop boardwalk begins at the visitor center and is a little more than 1.5 miles, with nine rest stops and two rain shelters along the way. Canoe trips are also available.

The visitor center exhibits information to encourage a deeper appreciation of the area. A self-guided tour book describes the animals and plants that you may encounter. A slide show and other pictures are also on display to help you understand and appreciate the swamp and its inhabitants.

The visitor center and boardwalk are both handicapped accessible. The park is open Tuesday through Sunday from 9:00 A.M. to 5:00 P.M. It is closed on Mondays, Thanksgiving, Christmas Eve, Christmas, New Year's Eve, and New Year's Day. There is a small admission fee.

ACE Basin

WALTERBORO TO OLD SHELDON CHURCH

GENERAL DESCRIPTION: This trip begins in the historic, charming, well-preserved town of Walterboro, then takes you through the watershed of the enchanting Ashepoo, Combahee, and Edisto Rivers, one of the largest unspoiled wetlands areas in the nation, featuring lush forests and rich saltwater and freshwater coastal marshes.

SPECIAL ATTRACTIONS: Historic Walterboro, Ashepoo and Combahee Rivers, Bear Island and Donnelley Wildlife Management Areas, Bennetts Point, ACE Basin National Wildlife Refuge, Yemassee, Old Sheldon Church.

LOCATION: Southern Coast.

DRIVE ROUTE NUMBERS: Wichman Street/ Alternate US 17, Lucas Street, S-15-55/East Washington Street, SC 64, US

17/ACE Basin Parkway, Donnelly Road, Blocker Run Road, S-15-26/Bennett's Point Road, Ti Ti Road, S-7-33/River Road, Railroad Avenue, S-25-13, S-7-3, S-7-21/Old Sheldon Church Road, S-7-235/Bailey Road.

TRAVEL SEASON: All year, but fall, winter and spring are best. Heat and insects can be a problem in summer. Yemassee's Annual Shrimp Festival is held in September.

SERVICES: Motels, hotels, and other services are abundant in Walterboro and Beaufort. Limited services are offered in Jacksonboro and Yemassee.

See For More Information in the appendix for addresses and phone numbers of Attractions, Camping, Neat Places to Stay, Restaurants, Shops, Tours, and Nature-Based Services.

THE DRIVE

This 65–mile drive begins with a tour of old homes and buildings in lovely, historic Walterboro. It then winds you through dark, serene roads lined with Spanish-moss-strewn oaks and wildlife-filled estuarine wetlands of the ACE Basin, including stops in the Donnelley and Bear Island Wildlife Management Areas, remote Bennetts Point, and the Combahee Unit of the ACE Basin National Wildlife Refuge. You conclude by driving through the environs of lazy Yemassee and arriving at the ruins of Old Sheldon Church, truly splendor in the grass.

ACE Basin

WALTERBORO TO BENNETTS POINT

Walterboro is the county seat and most populous town of rural Colleton County. Named for Sir John Colleton, Lord Proprietor, whose land grant was bestowed by King Charles II in 1663, Colleton County is one of the oldest counties in America, dating back to 1682. Lowcountry plantations produced cotton, indigo, and primarily rice in Colleton County, making it one of the wealthiest areas in the state and one of the leading rice producers in America during the eighteenth century. Needing a summer retreat from harsh plantation life and the malaria brought on during the summer months, plantation owners Paul and Jacob Walter established Walterboro in 1783. Hickory Valley, Walterboro's historic district, was built between 1821 and 1929. Here you'll find the homes of some of the town's founders and prominent families, offering a glimpse of the wealth and lifestyle of that time. Many of these nineteenth-century structures are on the National Register of Historic Places.

Begin this drive at the **South Carolina Artisans Center** at 334 Wichman Street/ Alternate US 17 in the heart of downtown Walterboro. The center, housed in a historic home with a quaint wraparound porch, showcases and markets the finest handcrafted works of South Carolina's leading artisans. The mission of the center is to interpret, market, preserve, and perpetuate the folk art and fine craftsman-ship of South Carolina's artisans while creating a better understanding of our state's rich and diverse cultural heritage.

Handcrafted jewelry, pottery, baskets, furniture, elaborate teapots, sweet grass baskets, kudzu vine baskets, handmade paper, and woodcarvings made by South Carolina artists and craftsmen are marketed here. Prices range from $5.00 to more

South Carolina Artisans Center

than $500, and all purchases help support the educational programs, craft demonstrations, year-round special events, and ongoing operation of the center. The Artisans Center is open Monday through Saturday from 10:00 A.M. to 7:00 P.M. and Sunday from 1:00 to 6:00 P.M. No admission is charged, and the center is handicapped accessible.

To exit the center, turn left onto Lucas Street and follow it to the intersection with Washington. On your right at 373 Washington Street is Hiott's Pharmacy, where you can stop in for lunch or an ice-cream float. This pharmacy, housed in an 1890s building decorated with traditional black and white tiles, still fills prescriptions while you pull up to the lunch counter for a snack and an old-fashioned soda.

The historic shopping district of Walterboro is best seen on foot, so begin your stroll down Washington Street. Novit's Antique Mall is filled with numerous antique and collectible shops, Walterboro's City Plaza has a beautiful clock that chimes every quarter hour, and Sweet Grass Basket and Things, at 206 Washington, sells authentic sweet grass baskets. You'll pass other shops, coffeehouses, and bookstores, as you make your way to the *Press and Standard*, Walterboro's newspaper since 1877, at 113 Washington. This particular building was built in the 1920s and is a candidate for the National Register of Historic Places. The grounds are locally recognized as a meeting place for the community. If you're hungry, step into the Judges Chamber at 115 Washington Street or A Taste in Time Cafe at 242 Washington.

On your left at the end of Washington Street is the **Colleton County Courthouse**. Completed in the fall of 1822, this Greek Revival–style structure has outside walls that are three bricks (28 inches) thick. The courthouse is noted for hosting the first nullification meeting in South Carolina, when Robert Barnwell Rhett called for immediate secession in protest of federal tax laws in 1828.

Stroll back up Washington Street toward Hiott's. Resume the drive, following Washington Street all the way to Wichman Street. On your left at 521–545 East Washington Street is the **Albert House**. This building, constructed around 1890, served as the Farmers and Merchants Bank for many years. The current owners have restored the building and opened the Shops at Albert House on the ground floor and upscale apartments on the second story.

Look to your left as you pull out onto Wichman Street. At 418 Wichman is the **Jones-McDaniel-Hiott House**. The front of this house was built prior to 1838; the back of the house was added in the early 1860s. The second story and piazza were added in 1935. The surrounding gardens are said to have two *Camellia japonica* trees that are estimated to be more than 150 years old and have been featured in *Southern Living* magazine. One famous former owner of this home was Mrs. Elizabeth Ann Horry Dent, widow of Captain J. Herbert Dent, commander of the frigate *Constitution* ("Old Ironsides").

Turn right onto Wichman and travel 0.6 mile to the Little Library Park, a nice green space to stop for a rest and to enjoy downtown Walterboro. To the left of the park is the Bedon-Lucas House at 205 Church Street. Constructed in 1820, this home is under renovation now to be used as a house museum.

Just past the park, at 907 Wichman Street, is St. Judes Episcopal Church, a beautiful, tan wooden church built in 1882. It replaced an earlier structure that was destroyed by the cyclone of 1879. The stained glass windows of the church were made in Munich, Germany.

Fishburne Street to the left leads to Historic Hickory Valley, where Paul and Jacob Walter built summer homes in a hickory grove that formed the nucleus of a summer colony and began the town of Walterboro.

Continue 0.2 mile on Wichman to a stoplight. Turn right and travel 0.2 mile farther, to where the road forks. Bear to the right onto SC 64 toward Charleston. Travel 0.4 mile to a stop sign. Turn left to remain on SC 64, a dark, lazy, two-lane road lined with thick woods, fields, and pastures with grazing cows and horses.

Almost 6 miles from your last turn is Bonnie Doone Road, on your right, which leads you to Bonnie Doone Plantation. The 132-acre plantation is home to a Georgian–style mansion erected in 1931 that was featured as Rhett Butler's estate in the movie *Scarlett*. The plantation house now serves as a meeting place that offers rustic cabins on-site, picnic shelters, canoeing, fishing, nature trails, plantation gardens, and primitive camping.

Traveling past wetlands, cross Chessey Creek almost a mile past Bonnie Doone Road, and Horseshoe Creek 3 miles farther on SC 64. Continue another 2.7 miles to the old **Bethel Church** on your left (east). A historical marker to the left of the highway shows you where to stop to enjoy a walk through the mossy, overgrown cemetery.

Bethel Presbyterian Church, founded on this site in 1728 by the Reverend Archibald Stobo, served a large Presbyterian congregation here until being re-placed by Bethel Presbyterian Church in Walterboro. The church's original bell was moved to the new site. The cemetery contains the grave of Captain John Herbert Dent, a U.S. naval officer born in Maryland in 1782. Dent served as act-ing captain of the frigate *Constitution* in 1804 during the war with Tripoli and was senior officer in charge of naval affairs in Charleston during the War of 1812 against the British. He settled in Walterboro and died in 1823. His former home stands next to the Artisans Center at 418 Wichman Street in Walterboro.

Almost a mile farther down SC 64 is another historical marker noting Hayne Hall. The historical marker tells you that one mile north is the site of Hayne Hall, owned by the Hayne family during the Colonial and American Revolu-tion era. Colonel Isaac Hayne, a local planter and iron manufacturer turned Pa-triot soldier, was captured and executed by the British in 1781. His grave is in the family plot. *You may choose to turn left (east) onto Sparks Hall Road, a dirt road that's a bit rough, so take care if you decide to venture down it.*

Travel 1.5 miles farther on SC 64 to reach the western edge of Jacksonboro and the intersection with US 17.

If you are interested in visiting the short, excellently interpreted Edisto Nature Trail, an easy 1-mile loop aside the Edisto River, turn left (northeast) and travel 1 mile through town. The trailhead parking lot will be on your left (north) just before the road reaches the bridge over the Edisto River.

Turn right (southwest) onto US 17/Ace Basin Parkway. The roadside is lush and green, lined with marsh and woods. About 5 miles along US 17, you'll cross over the **Ashepoo River**, the middle waterway in the heart of the ACE Basin.

Named for the three rivers that drain the watershed—the Ashepoo, the Combahee, and the Edisto—the **ACE Basin** is home to many endangered or threatened species, including shortnose sturgeon, wood storks, loggerhead sea turtles, and southern bald eagles. From the early 1700s to the mid 1800s, the ACE Basin was home to large plantations owned by a small number of individuals who managed their wetlands primarily to grow rice. After the rice culture declined in the late 1800s, wealthy sportsmen purchased many of these plantations as hunting retreats and wildlife refuges. These owners tended this area so wisely that today much of the undeveloped, unpolluted lands provide refuge for a diverse and extremely productive population of wildlife.

The intricate network of marshes, tidal creeks, uplands, and wetlands has supported myriad plants and animals, including waterfowl, songbirds, fish, shellfish, and upland animals. The refuge lies along the Atlantic Flyway, "the highway in the sky." Vast numbers of shorebirds, neotropical songbirds, waterfowl, and birds of prey migrate here from throughout eastern North America. From late fall through early spring, the refuge is a haven for wood ducks, pintails, shovelers, mallards, and widgeons. Neotropical songbirds such as painted buntings and ruby-throated hummingbirds find haven here.

Endangered wood storks are moving north to places such as the ACE Basin to nest due to loss of habitat in more southern regions. The peregrine falcon, bald eagle, shortnose sturgeon, and alligators all thrive in the area. Wading birds such as egrets, herons, ibis, sandpipers, plovers, yellowlegs, and black-necked stilts populate the vicinity; white-tailed deer, raccoons, bobcats, river otters, gray foxes, rabbits, and squirrels roam the forests and marshlands.

Just past the bridge over the Ashepoo is Out Post Moe's ACE Basin Adventures, on your right which offers kayaking and wildlife tours throughout the Basin. At the first paved road, Clover Hill Road, you'll find the entrance to Cap'n Richards ACE Basin Escapes. Follow the arrows to his establishment.

Pass by S-15-26/Bennetts Point Road on your left (south) after a little over a mile, and continue 3 more miles to the entrance to **Donnelley Wildlife Management Area**, on your left (south). Proceed 0.6 mile down Donnelley Road to the trailhead for the 1.4-mile Backwater Trail loop on your left (east), and the headquarters and information kiosk just beyond.

Donnelley WMA is open for wildlife observation, bird-watching, photography, nature study, and hiking Monday through Saturday from 8:00 A.M. to 5:00 P.M. It is closed on Sunday, as well as from November 1 through January 20 in order to minimize disturbance to waterfowl. The Backwater Trail is open at all times.

During times that Donnelley WMA is closed, followers of this drive should simply turn southward down S-15-26/Bennetts Point, 3 miles northeast of the Donnelley WMA entrance, and head directly to Bear Island Wildlife Management Area.

The 8,000-acre Donnelley WMA, managed by the South Carolina Department of Natural Resources, is a cross section of the Lowcountry. Waterfowl, wildflowers, alligators, wild turkeys, and white-tailed deer are among the natural attractions of this outing through woodlands and along dikes that cross the old rice fields of the former St. Mary's Plantation. It encompasses a diversity of wetland and upland habitats, including managed rice fields, forested wetlands, tidal marshes, and agricultural lands. You'll find a variety of upland forest types here, including a natural stand of longleaf pines.

The area protects and enhances the diverse wetland and upland habitats for resident and migratory species of wildlife, provides quality hunting and other wildlife-related recreation opportunities, maintains and restores representative natural plant communities, and provides an area for natural-resource-related research and education programs.

Continue 2 miles southward past the kiosk and look for a nature trail sign on your right (west). Turn right and drive a few hundred yards to the beginning of the **Boynton Nature Trail**, at a parking lot beside an abandoned house.

The trail leads you to a backwater tupelo swamp that's favored by wood ducks, across rice field dikes with expansive wetland views, and through uplands filled with songbirds and forested with loblolly and spruce pines, live oaks, magnolias, hickories, ferns, red bays, holly, dogwoods, trumpet honeysuckle, yellow jessamine, pink azaleas, switch cane, and dwarf palmettos. The loop trail is 2.2 miles, but you need only to walk a few hundred feet to enjoy fascinating views of the rice fields and the tupelo swamp.

Bald eagles, turkey vultures, ospreys, wood storks, gallinules, coots, cormorants, eastern kingbirds, red-winged blackbirds, anhingas, and varieties of geese, grebes, loons, terns, vireos, ducks, sparrows, wrens, mergansers, warblers, hawks, herons, vultures, and many others make Donnelley WMA a mother lode of birds. Alligators, turtles, otters, and frogs populate the waterways, and the woods teem with deer, raccoons, turkeys, and foxes.

Donnelley Road ends at Blocker Run Road after 1.4 more miles. Turn left (east) onto Blocker Run Road and drive 2 dirt-road miles through forest punctuated by wetlands to reach S-15-26/Bennetts Point Road. Turn right (south), and head toward Bear Island and the isolated fishing village of Bennetts Point,

South Carolina's coastal outback. This winding roadway is lined with thick ancient oaks, forestland, and Ashepoo River wetlands.

After 7.5 miles, cross the Frank E. Baldwin Jr. Bridge over the Ashepoo River, where you'll have a terrific panoramic view of the river and its marshlands. A designated nature observation area is on your right once you transit the bridge, offering a closer look at the Ashepoo and its wading birds and other wildlife. Across the street is a parking area that provides one point of access for the hiking trails along the rice field dikes in **Bear Island Wildlife Management Area**.

The main entrance to Bear Island WMA is 2 miles farther southeast. Turn left (northeast) on unpaved Ti Ti Road. You'll see a kiosk on your left (north) with a map of the area. Here you'll find information about Mary's House Pond, where you can picnic or fish if you have a license.

Continue 1.5 miles northeast on Ti Ti Road, past Ashepoo and Sara Impoundments on your left (west), then turn left (east) along a rough dike-top road. After a half mile you will reach a forested hammock island with fishing holes and pleasant nature walking options.

Bear Island offers more than 20 miles of walks through mixed pine and hardwood forests, upland pines, and old rice field impoundments. Expansive views across beautiful wetlands are common, and many varieties of wildlife, especially alligators, can be seen.

Bear Island WMA features the state's largest expanse of publicly owned and easily accessible marshland. It contains about 10,500 acres of tidal marshes and freshwater marsh impoundments, with an additional 1,200 acres of maritime forests and 400 acres of tilled land. This area is excellent year-round for wildlife viewing.

There are a number of dikes, woodland paths, and dirt roads available for hiking. The dike trails are the primary attraction for hikers. One of the most pleasant outings is the 3-mile walk from Bennetts Point Road near the Ashepoo River Bridge to the dike's intersection with Ti Ti Road between Minkey Island and Upper Hog Impoundments. Giant cordgrass, blackberries, and a variety of wildflowers grow abundantly, and thick stands of cattails inhabit the shallows. Black needle rush and sawgrass can be found in the wetlands, and the island supports small forests of oaks, palmettos, pines, and wax myrtles. Wigeon grass, wild rice, and other avian food plants fill the freshwater impoundments.

Bear Island is managed for waterfowl, other migratory birds, and terrestrial wildlife. Alligators are plentiful and frequently seen, and woodlands teem with white-tailed deer, raccoons, fox squirrels, and wild turkeys. A variety of ducks visit or live here, including an introduced flock of mottled ducks. Fall and winter visitors include wigeons, teals, pintails, mallards, black, and other puddle ducks. Bald eagles, golden eagles, ospreys, great horned owls, vultures, swallows, wood storks, egrets, herons, cormorants, moorhens, rails, marsh wrens, purple martins, coots, eastern kingbirds, yellowlegs, peregrine falcons, red-tailed and red-shouldered hawks, Cooper's hawks, and great varieties of swallows and shorebirds are in residence year-round or part-time. Tens of thousands of ducks and other seasonal visitors are present in late winter.

Fishing is allowed from April through September. Nature observation is allowed Monday through Saturday from January 21 to October 31. The area is closed November 1 to January 20 and on Sundays. There is no admission fee.

Return from the rice field hammock the way you came and exit Ti Ti Road by turning left (south) back onto S-15-26/Bennetts Point Road. Drive southward for 3 miles to reach the remote fishing village of **Bennetts Point**. A small tackle and bait shop, B&B Seafood, will be on your left at the end of Bennetts Point Road, beside a boat landing on Mosquito Creek. Stop here for a view of the creek as it flows into the Ashepoo River to your right (west). Across Mosquito Creek is part of the ACE Basin National Estuarine Research Preserve. This is a good place to watch for brown pelicans, gulls, terns, horned grebes, red-breasted mergansers, and double-breasted cormorants.

Shrimp boats dock around the small residential homes and trailers scattered across the flat, marshy landscape. Commercial fishing and shrimping boats make their home here, daily following Mosquito Creek and the Ashepoo River a short distance south to St. Helena Sound and the open sea.

BENNETTS POINT TO OLD SHELDON CHURCH

Turn around and head back out on S-15-26/Bennetts Point Road, returning 14 miles northward to US 17. The last few miles on Bennetts Point Road are especially dark underneath thick oak canopies.

Turn left (southwest) onto US 17 and proceed 9 miles through verdant wetlands and forests to a bridge across the **Combahee River**, the westernmost major stream of the ACE Basin. As you cross the bridge, you leave Colleton County and enter Beaufort County. The bridge provides great north-south views of this river at a vantage point that has unusually high land on both sides. On your right, just past the bridge, is the Steel Bridge Boat Landing where picnicking and fishing are encouraged.

Turn right (north) onto S-7-33/River Road, 1.5 miles past the bridge. Drive 1.6 miles north to the entrance to the rice fields and dikes of the **Combahee Unit of the ACE Basin National Wildlife Refuge** on the right (northeast). You are welcome to walk the dikes of these wetlands that border the Combahee River, but heavy boots are probably needed on the overgrown pathways.

An easier walking option is to proceed a few yards farther along S-7-33 and look for a parking lot on the left (southeast) after the pedestrian crossing sign, almost directly across the highway from a lovely white plantation house. The parking lot sits among shade trees adjacent to a green, duckweed-covered pond and a dark and foreboding canal stream. You need only venture a few feet to reach a wooden footbridge across the canal in order to experience the splendor of this locale. The tea-black waters of the canal beautifully set off the white spider lilies overhanging it. The rice field wetlands in front of you are alive with birds, alligators, turtles, and frogs. If you want to exercise a little, continue on the trail along the dike and complete a 3-mile loop that takes you past canals, rice fields, and mixed pine/hardwood forest.

Continue northwest on S-7-33/River Road. This dark, wooded road was once dotted with the Combahee River rice plantations of eighteenth- and nineteenth-century South Carolina aristocrats. As you traverse this route, glimpses of vegetation let you know that the good life continues behind lush pastures and oak groves.

One site you can't miss is **Auldbrass Plantation**, 6 miles from your last stop, on the right (northeast). The modern, geometric brown fence catches your eye against the natural landscape and creates an interesting pattern as you drive past the plantation. This famous Frank Lloyd Wright home, built in 1939, has no right angles. It is privately owned and not open for public tours, but a number of structures, such as the caretaker's quarters, chicken run, two cottages, and the granary, can be seen from the road if you are willing to stop and peek over the chest-high fence. The orange rocks decorating the triangular entrance provide an interesting contrast to the brown fence and verdant grass behind it. The home looks as if it would be more at home in the western desert.

More segments of the Combahee Unit of the ACE Basin NWR are just past Auldbrass. Entrances to these segments begin with the second dirt road on the right (northeast) after Auldbrass; additional dirt road entrances are 0.6 mile and 1.1 miles farther up the road. Short walking trails are available at the end of each of these roads, taking visitors to the backwaters of the Combahee River. Bald cypress trees and knees, bobwhites, wild turkeys, deer, and mourning doves are among the sights.

Continue almost a mile farther northwest into Yemasee and turn left (southwest) on Railroad Avenue. Drive 0.3 mile, turn right (north), and cross the railroad tracks onto Salkehatchie Road/S-25-13.

Yemassee is a small railroad village that looks like a throwback to the 1950s. Located astride the boundary between Beaufort and Hampton Counties, the town is one of few in South Carolina that can still boast a rail passenger stop.

The community is, however, steeped in history, reaching far into South Carolina's past. It is named for one of the most powerful and extensive Native American tribes of the late seventeenth century. The Yemasee fought fiercely against European settlers in the early eighteenth century. The tribe's territory stretched along the coast from southern Georgia to the Edisto River, and its two major centers of power between the Savannah and Combahee Rivers were at Pocataligo and Coosawhatchie, nearby villages that retain those names to this day.

Toward the end of the Civil War, Sherman's army came through this area and burned most of the churches in the vicinity. A Presbyterian church that survived was used as a hospital by the Union army, and bloodstains can still be seen on the floor today.

Drive 0.3 mile on S-25-13 and turn right (northeast) on Alternate US 17. Cross the Combahee River almost 2 miles up the road, then pull over and enjoy the beauty of this wetland wonderland. The Combahee Boat Landing is one of the best roadside places to glimpse the waterway splendor of the ACE Basin.

Backtrack southwest across the bridge. You may want to turn right (north) just after recrossing the bridge to explore a short dirt road and two more short trails in the Combahee Unit of the ACE Basin NWR. A small pond, deer, alligators, and blue flag irises are among the attractions.

Old Sheldon Prince William's Parish Church

Retrace your route back into Yemassee. After you cross the railroad tracks again, however, bear right (southwest). At the stop sign, turn left onto S-7-3 toward Beaufort, and after almost 1 mile, bear left (southwest) on S-7-21/Old Sheldon Church Road.

Drive 5.5 miles and turn right (west) on Bailey Road/S-7-235. Travel a few yards along this road to glimpse some beautiful marshes, where flocks of birds, including vultures, egrets, waterfowl, and small songbirds, are frequently seen.

Return to S-7-21/Old Sheldon Church Road and turn right (southwest). On your left is your final stop, the beautiful ruins of Old Sheldon Church. This road is very dark because of the dense canopy of trees. Very little light can peek through, but when it does, the sight is one to behold. Well-outlined rays beam down through the black bark overhead. You'll see a historical marker for the church on your left (east). On your right (west), across the street from the ruins, is a tract of land preserved by the Low Country Land Trust, also worth a peek.

The ruins of **Old Sheldon Prince William's Parish Church**, first built in 1748, stand tall to this day. The church was burned in 1780 by the British, rebuilt in 1826, and burned again in 1865 by Sherman's troops. It was named for the ancestral home of the Bull family in Warwickshire, England. Annual services are still held on the second Sunday after Easter. The brick columns and fragile arches of the former church, surrounded by enormous oaks, maintain their grace and beauty in this idyllic grassy clearing amid an enchanting, dark forest. A small, shaded picnic area on the grounds provides a place to contemplate the ruins and the Lowcountry life of the nineteenth century.

Historic Beaufort and Sea Islands

BEAUFORT TO HUNTING ISLAND STATE PARK

GENERAL DESCRIPTION: This 30-mile trip begins in the historic, picturesque waterfront town of Beaufort and carries sightseers across salt marshes, creeks, and the Beaufort River to the quaint town of Port Royal, through truck farms on St. Helena Island to wild and beautiful Hunting Island State Park on the shores of the Atlantic Ocean.

SPECIAL ATTRACTIONS: Historic Beaufort, Port Royal, Beaufort River, Penn Center, St. Helena Sound, Hunting Island State Park.

LOCATION: Southern coast.

DRIVE ROUTE NUMBERS: Bay Street, New Street, Craven Street, East Street, Federal Street, Pinckney Street, King Street, Short Street, Laurens Street, Hancock Street, Prince Street, Carteret Street, Church Street, US Business 21, Meridian Road/S-7-36, Lady's Island Drive, US 21, SC 802, Old Shell Road, S-7-124/London Avenue, Sands Beach Road, Eighth Street, Paris Avenue, Eleventh Street, S-7-45/Martin Luther King Boulevard, S-7-195/Ephram Road, S-7-77/Sea Side Road, S-7-762/Hunting Island Drive, S-7-406.

TRAVEL SEASON: All year.

SERVICES: Beaufort offers plentiful hotels, motels, and other services.

See For More Information in the appendix for addresses and phone numbers of Attractions, Camping, Neat Places to Stay, Restaurants, Shops, Tours, and Nature-Based Services.

THE DRIVE

The setting for *The Big Chill* and many other movies, Beaufort is a charming old waterfront town that provides the beginning point for this 30-mile trip on South Carolina southern Sea Islands. After winding through Beaufort and the adjacent port community of Port Royal, visitors ride across salt marshes, pausing on the grounds of the historic Penn Center, symbol of African-American freedom, before continuing on to the wild beauty of Hunting Island State Park on the Atlantic Ocean, with its enchanting lighthouse.

Beaufort, the second oldest town in the state, is a lovely community on Port Royal Island beside the Beaufort River. It is blessed with a spectacular natural beauty and an exciting, turbulent history that make the area one of the most

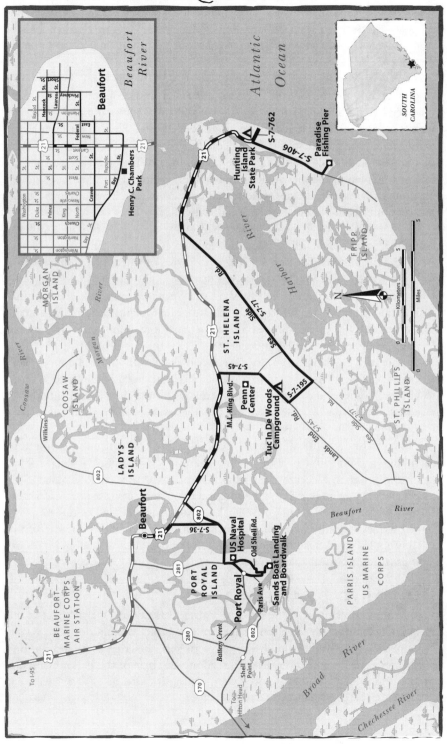

Beaufort River

Beaufort

Short St.
Pinckney St.
Hancock St.
Laurens St.
Bayard St.
Hamilton St.
East St.
Federal St.
New St.
Carteret St.
21
21
Scott St.
West St.
Republic St.
Port St.
Bay St.
Washington St.
Newcastle St.
Craven St.
Prince St.
Duke St.
King St.
North St.
Church St.
Hamilton St.
Bay St.
Wilmington St.

Henry C. Chambers Park

Atlantic Ocean

SOUTH CAROLINA

Paradise Fishing Pier
S-7-762
S-7-406

Hunting Island State Park

21

FRIPP ISLAND

MORGAN ISLAND

Morgan River

Coosaw River

COOSAW ISLAND

Wilkins

LADYS ISLAND

802

21

Harbor River

St. Helena Sound

S-7-77

ST. HELENA ISLAND

21

Sea Side Rd.

S-7-45

M.L. King Blvd.
Penn Center

Tuc In De Woods Campground
S-7-195

Sea Side Rd.

Lands End Rd.

S-7-45

ST. PHILLIPS ISLAND

N

5
5
5
Kilometers
Miles
0
0

Beaufort

21

Beaufort River

802

S-7-36

US Naval Hospital
Old Shell Rd.

281

Sands Boat Landing and Boardwalk

PORT ROYAL ISLAND

Port Royal
Paris Ave.

PARRIS ISLAND US MARINE CORPS

BEAUFORT MARINE CORPS AIR STATION

21

280

Battery Creek

802

Shell Point

To I-95

21

170

To Hilton Head

Broad River

Chechessee River

intriguing places in South Carolina. The picturesque landscape of ancient live oaks, saltwater marshes, creeks, rivers, and deep harbor waters enhances the splendor of Beaufort's antebellum homes. Centuries ago, the natural beauty made the area an attractive locale for Spanish, French, and English explorers to "conquer."

Pedro de Salaza, a Spanish explorer, visited Port Royal Island in 1514, the second landing on the North American continent by Europeans. He was soon followed by another Spaniard, Francisco Cordillo, in 1520, and then by Captain Jean Ribaut, a French Huguenot, in 1562. Ribaut attempted to establish a settlement near the present-day town of Port Royal, the first Protestant settlement in the United States, but it was soon abandoned. When Ribaut returned to France to replenish supplies, he left some soldiers behind. Frustrated, the soldiers built their own ship and attempted to sail back to France. They made it home, but only after being rescued by an English ship.

In 1566, Spaniards established a fort, San Felip, and a military port, St. Elena, considered the capital of La Florida Province for twenty-one years. Native Americans destroyed this fort, but the Spaniards remained; they built a larger fort, San Marcos, in 1587, the same year that England sent Sir Francis Drake to take the land. Drake successfully pushed the Spaniards back to St. Augustine, making room for the English to settle the area. The town of Beaufort was established in 1711 and named for one of the original lords proprietor of Carolina, Henry Somerset, Duke of Beaufort (1684–1714).

During the eighteenth century, Beaufort thrived as indigo and cotton plantation owners of St. Helena and Parris Island began to build homes here in order to visit each other and to enjoy cultural activities during the summer months. In fact, before the Civil War, Beaufort was considered the wealthiest and most aristocratic town of its size in America.

Beaufort was a political hotbed as well. The first Ordinance to Secede from the Union was drafted here at the Milton Maxey House. South Carolina seceded from the Union on December 20, 1860. Almost a year later, in November 1861, a Federal fleet circled Port Royal Sound, and the Confederates abandoned Beaufort. By December 1861, Union General Isaac Stevens occupied Beaufort's abandoned homes, turning them into hospitals and offices for the remainder of the Civil War. This saved Beaufort from being burned by Sherman's troops on his infamous march from Atlanta.

HISTORIC BEAUFORT

Begin your 2-mile drive of the historic district of Beaufort on Bay Street at the **Henry C. Chambers Waterfront Park** on the banks of the Beaufort River. Within the park, you'll find shady places to rest, a playground, and an amphitheater beneath enormous oak trees. Along the rear of the park, restaurants such as Plums and the John Cross Tavern, dating back to the 1700s, have back

View of the Beaufort River from the Henry C. Chambers Waterfront Park

porches that allow you to dine and enjoy a scenic view of the Beaufort River. Unique shops are also accessible from the park through brick alleys that lead to Bay Street and Beaufort's Visitor Center, at 1006 Bay, where visitors can find information on riverboat tours, self-guided walking tours, and nearby attractions.

Across from the park, at 801 Bay Street, is the **John Mark Verdier House Museum**. One of the few homes open to the public, this Federal-style historic home, built in the 1790s, stands out amid the hustle and bustle of Bay Street. This historic home played host to the Marquis de Lafayette in 1825 on his tour of the States, and during the Civil War served as headquarters for Union troops. Today its first floor houses the Historic Beaufort Foundation. Visitors can tour the Verdier House Museum Monday through Saturday from 11:00 A.M. to 4:00 P.M.

Head east on Bay Street, past upscale antique, jewelry, book, and clothing stores, and cross over Carteret Street. The bridge to Lady's Island is to your right. The second house on your left, at 601 Bay Street, is the **Lewis Reeve Sams House**, circa 1852. Sitting on the corner of Bay and New Streets, this white wooden home, surrounded by a meek picket fence, is most famous for the bucket brigade that saved the home from burning during the 1907 fire that destroyed many of Beaufort's homes.

Across the street from the Lewis Reeve Sams House is a shaded park on the Beaufort River and the Stephen Elliott, CSA, Memorial. Old oaks canopy com-

Historic Beaufort and Sea Islands   **217**

fortable benches and a cannon that recognizes Brigadier General Stephen Elliott for his bravery and leadership in the Confederate defense of Beaufort.

Continue by turning left (north) onto New Street. At the next block, on the corner of New and Port Republic Streets, the **Thomas Hepworth House**, the oldest home in Beaufort, is on your left. Built in 1717, this two-story putty-colored wooden house sits atop a stucco base. Like so many of the homes in this area, its yard is enclosed by a brick wall.

Continue north for another block on New Street, and take a right onto Craven Street and then an immediate left (north) onto East Street. On your right, tucked between Craven and Federal Streets, is the Joseph Johnson House, circa 1859. This natural-colored medieval-style stone and brick structure, known as **"The Castle,"** is hidden behind palmetto trees and an ivy-covered wall. Used as a hospital by Federal troops during the Civil War, the home overlooks the Beaufort River and is surrounded by colorful gardens and olive trees brought from the Mount of Olives in the Holy Land. Built on palmetto logs, with more than seventy windows and four triple chimneys, it is one of the most photographed homes in America. Remain on New Street to get the best view of the home.

At Federal Street take a right (east). You'll get a good look of the back of The Castle here. After crossing a small creek, the first house on your left is **Cassena**, at 315 Federal Street. Built in the 1800s by John Blythewood, the home's front yard is filled with camellias, magnolias, and old oak trees. The white wooden home is made brighter by Key West blue porch ceilings. Like many of the homes in Beaufort, Cassena was purchased by one of the family's slaves after the Civil War.

At 303 Federal Street, on the corner of Federal and Pinckney Streets, is the James Rhett House. Construction began on the home in 1884, with Mr. Rhett intending to build his home two rooms deep. Rhett did not anticipate the actual cost of his original design, however, and he was forced to pare down his initial plan substantially. Today the home is referred to as **"Rhett's Folly."** Its facade is graced with long glass windows and upstairs and downstairs porches. Encircled by an iron and brick gate, the house has a commanding presence.

Across the street is the William Fripp House, circa 1830. Also known as **Tidewater**, this white, two-story Federal-style home faces the Beaufort River and was built by William Fripp, owner of nine plantations.

At 501 Pinckney Street, directly in front of you, is the James Robert Verdier House, circa 1814. Called the **Marshlands**, this two-story home faces the Beaufort River and is decorated with a porch that wraps entirely around the home. Sprawling oaks fill the front and side yards.

Take a left onto Pinckney Street and continue north for one block. Turn right (east) onto King Street, the first paved road on your right, and follow it to Short Street. Here you have the best view of the Paul Hamilton House, circa 1856, also known as **The Oaks**. This beautiful home was abandoned when Union forces occupied Beaufort, and when the Hamilton family returned after the war to reclaim their home, they did not have the money needed to purchase it. Friends and family in the community helped collect the necessary funds, and the Hamiltons were able to reclaim their house. This private home is haunted by a French Huguenot ghost, who opens and closes doors, taps sleeping visitors on the shoulder during the night, and moves furniture at his whim.

Follow Short Street past The Oaks to Laurens Street. Take a right here. You'll see the back of The Oaks to your right. At the end of Laurens Street is **Tidalholm**, the summer home of Edgar Fripp, circa 1853, at 1 Laurens Street on your left. This home on the Beaufort River, which has been used in several movies, including *The Big Chill* and *The Great Santini*, is the only house in town with water on three sides and a widow's watch.

Return to Short Street and turn right. Continue north for one more block, then turn left onto Hancock Street. On your right at 207 Hancock Street is the **Elizabeth Hext House**, circa 1720, the second oldest home in Beaufort. The home's red tin roof contrasts with the whitewashed boards of the home's facade and its black shutters. A gate engulfed by ivy and confederate jasmine sits beneath gaslights that flicker even in the light of day, making for an eerie experience, especially since the ghosts of pirates are said to haunt this dwelling.

Continue west on Hancock Street past Pinckney and Hamilton Streets to East Street. Take a left on East Street, and then a quick right onto Prince Street. On the corner of Prince and New Streets, at 511 Prince Street, is the **Henry McKee House** (circa 1834). After the Civil War, Robert Smalls, a freed slave who became the first black United States congressman, purchased this home at a tax sale. The McKee family contested Smalls's ownership, and the case went all the way to the Supreme Court. Smalls prevailed, and apparently didn't harbor ill feelings. When a member of the McKee family wandered into the home, Smalls allowed her to reside here until her death. The home remained in the Smalls family until 1940.

Continue west on Prince Street to Carteret Street, a main thoroughfare. Turn left and continue south for three blocks to Craven Street. Take a right (west) onto Craven Street. Immediately, you'll see on your right the **Beaufort Arsenal Museum** at 713 Craven Street. This blond, castlelike structure, built in 1798 and rebuilt in 1852, holds many relics of nature, war, and early industry. Visitors can tour the arsenal on Monday, Tuesday, Thursday, Friday, and Saturday from 10:00 A.M. to 5:00 P.M.

On the next block is the Tabernacle Baptist Church on your right, where Robert Smalls is buried; a bronze bust of the leader greets visitors in the church's front yard. Not only was Smalls a freed slave who served as a U.S. congressman for nine years, but he also served as Captain of the *Planter* during the Civil War, as a delegate to state constitutional conventions in 1868 and 1895, and as a member of South Carolina's Senate and House of Representatives. Smalls died in 1915 and is honored at this tall, whitewashed church that has been in service since 1811.

Continue on Craven over West Street. On your right at 1009 Craven is the Rhett House Inn, a stately white mansion with first- and second-floor front porches where guests may rest in the shade of the oaks that surround the inn.

Past Newcastle Street, the Craven Inn is set off of the road at 1103 Craven Street. Delicate garden plots splash color across the inn's immaculate yard. White roses hang from the second-story wall, inviting visitors to its front door.

At the next corner, Craven ends at Church Street. Take a left here toward the Beaufort River, then another left onto Bay Street to visit Beaufort's quaint downtown. *(Turn right on Bay Street if you wish to see more magnificent, waterfront homes, such as the **William Elliott House**, a three-story pre-Revolutionary tabby house, known today as the Anchorage House. The **Leverett House**, a two-story pre-revolutionary home enclosed by a beautiful iron gate; the Thomas Fuller House, circa 1786, called the **Tabby Manse**; and the **John A. Cuthbert House**, circa 1810, are along this route.)*

Just after turning left (east) onto Bay Street, Carriage Tours ticket sales and Historic Tours Shops are on your right, at the front of the Henry C. Chambers Park. Park in the public parking area and stroll down Bay Street to experience Beaufort's downtown on foot. You have numerous places to eat, such as the Bank Waterfront Grill and Bar, housed in the old Beaufort Bank, as well as Hemingways, Luthers, Plums, Ollie's by the Bay, and Harry's in the historic John Cross Tavern. All of these waterfront eateries offer relaxing back porch dining with terrific views of the Beaufort River. Beaufort also offers a wide variety of unique clothing, jewelry, art galleries, and gift shops. Be sure to visit High Cotton, the Rhett Gallery Art and Framing, the Indigo Gallery, the Craftseller, Bay Street Trading Company, Beaufort Clothing Company, and The Picket Fence.

Exit downtown Beaufort by turning right (southeast) off of Bay Street onto Business US 21 South to cross the drawbridge that affords a terrific view of the **Beaufort River** and its lush marshlands.

PORT ROYAL

Once over the bridge, you'll be on Lady's Island. Go about a mile on US Business 21 South/Sea Island Parkway and turn right (south) on Meridian Road/S-7-36. Ride 1.5 miles where, at a major intersection, you take a right (southwest) onto Lady's Island Drive/US 21/SC 802 to visit the charming town of Port Royal, 1.5 miles away.

As you reach the highest point of the McTeer Memorial Bridge over the Beaufort River, the river and its marshlands extend as far as you can see along the horizon to your left. Beaufort can be seen to your right near a bend in the waterway. Its church steeples peek above the treetops, and a marina full of fancy yachts and sailboats bounces at the base of the bridge.

After crossing the bridge, you're back on Port Royal Island. Take a left (south) at the first intersection to continue on SC 802, which becomes Ribaut Road. Travel 0.2 mile down Ribaut Road, then turn left (south) onto Old Shell Road. The United States Naval Hospital is on your left. Here you can visit the ruins of Fort Frederick, named after the eldest son of King George II of England. Built around 1753 to replace the older Beaufort Fort (circa 1706), Fort Frederick fell to ruins twenty years later. It was then replaced by Fort Lyttleton, which is also located on the hospital grounds.

Continue over Pinckney Street on Old Shell Road, traveling through a shaded residential area for a little more than a mile. Cute old bungalows decorate this street. Old Shell Road curves to the right and intersects with London Avenue/S-7-124. Take a left on London. On your right is Live Oaks Park, a public park with a playground, tennis courts, basketball court, and a unique covered oyster shed with a fireplace and a barbecue pit. Live oaks adorn the rustic park.

Continue on London Street for six blocks. Take a left (east) onto Sands Beach Road and follow it to the Sands Boat Landing and Boardwalk at the southern tip of Port Royal Island.

The expansive boardwalk extends into the water where the Beaufort River and Battery Creek intersect. At the tip of the island, you have a fantastic view of Battery Creek and the Beaufort River. Vibrant marshlands reach out into the water. If you happen to visit when others are not around, you can enjoy the serenity of hearing only the lapping of water on the dock. This is a great place for bird viewing.

Backtrack on Sands Beach Road and take a right on London Avenue. Drive one block to Eighth Street, turn left (west), and drive past nicely decorated homes in downtown Port Royal. Eighth Street ends at Paris Avenue. The Town Hall of Port Royal is on your left at 700 Paris Avenue, along with an ornate Memorial Clock commemorating the fiftieth anniversary of V-J Day and the end of World War II.

Take a right (north) on Paris Avenue to continue through town. Turn left on 11th Street to see the Port Royal Playhouse, a century-old former church building. The whitewashed wooden church is elegantly placed among huge live oaks. Follow 11th Street over Madrid Avenue all the way to its end at Port Royal Seafood, Inc. a local seafood market, and Dockside Restaurant on the banks of Battery Creek. Step inside for fresh local seafood dinners and spectacular views of shrimp boats and shimmering Battery Creek.

Backtrack on 11th Street 0.3 mile to Paris Avenue, and turn left. Travel north on Paris Avenue for a half mile, passing small businesses and restaurants and the Port Royal Police Department and Fire Station. Paris Avenue intersects with Ribaut Road/SC 802; continue 0.8 mile to the next intersection, and turn right at the light (east) to continue on SC 802 toward US 21 and cross back over McTeer Memorial Bridge and onto Lady's Island.

If you wish to visit the U.S. Marine Base on Parris Island, turn left (west) at the intersection of Paris Avenue and SC 802. The Russell Bell Bridge connects Port Royal Island with Parris Island and the Shell Point area of Beaufort County. Lights on the bridge provide a scenic drive at night.

ST. HELENA ISLAND

Three and a half miles from Port Royal, Lady's Island Drive intersects with Sea Island Parkway/US 21. Take a right (southeast) to travel on US 21/Sea Island Parkway. St. Helena Island is 2.5 miles ahead, on the other side of Cowan Creek.

First called Santa Elena by the Spanish, this small rural island was later named **St. Helena** by the English. In the eighteenth century, plantation owners became wealthy growing Sea Island cotton here. Slaves greatly outnumbered plantation owners and their families. When Union soldiers captured St. Helena and other Sea Islands, the slaves remained and later were given land of their own.

Today on St. Helena, you'll find quaint stores and a sense of the old South. Change comes slowly on this agricultural island. The roads are lined with Spanish-moss-draped oak trees, old cottages, and sandy soils that support fields of corn and tomatoes.

Fruit stands dapple the highway with Sea Island produce along the drive toward the Frogmore community. An inviting old antique/junk shop, Peddlers Porch, sits to the right of the highway. A half mile farther on your right is the Gullah Welcome Center. Slow down and notice the curious stores along both sides of the road. Frogmore Frolics and What's In Store sell one-of-a-kind original art pieces, crafts, and gifts. The No Pork Cafe offers delicious fresh fruit drinks and authentic vegetarian meals, and houses the Afrikan Universal Library Museum, where you can browse an array of texts on African culture. Across the street the Sandwich Shoppe offers fresh deli sandwiches. The Royal Frogmore Inn and Restaurant, where you can enjoy blues and jazz music in the evenings, is also on your left. Continue south past Gullah Grub to 869 Sea Island Parkway. Here at the Ibile Indigo House you can meet an artist who works solely with indigo, creating beautiful crafts and clothes. The Red Piano Gallery Too beckons visitors at 870 Sea Island Parkway with its displays of some of the South's most important collections of folk art.

To visit the **Penn Center**, one of the nation's most historically significant African-American educational and cultural institutions, take a right (west) on S-7-45/Martin Luther King Boulevard and drive a half mile to the center.

During the Civil War, Union troops occupied the Sea Islands and made concerted efforts not only to free slaves, but to educate them as well. The Penn Center was established in 1862 by the Quaker Freedman's Society of Pennsylvania in an effort, sometimes called the Port Royal Experiment, to bring formal education to freed slaves. Laura Towne and Ellen Murray, teachers from Pennsylvania, helped found Penn Center and devoted forty years of their lives to educating the Sea Islands' freed slaves.

Classes were first held in a single room on Oaks Plantation, but the instruction was later relocated to the **Brick Baptist Church**, which is on your left, directly across from the Penn Center grounds. In 1864, a prefabricated building was sent from Pennsylvania and placed on a fifty-acre tract of land across from the church. The building erected on this land became the first Penn School building. Today there are nineteen buildings at the Penn School National Historic Landmark.

In the early 1900s, the school adopted the Tuskegee Curriculum, which emphasized agricultural and home economics classes. It worked under this curriculum until the center was absorbed into the South Carolina public school system in 1948. The last class was graduated in 1953. In spite of the center closing as a school, it continued to play a central role in the Sea Island community. Dr. Martin Luther King Jr. and the Southern Christian Leadership Conference held annual civil rights movement meetings here. Today the school continues to work on community-based projects, such as bringing public water to the islands, helping farmers to buy and market through cooperatives, and advocating better housing and health care for low-income people.

At the center's grounds, you can visit the York W. Bailey Museum, dating back to 1862. Penn School students built it in the Lowcountry's unique tabbylike style structure with oyster shells, concrete, and sand. The museum houses artifacts, photographs, personal and institutional papers, and published materials, as well as video- and audiotapes that interpret the history of Penn Center, the Gullah culture, and the African-American connection between West Africa and the Sea Islands.

Another interesting building you might want to explore is **Darrah Hall**, the oldest building on the Penn Center campus, built as a memorial to Sophia Towne Darrah. Originally located on "the green" at the intersection of US 21 and Lands End Road, Darrah Hall was moved to the center of Penn's campus in 1940. It was first used as a gymnasium and later as a tomato-packing house. It became the site of temperance meetings, farmer fairs, community sings, and plays. The hall's original basketball scoreboard can still be seen.

Also on the Penn Center grounds is the Laura Towne Library and Archives; the Brick Church, built by slaves in 1855; the Old Burial Ground; a kitchen; and dorm rooms. More than 20,000 people visit the Penn Center annually to learn about the history of the Gullah and Sea Island culture, participate in community programs, and attend conferences and family reunions.

The grounds are open Monday through Friday; the museum is open Tuesday through Friday from 11:00 A.M. to 4:00 P.M. and Saturday from 10:00 A.M. to 4:00 P.M.

Exit the Penn Center to your right to continue west on S-7-45/Martin Luther King Boulevard. The road forks less than a half mile from the Penn Center, where S-7-45 becomes Lands End Road. Take the right fork. Drive slowly because 0.1 mile past Penn Center on your left are the ruins of the Chapel of Ease to St. Helena Church in Beaufort, built in the 1740s.

Tuc In De Woods Campground is on your left less than a mile past the Chapel of Ease. Continue down Lands End Road, which is shaded by oak canopies, before opening up to bright fields full of tomatoes and corn.

Drive 0.7 mile farther and look for the first paved road on your left, Ephram Road/S-7-195. Turn left and travel a mile to where the road ends at Sea Side Road/S-7-77.

Take a left (east) onto S-7-77/Sea Side Road, and travel 7 miles to the junction with US 21/Sea Island Parkway South. Agricultural fields, pecan groves lined with whitewashed fences, fields of colorful wildflowers, and forestlands decorate this quiet, rural road. The homes to the right sit on Station Creek, but you can't see the creek until you pass over Club Bridge Creek and then get a good glimpse to your right.

HUNTING ISLAND

When you reach US 21/Sea Island Parkway, take a right (southeast) to visit Hunting Island State Park, 4 miles ahead.

After a mile, you'll see the Gay Fish Company's shrimp boats docked or making their way through the inlet marshlands of the Harbor River. Seagulls dip down, trying to catch stray shrimp on deck. A mile farther, you cross the Harbor River and you have a terrific view of St. Helena Sound and Harbor Island's residential development. Once you cross Harbor River on a blue drawbridge, you are on Harbor Island. Travel 2 miles on Harbor Island, enjoying beautiful views of the Harbor River and marshlands on your right.

Next you cross over Johnson Creek to reach **Hunting Island State Park**, one of the most popular state parks in South Carolina. The 5,000-acre island was so named because the land was once primarily used for hunting deer, raccoon and other small game, and waterfowl.

At Hunting Island State Park, you can enjoy 3 miles of beach, maritime forest, and saltwater marshes. The park provides 200 campsites, 15 completely supplied cabins, picnic shelters, and a visitor center and park store that provide educational programs and nature walks year-round. Visitors can fish in a lagoon for whiting, spot, trout, bass, and drum, or, at the southern end of the island, dangle lines from the Paradise Fishing Pier.

Nature trails take you throughout this barrier island. A 1-mile nature trail leads from the park's lighthouse, and a 4-mile hiking trail guides you throughout the island's pristine habitats, the best-developed slash pine–palmetto forest in the state. White-tailed deer and raccoons find refuge on this barrier island, as well as more than 125 species of birds, including herons, gulls, terns, and egrets.

Visitors also have terrific shelling opportunities at Hunting Island Beach. Clam shells, Atlantic cockles, angel wings, sand dollars, and sea horses abound. Unlike many of the state's barrier islands, Hunting Island still appears much as it did to Europeans when they arrived in America. Unfortunately, the beach is

Hunting Island Beach

quickly eroding. Between 1830 and 1930, erosion took 1.3 miles from the island. The island has eroded at an average annual rate of 25 feet on the northern tip and 10 feet on the central beach. The presence of a mature forest at the edge of the shore is clear evidence that the sea is rapidly reclaiming the land.

Just after you cross the bridge, Campground Road on your left is the first entrance road to the park. Turn here to reach one of the park's campgrounds. To visit one of the most famous sites of Hunting Island, its lighthouse, continue south for 1.2 miles until you see the green sign noting the left turn to the park office, beach access, and lighthouse. Turn left into the park on S-7-762/Hunting Island Drive. Follow the dark, winding road for 1 mile through thick woods of palms, palmettos, pines, and oaks; the park's visitor center is on your right. Continue left at North Beach Road to visit the 1875 lighthouse. This National Historic Landmark is enjoyed by guests who climb to the top for panoramic views of Hunting Island.

The first lighthouse on the island was a brick structure built in 1859. That tower was destroyed during the Civil War. A new lighthouse, made of cast iron and designed to be moved if necessary, was constructed in 1875. The bottom two-thirds of this conical, 136-foot lighthouse is painted white; its top is black.

Historic Beaufort and Sea Islands

In 1889, the lighthouse was relocated 1.25 miles southeast of the first location because of erosion, and by 1890 the keeper's dwelling, oil house, and other buildings were also moved to the new lighthouse site. A dock and tram road were built to transport oil to the lighthouse. Two other original structures, the oil house and the cistern, remain on-site. Both are listed on the National Register of Historic Places.

Hunting Island Lighthouse

After you have toured the lighthouse complex and walked on the beach, with its tall palmetto trees bending over the short stretch of sand, head back out on S-7-762/Hunting Island Drive and turn left (south) on S-7-406. A marsh boardwalk is on your right almost 2 miles from Hunting Island Drive, offering a nice parking area and a boardwalk that extends far into Johnson Creek and its hammock islands. This is a good place for wildlife viewing.

The end of Hunting Island is a half mile past the marsh boardwalk. Turn left to visit the nature center and fishing pier, just before the bridge to Fripp Island, a private, gated community. On your right is Russ Point Road, which leads to Russ Point Boat Landing.

The nature center features live native snakes and turtles, a small saltwater aquarium, daily programs, and sea turtle exhibits. The center is open daily from 9:00 A.M. to 5:00 P.M. Paradise Fishing Pier extends 1,120 feet into Fripp Inlet, providing a terrific place for fishing and unobstructed views of the inlet and the great Atlantic Ocean beyond. A nominal fee is required to access the nature center and the fishing pier.

Hunting Island Park is open daily during standard time from 6:00 A.M. to 6:00 P.M. During daylight saving time, the park is open daily from 6:00 A.M. to 9:00 P.M.

Lower savannah River Valley

ESTILL TO HILTON HEAD ISLAND

GENERAL DESCRIPTION: Beginning in the rural town of Estill and ending at the edge of the popular seaside resort of Hilton Head Island, this 97-mile drive in the Lower Savannah River Valley takes visitors through remote communities, old plantation lands, and a variety of low-lying habitats full of fascinating vegetation and wildlife.

SPECIAL ATTRACTIONS: Webb Wildlife Center, Tillman Sand Ridge Heritage Preserve, Purrysburgh Monument, Savannah National Wildlife Refuge, Bluffton, Pinckney Island National Wildlife Refuge.

LOCATION: Southern coast.

DRIVE ROUTE NUMBERS: US 321/East Railroad Avenue, S-25-20/Augusta Stage Coach Road, S-27-119, S-27-31, S-27-34,

SC 46, US 17, SC 170, Laurel Hill Wildlife Drive, May River Road, S-07-66/Boundary Street, Water Street, S-07-11/Calhoun Street, US 278, S-07-744/Sawmill Creek Road.

TRAVEL SEASON: All year. Winters are mild, and early spring and late fall are delightful. Summers can be a bit hot and humid.

SERVICES: Hotels, motels, and other services are abundant in Hardeeville, Bluffton, Hilton Head, and Beaufort.

See For More Information in the appendix for addresses and phone numbers of Attractions, Camping, Neat Places to Stay, Restaurants, Shops, Tours, and Nature-Based Services.

THE DRIVE

This tour of low-lying country habitats provides a peek at areas near the Hilton Head Island resort community that are seldom seen by most of the millions who visit the area each year. It begins well off the beaten path, in the small town of Estill, and takes visitors into the heart of that part of the Lowcountry where nature still reigns. Wetlands and forests dominate the drive, which passes through three protected state wildlife areas, two national wildlife refuges, one state park, and several small towns.

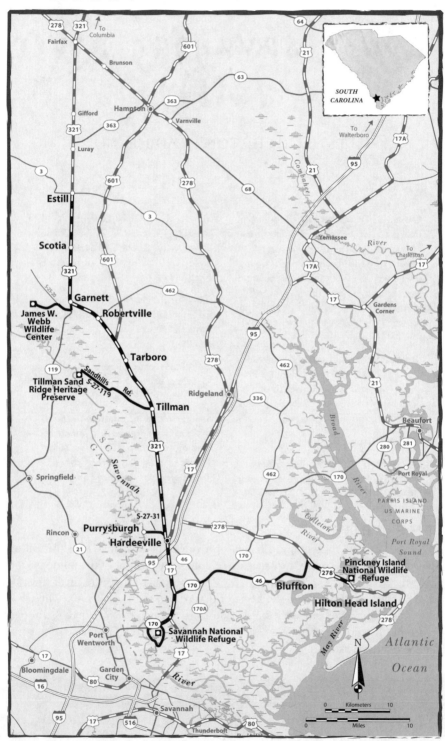

ESTILL TO WEBB WILDLIFE CENTER

Begin this drive on US 321/East Railroad Avenue at the corner of Third Street West, in the heart of **Estill**, a small, rural railroad town tucked into the western portion of Hampton County.

Estill, founded by William Caryler Johnson Jr., began as the small community of Lawtonville on land that Johnson deeded to the railroad. Incorporated in 1905, the town was named after the Southbound Holding Company's president, Colonel James Holbrook Estill. The town, which faces the railroad along US 321, remains quaint today. Only two blocks of downtown, gas stations, and a few empty storefronts line the highway, typical of many rural towns throughout the state. Such towns flourished in the days when train travel was popular.

Head south on US 321 into the countryside of **Hampton County**, South Carolina's watermelon capital and proud possessor of the state's largest white-tailed deer population and its longest hunting season. Change comes slowly here, and the county continues to reflect the landscapes and lifestyle of the rural Low-country. Named for Wade Hampton, a confederate general and governor of South Carolina, Hampton County was formed in 1878 shortly after Wade Hampton became governor.

This Lowcountry county of sandy bluffs, freshwater lakes, and the salty Savannah River is a haven for wildlife. Migratory songbirds, shorebirds, water-fowl, and reptiles find refuge in the old plantation rice fields, swamps, and pine forests, and native flora, such as the sweet magnolia, thick Spanish moss, and vi-brant resurrection ferns that adorn ancient, sprawling live oaks, decorate this lovely drive.

Continue through tiny Scotia, 5 miles from Estill, and on to Garnett, 5 more miles down US 321. In Garnett, bear right (south) on SC 119, travel less than 0.1 mile, and turn right (west) onto S-25-20/Augusta Stage Coach Road. Travel 2.8 miles and look for a large brick sign for the Webb Wildlife Center on your left. Turn left (west) onto this dirt road, and travel about 1.4 miles to the Bel-mont Lodge, a green plantation home on the right, and South Carolina Depart-ment of Natural Resources (DNR) offices and an education center.

The 5,866-acre **Webb Wildlife Center** is operated by DNR as a management and research facility designed to demonstrate multiple-use wildlife and timber management. It occupies land granted by the King of England to John Tison in 1737, who then turned the land into a working plantation. The Tison family held onto the land for nearly 150 years. Around 1882, John King Garnett constructed the present lodge, now named for the Belmonts, a New York family of bankers and horse racing enthusiasts who acquired the plantation in 1890.

The Webb Center offers terrific fishing for bass, bream, crappie, and catfish, hunting of deer, turkey, and quail, canoeing down black-water streams, and hik-ing through pine forests and cypress swamps on shady nature trails, as well as bird and wildlife viewing.

Visitors can wind through the thick woods on sandy roads. At the Belmont Lodge area, take a left or right to ride through the center's grounds. To your left is the Palachucholo Wildlife Management Area and Camping Station. The United States Army Corps of Engineers and the South Carolina Department of Natural Resources manage this densely wooded area. An interesting old house that now serves as a check station is just off of the road, as is the home for the on-site manager. Directly in front of you is the road to the Webb lakes; to the right is a road that will take you through the woods (approximately 2 miles) back to S-25-20/Stage Coach Road at a point slightly north of the main entrance.

Bald cypresses, water tupelos, laurel oaks, overcup oaks, willow oaks, white oaks, sycamores, ashes, hackberries, elms, river birches, hickories, poplars, black gums, longleaf pines, slash pines, loblolly pines, pond pines, willow oaks, red oaks, live oaks, elm maples, and sweet gums thrive in the swamp-hardwood floodplain and surrounding flat terrain. The forest provides a home for white-tailed deer, gray fox squirrels, flying squirrels, bobcats, river otters, raccoons, beavers, feral hogs, gray foxes, red foxes and opossums. Numerous reptiles such as alligators, turtles, rattlesnakes, toads, and frogs are found here too.

Game birds, birds of prey, wading birds, and waterfowl abound, including such species as wild turkey, bobwhite quail, mourning dove, woodcock, Wilson's snipe, osprey, red-tailed hawk, red-shouldered hawk, marsh hawk, kestrel, bald eagle, broad-winged hawk, Cooper's hawk, sharp-shinned hawk, great blue heron, little blue heron, green heron, great egret, cattle egret, white ibis, wood stork, wood duck, mallard, ring-necked duck, merganser, coot, and blue-winged teal.

Bird-voiced tree frogs, swallow-tailed kites, and red-cockaded woodpeckers are rare and endangered species that find a safe haven here. Protected rare plants at the Webb Center are the woolly dutchman's pipe, Chapman's sedge, green-fly orchid, silverbell, Virginia bunchflower, wild coco, long-horn orchid, and the hooded pitcher plant.

WEBB WILDLIFE CENTER TO TILLMAN SAND RIDGE HERITAGE PRESERVE

Whether you exit the Webb Wildlife Center on the main entrance road or on the side road slightly north of the entrance, turn right (southeast) on S-25-20/Augusta Stage Coach Road. Backtrack to Garnett, 2.8 miles ahead, cross over SC 119, and take a right at the second stop sign to continue your ride southward on US 321.

You enter **Jasper County**, named for Revolutionary War hero Sergeant William Jasper, a mile from Garnett. Steeped in Revolutionary and Civil War history, Jasper County was the site of colonial-era battles and a Civil War confrontation during which Union troops trampled the Confederates after their seizure of Savannah. It was home to the Yemassee and Coosaw Indians until colonial times, when a Swiss-German settlement, Purrysburgh, sprang up on the

Savannah River. Settlers built extensive rice plantations on the river, some of which are now part of the Savannah River National Wildlife Refuge.

Comprising 622 square miles, Jasper, perhaps the state's most rural county, is home to numerous hunting clubs and plantation grounds full of freshwater and saltwater lakes and streams, all of which foster abundant wildlife. Species range from ducks and marsh hens to deer, quail, and boar, making this area a sportsman's paradise.

Three miles from Garnett, you pass over a swamp and then enter Robertville, a crossroads town marked only by a few homes, a gas station, and the **Robertville Baptist Church**. The church, to the right of the highway, was constructed in 1848 as an Episcopal church in nearby Gillisonville. During the Civil War, members of the church believed Union troops were coming, so they dismantled the building, numbered the boards, and hid them in the woods until they were ready to put the church back together. Robertville did fall prey to Sherman's army, and the entire town was burned in 1865. The church was erected here by Black Swamp Baptists in 1871.

A historical marker on the church grounds describes the town's namesake, Henry Martyn Robert (1837–1923), a military engineer and 1857 graduate of West Point who is best known for his manual on parliamentary law, *The Pocket Manual of Rules of Order for Deliberative Assemblies* (1876). A revision appeared in 1915 as *Robert's Rules of Order*.

Leaving Robertville, continue south on US 321, passing through Tarboro after 5 miles. At Garbade's General Store, the only commerce in this sleepy town, you can pick up film, hunting licenses, and supplies, as well as snacks for your ride.

Continue 5 more miles to Tillman, then drive another half mile and turn right (west) on S-27-119/Sandhills Road toward the **Tillman Sand Ridge Heritage Preserve**. After 4.8 miles, be sure to stay to the right at the fork in the road to remain on S-27-119; B and C Boat Landing is to your left on S-27-201.

Six miles from US 321, you'll see the entrance to the preserve on your left, marked by a large green sign. The preserve is open from daylight to dusk, and you may walk the trails, or drive on them if you are in a four-wheel-drive vehicle.

The 953-acre tract has more than a half mile of frontage on the Savannah River. The preserve protects South Carolina's most endangered reptile, the gopher tortoise, and several species of rare plants that inhabit a 300-acre sand ridge portion of the property. The best time to visit is in spring, when the tortoises emerge from their burrows.

The Tillman Sand Ridge Heritage Preserve is composed primarily of two habitat types: xeric sand ridges and mixed bottomland hardwood/cypress swamp. The sandy ridges provide a home to the large, land-dwelling gopher tortoise and several rare plant species such as the gopher apple, southern twayblade, and soft-haired coneflower. The burrows these tortoises make can be 30 feet long and 15 feet deep, providing homes to more than one hundred other species, including the gopher frog. Slash pines and some longleaf pines make up the forest here, and a mixed bottomland hardwood/cypress swamp lies next to the Savannah River. Numerous tree species grow here, including bald cypress, tupelo gum, red maple, water oak, and water hickory; a number of very large cypress trees are scattered in the swamp.

Habitats from the sand ridge to the Savannah River support a wide variety of birds. You might see prothonotary warblers, painted buntings, pileated and hairy woodpeckers, vieros, and blue grosbeaks. If you are lucky (or maybe unlucky, depending on your perspective), you might come across an eastern diamondback rattlesnake.

TILLMAN SAND RIDGE HERITAGE PRESERVE TO SAVANNAH NATIONAL WILDLIFE REFUGE

Exit the Tillman Sand Ridge Heritage Preserve right (east) onto S-27-119, and backtrack 6 miles to US 321 in Tillman. Take a right (south) on US 321 toward Hardeeville, 13 miles ahead. This is a lovely drive through forested wetlands, swamps, and pinelands offset by a blanket of ferns that glow an incandescent green.

As you come upon the outskirts of Hardeeville, slow down and bear right to remain on US 321 when the road forks as SC 46 goes off to the left. Turn right (west) on S-27-31/Church Road, the first paved road after the fork, and visit the community of Purrysburgh. A brown sign SAVANNAH RIVER ACCESS marks the turn. Purrysburgh was the first settlement in the area, antedating Hardeeville by more than a century. To visit the cross monument that was erected in the 1940s, drive 2.2 miles to the end of the road, take a right on S-27-34 and travel 0.6 mile to a historical marker to the left of the road. Turn left onto a dirt road just before the marker and pass under huge oak trees as you drive a few tenths of a mile to the Savannah River. You'll see the stone cross that commemorates the site of the Purrysburgh settlement of Swiss and Huguenots in 1733.

Backtrack to S-27-34, turn right, and travel 0.6 mile. Take a left onto S-27-31/Church Road. If you were to continue past Church Road, you'd reach Millstone Landing a few tenths of a mile ahead on your right, the site of the annual Catfish Festival and Boat Races.

Drive back east on S-27-31/Church Road for 2.2 miles. At the stop sign, cross over US 321 and merge onto SC 46 toward the town of Hardeeville. Cross over US 17 after 0.3 mile, and continue 0.2 mile to Hardeeville's modest city hall and the Argent Train Engine No. 7, built by the H. K. Porter Company in 1910. Walk completely around the black engine, which is protected by a shed cover, to get a close look at its unique design.

Continue 0.1 mile on SC 46 to the antebellum Hardeeville Methodist Church on your left. Hardeeville somehow survived Sherman's fires in 1865, and the bell in the church towers is said to have been taken from the last slave ship to sail up the Savannah River.

Turn around at the church and drive 0.3 mile back to US 17. At the lighted intersection, turn left (south) onto US 17 and travel past a commercial area near the I–95/US 17 intersection where numerous fast-food restaurants, hotels, motels, and gas stations line the highway. Cross over I–95, remaining on US 17 south for 6 miles, then bear to the right (west) onto SC 170 to enter the **Savannah National Wildlife Refuge**.

Drive 3 miles to the left turn onto Laurel Hill Wildlife Drive. You can drive a 4-mile loop through the 26,295-acre preserve. Once a community of rice plantations, it's now a sanctuary for migratory birds, waterfowl, and innumerable species of wildlife. The driving tour takes you through managed freshwater pools and hardwood hammocks.

The refuge consists of freshwater marshes, tidal rivers and creeks, and bottomland hardwoods. The 3,000 acres of freshwater impoundments managed for migratory waterfowl were formerly the rice fields of plantations dating back to the mid- or late-1700s. Many of the dikes that enclose the pools were originally built with slave labor and Irish immigrant help. Thirty-six miles of dikes are open for foot travel during daylight hours, providing excellent observation opportunities for alligators, birds, and fascinating vegetation. Half of the refuge is bottomland, composed primarily of cypress, gum, and maple species.

Savannah River National Wildlife Refuge

Dozens of miles of river, streams, and creeks wind their way through the refuge boundaries, supporting habitats of bottomland hardwoods and paludal, estuarine, and tidal freshwater wetlands. Upland hardwoods border the eastern boundary.

Waterfowl, most abundant from November to February, include ducks, geese, wading birds, shorebirds, and several endangered and/or threatened species, such as bald eagles, wood storks, manatees, and the shortnose sturgeon. Wood ducks, great horned owls, bald eagles, ospreys, and swallow-tailed kites find year-round refuge here, as do alligators and other reptiles.

Once you begin the drive from the parking area off of SC 170, you cannot turn around, so be sure to stop at the rest rooms to the right, and at the kiosk loaded with pamphlets that describe the area and the wildlife you might see here. The drive through the refuge is slow and meandering, providing excellent opportunities to see interesting wildlife and plants.

You may walk through the refuge on designated trails open from November 1 to March 15. Fishing is permitted in the freshwater pools from March 15 to October 25, and hunts are administered for deer, turkey, feral hogs, and squirrels during fall and winter. The refuge is open from 7:00 A.M. to 8:00 P.M., and no admission fee is required.

SAVANNAH NATIONAL WILDLIFE REFUGE TO PINCKNEY ISLAND NATIONAL WILDLIFE REFUGE

When you complete the Savannah National Wildlife Refuge loop, take a right (east) on SC 170, reaching US 17 after a mile. Continue straight (north) on US 17/SC 170 and follow the signs to Hilton Head.

After 2 miles, turn to the right to stay on SC 170 east toward Hilton Head. In 0.7 mile, the road forks; bear to the right, now following the signs to Bluffton, 14 miles ahead. You'll reach a stop sign 3.2 miles farther, where you turn left onto SC 46 toward Bluffton. Cross the New River and enter Beaufort County after another 0.7 mile. About 2 miles farther, continue traveling straight to stay on SC 46, as SC 170 forks left. Bluffton is 7 miles ahead on SC 46.

Settled in 1825 as a summer resort for rice and cotton planters, **Bluffton** is situated on a bluff overlooking the May River. The town provided a refuge from the harsh plantation environment and diseases such as yellow fever, and it became a commercial center for isolated plantations in the vicinity. Ten antebellum homes and a number of other nineteenth-century buildings remain today.

Bluffton was once a hotbed for political rhetoric. In 1844, cries of secession were first given voice here, and a debate spawned the Bluffton Movement in response to the federal tariff. The town was abandoned during the Civil War when Union forces occupied Hilton Head. Bluffton was pillaged and partially burned.

Around the turn of the twentieth century, Bluffton began to grow. With the construction in 1962 of the Talmadge Bridge that connects Savannah to South

Church of the Cross

Carolina via US 17, commercial trade by water ended, changing Bluffton forever. Trading was over, and the town became a summer resort again.

When you enter Bluffton, SC 46 becomes May River Road. On your way into town you'll pass unique antique shops, gardening centers, and lively restaurants like Pepper's Porch. At the first stop sign, take a right (south) on S-07-66/Boundary Street to pass cute bungalows and visit the historic district of Bluffton. After 0.4 mile, take a right (west) on Water Street, which intersects with S-07-11/Calhoun Street. Directly in front of you is the Episcopal Church, **Church of the Cross**, established in 1767. Built in 1854, the church is the most historic structure in Bluffton. It was designed by a French architect, and constructed of black cypress. A fan motif of palmetto fronds is found over the windows, and a birdhouse on the grounds resembles the church. Park here and walk around on the grounds, where you'll have spectacular views of the May River.

From the church, turn right and head north along S-07-11/Calhoun Street until it intersects with SC 46 after seven blocks. Take a right (east) and then an immediate left (north) at a stop sign to remain on SC 46. Travel 2 miles north on SC 46/Bluffton Road, then merge to your right onto US 278 east toward Hilton Head Island. The Island Visitors Center is immediately on your right. Stop here for lodging and visitor information.

After 1.5 miles, you may choose to turn left on S-07-744/Sawmill Creek Road. The turn is marked with a sign for the Waddell Mariculture Center and the 1,111-acre Victoria Bluff Wildlife Management Area bordering the Colleton River.

From the visitors center, travel 3 miles farther on US 278 and cross the bridge over the Intracoastal Waterway. Enjoy the great views of the water and of Pinckney and Hilton Head Islands straight ahead. Immediately after crossing the bridge, look for signs for **Pinckney Island National Wildlife Refuge** on your left (northeast).

Wildlife observation, hiking, and biking are permitted at the refuge. Fourteen miles of trails are open to hiking and bicycling, providing access to maritime forest, salt marsh, open fields, and freshwater ponds. No motorized vehicles are allowed north of the public parking lot.

Pinckney Island, inhabited for some 10,000 years, is now a 4,000-acre salt marsh and small island refuge. Prior to 1775, the island was known as Espalanga Lookout and then Mackey's Island. Alexander Mackey received two proprietary grants for land on this island in 1710. Charles Pinckney later owned the land and willed it in 1769 to his son Charles Coatesworth Pinckney, a successful planter who was educated in England. The younger Pinckney served in the First and Second Provincial Congresses, as a commander in the Revolution, and later in the South Carolina General Assembly. He was a signer of the United States Constitution in Philadelphia in 1787 and was a delegate to the South Carolina Constitutional Convention of 1790 in Columbia.

Charles Coatesworth Pinckney retired to this island in 1801 and began experimenting with exotic seed from all over the world. In addition to breeding sheep and raising cattle, hogs, chickens, and horses, he also maintained a nursery filled with exotic plants and a laboratory. Pinckney built a home here, but it was wiped out by a hurricane after his death, and no trace of it remains.

Pinckney Island is the largest of several islands in the refuge, and the only one open to the public. The refuge also includes Corn Island, Big and Little Harry Islands, Buzzard Island, and numerous small hammocks. The majority of the refuge consists of salt marsh and tidal creeks, but there are several other land types here, including forestland, brushland, fallow field, and freshwater ponds. These habitats support a diversity of wildlife and bird and plant life.

Birds making their homes here include white ibis, herons, and egrets. Waterfowl, shorebirds, wading birds, raptors, and neotropical migrants are commonly seen in the refuge. An active bald eagle nest is nearby, so these birds are not an uncommon sight. The refuge is open during daylight hours, usually 6:00 A.M. to 8:00 P.M.

To visit Hilton Head Island, take a left (southeast) on US 278 and continue east over the J. Wilton Graves Memorial Bridge. Hilton Head Island, a resort community, has 12 miles of beach and offers fishing, biking, boating, shopping, and horseback riding. Restaurants range from casual to fine dining, offering everything from Lowcountry seafood to high-style Italian. Although there has been much development, the island remains predominantly "green." Local ordinances prohibit buildings that are taller than the trees, and no billboards are allowed on the island. Step into the Hilton Head Visitors Center on your right just past the bridge to pick up brochures on nature-based services and other recreational activities, restaurants, inns and rental units.

For More Information

CHAPTER ONE: BLUE RIDGE MOUNTAINS

ATTRACTIONS
Andrew Pickens Ranger District
Sumter National Forest
112 Andrew Pickens Circle
Mountain Rest, SC 29664
(864) 638–9568
www.fs.fed.us/r8/fms

Bad Creek Reservoir
7812 Rochester Highway
Seneca, SC 29672
(864) 885–4600

Brasstown Creek Heritage Preserve
Buzzard Roost Heritage Preserve
South Carolina Heritage Trust Program
South Carolina Department of Natural
Resources
P.O. Box 167
Columbia, SC 29202
(803) 734–3888
www.dnr.state.sc.us

Foothills Trail Conference
P.O. Box 3041
Greenville, SC 29602
(864) 467–9537

Oconee State Park
624 State Park Road
Mountain Rest, SC 29664
(864) 638–5353
www.southcarolinaparks.com

Oconee Station State Historic Site
500 Oconee Station Road
Walhalla, SC 29691
(864) 638–0079
www.southcarolinaparks.com

Walhalla State Fish Hatchery
198 Fish Hatchery Road
Mountain Rest, SC 29664
(864) 638–2866
www.fs.fed.us/r8/fms

CAMPING
Chau Ram County Park
1220 Chau Ram Park Road
Westminster, SC 29693
(864) 638–4212

Cherry Hill Recreation Area
Andrew Pickens Ranger District
Sumter National Forest
112 Andrew Pickens Circle
Mountain Rest, SC 29664
(864) 638–9568
www.fs.fed.us/r8/fms

Devils Fork State Park
161 Holcombe Circle
Salem, SC 29676
(864) 944–2639
www.southcarolinaparks.com

Keowee-Towaway State Natural Area
108 Residence Drive
Sunset, SC 29685
(864) 868–2605
www.southcarolinaparks.com

Mile Creek County Park
757 Keowee Baptist Church Road
Six Mile, SC 29682
(864) 868–2196

Oconee State Park
624 State Park Road
Mountain Rest, SC 29664
(864) 638–5353
www.southcarolinaparks.com

Table Rock State Park
158 East Ellison Lane
Pickens, SC 29671
(864) 878–9813
www.southcarolinaparks.com

NEAT PLACES TO STAY
Chauga River House Bed and Breakfast
1099 Cobb's Bridge Road
Long Creek, SC 29658
(864) 647–9587 or (800) 451–9972

www.jus4funusa.com/sc/bedandbreakfasts.
html

Devils Fork State Park
161 Holcombe Circle
Salem, SC 29676
(864) 944–2639
www.southcarolinaparks.com

Keowee-Towaway State Natural Area
108 Residence Drive
Sunset, SC 29685
(864) 868–2605
www.southcarolinaparks.com

Liberty Hall Inn
621 South Mechanic Street
Pendleton, SC 29670
(864) 646–7500 or (800) 643–7944
www.bbonline.com/sc/liberty

Magnolia Manor Bed and Breakfast
207 Westminster Highway (SC 183)
Westminster, SC 29693
(864) 647–8559
www.bbonline.com/sc/magnoliamanor

Oconee State Park
624 State Park Road
Mountain Rest, SC 29664
(864) 638–5353
www.southcarolinaparks.com

Rocky Retreat Bed and Breakfast
1000 Milwee Creek Road
Pendleton, SC 29670
(864) 225–3494
www.bbonline.com/sc/rockyretreat/

The Schell Haus B&B
117 Hiawatha Trail
Pickens, SC 29671
(864) 878–0078
schellhs@bellsouth.net
www.schellhaus.com

Sunrise Farm Bed and Breakfast
325 Sunrise Drive
Salem, SC 29676
(864) 944–0121
sfbb@bellsouth.net

Table Rock State Park
158 East Ellison
Pickens, SC 29671
(864) 878–9813
www.southcarolinaparks.com

Wildwater Cabins
1251 Academy Road
Long Creek, SC 29658
(864) 647–9587
www.wildwaterrafting.com

RESTAURANTS AND SHOPS
Antiques Etc.
120 East Main Street
Walhalla, SC 29691
(864) 638–8777

The Apple Bin
122 East Main Street
Walhalla, SC 29691
(864) 718–7324

Candlelight Antiques
124 East Main Street
Walhalla, SC 29691
(864) 638–7346

Especially For You
124-B East Main Street
Walhalla, SC 29691
(864) 718–9300

Farm House Gallery
124-F East Main Street
Walhalla, SC 29691
(864) 718–7171

Foothills Antique Mall
112 West Main Street
Walhalla, SC 29691
(864) 638–0459
antiquesleuth@mindspring.com

Hidden Treasures
208 East Main Street
Walhalla, SC 29691
(864) 638–0850

Joanne's Sweet Shoppe and Cafe
107 East Main Street
Walhalla, SC 29691
(864) 638–0038

The Steak House Cafeteria
316 East Main Street
Walhalla, SC 29691
(864) 638–3311

Warther's Originals
308 East Main Street
Walhalla, SC 29691
(864) 638–0200
members.aol.com/warthersor/

TOURS AND NATURE-BASED SERVICES
Grady's Great Outdoors
3440 Clemson Boulevard
Anderson, SC 29621
(864) 226–5283
www.gradysoutdoors.com

Nantahala Outdoor Center
851-A Chattooga Ridge Road
Mountain Rest, SC 29664
(800) 232–7238
www.nocweb.com

Wildwater Ltd.
P.O. Box 309
Long Creek, SC 29658
(800) 451–9972
www.wildwaterrafting.com

CHAPTER TWO: MOUNTAIN BRIDGE NATURAL AREA

ATTRACTIONS
Andrew Pickens Ranger District
Sumter National Forest
112 Andrew Pickens Circle
Mountain Rest, SC 29664
(864) 638–9568
www.fs.fed.us/r8/fms

Caesars Head State Park
8155 Greer Highway
Cleveland, SC 29635
(864) 836–6115
www.southcarolinaparks.com

Oconee Station State Historic Site
500 Oconee Station Road
Walhalla, SC 29691
(864) 638–0079
www.southcarolinaparks.com

Paris Mountain State Park
2401 State Park Road
Greenville, SC 29609
(864) 244–5565
www.southcarolinaparks.com

Pickens County Museum of Art and History
307 Johnson Street
Pickens, SC 29671
(864) 898–5963
picmus@co.pickens.sc.us

Pretty Place
Camp Greenville YMCA
P.O. Box 390
Cedar Mountain, NC 28718
(864) 836–3291
www.campgreenville.com

CAMPING
Caesars Head State Park
8155 Geer Highway
Cleveland, SC 29635
(864) 836–6115
www.southcarolinaparks.com

Jones Gap State Park
303 Jones Gap Road
Marietta, SC 29661
(864) 836–3647
www.southcarolinaparks.com

Keowee-Toxaway State Natural Area
108 Residence Drive
Sunset, SC 29685
(864) 868–2605
www.southcarolinaparks.com

Mile Creek County Park
757 Keowee Baptist Church Road
Six Mile, SC 29682
(864) 868–2196
(open March to October)

Table Rock State Park
158 East Ellison Lane
Pickens, SC 29671
(864) 878–9813
www.southcarolinaparks.com

Neat Places to Stay

Foxfire Mountain Cabins
P.O. Box 578
Cedar Mountain, NC 28718
www.foxfiremtcabins.com

Pettigru Place Bed and Breakfast
302 Pettigru Street
Greenville, SC 29601
(864) 242–4529 or (877) 362–4644
info@pettigruplace.com
www.pettigruplace.com

The Schell Haus B&B
117 Hiawatha Trail
Pickens, SC 29671
(864) 878–0078
schellhs@bellsouth.net
www.schellhaus.com

The Season Cabin Rentals
Hank or Debbie Byrd
2044 Table Rock Road
Pickens, SC 29671
(864) 878–4894
www.theseasoncabins.com

Sunrise Farm Bed and Breakfast
325 Sunrise Drive
Salem, SC 29676
(864) 944–0121
sfbb@bellsouth.net
www.bbonline.com/sc/sunrise

Restaurants and Shops

Aunt Sue's Country Corner Restaurant
107 A Country Creek Drive
Pickens, SC 29671
(864) 878–4366 or 878–5020
www.auntsues.com
(open April to November)

Mountain House Restaurant
US 276
Cleveland, SC 29635
(864) 836–7330
(open Friday and Saturday, April to November)

Perdue's Mountain Fruit Farm
302 Sassafras Drive
Taylors, SC 29687
(864) 244–5809 or 895–5002

Tours and Nature-Based Services

Grady's Great Outdoors
3440 Clemson Boulevard
Anderson, SC 29621
(864) 226–5283
www.gradysoutdoors.com

Greenville Rocks and Ropes
218 Pendleton Street
Greenville, SC 29601
(864) 271–9557
www.rocksandropes.net

Nantahala Outdoor Center
Chattooga Outpost
851-A Chattooga Ridge Road
Mountain Rest, SC 29664
(800) 232–7238
www.noc.com

Wildwater Ltd.
1251 Academy Road
Long Creek, SC 29658
(800) 457–9587
www.wildwaterrafting.com

CHAPTER THREE: CHEROKEE FOOTHILLS SCENIC HIGHWAY

Attractions

Cowpens National Battlefield
National Park Service
U.S. Department of the Interior
P.O. Box 308
Chesnee, SC 29328
(864) 461–2828
www.nps.gov/cowp

Eastatoe Creek Heritage Preserve
South Carolina Heritage Trust Program
South Carolina Department of Natural Resources
P.O. Box 167
Columbia, SC 29202
(803) 734–3893
www.dnr.state.sc.us

Kings Mountain National Battlefield Park
2625 Park Road
Blacksburg, SC 29702
(864) 936–7921
www.nps.gov

Lake Hartwell State Recreation Area
19138-A South Highway 11
Fair Play, SC 29643
(864) 972–3352
www.southcarolinaparks.com

Oconee Station State Historic Site
500 Oconee Station Road
Walhalla, SC 29691
(864) 638–0079
www.southcarolinaparks.com

Paris Mountain State Park
2401 State Park Road
Greenville, SC 29609
(864) 244–5565
www.southcarolinaparks.com

CAMPING

Coneross Campground
(Townville, SC)
US Army Corps of Engineers
Hartwell Project Office
P.O. Box 278
Hartwell, GA 30643
(877) 444–6777
www.reserveusa.com

Devils Fork State Park
161 Holcombe Circle
Salem, SC 29676
(864) 944–2639
www.southcarolinaparks.com

High Falls County Park
671 High Falls Road
Seneca, SC 29678
(864) 882–8234
www.oconeesc.com

Jones Gap State Park
303 Jones Gap Road
Marietta, SC 29661
(864) 836–3647
www.southcarolinaparks.com

Lake Hartwell State Recreation Area
19138-A South Highway 11
Fair Play, SC 29643
(864) 972–3352
www.southcarolinaparks.com

Pendleton District Commission in
Hunter's Store
125 East Queen Street
Pendleton, SC 29670
(864) 646–3782 or (800) 862–1795
www.pendleton-district.org

South Cove County Park
1099 South Cove Road
Seneca, SC 29672
(864) 882–5250
www.oconeesc.com
(open March to November)

Table Rock State Park
158 East Ellison Lane
Pickens, SC 29671
(864) 878–9813
www.southcarolinaparks.com

NEAT PLACES TO STAY

Bell Tower Inn Bed and Breakfast
501 Depot Street
Campobello, SC 29322
(864) 468–4266 or (877) BELLTOWER
www.bbonline.com/sc/belltower

C'est Voila B&B Suite
191 Doctor's Cove Road
Inman, SC 29349
(864) 592–3424
www.bbonline.com/sc/c'estvoila

The Country Mouse Inn
120 North Trade Avenue
Landrum, SC 29356
(864) 457–4061
www.bbonline.com/sc/countrymouse

Jolly Place–A Bed and Breakfast Inn
405 College Drive
Gaffney, SC 29340
(864) 489–4638
www.bbonline.com/sc/jolly

Lakeshore Bed and Breakfast
1026 East Lakeshore Drive
Landrum, SC 29356
(864) 457–5330
lakeshorebb@aol.com

The Red Horse Inn
310 North Campbell Road
Landrum, SC 29356
(864) 895–4968
theredhorseinn@aol.com

Walnut Lane Inn
110 Ridge Road
Lyman, SC 29365
(864) 949–7230
walnutlaneinn@charter.net
www.walnutlaneinn.com

RESTAURANTS AND SHOPS
Aunt Sue's Country Corner
107 A Country Creek Drive
Pickens, SC 29671
(864) 878–4366
www.auntsues.com

Country Kitchen
SC Highway 130 South
Stamps Creek Road
Salem, SC 29676
(864) 944–7888

Country Peddler
305 Depot Street
Campobello, SC 29322
(864) 468–5200

Perdue's Mountain Fruit Farm
302 Sassafras Drive
Taylors, SC 29687
(864) 244–5809 or 895–5002

Table Rock Lodge Restaurant
Table Rock State Park
158 East Ellison Lane
Pickens, SC 29671
(864) 878–9065

TOURS AND NATURE-BASED SERVICES
Fish Inc.
15071 North Highway 11
Salem, SC 29676
(864) 944–9292

Grady's Great Outdoors
3440 Clemson Boulevard
Anderson, SC 29621
(864) 226–5283
sales@gradysoutdoors.com

Hoyett's Grocery and Tackle
516 Jocassee Lake Road
Salem, SC 29676
(864) 944–9016
www.carol.net/hoyetts

Nantahala Outdoor Center
851-A Chattooga Ridge Road
Mountain Rest, SC 29664
(800) 232–7238
www.nocweb.com

River Bend Sportsman's Resort
P.O. Box 279
Fingerville, SC 29338
(864) 592–1348
www.rvrbend.com

The Season Hunting/Guide Service
2044 Table Rock Road
Pickens, SC 29671
(864) 878–4894 or 918–2470
www.theseasoncabins.com

Sunrift Adventures
1 Center Street
Travelers Rest, SC 29690
(864) 834–3019
www.sunrift.com

Wildwater Ltd.
1251 Academy Road
Long Creek, SC 29658
(800) 451–9587
www.wildwaterrafting.com

CHAPTER FOUR: UPPER SAVANNAH RIVER VALLEY

ATTRACTIONS
Baker Creek State Park
Route 3, Box 59
McCormick, SC 29835
(864) 443–2457
baker_creek_sp@prt.state.sc.us
www.southcarolinaparks.com

Calhoun Falls State Recreation Area
46 Maintenance Shop Road
Calhoun Falls, SC 29628
(864) 447–8267
www.southcarolinaparks.com

Dorn Mill Center for History and Art
200 North Main Street
McCormick, SC 29835
(864) 465–3216

Erskine College
Bowie Arts Center
Bonner Street
Due West, SC 29639
(864) 379–8867
www.erskine.edu

Hickory Knob Resort State Park
Route 4, Box 199-B
McCormick, SC 29835
(800) 491–1764
www.southcarolinaparks.com

John de la Howe Barn and Tract
Route 1, Box 154
Highway 81 South
McCormick, SC 29835
(864) 391–2131

Joseph Jennings Dorn House
206 East Gold Street
McCormick, SC 29835
(864) 465–2225

Long Cane District
Sumter National Forest
810 Buncombe Street
Edgefield, SC 29824
(803) 637–5396 or 561–4072
www.fs.fed.us/r8/fms

MACK Art Gallery
The Old Keturah Hotel
115 South Main Street
McCormick, SC 29835
(864) 465–3216
www.marts@infoave.net

Sadlers Creek State Park
940 Sadlers Creek State Park Road
Anderson, SC 29626
(864) 226–8950
www.southcarolinaparks.com

South Carolina Botanical Gardens
Clemson University
102 Garden Trail
Clemson, SC 29634

(864) 656–3405
www.clemson.edu

Stevens Creek Heritage Preserve
South Carolina Heritage Trust Program
South Carolina Department of Natural
Resources
P.O. Box 167
Columbia, SC 29200
(803) 734–3893
www.dnr.sc.state.us

Strom Thurmond Dam and Lake
Route 1, Box 12
Clarks Hill, SC 29821-9701
(864) 333–1100

CAMPING
Baker Creek State Park
Route 3, Box 50
McCormick, SC 29835
(864) 443–2457
www.southcarolinaparks.com

Calhoun Falls State Recreation Area
46 Maintenance Shop Road
Calhoun Falls, SC 29628
(864) 447–8267
www.southcarolinaparks.com

Carolina Landing
120 Carolina Landing
Fair Play, SC 29643
(864) 972–9892

Hawe Creek Campground
(Corps of Engineers)
Route 3, Box 235
McCormick, SC 29835
(877) 444–6777
(open March to November)

Hickory Knob Resort State Park
Route 4, Box 199B
McCormick, SC 29835
(800) 491–1764 or (864) 391–2450
www.southcarolinaparks.com

Lake Hartwell KOA
200 Wham Road
Anderson, SC 29625
(864) 287–3161 or (800) 562–5804
www.koa.com

Lake Hartwell State Recreation Area
19138-A Highway 11 South
Fair Play, SC 29643
(864) 972–3352

Modoc Campground
(Corps of Engineers)
Route 1, Box 2-D
Modoc, SC 29838
(877) 444–6777
(open April to October)

Sadlers Creek State Recreation Area
940 Sadlers Creek State Park Road
Anderson, SC 29626
(864) 226–8950
www.southcarolinaparks.com

NEAT PLACES TO STAY
Abbewood Bed and Breakfast
509 North Main Street
Abbeville, SC 29620
(864) 459–5822

Bar Mel Inn
Route 1, Box 329
McCormick, SC 29835
(864) 465–2971

Hickory Knob State Resort Park
The Guillebeau House
Route 1, Box 199-B
McCormick, SC 29835
(864) 391–2450 or (800) 491–1764
www.southcarolinaparks.com

The Latimer Inn
1387 Scenic Highway 81 North
Calhoun Falls, SC 29628
(864) 391–2747
www.latimerinn.com

Liberty Hall Inn Bed and Breakfast
621 Mechanic Street
Pendleton, SC 29670
(864) 646–7500 or (800) 643–7944
libertyhallinn@aol.com
www.bbonline.com/sc/liberty

Oakwood Bed and Breakfast
484 Boulevard
Anderson, SC 29621
(864) 964–9462

oakwoodbandb@msn.com
www.oakwoodbandb.com

Rocky Retreat Bed and Breakfast
1000 Milwee Creek Road
Pendleton, SC 29670
(864) 225–3494
jtligon@aol.com

The Vintage Inn
1206 North Main Street
Abbeville, SC 29620
(864) 459–4784 or (800) 890–7312
www.thevintageinn.com

RESTAURANTS AND SHOPS
Bordeaux Country Store
Hickory Knob Resort State Park
Route 4, Box 199-B
McCormick, SC 29835
(800) 491–1764
www.southcarolinaparks.com

C.C. Blair's Family Restaurant
108 West Gold Street
McCormick, SC 29835
(864) 465–3667

Fannie Kate's Inn, Restaurant, and Pub
127 South Main Street
McCormick, SC 29835
(864) 465–0061 or (800) 965–0061
www.fanniekates.com

John de la Howe Barn
Highway 28
Route 1, Box 154
McCormick, SC 29835
(864) 391–2131, ext. 124

McCormick Arts Council Gallery Shop
Keturah Hotel
115 South Main Street
McCormick, SC 29835
(864) 465–3216

Rubbies Barbecue
Highway 378
McCormick, SC 29835
(open Thursday through Saturday nights)

Sadlers Creek Barbecue
1721 South Highway 187

Anderson, SC 29626
(864) 225–2425
(Saturday only)

Strom's Drug Store
124 South Main Street
McCormick, SC 29835
(864) 465–2011

TOURS AND NATURE-BASED SERVICES

Grady's Great Outdoors
3440 Clemson Boulevard
Anderson, SC 29621
(864) 226–5283
sales@gradysoutdoors.com
www.gradysoutdoors.com

River Bend Sportsman's Resort
Wilkie Bridge Road
P.O. Box 279
Fingerville, SC 29338
(864) 592–1348
www.rvrbend.com

CHAPTER FIVE: LONG CANE FOREST AND THE EIGHTEENTH-CENTURY FRONTIER

ATTRACTIONS

Abbeville County Library
201 South Main Street
Abbeville, SC 29620
(864) 459–4009

Abbeville County Museum
Poplar and Henry M. Turner Streets
Abbeville, SC 29620
(864) 459–4600

Abbeville Opera House
100 Court Square
Abbeville, SC 29620
(864) 459–2157
operahouse@wctel.net

Belmont Inn
104 East Pickens Street
Abbeville, SC 29620
(864) 459–9625
www.belmontinn.net

Burt-Stark House
400 Main Street
Abbeville, SC 29620
(864) 459–4297 or 459–4688

Emerald Farm
409 Emerald Farm Road
Greenwood, SC 29646
(864) 223–2247 or (888) 290–9246
www.emeraldfarm.com

Erskine College
Bowie Arts Center
Bonner Street
Due West, SC 29639
(864) 379–8867
www.erskine.edu

Historic Ninety Six Visitors Center
97 Main Street
Ninety Six, SC 29666
(864) 543–4820

Lake Greenwood State Recreation Area
302 State Park Road
Ninety Six, SC 29666
(864) 543–3535
www.southcarolinaparks.com

Long Cane Ranger District
Sumter National Forest
810 Buncombe Street
Edgefield, SC 29824
(803) 637–5396
www.fs.fed.us/r8/fms

Magnolia Dale
P.O. Box 174
Edgefield, SC 29824
(803) 637–5306

National Wild Turkey Federation Center
and Museum
770 Augusta Road
Edgefield, SC 29824
(803) 637–3106 or (800) THE–NWTF
www.nwtf.org

Ninety Six National Historic Site
1103 Highway 248 South
Ninety Six, SC 29666
(864) 543–4068
www.nps.gov/nisi

Oakley Park Museum
300 Columbia Road
Edgefield, SC 29824
(803) 637–4027

Old Edgefield Pottery
230 Simkins Street
Edgefield, SC 29824
(803) 637–2060
www.edgefieldpottery.com

Park Seed Company
1 Parkton Avenue
Greenwood, SC 29649
(864) 223–8555 or (800) 213–0076
www.parkseed.com

Parson's Mountain Recreation Area
(Abbeville)
Sumter National Forest
810 Buncombe Street
Edgefield, SC 29824
(803) 637–5396
www.fs.fed.us/r8/fms

Tompkins Memorial Library and Edgefield Welcome Center
104 Courthouse Square
Edgefield, SC 29824
(803) 637–4010

CAMPING

Baker Creek State Park
Route 3, Box 50
McCormick, SC 29835
(864) 443–2457
www.southcarolinaparks.com

Long Cane Ranger District Fell Hunt
Camp
Lick Fork Lake Recreation Area
Sumter National Forest
810 Buncombe Street
Edgefield, SC 29824
(803) 637–5396
www.fs.fed.us/r8/fms

Hawe Creek Campground
Route 3, Box 235
McCormick, SC 29835
(877) 444–6777
(open March to November)

Hickory Knob State Park
Route 4, Box 199-B
McCormick, SC 29835
(800) 491–1764
www.southcarolinaparks.com

Lake Greenwood State Recreation Area
302 State Park Road
Ninety Six, SC 29666
(864) 543–3535
www.southcarolinaparks.com

NEAT PLACES TO STAY

Abbewood Bed and Breakfast
509 North Main Street
Abbeville, SC 29620
(864) 459–5822

Belmont Inn
104 East Pickens Street
Abbeville, SC 29620
(864) 459–9625 or (877) 459–8118
www.belmontinn.net

Cox House Inn
602 Lee Street
P.O. Box 486
Johnston, SC 29832
(803) 275–2707
www.thecoxhouseinn.com

Edgefield Inn
P.O. Box 420
702 Augusta Road
Edgefield, SC 29824
(803) 637–2001
edgefieldinn@jetbn.net
www.edgefieldinn.com

Grace Place B&B
115 Grace Street
Greenwood, SC 29649
(864) 229–0053

Inn on the Square
104 Court Avenue East
Greenwood, SC 29646
(864) 223–4488

Mile Rock Bed and Breakfast
1300 North Main Street
Abbeville, SC 29620
(864) 459–9931

Southwood Manor Bed and Breakfast
100 East Main Street
Ridge Spring, SC 29129
(803) 685–5100 or (800) 931–1786
southent@pbtcomm.net

The Vintage Inn
1206 North Main Street
Abbeville, SC 29620
(864) 459–4784 or (800) 890–7312
www.thevintageinn.com

RESTAURANTS AND SHOPS
Belmont Inn
104 East Pickens Street
Abbeville, SC 29620
(864) 459–9625 or (877) 459–8118
www.belmontinn.net

Ferrell's Antiques and Museum
101 Courthouse Square
Edgefield, SC 29824
(803) 637–4618
terrymferrell@yahoo.com
www.oldedgefieldpottery.com

Log Cabin Antiques
Main Street (in the old train depot)
Donalds, SC 29638
(864) 379–2575

Old Edgefield Pottery
230 Simkins Street
Edgefield, SC 29824
(803) 637–2060
www.edgefieldpottery.com

Park Seed Company
1 Parkton Avenue
Greenwood, SC 29649
(864) 223–8555 or (800) 213–0076
www.parkseed.com

The Rough House
116 Court Square
Abbeville, SC 29620
(864) 459–1932

Ten Governors Cafe
109 Court House Square
Edgefield, SC 29824
(803) 637–9050

Yoder's Dutch Kitchen
809 East Greenwood Street
Abbeville, SC 29620
(864) 459–5556

TOURS AND NATURE-BASED SERVICES
Grady's Great Outdoors
3440 Clemson Boulevard
Anderson, SC 29621
(864) 226–5283
www.gradysoutdoors.com

River Bend Sportsman's Resort
Wilkie Bridge Road
P.O. Box 279
Fingerville, SC 29338
(864) 592–1348
www.rvrbend.com

CHAPTER SIX: THOROUGH-BRED COUNTRY

ATTRACTIONS
Aiken Center for the Arts
122 Laurens Street SW
Aiken, SC 29801
(803) 641–9094

Aiken County Historical Museum
433 Newberry Street SW
Aiken, SC 29801
(803) 642–2015

Aiken Gopher Tortoise Heritage Preserve
South Carolina Heritage Trust Program
South Carolina Department of Natural Resources
P.O. Box 167
Columbia, SC 29202
(803) 734–3893
www.dnr.state.sc.us

Aiken State Natural Area
1145 State Park Road
Windsor, SC 29856
(803) 649–2857
www.southcarolinaparks.com

Aiken Thoroughbred Hall of Fame and Hopeland Gardens
Whiskey Road and Dupree Place
Aiken, SC 29801

(803) 642–7758
www.aikencounty.net

Barnwell County Museum
Marlboro Avenue
Barnwell, SC 29812
(803) 259–1916

Barnwell State Park
223 State Park Road
Blackville, SC 29817
(803) 284–2212
www.southcarolinaparks.com

Carriage Museum at Rye Patch
100 Berrie Road
Aiken, SC 29801
(803) 642–7630

Hitchcock Woods
The Hitchcock Foundation
P.O. Box 1702
Aiken, SC 29802
(803) 642–0528

Legare-Morgan House
241 Laurens Street
Aiken, SC 29801

Montmorenci Vineyards
2989 Charleston Highway
Aiken, SC 29801
(803) 649–4870

Original Graniteville Mill and Blue Row
Homes
Gregg Street
Graniteville, SC 29829

Redcliffe Plantation State Historic Site
181 Redcliffe Road
Beech Island, SC 29842
(803) 827–1473
www.southcarolinaparks.com

Salley Old School Museum
218 Pine Street
Salley, SC 29137
(803) 258–3301

Willcox Inn
100 Colleton Avenue
Aiken, SC 29801

(803) 648–1898 or (877) 648–2200
www.thewillcox.com

CAMPING

Aiken RV Park
2424 Columbia Highway North
Aiken, SC 29801
(803) 648–4056

Aiken State Natural Area
1145 State Park Road
Windsor, SC 29856
(803) 649–2857
www.southcarolinaparks.com

Barnwell State Park
233 State Park Road
Blackville, SC 29817
(803) 284–2212
www.southcarolinaparks.com

NEAT PLACES TO STAY

Annie's Inn Bed and Breakfast
3083 Charleston Highway
Montmorenci, SC 29839
(803) 649–6836
www.anniesinnbnb.com

Bloom Hill
772 Pine Log Road
North Augusta, SC 29841
(803) 593–2573

The Briar Patch
544 Magnolia Lane SE
Aiken, SC 29801
(803) 649–2010
briarfox@prodigy.net

The Confederate Manor
3663 Dexter Street
Blackville, SC 29817
(803) 284–2170

Crossways Plantation Bed and Breakfast
450 East Boundary Street
Aiken, SC 29801
(803) 644–4746
www.crosswaysplantation.com

Hotel Aiken
235 Richland Avenue
Aiken, SC 29801
(803) 648–4265

Rosemary and Lookaway Halls Bed and Breakfast
804 Carolina Avenue
North Augusta, SC 29841
(803) 278–6222 or (800) 531–5578
sandhurst@scescape.net
www.bbonline.com/sc/rosemary-lookaway/

Sandhurst Estate Bed and Breakfast Inn
215 Dupree Place
Aiken, SC 29801
(803) 642–9259
innkeeper@sandhurtstestate.com
www.sandhurstestate.com

Town and Country Inn
2340 Sizemore Circle
Aiken, SC 29803
(803) 642–0270
info@towncountrybb.com
www.bbonline.com/sc/towncountry

Willcox Inn
100 Colleton Avenue
Aiken, SC 29801
(803) 648–1898 or (877) 648–2200
www.thewillcox.com

RESTAURANTS AND SHOPS

Aiken Antique Mall
112-114 Laurens Street
Aiken, SC 29801
(803) 648–6700

Aiken Center for the Arts
122 Laurens Street
Aiken, SC 29801
(803) 641–9094
www.aikencenterforthearts.org

The Arnold Gallery
321 Richland Avenue West
Aiken, SC 29807
(803) 502–1100
www.trisharnold.com

Ballard's Cafe
114 Main Street
Barnwell, SC 29812
(803) 259–1245

Birds and Butterflies of Aiken
117A Laurens Street, NW

Aiken, SC 29801
(803) 649–7999

The Bookworm
49 Jefferson Street
Barnwell, SC 29812
(803) 259–2665 or 259–9676
www.officepros.com/bookworm

Miller's Bread Basket
483 Main Street
Blackville, SC 29817
(803) 284–3117

Miller's Mini Mall
477 Main Street
Blackville, SC 29817
(803) 284–5000

New Moon Cafe
116 Laurens Street
Aiken, SC 29801
(803) 643–7088

Number 10 Downing Street
241 Laurens Street
Aiken, SC 29801
(803) 642–9062

Parrot's on L'Artigue Antiques and Gifts
5575 L'Artigue Street
Blackville, SC 29817
(803) 284–3670

Paw Print Pottery at the Little Red Barn
12080 Highway 278
Barnwell, SC 29812
(803) 541–7900

Plum Pudding
101 Laurens Street
Aiken, SC 29801
(803) 648–2744

Polo Tavern
225 Richland Street
Aiken, SC 29801
(803) 648–4265

West Side Bowery
151 Bee Lane
Aiken, SC 29801
(803) 648–2900

For More Information   **249**

The Winton Inn
8273 Marlboro Avenue
Barnwell, SC 29812
(803) 259–7181

York Cottage Antiques
409 Hayne Street
Aiken, SC 29801
(803) 642–9524

TOURS AND NATURE-BASED SERVICES
Aiken Visitors Center
121 Richland Avenue East
Aiken, SC 29801
(803) 641–1111 or (800) 542–4536
www.aikenchamber.net

CHAPTER SEVEN: MIDLANDS FOREST AND RIVERS

ATTRACTIONS
Dreher Island State Recreation Area
3677 State Park Road
Prosperity, SC 29127
(803) 364–4152
www.southcarolinaparks.com

Enoree/Tyger Ranger District
Sumter National Forest
20 Work Center Road
Whitmire, SC 29178
(803) 276–4810
www.fs.fed.us/r8/fms

Musgrove Mill State Historic Site
398 State Park Road
Clinton, SC 29325
(864) 938–0100
www.southcarolinaparks.com

Newberry College
2100 College Street
Newberry, SC 29108
(803) 276–5010
www.newberry.edu

Newberry Opera House
1201 McKibben Street
Newberry, SC 29108
(803) 276–5179
www.newberryoperahouse.com

Old Newberry County Courthouse
Main Street
P.O. Box 396
Newberry, SC 29108
(803) 276–0513

Riverbanks Zoo and Botanical Garden
I-26 at Greystone Boulevard
Columbia, SC 29210
(803) 779-8717
www.riverbanks.org

Rose Hill State Historic Site
2677 Sardis Road
Union, SC 29379
(864) 427–5966
www.southcarolinaparks.com

CAMPING
Dreher Island State Recreation Area
3677 State Park Road
Prosperity, SC 29127
(803) 634–4152
www.southcarolinaparks.com

Enoree/Tyger Ranger District
Sumter National Forest
20 Work Center Road
Whitmire, SC 29178
(803) 276–4810
www.fs.fed.us/r8/fms

Sesquicentennial State Park
9564 Two Notch Road
Columbia, SC 29223
(803) 788–2706
www.southcarolinaparks.com

NEAT PLACES TO STAY
Barklin House
1710 College Street
Newberry, SC 29108
(803) 321–9155
www.barklinhouse.com

Inn at Merridun
100 Merridun Place
Union, SC 29379
(803) 427–7052 or (888) 892–6020
info@merridun.com
www.merridun.com

Inn on Main
921 Main Street
Newberry, SC 29108
(803) 637–9092

Juxa Plantation
143 Wilson Road
Union, SC 29379
(864) 427–8688
nolaxjuxa@aol.com

Maybin House Bed and Breakfast
1727 Harrington Street
Newberry, SC 29108
(803) 276–2266

RESTAURANTS AND SHOPS
Antiques Etc.
1213 Main Street
Newberry, SC 29108
(803) 276–1073

The Back Porch
Main Street
Prosperity, SC 29127
(803) 364–3556

Cabana Cafe
1215 Boyce Street
Newberry, SC 29108
(803) 405–0030

Dawkins' Mercantile
112 Grace Street (in Town Square)
Prosperity, SC 29127
(803) 364–2736

Delamator's
1117 Boyce Street
Newberry, SC 29108
(803) 276–3555

Juxa Plantation Antiques and Accessories
143 Wilson Road
Union, SC 29379
(864) 427–8688
www.virtualcities.com/ons/sc/e/sce6701.htm

The Lamplighter Gallery
1104 Caldwell Street
Newberry, SC 29108
(803) 276–1500

Liberty Antiques and Auctions
934 Main Street
Newberry, SC 29108
(803) 276–8600

Market Basket Antiques and Collectibles
1107 Harrington Street
Newberry, SC 29108
(803) 321–6000

Midlands Antique Mall
1510 Main Street
Little Mountain, SC 29075
(803) 345–9793
www.indo/pacific.com

Out on a Whim Functional Art
1118 Main Street
Newberry, SC 29108
(803) 321–6650

Showcase Antiques
1737 Johnstone Street
Newberry, SC 29108
(803) 276–0396
www.putnam@backroads.net

Steven W's Downtown Bistro
1100 Main Street
Newberry, SC 29108
(803) 276–7700

Trader John's Antiques
11213 Highway 121
Newberry, SC 29108
(803) 276–0432

TOURS AND NATURE-BASED SERVICES
Adventure Carolina Canoes and Touring Kayaks
1107 State Street
Cayce, SC 29033
(803) 796–4505
www.adventurecarolina.com

The Back Packer
1215 Wayne Street
Columbia, SC 29202
(803) 799–7571
www.backpackerqualitygear.com

Moe Levy's Wilderness Station
1105 Lady Street

Columbia, SC 29201
(803) 252–7102

River Runner Outdoor Center
905 Gervais Street
Columbia, SC 29201
(803) 771–0353

CHAPTER EIGHT: COTTON AND SAND HILLS

ATTRACTIONS
Bishopville Opera House
Lee County Arts Foundation
P.O. Box 313
Bishopville, SC 29010
(803) 484–5090

Camden Archives and Museum
1314 Broad Street
Camden, SC 29020
(803) 425–6050
www.mindspring.com/camdenarchives

Carolina Sandhills National Wildlife Refuge
23734 US 1
McBee, SC 29101
(843) 335–8401
www.carolinasandhills.fws.gov

Cheraw Fish Hatchery
Route 2, Box 620
Cheraw, SC 29520
(843) 537–7628

Cheraw State Recreation Area
100 State Park Road
Cheraw, SC 29520
(843) 537–9656 or (800) 868–9630
www.southcarolinaparks.com

Coker College
300 East College Avenue
Hartsville, SC 29550
(843) 383–8050
www.coker.edu

Fine Arts Center of Kershaw County
810 Lyttleton Street
Camden, SC 29020
(803) 425–7676

Historic Camden
P.O. Box 710
Camden, SC 29020
(803) 432–9841
www.historic-camden.org

Historic Camden Revolutionary War Site
222 Broad Street
Camden, SC 29020
(803) 432–9841
www.historic-camden.org

Historic Cheraw
Cheraw Visitors Bureau
221 Market Street
Cheraw, SC 29520
(843) 537–8425
www.cheraw.com

Lee State Natural Area
487 Loop Road
Bishopville, SC 29010
(803) 428–5307
www.southcarolinaparks.com

Old St. David's Episcopal Church
91 Church Street
Cheraw, SC 29520
(843) 537–8425 or (888) 537–0014
www.cheraw.com

Pee Dee River Artifacts Room
204 Market Street
Cheraw, SC 29520
(843) 537–6565

Sand Hills State Forest
16218 Highway 1
P.O. Box 128
Patrick, SC 29584
(843) 498–6478
www.state.sc.us/forest

Swan Lake and Iris Gardens
West Liberty Street Extension
Sumter, SC 29150
(803) 436–2640 or (800) 688–4748
www.sumter-sc-tourism.com

Woods Bay State Natural Area
11020 Woods Bay Road
Olanta, SC 29114
(843) 659–4445
www.southcarolinaparks.com

CAMPING
Cheraw State Recreation Area
100 State Park Road
Cheraw, SC 29520
(843) 537–9656 or (800) 868–9630
www.southcarolinaparks.com

Lee State Natural Area
487 Loop Road
Bishopville, SC 29010
(803) 428–5307
www.southcarolinaparks.com

Poinsett State Park
6660 Poinsett Park Road
Wedgefield, SC 29168
(803) 494–8177
www.southcarolinaparks.com

Sand Hills State Forest
P.O. Box 128
Patrick, SC 29584
(843) 498–6478
www.state.sc.us/forest

Sesquicentennial State Park
9564 Two Notch Road
Columbia, SC 29223
(803) 788–2706
www.southcarolinaparks.com

NEAT PLACES TO STAY
Breeden Inn, Carriage House,
and Garden Cottage
404 East Main Street
Bennettsville, SC 29512
(843) 479–3665 or (888) 335–2996
www.breeden.com

Carriage House of Sumter
431 North Main Street
Sumter, SC 29150
(803) 773–5829

Cheraw State Recreation Area
100 State Park Road
Cheraw, SC 29520
(843) 537–9656 or (800) 868–9630
www.southcarolinaparks.com

Magnolia House Bed and Breakfast
230 Church Street
Sumter, SC 29150

(803) 775–6694 or (888) 666–0296
www.bbonline.com/sc/magnolia

Missouri Inn
314 East Home Avenue
Hartsville, SC 29550
(843) 383–9553

Nealcrest Farm Bed and Breakfast
1245 Windsor Farm Lane
Hartsville, SC 29550
(843) 383–6677

Spears Guest House
228 Huger Street
Cheraw, SC 29540
(843) 537–7733 or (888) 4CHERAW

314 Market Street Bed and Breakfast
314 Market Street
Cheraw, SC 29520
(843) 537–5797

RESTAURANTS AND SHOPS
The Country Kitchen
Highway 9 West
Cheraw, SC 29520
(843) 537–3662

Dixie Cafe
311 South Main Street
Bishopville, SC 29010
(803) 484–9148

Hard Times Cafe
2859-A US 1 North
Cassatt, SC 29032
(803) 425–7308

Mary's Restaurant
134 Market Street
Cheraw, SC 29520
(843) 537–6790

The New Butterfly Shop
148 Market Street
Cheraw, SC 29520
(843) 921–0261

Sentimental Journey Antiques
242 Second Street
Cheraw, SC 29520
(843) 537–0461

Shiloh Fish House
3388 Highway 102
Shiloh Community
Chesterfield, SC 29709
(843) 623–7204

South Carolina Cotton Museum
Company Store
121 West Cedar Lane
Bishopville, SC 29010
(803) 484–4497
www.sccotton.org

Thomas Antiques Company
92 Powe Street
Cheraw, SC 29520
(843) 537–5762 or 537–3422
othomasjr@aol.com

TOURS AND NATURE-BASED SERVICES

Adventure Carolina Canoes and Touring
Kayaks
1107 State Street
Cayce, SC 29033
(803) 796–4505
www.adventurecarolina.com

Betwixt the River Outfitters
234 Schofield Road
Marion, SC 29571
(843) 423–1919
btxrivers@aol.com
www.betwisttherivers.com

Cheraw Visitors Bureau
221 Market Street
Cheraw, SC 29520
(843) 537–8425 or (888) 537–0014
www.cheraw.com

River Rats Guided Scenic Eco-River Trips
1660 Alford Road
Conway, SC 29526
(843) 365–1717
eleebysea@aol.com
www.river-rats.net

River Runner Outdoor Center
905 Gervais Street
Columbia, SC 29201
(803) 771–0353

CHAPTER NINE: TOBACCO ROAD

ATTRACTIONS

Black River Swamp Preserve
Pine Tree Landing
South Carolina Heritage Trust Program
South Carolina Department of Natural
Resources
P.O. Box 167
Columbia, SC 29200
(803) 734–3893

Cooper's Country Store
6945 US Highway 521
Salters, SC 29590
(843) 387–5772
coopercs@wpmedia.com
www.cooperscountrystore.com

South Carolina Tobacco Museum
104 Northeast Front Street
Mullins, SC 29574
(843) 464–8194 or (800) 207–7967
farmer@marketplace.com
www.mullinssc.com

Springbank Center
1345 Springbank Road
Kingstree, SC 29556
(800) 671–0361
www.springbankretreat.org

Thorntree House
421 South Virginia Street
Kingstree, SC 29556
(843) 354–6431

Williamsburg County Arts Council and
Gallery
108 West Main Street
Kingstree, SC 29556
(843) 354–7247
www.williamsburgsc.org

Williamsburg Historical Museum
Old Carnegie Library
135 Hampton Avenue
Kingstree, SC 29556
(843) 355–3306
history1@ftc-i.net
(open Tuesday through Thursday)

CAMPING

Francis Marion National Forest
Wambaw Ranger District
P.O. Box 788
McClellanville, SC 29458
(843) 887–3257
www.fs.fed.us/r8/fms

Huntington Beach State Park
16148 Ocean Highway
Murrells Inlet, SC 29576
(843) 237–4440
www.southcarolinaparks.com

Lee State Natural Area
487 Loop Road
Bishopville, SC 29010
(803) 428–5307
www.southcarolinaparks.com

RESTAURANTS AND SHOPS

Brown's Bar-B-Que
809 Highway 52 North
Kingstree, SC 29556
(843) 382–2753

Cooper's Country Store
6945 US 521
Salters, SC 29590
(843) 387–5772
coopercs@wpmedia.com
www.cooperscountrystore.com

The Cornerstone
141 North Academy Street
Kingstree, SC 29556
(843) 355–6015

The Palmetto House
124 South Academy Street
Kingstree, SC 29556
(843) 354–2213 or 355–3201

The Station House
134 East Main Street
Kingstree, SC 29556
(843) 354–3337

TOURS AND NATURE-BASED SERVICES

Black River Outdoors Center
Expeditions
21 Garden Avenue
Georgetown, SC 29440

(843) 546–4840
www.blackriveroutdoors.com

Blackwater Adventures and Kayak Tours
1944 Pinopolis Road
Pinopolis, SC 29469
(843) 761–1850 or (800) 761–1850
www.blackwateradventure.com

CHAPTER TEN: WACCAMAW NECK

ATTRACTIONS

Brookgreen Gardens
1931 Brookgreen Drive
Murrells Inlet, SC 29576
(843) 235–6000 or (800) 849–1931
www.brookgreen.org

Hobcaw Barony and Bellefield Nature
Center
22 Hobcaw Road
Georgetown, SC 29440
(843) 546–4623
www.hobcawbarony.com

Huntington Beach State Park
16148 Ocean Highway
Murrells Inlet, SC 29576
(843) 237–4440
www.southcarolinaparks.com

Myrtle Beach State Park
4401 South Kings Highway
Myrtle Beach, SC 29575
(843) 238–5325
www.southcarolinaparks.com

CAMPING

Huntington Beach State Park
16148 Ocean Highway
Murrells Inlet, SC 29576
(843) 237–4440
www.southcarolinaparks.com

Lakewood Camping Resort
5901 South Kings Highway
Myrtle Beach, SC 29577
(843) 238–5161
www.lakewoodcampground.com

Myrtle Beach State Park
4401 South Kings Highway
Myrtle Beach, SC 29575
(843) 238–5325
www.southcarolinaparks.com

Myrtle Beach Travel Park
10108 Kings Road
Myrtle Beach, SC 29572
(843) 449–3714 or (800) 255–3568
www.myrtlebeachtravelpark.com

Ocean Lakes Family Campground
6001 US 17 South
Myrtle Beach, SC 29577
(843) 238–5636
www.oceanlakes.com

Pirateland Family Campground
5401 South Kings Highway
Myrtle Beach, SC 29577
(843) 238–5155

Neat Places to Stay
Brustman House
400 25th Avenue South
Myrtle Beach, SC 29577
(843) 448–7699 or (800) 448–7699
bebrustman@att.net
www.brustmanhouse.com

Cypress Inn
16 Elm Street
P.O. Box 495
Conway, SC 29528
(843) 248–8199 or (800) 575–5307
innkeeper@cypressinn.com
www.acypress.inn

The Pelican Inn
506 Myrtle Avenue
Pawleys Island, SC 29585
(843) 237–2298

Restaurants and Shops
Admiral's Flagship
US 17 Business
Murrells Inlet, SC 29576
(843) 651–3016

Broadway at the Beach
1325 Celebrity Circle
Myrtle Beach, SC 29577

(843) 444–3200
www.broadwayatthebeach.com

Bucksport Marina Restaurant
135 Bucksport Road
Conway, SC 29527
(843) 397–6300

Dockside Restaurant
4037A US 17 Business
Murrells Inlet, SC 29576
(843) 651–5850
www.captaindavesdockside.com

Frank's Restaurant and Bar
10434 Ocean Highway
Pawleys Island, SC 29585
(843) 237–3030

Hanser House
14360 Ocean Highway
Pawleys Island, SC 29585
(843) 235–3021

Lee's Inlet Kitchen
4460 US 17 Business
Murrells Inlet, SC 29576
(843) 651–2881

Litchfield Beach House
13060 Ocean Highway
Litchfield Beach, SC 29585
(843) 237–3949

The Mayor's House
13089 US 17 South
Litchfield Beach, SC 29585
(843) 237–9082
www.discovermyrtlebeach.com

Myrtle Beach Factory Stores
4635 Factory Stores Boulevard
Myrtle Beach, SC 29579
(843) 236–5100 or (888) SHO–P333

Nance's Creek Front Restaurant
P.O. Box 44
Highway 17 Business
Murrells Inlet, SC 29576
(843) 651–2696

Oliver's Lodge Restaurant
Business Highway 17 and Belin Drive

Murrells Inlet, SC 29576
(843) 651–2963

Pawleys Island Hammock Shop Complex
US 17
Pawleys Island, SC 29585
(843) 237–7706

Webster's Lowcountry Grill and Tavern
Litchfield Beach and Golf Resort
14276 Ocean Highway
Litchfield Beach, SC 29585
(843) 237–3000
www.litchfieldbeach.com

TOURS AND NATURE-BASED SERVICES
Black River Outdoors Center
Expeditions
21 Garden Avenue
Georgetown, SC 29440
(843) 546–4840
www.blackriveroutdoors.com

Blackwater Adventures and Kayak Tours
1944 Pinopolis Road
Pinopolis, SC 29469
(843) 761–1850 or (800) 761–1850

Captain Dick's Deep Sea Fishing
Captain Dick's Marina
4123 Waterfront 17 Business
Murrells Inlet, SC 29576
(843) 651–3676 or (866) 557–3474
www.captdicks.com

Captain Sandy's Tours, Inc.
P.O. Box 186
Georgetown, SC 29442
(843) 527–4106
capsandy@sccoast.net
www.cruisecaptsandy.com

Carolina Safari and Jeep Tours
4866 US 17, Suite 29
North Myrtle Beach, SC 29582
(843) 272–1177

Pawley's Island Beach Service
10570 Ocean Highway 17
Pawleys Island, SC 29585
(843) 237–4666

Rip's Small Boats
2452 Waterford Road
Pawleys Island, SC 29585
(843) 237–8301

Tall Ship Jolly Rover and Carolina Rover
735 Front Street
Georgetown, SC 29440
(843) 546–8822 or (800) 705–9063
www.seaportgeorgetown.com/jolly_rover.
htm

CHAPTER ELEVEN: WINYAH BAY AND SANTEE RIVER DELTA

ATTRACTIONS
Cape Romain National Wildlife Refuge
5801 US 17 North
Awendaw, SC 29429
(843) 928–3264

Francis Marion National Forest
P.O. Box 788
McClellanville, SC 29458
(843) 887–3257
www.fs.fed.us/r8/fms

Hampton Plantation State Historic Park
1950 Rutledge Road
McClellanville, SC 29458
(843) 546–9361
www.southcarolinaparks.com

Heriot-Tarbox House
15 Cannon Street
Georgetown, SC 29440

Hobcaw Barony and Bellefield Nature
Center
22 Hobcaw Road
Georgetown, SC 29440
(843) 546–4623
www.hobcawbarony.com

Hopsewee Plantation
494 Hopsewee Road
Georgetown, SC 29440
(843) 546–7891
www.hopsesewee.com

Kaminski House Museum
1003 Front Street
Georgetown, SC 29440
(843) 546–7706
(888) 233–0383

Little Wambaw Swamp Wilderness
Tibwin Plantation
Francis Marion National Forest
P.O. Box 788
McClellanville, SC 29458
(843) 887–3257
www.fs.fd.us/r8/fms

Maritime Museum Gallery
Old Market Building
633 Front Street
Georgetown, SC 29440
(843) 546–7423
www.ricemuseum.com

Prince George Winyah Episcopal Church
708 High Market Street
Georgetown, SC 29440
(843) 546–4358

Rice Museum
Old Market Building
637 Front Street
Georgetown, SC 29440
(843) 527–7964

Santee Coastal Reserve
220 Santee Gun Club Road
McClellanville, SC 29458
(843) 546–8665

Sewee Visitor and Environmental
Education Center
5821 US 17 North
Awendaw, SC 29429
(843) 928–3368
TDD (843) 928–3833
www.seweecenter.fws.gov

Tom Yawkey Wildlife Center Heritage
Preserve
South Carolina Heritage Trust Program
South Carolina Department of Natural
Resources
1 Yawkey Way South
Georgetown, SC 29440
(843) 546–6814 or (803) 734–3893

Village Museum
P.O. Box 595
405 Pinckney Street
McClellanville, SC 29458
(843) 887–3030

CAMPING
Buck Hall Recreation Area
Guillard Lake Recreation Area
Francis Marion National Forest
P.O. Box 788
McClellanville, SC 29458
(843) 887–3257 or 336–3248
www.fs.fed.us/r8/fins

Huntington Beach State Park
16148 Ocean Highway
Murrells Inlet, SC 29576
(843) 237–4440
www.southcarolinaparks.com

Santee Coastal Reserve
220 Santee Gun Club Road
McClellanville, SC 29458
(843) 546–8665
(open February to October)

NEAT PLACES TO STAY
Alexander's Inn Bed and Breakfast
620 Prince Street
Georgetown, SC 29440
(843) 527–0233 or (888) 557–0233
www.alexanderinn.com

DuPre House Bed and Breakfast
921 Prince Street
Georgetown, SC 29440
(877) 519–9499 or (843) 546–0298
richard.barnett@gte.net
www.duprehouse.com

King's Inn at Georgetown
230 Broad Street
Georgetown, SC 29440
(843) 527–6937

Live Oak Bed and Breakfast
515 Prince Street
Georgetown, SC 29440
(843) 545–8658 or (888) 730–6004
www.liveoak.inn

Mansfield Plantation Bed
and Breakfast Inn
Highway 701 North
Route 8, Box 590
Georgetown, SC 29440
(843) 546–6961 or (800) 355–3223
www.mansfieldplantation.com

1790 House Bed and Breakfast
630 High Market Street
Georgetown, SC 29440
(843) 546–4821 or (800) 890–7432
1790house.com

The Shaw House Bed and Breakfast
613 Cypress Court
Georgetown, SC 29440
(843) 546–9663
www.firstchoice.com

Winyah Bay Inn
3030 South Island Road
Georgetown, SC 29440
(843) 546–0464 or (866) 394–6924
www.winyahbayinn.com

RESTAURANTS AND SHOPS
Angels Touch Tea Room
1790 House Bed and Breakfast Inn
630 High Market Street
Georgetown, SC 29440
(843) 546–4821 or (800) 890–7432

Augustus and Carolina European
Antiques
830 Front Street
Georgetown, SC 29440
(843) 545–9000

C&C Farms
8832 North Highway 17
McClellanville, SC 29458
(843) 887–3833

Carolina Interior Design
717 Front Street
Georgetown, SC 29440
(843) 546–3650

Christopher's Fine Jewelry and Gallery
724 Front Street

Georgetown, SC 29440
(843) 527–8181

The Crab Pot
10024 US 17 North
McClellanville, SC 29458
(843) 887–3156
www.thecrabpot.net

Emma Marie's Antique Shoppe
1103 Front Street
Georgetown, SC 29440
(843) 545–8030

Front Street Deli
809 Front Street
Georgetown, SC 29440
(843) 546–2008

Harborwalk Books
723 Front Street
Georgetown, SC 29440
(843) 546–8212

Hathaway's
9905 North Highway 17
McClellanville, SC 29458
(843) 887–3837

Independent Seafood Company
1 Cannon Street
Georgetown, SC 29440
(843) 546–6642

Kudzu Bakery
120 King Street
Georgetown, SC 29440
(843) 546–1847

Orange Blossom Cafe
107 Orange Street
Georgetown, SC 29440
(843) 527–5060

Pink Magnolia
719 Front Street
Georgetown, SC 29440
(843) 527–6506

Prince George Framing Art Gallery
805 Front Street

Georgetown, SC 29440
(843) 527–8413
www.princegeorgeframing.com

Rice Paddy Restaurant
732 Front Street
Georgetown, SC 29440
(843) 546–2021

The River Room
801 Front Street
Georgetown, SC 29440
(843) 527–4110

Roycroft Daylily Nursery
942 White Hall Avenue
Georgetown, SC 29440
(843) 527–1533
www.roycroftdaylilies.com

Syd and Luther's
713 Front Street
Georgetown, SC 29440
(843) 527–3106

Thomas Cafe
703 Front Street
Georgetown, SC 29440
(843) 546–7776

Tosh Antiques
802 Church Street
Georgetown, SC 29440
(843) 527–8537

TOURS AND NATURE-BASED SERVICES
Black River Outdoors Center
Expeditions
21 Garden Avenue (US 701 North)
Georgetown, SC 29440
(843) 546–4840
www.blackriveroutdoors.com

Blackwater Adventures and Kayak Tours
1944 Pinopolis Road
Pinopolis, SC 29469
(843) 761–1850 or (800) 761–1850
www.blackwateradventure.com

Boat Shed (Marina)
18 South St. James Street
Georgetown, SC 29440
(843) 546–4415

Bulls Bay Supply
10086 US 17 North
McClellanville, SC 29458
(843) 887–3251

Captain Dick's Marina and Explorer Fleet
4123 Highway 17 Waterfront
Murrells Inlet, SC 29576
(843) 651–3676 or (866) 557–FISH (3474)
www.captdicks.com

Captain Sandy's Tours, Inc.
P.O. Box 186
Georgetown, SC 29442
(843) 527–4106
capsandy@sccoast.net

Carolina Rover
Broad Street on the Boardwalk
Georgetown, SC 29940
(843) 546–8822 or (800) 705–9063
www.rovertours.com

Coastal Expeditions, Inc.
Cape Romain National Wildlife Refuge
and Bull Island
5801 Highway 17 North
Awendaw, SC 29429
(843) 881–4582

Miss Nell Tours
308 Front Street
Georgetown, SC 29440
(843) 546–3975
www.seaportgeorgetown.com/miss_nell_
tours.htm

Nature Adventures Outfitters
1900 I'on Swamp Road
Awendaw, SC 29429
(843) 928–3316 or (800) 673–0679
www.natureadventuresoutfitters.com

Sewee Visitor and Environmental Education Center
5821 Highway 17 North
Awendaw, SC 29429
(843) 928–3368
TDD (843) 928–3833
www.seweecenter.fws.gov

CHAPTER TWELVE: FRANCIS MARION NATIONAL FOREST

ATTRACTIONS

Cape Romain National Wildlife Refuge
5801 Highway 17 North
Awendaw, SC 29429
(843) 928–3264

Capers Island Heritage Preserve
South Carolina Heritage Trust Program
South Carolina Department of Natural
Resources
P.O. Box 167
Columbia, SC 29202
(803) 734–3893

Francis Marion National Forest
P.O. Box 788
McClellanville, SC 29458
(843) 887–3257
www.fs.fed.us/r8/fms

Hampton Plantation State Historic Park
1950 Rutledge Road
McClellanville, SC 29458
(843) 546–9361
www.southcarolinaparks.com

Huger Recreation Area
Witherbee Ranger Station
2421 Witherbee Road
Cordesville, SC 29434
(843) 336–3248
www.fs.fed.us/r8/fms

Mepkin Abbey
1098 Mepkin Abbey Road
Moncks Corner, SC 29461
(843) 761–8509
mepkin@infoave.net
www.mepkinabbey.org

Old Santee Canal Park
900 Stoney Landing Road
Moncks Corner, SC 29461
(843) 899–5200
www.oldsanteecanalpark.org

Santee Coastal Reserve
220 Santee Gun Club Road
P.O. Box 37

McClellanville, SC 29458
(843) 546–8665

Sewee Visitor and Environmental
Education Center
5821 US 17 North
Awendaw, SC 29429
(843) 928–3368 or 928–3883
seweecenter.fws.gov

Tibwin Plantation
Francis Marion National Forest
Wambaw Ranger District
P.O. Box 788
McClellanville, SC 29458
(843) 887–3257
www.fs.fed.us/r8/fms

CAMPING

Black's Fish Camp
Francis Marion National Forest
1370 Black's Camp Road
Cross, SC 29436
(843) 753–2231

Buck Hall Recreation Area
Francis Marion National Forest
P.O. Box 788
McClellanville, SC 29458
(843) 887–3257 or 336–3248
www.fs.fed.us/r8/fms

Francis Marion National Forest
Witherbee Ranger Station
2421 Witherbee Road
Cordesville, SC 29434
(843) 336–3248
www.fs.fed.us/r8/fms

James Island County Park
871 Riverland Drive
Charleston, SC 29412
(800) 743–PARK or (843) 795–9884
jicpcg@bellsouth.net
www.charlestoncampgrounds.com

S&S Campground
867 S&S Campground Lane
P.O. Box 1
Cross, SC 29436
(843) 753–7228

Neat Places to Stay

Rice Hope Plantation Inn
206 Rice Hope Drive
Moncks Corner, SC 29461
(800) 569–4038 or (843) 761–4832
www.ricehope.com

Restaurants and Shops

The Dock Seafood Restaurant and Bar
Highway 52 Tailrace Canal
Moncks Corner, SC 29461
(843) 761–8080

Sewee Restaurant
4808 Highway 17 North
Awendaw, SC 29429
(843) 928–3609

Tours and Nature-based Services

Blackwater Adventures and Kayak Tours
1944 Pinopolis Road
Pinopolis, SC 29469
(843) 761–1850 or (800) 761–1850
www.blackwateradventure.com

Coastal Expeditions, Inc.
Bull Island
514-B Mill Street
Mt. Pleasant, SC 29464
(843) 884–7684

Nature Adventures Outfitters
I'on Swamp Road
Awendaw, SC 29429
(800) 673–0679 or (843) 928–3316
www.natureadventuresoutfitters.com

Truman's Guide Service
806 Bowfin Drive
Moncks Corner, SC 29461
(843) 899–4325 or 729–2212
truman@homeexpressway.net
www.spav.com/progc/truml/default.html

CHAPTER THIRTEEN: LAKE MOULTRIE LOOP

Attractions

Cypress Gardens
3030 Cypress Gardens Road
Moncks Corner, SC 29461

(843) 553–0515
www.cypressgardens.org

Eutaw Springs Battlefield Park
SC Highway 6
Southeast of Eutawville
(no contact information)

Francis Marion National Forest
1015 North Pinckney Street
P.O. Box 788
McClellanville, SC 29458
(843) 887–3257
www.fs.fed.us/r8/fms

Mepkin Abbey
1098 Mepkin Abbey Road
Moncks Corner, SC 29461
(843) 761–8509
mepkin@infoave.net
www.mepkinabbey.com

Old Santee Canal Park
900 Stoney Landing Road
Moncks Corner, SC 29461
(843) 899–5200
www.oldsanteecanalpark.org

Palmetto Trail
Palmetto Conservation Foundation
1314 Lincoln Street, Suite 213
Columbia, SC 29201
(803) 771–0870
www.palmettoconservation.org

Camping

Angel's Landing
1556 Viper Road
Pineville, SC 29468
(843) 351–4274 or (800) 315–3087

Black's Fish Camp
Francis Marion National Forest
1370 Black's Camp Road
Cross, SC 29436
(843) 753–2231

Francis Marion National Forest
P.O. Box 788
McClellanville, SC 29458
(843) 887–3257
www.fs.fed.us/r8/fms

Harry's Fish Camp
320 Harry's Camp Circle
Pineville, SC 29468
(843) 351–4561

S&S Campground
867 S&S Campground Lane
P.O. Box 1
Cross, SC 29436
(843) 753–7228

Santee State Park
251 State Park Road
Santee, SC 29142
(803) 854–2408
www.southcarolinaparks.com

NEAT PLACES TO STAY
Rice Hope Plantation Inn
206 Rice Hope Drive
Moncks Corner, SC 29461
(800) 569–4038 or (843) 761–4832
www.ricehope.com

RESTAURANTS AND SHOPS
Black's Fish Camp
Francis Marion National Forest
1370 Black's Camp Road
Cross, SC 29436
(843) 753–2231

The Berkeley Restaurant
399 North Highway 52
Moncks Corner, SC 29461
(843) 761–8400

The Dock Seafood Restaurant and Bar
US Highway 52 Tailrace Canal
Moncks Corner, SC 29461
(843) 761–8080

Howard's
336 East Main Street
Moncks Corner, SC 29461
(843) 761– 8565

TOURS AND NATURE-BASED SERVICES
Blackwater Adventures and Kayak Tours
1944 Pinopolis Road
Pinopolis, SC 29469
(843) 761–1850 or (800) 761–1850
www.blackwateradventure.com

Fisheagle Wildlife Adventures
P.O. Box 1086
Santee, SC 29142
(803) 492–9085 or (800) 967–7739

Nature Adventures Outfitters
1900 I'on Swamp Road
Awendaw, SC 29429
(800) 673–0679 or (843) 928–3316
www.natureadventuresoutfitters.com

Truman's Guide Service
806 Bowfin Drive
Moncks Corner, SC 29461
(843) 899–4325 or 729–2212
truman@homeexpressway.net
www.spav.com/progc/truml/default.html

CHAPTER FOURTEEN:
WATEREE BASIN

ATTRACTIONS
Boykin Mill
Boykin Mill Road
Boykin, SC 29128
(803) 432–2786

Congaree Swamp National Monument
100 National Park Road
Hopkins, SC 29061
(803) 776–4396
www.nps.gov

Fort Watson/Santee Indian Mound
Santee National Wildlife Refuge
Route 2, Box 370
Summerton, SC 29148
(803) 478–2217

Historic Camden
222 Broad Street
P.O. Box 710
Camden, SC 29020
(803) 432–9841
www.historic-camden.org

Manchester State Forest
6740 Headquarters Road
Wedgefield, SC 29168
(803) 494–8196 or (800) 688–4748
manchestert@ftc-i.net

Poinsett State Park
6660 Poinsett Park Road
Wedgefield, SC 29168
(803) 494–8177
www.southcarolinaparks.com

Santee National Wildlife Refuge
2125 Fort Watson Road
Summerton, SC 29148
(803) 478–2217
www.southeast.fws.gov/santee

Santee State Park
251 State Park Road
Santee, SC 29142
(803) 854–2408
www.southcarolinaparks.com

Sumter County Museum
122 North Washington Street
Sumter, SC 29150
(803) 775–0908

Sumter Gallery of Art
200 Hasel Street
Sumter, SC 29150
(803) 775–0543

Swan Lake and Iris Gardens
West Liberty Street Extension
Sumter, SC 29150
(803) 436–2640 or (800) 688–4748

CAMPING
Campers Paradise
2449 Raccoon Road
Manning, SC 29102
(803) 473–3550

Lee State Natural Area
487 Loop Road
Bishopville, SC 29010
(803) 428–5307
www.southcarolinaparks.com

Lighthouse Point Campground
1567 Harborhouse Road
Manning, SC 29102
(803) 478–2138

Mill Creek County Park
Sumter County Recreation Department
7975 Milford Plantation Road

Pinewood, SC 29125
(803) 436–2248

Poinsett State Park
6660 Poinsett Park Road
Wedgefield, SC 29168
(803) 494–8177
www.southcarolinaparks.com

Santee Lakes Campground
1268 Gordon Road
Summerton, SC 29148
(803) 478–2262

Santee State Park
251 State Park Road
Santee, SC 29142
(803) 854–2408
www.southcarolinaparks.com

Sesquicentennial State Park
9564 Two Notch Road
Columbia, SC 29223
(803) 788–2706
www.southcarolinaparks.com

Taw Caw Campground and Marina
1328 Joyner Drive
Summerton, SC 29148
(803) 478–2171

NEAT PLACES TO STAY
A Camden Bed and Breakfast
127 Union Street
Camden, SC 29020
(803) 432–2366
www.camden.sc.bnb.com

Candlelight Inn
1904 Broad Street
Camden, SC 29020
(803) 424–1057
www.candlelightinn.org

Greenleaf Inn
1308 Broad Street
Camden, SC 29020
(803) 425–1806 or (800) 437–5874
www.greenleafinncamden.com

Magnolia House Bed and Breakfast
230 Church Street
Sumter, SC 29150

(803) 775–6694 or (888) 666–0296
www.bbonline.com/sc/magnolia

RESTAURANTS AND SHOPS
Antique Row
Broad Street
Sumter, SC 29150

Boykin Mill General Store
81 Boykin Mill Road
Rembert, SC 29128
(803) 424–4731
www.boykinmillpond.com

The Broom Place
P.O. Box 74
Rembert, SC 29128
(803) 425–0933

LeNoir Country Store and Post Office
3240 Horatio Hagood Road
Horatio, SC 29062
(803) 499–4023

Mill Pond Restaurant
73 Boykin Mill Road
Rembert, SC 29128
(803) 425–8825
www.boykinmillpond.com

Old South Restaurant
402 East Dekalb Street
Camden, SC 29020
(803) 713–0009

Summerton Diner
32 South Church Street
Summerton, SC 29148
(803) 485–6835

TOURS AND NATURE-BASED SERVICES
Adventure Carolina Canoes and Touring
Kayaks
1107 State Street
Cayce, SC 29033
(803) 796–4505
www.adventurecarolina.com

The Back Packer
1215 Wayne Street
Columbia, SC 29202
(803) 799–7571
www.backpackerqualitygear.com

Fisheagle Wildlife Adventures
P.O. Box 1086
Santee, SC 29142
(803) 492–9085 or (800) 967–7739

Great Wide Open Outfitters
35 Grier Street
Sumter, SC 29150
(803) 775–6103
www.greatwideopen.com

Moe Levy's Wilderness Station
1105 Lady Street
Columbia, SC 29201
(803) 252–7102

River Runner Outdoor Center
905 Gervais Street
Columbia, SC 29201
(803) 771–0353

CHAPTER FIFTEEN: CONGAREE BASIN AND LAKE MARION

ATTRACTIONS
Calhoun County Museum
303 Butler Street
St. Matthews, SC 29135
(803) 874–3964

Congaree Swamp National Monument
100 National Park Road
Hopkins, SC 29061
(803) 776–4396
www.nps.gov/cosw

Kensington Mansion
US Highway 601
Eastover, SC 29044
(803) 353–0456

Santee State Park
251 State Park Road
Santee, SC 29412
(803) 854–2408
www.southcarolinaparks.com

Santee National Wildlife Refuge
2125 Fortwatson Road
Summerton, SC 29148
(803) 478–2217
www.fws.gov

CAMPING

Bell's Marina
12907 Old Highway 6
Eutawville, SC 29048
(803) 492–7924
www.bellsmarina.com

Congaree Swamp National Monument
100 National Park Road
Hopkins, SC 29061
(803) 776–4396
www.nps.gov/cosw

Mill Creek Marina and Campground
216 Lake Marion Lane
Vance, SC 29163
(803) 492–7746
www.millcreekmarinacampground.com

Mountaineer Campground
Route 2, Box 204, US 301
Cameron, SC 29030
(803) 534–6453

Poinsett State Park
6660 Poinsett Park Road
Wedgefield, SC 29168
(803) 494–8177
www.southcarolinaparks.com

Rocks Pond Campground and Landing
235 Rocks Pond Road
Eutawville, SC 29048
(803) 492–7711
www.rockspondcampground.com

Santee State Park
251 State Park Road
Santee, SC 29412
(803) 854–2408
www.southcarolinaparks.com

Sesquicentennial State Park
9564 Two Notch Road
Columbia, SC 29223
(803) 788–2706
www.southcarolinaparks.com

Stumphole Landing Campground
18 Halter Court
Elloree, SC 29047
(803) 826–6111

NEAT PLACES TO STAY

Claussen's Inn
2003 Greene Street
Columbia, SC 29205
(803) 765–0440
www.claussensinn.com

Chestnut Cottage Bed and Breakfast
1718 Hampton Street
Columbia, SC 29201
(803) 256–1718
ggarrett@logicsouth.com
www.bbonline.com/sc/chestnut

Rose Hall Bed and Breakfast
1006 Barnwell Street
Columbia, SC 29201
(803) 771–2288 or (866) 771–2288
stay@rosehallbb.com
www.rosehallbb.com

Santee State Park
251 State Park Road
Santee, SC 29142
(803) 854–2408
www.southcarolinaparks.com

Two Lora's Guest House
153 West Bridge Street
St. Matthews, SC 29135
(803) 655–9048 or (800) 913–3131
lfogle9424@aol.com
www.bbonline.com/sc/twoloras/

RESTAURANTS AND SHOPS

Al Amir
2930 Devine Street
Columbia, SC 29205
(803) 771–6292

Basil Pot
928 Main Street
Columbia, SC 29201
(803) 799–0928
www.basilpot.com

Clark's Restaurant
8920 Old Number Six Highway and
Bradford Boulevard
Santee, SC 29412
(803) 854–2101
www.clarksinnrestaurant.com

Hunter-Gatherer Brewery and Ale House
900 Main Street
Columbia, SC 29201
(803) 748–0540

Immaculate Consumption
933 Main Street
Columbia, SC 29201
(803) 799–9053

Mr. Friendly's New Southern Cafe
2001-A Green Street
Columbia, SC 29205
(803) 254–7828
www.mrfriendlys.com

Rockaway Athletic Club
2719 Rosewood Drive
Columbia, SC 29205
(803) 252–6931

Villa Tronco
1213 Blanding Street
Columbia, SC 29201
(803) 256–7677
www.villatronco.com

Yesterday's Restaurant and Tavern
2030 Devine Street
Columbia, SC 29205
(803) 799–0196
www.yesterdayssc.com

Za's Brick Oven Pizza
2930 Devine Street
Columbia, SC 29205
(803) 771–7334

TOURS AND NATURE-BASED SERVICES
Adventure Carolina Canoes and Touring
Kayaks
1107 State Street
Cayce, SC 29033
(803) 796–4505
www.adventurecarolina.com

The Back Packer
1215 Wayne Street
Columbia, SC 29202
(803) 799–7571
www.backpackerqualitygear.com

Fisheagle Wildlife Adventures
P.O. Box 1086
Santee, SC 29142
(803) 492–9085 or (800) 967–7739

Moe Levy's Wilderness Station
1105 Lady Street
Columbia, SC 29201
(803) 252–7102

River Runner Outdoor Center
905 Gervais Street
Columbia, SC 29201
(803) 771–0353

CHAPTER SIXTEEN: HISTORIC CHARLESTON

ATTRACTIONS
Aiken-Rhett House
48 Elizabeth Street
Charleston, SC 29403
(843) 723–1159
www.historiccharleston.org

Avery Research Center for African American History and Culture
125 Bull Street
Charleston, SC 29424
(843) 953–7608
www.cofc.edu

Boone Hall Plantation and Gardens
US Highway 17 North
Mount Pleasant, SC 29464
(843) 884–4371
www.boonehallplantation.com

Calhoun Mansion
16 Meeting Street
Charleston, SC 29401
(843) 722–8205
Historic Charleston Foundation
www.historiccharleston.org

Charles Pinckney National Historic Site
1254 Long Point Road
Mt. Pleasant, SC 29464
(843) 881–5516
www.nps.gov

Charleston IMAX Theatre
360 Concord Street, Aquarium Wharf
Charleston, SC 29401
(843) 725–IMAX (4629)
www.charlestonimax.com

Charleston Museum
360 Meeting Street
Charleston, SC 29403
(843) 722–2996
www.charlestonmuseum.org

Charleston Area Convention and Visitors
Bureau
81 Mary Street
Charleston, SC 29403
(843) 853–0444 or (800) 868–8118
www.charlestoncvb.com

Charles Towne Landing State Historic Site
1500 Olde Towne Road
Charleston, SC 29407
(843) 852–4200

Circular Congregational Church
150 Meeting Street
Charleston, SC 29401
(843) 577–6400

The Citadel
171 Moultrie Street
Charleston, SC 29409
(843) 953–5000
www.citadel.edu

College of Charleston
66 George Street
Charleston, SC 29424
(843) 953–5507
www.cofc.edu

Dock Street Theatre
135 Church Street
Charleston, SC 29401
(843) 720–3968
www.cityofcharleston.com

Drayton Hall
3380 Ashley River Road
Charleston, SC 29414
(888) 349–0588 or (843) 769–2600
www.draytonhall.org

Edmonston-Alston House
21 East Battery
Charleston, SC 29401
(843) 722–7171
www.middletonplace.org

First Scots Presbyterian Church
53 Meeting Street
Charleston, SC 29401
(843) 722–8882

Folly Beach County Park
West Ashley Avenue
Folly Beach, SC 29439
(843) 588–2426
www.ccprc.com

Fort Moultrie
1214 Middle Street
Sullivan's Island, SC 29482
(843) 883–3910 or 883–3123
www.nps.gov/fomo

Fort Sumter National Monument
Fort Sumter Tours Inc. and Spiritline
Cruises, LLC
360 Concord Street
Charleston, SC 29401
(843) 722–2628
www.spiritlinecruises.com

Francis Marion National Forest
P.O. Box 788
McClellanville, SC 29458
(843) 887–3257
www.fs.fed.us/r8/fms

Friends of the Hunley
Warren Lasch Conservation Center
1250 Supply Street, Building 255
North Charleston, SC 20405
(843) 722–2333 or (866) 866–9938
www.hunley.org

Gibbes Museum of Art
135 Meeting Street
Charleston, SC 29401
(843) 722–2706
gibbes1@charleston.net
www.gibbes.com

HCF Museum Shop and Bookstore
108 Meeting Street

Charleston, SC 29401
(843) 724–8484 (museum)
(843) 723–1623 (bookstore)
www.historiccharleston.org

Heyward-Washington House
87 Church Street
Charleston, SC 29401
(843) 722–0354
www.charlestonmuseum.org

Historic Charleston Foundation
40 East Bay Street
Charleston, SC 29401
(843) 723–1623

Isle of Palms County Park
One 14th Avenue
Isle of Palms, SC 29451
(843) 886–3863
www.ccprc.com

James Island County Park
871 Riverland Drive
Charleston, SC 29412
(800) 743–PARK or (843) 795–9884
jicpcg@bellsouth.net
www.charlestoncampgrounds.com

Joseph-Manigault House
350 Meeting Street
Charleston, SC 29403
(843) 723–2926
www.charlestonmuseum.org

Kahal Kadosh Beth Elohim Synagogue
86 Hasell Street
Charleston, SC 29401
(843) 723–1090
www.kkbe.org

Magnolia Plantations and Its Gardens
3550 Ashley River Road
Charleston, SC 29414
(843) 571–1266
www.magnoliaplantation.com

Middleton Place Foundation
4300 Ashley River Road
Charleston, SC 29414
(843) 556–6020 or (800) 782–3608
www.middletonplace.org

Nathaniel Russell House
51 Meeting Street
Charleston, SC 29401
(843) 724–8481
www.historiccharleston.org

Old Exchange and Provost Dungeon
122 East Bay Street
Charleston, SC 29401
(843) 727–2165
www.oldexchange.com

Old Powder Magazine
79 Cumberland Street
Charleston, SC 29401
(843) 805–6730

Old Slave Market Museum
6 Chalmers Street
Charleston, SC 29401
(843) 724–7395

Palmetto Islands County Park
444 Needlerush Park
Mt. Pleasant, SC 29464
(843) 884–0832
www.ccprc.com

Patriot's Point Naval and Maritime
Museum
40 Patriots Point Road
Mt. Pleasant, SC 29464
(800) 248–3508
www.state.sc.us/patpt/

Preservation Society of Charleston
147 King Street
Charleston, SC 29401
(843) 722–4630
www.preservationsociety.org

South Carolina Aquarium
100 Aquarium Wharf
Charleston, SC 29413-9001
(843) 720–1990
www.scaquarium.org

South Carolina Historical Society
100 Meeting Street
Charleston, SC 29401
(843) 723–3225
www.schistory.org

South Carolina Society Hall
72 Meeting Street
Charleston, SC 29401
(843) 723–9032
www.cr.nps.gov

St. Philip's Episcopal Church
142 Church Street
Charleston, SC 29401
(843) 722–7734

Unitarian Church in Charleston
4 Archdale Street
Charleston, SC 29401
(843) 723–4617

CAMPING
Buck Hall Recreation Area
Francis Marion National Forest
P.O. Box 788
McClellanville, SC 29458
(843) 336–3248
www.fs.fed.us/r8/fms

Charleston KOA
9494 Highway 78
Ladson, SC 29456
(843) 797–1045 or (800) KOA–5812

Fain's Campground
6309 Fain Boulevard
Charleston, SC 29418
(843) 744–1005

James Island County Park
871 Riverland Drive
James Island, SC 29412
(800) 743–PARK or (843) 795–7275
jicpcg@bellsouth.net
www.charlestoncampgrounds.com

KOA Mt. Pleasant
3157 Highway 17 North
Mt. Pleasant, SC 29464
(843) 849–5177 or (800) KOA–5796

Oak Plantation
3540 Savannah Highway
Johns Island, SC 29455
(843) 766–5936

NEAT PLACES TO STAY
1837 Bed and Breakfast
126 Wentworth Street
Charleston, SC 29401
(843) 723–7166 or (877) 723–1837
www.1837bb.com

27 State Street Bed and Breakfast
27 State Street
Charleston, SC 29401
(843) 722–4243
www.charleston-bb.com

A Bed and Breakfast
4 Unity Alley
Charleston, SC 29401
(843) 577–6660
unitybb@aol.com
www.unitybb.com

Anchorage Inn
26 Vendue Range
Charleston, SC 29401
(843) 723–8300 or (800) 421–2952
www.anchoragen.com

Ansonborough Inn
21 Hasell Street
Charleston, SC 29401
(843) 723–1655 or (800) 522–2073
www.ansonboroughinn.com
ansonboroughinn@cchat.com

Ashley Inn B&B
201 Ashley Avenue
Charleston, SC 29403
(843) 723–1848 or (800) 581–6658
ashleyinnbb@aol.com
www.charleston-sc-inns.com

Battery Carriage House Inn
20 South Battery
Charleston, SC 29401
(843) 727–3100 or (800) 775–5575
bch@mymailstation.com
www.batterycarriagehouse.com

Belvedere Bed and Breakfast
40 Rutledge Avenue
Charleston, SC 29401
(843) 722–0973 or (800) 816–1664
www.belvedereinn.com

Cannonboro Inn B&B
184 Ashley Avenue
Charleston, SC 29403
(843) 723–8572 or (800) 235–8039
cannonboroinn@aol.com
www.charleston-sc-inns.com

Elliott House Inn
78 Queen Street
Charleston, SC 29401
(843) 723–1855 or (800) 729–1855
www.elliotthouseinn.com

Fantasia Bed and Breakfast
11 George Street
Charleston, SC 29401
(843) 853–0201 or (800) 852–4466
mail@fantasiabb.com
www.fantasiabb.com

Governor's House Inn
117 Broad Street
Charleston, SC 29401
(843) 720–2070 or (800) 720–9812
innkeeper@govhouse.com
www.governorshouse.com

Guilds Inn
101 Pitt Street
Mt. Pleasant, SC 29464
(843) 881–0510 or (800) 569–4038
lou.edens@mindspring.com
www.guildsinn.com

Hayne House Bed and Breakfast
30 King Street
Charleston, SC 29401
(843) 577–2633
haynehouse@yahoo.com
www.haynehouse.com

Indigo Inn
One Maiden Lane
Charleston, SC 29401
(843) 577–5900 or (800) 845–7639
indigoinn@crabnet.com
www.indigoinn.com

John Rutledge House Inn
116 Broad Street
Charleston, SC 29401
(843) 723–7999 or (800) 476–9741
jrh@charminginns.com
www.charminginns.com

Kings Courtyard Inn
198 King Street
Charleston, SC 29401
(843) 723–7000 or (800) 845–6119
kci@charminginns.com
www.charminginns.com

The Kitchen House
126 Tradd Street
Charleston, SC 29401
(843) 577–6362
loisevans@worldnet.att.net
www.cityofcharleston.com/kitchen.htm

Long Point Inn Bed and Breakfast
1199 Long Point Road
Mt. Pleasant, SC 29464
(843) 849–1884
infor@charleston-longptinn.com
www.charleston-longptinn.com

Meeting Street Inn
173 Meeting Street
Charleston, SC 29401
(843) 723–1882 or (800) 842–8022
meetingstreetinn@crabnet.net
www.meetingstreetinn.com

Mills House Hotel
Meeting and Queen Street
Charleston, SC 29401
(800) 874–9600 or (843) 577–2400
stay@millshouse.com
www.millshouse.com

Phoebe Pember House
East Bay B&B
26 Society Street
Charleston, SC 29401
(843) 722–4186
www.phoebepemberhouse.com

Planters Inn
112 North Market Street
Charleston, SC 29401
(843) 722–2345 or (800) 845–7082
www.plantersinn.com

Rutledge Victorian Guest House
114 Rutledge Avenue
Charleston, SC 29401
(843) 722–7551 or (888) 722–7553
normlyn@prodigy.net
www.charlestonvictorian.com

Sunny Meadows
1459 Venning Road
Mt. Pleasant, SC 29464
(800) 569–4038 or (843) 881–0510
www.bbonline.com/sc/sunny

Thirty-Six Meeting Street B&B
36 Meeting Street
Charleston, SC 29401
(843) 722–1034
abrandt@awod.com
www.36meetingstreet.com

Thomas Lamboll House
19 King Street
Charleston, SC 29401
(843) 723–3212 or (888) 874–0793
lamboll@aol.com
www.lambollhouse.com/home.htm

Two Meeting Street Inn
2 Meeting Street
Charleston, SC 29401
(843) 723–7322
www.twomeetingstreet.com

Wentworth Mansion
149 Wentworth Street
Charleston, SC 29401
(843) 853–1886 or (888) INN–1886
mgr@wentworthmansion.com

Zero Water Street Bed and Breakfast
31 East Battery
Charleston, SC 29401
(843) 723–2841
bettygeer@aol.com
www.zerowaterstreet.com

RESTAURANTS AND SHOPS
Anson's Restaurant
12 Anson Street
Charleston, SC 29401
(843) 577–0551
www.ansonrestaurant.com

Blossom Cafe
171 East Bay Street
Charleston, SC 29403
(843) 722–9200
www.magnolias-blossom-cypress.com

The Boathouse
101 Palm Boulevard
Isle of Palms, SC 29451
(843) 886–8000
www.boathouserestaurant.com

Bocci's Italian Restaurant
158 Church Street
Charleston, SC 29401
(843) 720–2121
www.boccis.com

Bowen's Island Restaurant
1871 Bowen's Island Road
Charleston, SC 29412
(843) 795–2757

Carolina Galleries
188 King Street
Charleston, SC 29401
(843) 723–2266 or 577–9212
www.carolinagalleries.com

Charleston Gardens
61 Queen Street
Charleston, SC 29401
(843) 723–0252
www.charlestongardens.com

Circa 1886 Restaurant
149 Wentworth Street
Charleston, SC 29401
(843) 853–7828
www.circa1886.com

Coleman Fine Art
45 Hasell Street
Charleston, SC 29401
(843) 853–7000
www.colemanfineart.com

82 Queen
82 Queen Street
Charleston, SC 29401
(800) 849–0082 or (843) 723–7591
www.82queen.com

Fish
442 King Street
Charleston, SC 29401
(843) 722–3474
www.fishrestaurant.net

Garibaldi's Cafe
49 South Market Street
Charleston, SC 29401
(843) 723–7153

High Cotton
199 East Bay Street
Charleston, SC 29401
(843) 724–3815
www.mavericksouthernkitchens.com

Historic Charleston Museum Shop
108 Meeting Street
Charleston, SC 29401
(843) 724–8484
www.historiccharleston.org

Il Pescatore Restaurante
201 Coleman Boulevard
Mt. Pleasant, SC 29464
(843) 971–3931

Juanita Greenberg's Nacho Royale
439 King Street
Charleston, SC 29403
(843) 723–6224

Kahoal Kadosh Beth Elohim Judaica
Shop
86 Hasell Street
Charleston, SC 29401
(843) 723–7324
www.kkbe.org

The Library Restaurant and Rooftop Bar
23 Vendue Range
Charleston, SC 29401
(843) 723–0485

Magnolia's
185 East Bay Street
Charleston, SC 29401
(843) 577–7771
www.magnolias-blossom-cypress.com

Martin Gallery
57 Queen Street
Charleston, SC 29401
(843) 723–7378
www.martingallerycharleston.com

Moo Roo Handbags
316 King Street

Charleston, SC 29401
(843) 534–2233
www.mooroo.com

Noah's Nook
188 Meeting Street
Charleston, SC 29401
(843) 722–8002

One Eyed Parrot
1130 Ocean Boulevard
Isle of Palms, SC 29451
(843) 886–4360
questions@oneeyedparrot.com

Peninsula Grill
112 North Market Street
Charleston, SC 29401
(843) 723–0700
www.peninsulagrill.com

Poogan's Porch
72 Queen Street
Charleston, SC 29401
(843) 577–2337
www.poogansporch.com

Robert's of Charleston
182 East Bay Street
Charleston, SC 29401
(843) 577–7565

Slightly North of Broad
192 East Bay Street
Charleston, SC 29401
(843) 723–3424
www.slightlynorthofbroad.net

Vincenzo's
232 Meeting Street
Charleston, SC 29401
(843) 577–7953

The Wreck
106 Haddell Street
Mt. Pleasant, SC 29464
(843) 884–0052

Your Place
6 Market Street
Charleston, SC 29401
(843) 722–8360

Tours and Nature-Based Services

Aqua Safari, Inc.
P.O. Box 309
Isle of Palms, SC 29451
(843) 886–8133 or (800) 524–3444
www.aqua-safaris.com

Barrier Island Ecotours
P.O. Box 343
Isle of Palms, SC 29421
www.nature-tours.com
(843) 886–5000

Bohicket Yacht Charters and Boat Rentals
1880 Andell Bluff Boulevard
Bohicket Marina
Johns Island, SC 29455
(843) 768–7294
www.bohicketboat.com

Captain Richard Stuhr
547 Sanders Farm Lane
Charleston, SC 29492
(843) 881–3179
www.captstuhr.com

Charleston Harbor Tours
196 Concord Street
Charleston, SC 29401
(843) 722–1112 or (800) 344–4483

Coastal Expeditions, Inc.
Shem Creek Maritime Center
514B Mill Street
Mt. Pleasant, SC 29464
(843) 884–7684
www.coastalexpeditions.com

Doin' the Charleston Tours, Inc.
P.O. Box 31338
Charleston, SC 29417-1338
(843) 763–1233 or (800) 647–4487
mkatzen@dointhecharlestontours.com
www.dointhecharlestontours.com

Edwin S. Taylor Fishing Pier
101 East Artic Avenue
Folly Beach, SC 29439
(843) 588–FISH (3474)

Fort Sumter Tours Inc. and Spiritline
Cruises, LLC
360 Concord Street

Charleston, SC 29401
(843) 722–2628
www.spiritlinecruises.com

Gray Line of Charleston
29 Broad Street
Charleston, SC 29401
(843) 722–4444 or (800) 423–0444
grayline@bellsouth.net
www.graylineofcharleston.com

Old Towne Carriage Company
20 Anson Street
Charleston, SC 29401
(843) 722–1315
www.toursofcharleston.com

On the Market Tours
338 President Street
Charleston, SC 29401
(843) 883–8687
www.onthemarkettours.com

Outdoor Discovery Tours, Inc.
5900 Rivers Avenue
North Charleston, SC 29406
(843) 744–1224
www.dolphin-tours.com

Sandlapper Water Tours
1313 Wylls-Neck
Mt. Pleasant, SC 29464
(843) 849–TOUR

Tour Charleston, LLC
184 East Bay Street
Charleston, SC 29401
(843) 723–1670
www.tourcharleston.com

CHAPTER SEVENTEEN: WADMALAW, JOHNS, AND EDISTO ISLANDS

Attractions

Angel Oak Park
3688 Angel Oak Road
Johns Island, SC 29455
(843) 559–3496

Beachwalker Park
Beachwalker Drive
Kiawah Island, SC 29455
(843) 768–2395
www.ccprc.com

Caw Caw Interpretive Center
5200 Savannah Highway 17 South
Ravenel, SC 29470
(843) 889–8898
www.ccprc.com/cawcaw.htm

Charleston Tea Plantation
6617 Maybank Highway
Wadmalaw Island, SC 29487
(843) 559–0383 or (800) 443–5987
charstea@awod.com

Edisto Island Historic Preservation
Museum
2343 Highway 174
P.O. Box 393
Edisto Island, SC 29438
(843) 869–1954
haigandfrankedisto@yahoo.com

The Grove
ACE Basin National Wildlife Refuge
U.S. Fish and Wildlife Service
P.O. Box 848
Hollywood, SC 29449
(843) 889–3084

CAMPING
Edisto Beach State Park
8377 State Cabin Road
Edisto Island, SC 29438
(843) 869–2756 or 869–2156
www.southcarolinaparks.com

Fains Campground
63089 Fain Street
Charleston, SC 29406
(843) 744–1005

James Island County Park
871 Riverland Drive
Charleston, SC 29412
(800) 743–PARK or (843) 795–7275
jicpcg@bellsouth.net
www.charlestoncampgrounds.com

Lake Aire RV Campground
4375 Highway 162
Hollywood, SC 29449
(843) 571–1271
www.lakeairerv.com

Oak Plantation
3540 Savannah Highway
Johns Island, SC 29455
(843) 766–5936

NEAT PLACES TO STAY
Edisto Beach State Park
8377 State Cabin Road
Edisto Island, SC 29438
(843) 869–2756 or 869–2156
www.southcarolinaparks.com

Fairfield Ocean Ridge
1 King Cotton Road
Edisto Island, SC 29438
(843) 869–2561 or (800) 845–8500

James Island County Park
871 Riverland Drive
Charleston, SC 29412
(800) 743–PARK or (843) 795–7275
jicpcg@bellsouth.net
www.charlestoncampgrounds.com

Old Academy Bed and Breakfast
904 Hampton Street
Walterboro, SC 29488
(843) 549–3232
info@oldacademybandb.com
www.oldacademybandb.com

RESTAURANTS AND SHOPS
Bowen's Island Restaurant
1871 Bowen's Island Road
Charleston, SC 29412
(843) 795–2757

Charleston Tea Plantation
6617 Maybank Highway
Wadmalaw Island, SC 29487
(843) 559–0383 or (800) 443–5987
charstea@awod.com

Dock Side Restaurant
3730 Dock Site Road
Edisto Beach, SC 29438
(843) 869–2695

Farm House Antiques
4915 Savannah Highway
Ravenel, SC 29470
(843) 889–9829

Heron House Restaurant
21 Fairway Drive
Edisto Island, SC 29438
(843) 869–1112

Jackson's Antiques Gallery
3823 Savannah Highway
Johns Island, SC 29455
(843) 556–9008

Old Post Office Restaurant
1442 Highway 174
Edisto Island, SC 29438
(843) 869–2339

Pavilion Restaurant and Coot's Lounge
102 Palmetto Boulevard
Edisto Beach, SC 29438
(843) 869–3061
www.belledisto.com

The Privateer
1882 Andell Bluff Boulevard
Johns Island, SC 29455
(843) 768–1290

Red Sky Grill
1001 Landfall Way
Johns Island, SC 29455
(843) 768–0183

Robert Sarco Antiques
6317 Highway 162
P.O. Box 309
Hollywood, SC 29449
(843) 889–3007

Rosebank Farms Cafe
1886 Andell Bluff Boulevard
Johns Island, SC 29455
(843) 768–1807

Sea Cow Eatery
145 Jungle Road
Edisto Beach, SC 29438
(843) 869–3222

With These Hands Gallery
1444 SC Highway 174
Edisto Island, SC 29438
(843) 869–3509

TOURS AND NATURE-BASED SERVICES
ACE Basin Bioreserve Office
8675 Willtown Road
Hollywood, SC 29449
(843) 889–2427

ACE Basin Tours, Inc.
One Coosaw River Drive
Beaufort, SC 29907
(866) 521–3099
www.acebasintours.com

Captain Ivan's Island Charters
805 Duck Hawk Retreat
Charleston, SC 29412
(843) 762–2020

Carolina Heritage Outfitters
US Highway 15
Canadys, SC 29433
(843) 563–5051
www.canoesc.com
canoesc@mindspring.com

Edisto Island Marina
3702 Docksite Road
Edisto Beach, SC 29438
(843) 869–3504

Edisto Island Serpentarium
1374 Highway 174
Edisto Island, SC 29438
(843) 869–1171
eserpentarium@aol.com
www.edistoserpentarium.com

Edisto Watersports and Tackle, Inc.
3731 Dock Site Road
Edisto Beach, SC 29438
(843) 869–0663
www.luckystrikecharters.com

Kiawah Island Visitor Center
22 Beachwalker Drive
Kiawah Island, SC 29455
(843) 853–8000

Pon Pon Guides Unlimited
P.O. Box 441
Edisto Island, SC 29438
(843) 869–7929

Tullifany Joe's Outposts
Coosaw Way
Knowles Island, SC 29936
(843) 726–6468 or (800) 228–8420
kidco@hargray.com
www.palmkey.com

CHAPTER EIGHTEEN: EDISTO AND ASHLEY RIVERS

ATTRACTIONS
Bee City
1066 Holly Ridge Lane
Highway 61
Cottageville, SC 29435
(843) 835–5912
www.beecity.net

Charles Towne Landing State Historic Site
1500 Old Towne Road
Charleston, SC 29407
(843) 852–4200
www.southcarolinaparks.com

Colleton State Park
147 Wayside Lane
Canadys, SC 29433
(843) 538–8206
www.southcarolinaparks.com

Colonial Dorchester State Historic Site
300 State Park Road
Summerville, SC 29485
(843) 873–1740
www.southcarolinaparks.com

Drayton Hall
3380 Ashley River Road
Charleston, SC 29414
(888) 349–0588
(843) 769–2600
www.draytonhall.org

Francis Beidler Forest
336 Sanctuary Road
Harleyville, SC 29448

(803) 462–2150
www.pride-net.com/swamp

Givhans Ferry State Park
746 Givhans Ferry Road
Ridgeville, SC 29472
(803) 873–0692
www.southcarolinaparks.com

Magnolia Plantation and Its Gardens
3550 Ashley River Road
Charleston, SC 29414
(843) 571–1266
www.magnoliaplantation.com

Middleton Place Foundation
4300 Ashley River Road
Charleston, SC 29414
(843) 556–6020 or (800) 782–3608
www.middletonplace.org

CAMPING
Colleton State Park
147 Wayside Lane
Canadys, SC 29433
(843) 538–8206
www.southcarolinaparks.com

Givhans Ferry State Park
746 Givhans Ferry Road
Ridgeville, SC 29472
(843) 873–0692
www.southcarolinaparks.com

NEAT PLACES TO STAY
The Inn at Middleton Place
4300 Ashley River Road
Charleston, SC 29414
(843) 556–0500 or (800) 543–4774
www.middletonplace.org

Woodlands Resort and Inn
125 Parsons Road
Summerville, SC 29483
(843) 875–2600 or (800) 774–9999
reservations@woodlandsinn.com
www.woodlandsinn.com

RESTAURANTS AND SHOPS
Drayton Hall's Museum Shop
3380 Ashley River Road
Charleston, SC 29414

(888) 349–0588 or (843) 769–2600
www.draytonhall.org

Lowder's Ban Tam Chef
310 South Parler Avenue
St. George, SC 29477
(843) 563–2878

Magnolia Plantation's Art Gallery and
Gift Shop
3550 Ashley River Road
Charleston, SC 29414
(843) 571–1266
www.magnoliaplantation.com

Middleton Place Museum Shop and
Restaurant
4300 Ashley River Road
Charleston, SC 29414-7266
(843) 556–6020 or (800) 782–3608
www.middletonplace.org

Vaughan's General Store
437 South Railroad Avenue
Ridgeville, SC 29472
(843) 873–1716
www.vaughsinc@aol.com

TOURS AND NATURE-BASED SERVICES

Captain Ivan's Island Charters
805 Duck Hawk Retreat
Charleston, SC 29412
(843) 762–2020
www.captainivan.com

Carolina Heritage Outfitters
US Highway 15
Canadys, SC 29433
(843) 563–5051
www.canoesc.com
canoesc@mindspring.com

Edisto River Canoe and Kayak Trail
Walterboro-Colleton Chamber of Commerce
213 Jefferies Boulevard
P.O. Box 1763
Walterboro, SC 29488
(803) 549–9595

Middleton Place Plantation and Tours
4300 Ashley River Road

Charleston, SC 29414-7266
(843) 556–6020 or (800) 782–3608
www.middletonplace.org

CHAPTER NINETEEN: ACE BASIN

ATTRACTIONS

ACE Basin National Wildlife Refuge
Combahee Unit
P.O. Box 848
Hollywood, SC 29449
(843) 889–3084

Bear Island Wildlife Management Area
585 Donnelley Drive
Green Pond, SC 29446
(843) 844–8957
www.walterboro.org/ACE-Basin/
bearisland.html

Bedon-Lucas House Museum
Colleton County Historical Society
205 Church Street
Walterboro, SC 29488
(843) 549–1922

Colleton Museum
239 North Jeffries Boulevard
Walterboro, SC 29488
(843) 549–2303
museum@lowcountry.com

Donnelley Wildlife Management Area
585 Donnelley Drive
Green Pond, SC 29446
(843) 844–8957

Lowcountry Visitors Center and Museum
1 Lowcountry Lane
Point South, SC 29945
(843) 717–3090 or (800) 528–6870
come2sc@hargray.com
www.sclowcountry.com

South Carolina Artisans Center
334 Wichman Street
Walterboro, SC 29488
(843) 549–0011
artisan@lowcountry.com
www.scartisanscenter.org

CAMPING

Colleton State Park
147 Wayside Lane
Canadys, SC 29433
(843) 538–8206
www.southcarolinaparks.com

Edisto Beach State Park
8377 State Cabin Road
Edisto Island, SC 29438
(843) 869–2756
www.southcarolinaparks.com

Green Acres RV Park
396 Campground Road
Walterboro, SC 29488
(843) 538–3450 or (800) 474–3450

The Oaks
Route 1, Box 52-C
Yemassee, SC 29945
(843) 726–5728

Wood Brothers Campground
8446 ACE Basin Parkway
US Highway 17 South
Green Pond, SC 29446
(800) 547–9940

Yemassee Point South KOA
P.O. Box 1760, US 17
Yemassee, SC 29945
(843) 726–5733 or (800) KOA–2948

NEAT PLACES TO STAY

Old Academy Bed and Breakfast
904 Hampton Street
Walterboro, SC 29488
(843) 549–3232
info@oldacademybandb.com
www.oldacademybandb.com

RESTAURANTS AND SHOPS

Antique Mall at Warshaw's
220 East Washington Street
Walterboro, SC 29488
(843) 549–6954

Hiott's Pharmacy
373 East Washington Street
Walterboro, SC 29488
(843) 549–7222

Jacksonboro Antiques
16845 ACE Basin Parkway
Jacksonboro, SC 29452
(843) 893–2850

The Judges Chambers
115 East Washington Street
Walterboro, SC 29488
(843) 549–9397

South Carolina Artisans Center
334 Wichman Street
Walterboro, SC 29488
(843) 549–0011
artisan@lowcountry.com
www.scartisanscenter.org

Sweetgrass Baskets and Things
206 Washington Street
Walterboro, SC 29488
(843) 542–9083

Toomer's Restaurant
16804 ACE Basin Parkway
Jacksonboro, SC 29452
(843) 893–2014

TOURS AND NATURE-BASED SERVICES

Cap'n Richards ACE Basin Nature Trail
P.O. Box 31254
Charleston, SC 29417
(843) 766–9664
www.acebasinescapes.com

Carolina Heritage Outfitters
US Highway 15
Canadys, SC 29433
(843) 563–5051
www.canoesc@mindspring.com

Coastal Expeditions, Inc
514-B Mill Street
Mt. Pleasant, SC 29464
(843) 884–7684
www.coastalexpeditions.com

Tullifany Joe's Outposts
Coosaw Way
Knowles Island, SC 29936
(800) 228–8420 or (843) 726–6468
kidco@hargray.com
www.palmkey.com

CHAPTER TWENTY: HISTORIC BEAUFORT AND SEA ISLANDS

ATTRACTIONS

Historic Beaufort Foundation
202 Scott Street
Beaufort, SC 29902
(843) 379–3331
www.beaufortcitysc.com

Hunting Island State Park
2555 Sea Island Parkway
Hunting Island, SC 29920
(843) 838–2011
www.southcarolinaparks.com

John Mark House Museum
801 Bay Street
Beaufort, SC 29902
(843) 524–6334 or 379–3331

Lowcountry Estuarium
1402 Paris Avenue
Port Royal, SC 29935
(843) 524–6600
www.lowcountryestuarium.org

Penn Center, Inc.
Cultural Center Museum
P.O. Box 126
16 Penn Center Circle West
St. Helena Island, SC 29920
(843) 838–2474

U.S. Marine Corps Recruit Depot
Museum
Building 111 Panama Street
Parris Island, SC 29905
(843) 228–2951
www.parrisisland.com

CAMPING

Hunting Island State Park
2555 Sea Island Parkway
Hunting Island, SC 29920
(843) 838–2011
www.southcarolinaparks.com

Stoney Crest Plantation Campground
419 May River Road
Bluffton, SC 29910
(843) 757–3249

Tuc In De Woods
#22 Tuc In De Woods
St. Helena's Island, SC 29920
(843) 838–2267

NEAT PLACES TO STAY

The Beaufort Inn
809 Port Republic Street
Beaufort, SC 29902
(843) 521–9000
www.beaufortinn.com

Beaulieu House at Cat Island
3 Sheffield Court
Beaufort, SC 29902
(843) 770–0303

Craven Street Inn
1103 Craven Street
Beaufort, SC 29902
(843) 522–1668
www.thecravenstreetinn.com

The Cuthbert House Inn
1203 Bay Street
Beaufort, SC 29902
(843) 521–1315 or (800) 327–9275
www.cuthberthouseinn.com

Hunting Island State Park
2555 Sea Island Parkway
Hunting Island, SC 29920
(843) 838–2011
www.southcarolinaparks.com

Old Point Inn
212 New Street
Beaufort, SC 29902
(843) 524–3177
www.oldpointinn.com

Rhett House Inn
1009 Craven Street
Beaufort, SC 29902
(843) 524–9030
www.rhetthouseinn.com

Two Suns Inn Bed and Breakfast
1705 Bay Street
Beaufort, SC 29902
(843) 522–1122 or (800) 532–4244
www.twosunsinn.com

RESTAURANTS AND SHOPS

The Bank Waterfront Grill and Bar
926 Bay Street
Beaufort, SC 29902
(843) 522–8831

Bay Towne Hall Grille
310 West Street
Beaufort, SC 29902
(843) 522–3880

Boombears
501 Carteret Street
Beaufort, SC 29902
(843) 524–2525

The Chocolate Tree
507 Carteret Street
Beaufort, SC 29902
(843) 524–7980

The Craftseller
818 Bay Street
Beaufort, SC 29902
(843) 525–6104

Dockside Restaurant
1699 11th Street
Port Royal, SC 29935
(843) 524–7433

Frogmore Frolics
849 Sea Island Parkway
St. Helena Island, SC 29920
(843) 838–9102

Harry's Restaurant
John Cross Tavern
812 Bay Street
Beaufort, SC 29902
(843) 524–3993

Magnolia Bakery and Cafe
703 Congress Street
Beaufort, SC 29902
(843) 524–1961

Michael Rainey Antiques and Bellavista
Antiques
702 Craven Street
Beaufort, SC 29902
(843) 521–4532

Plums
904½ Bay Street
Beaufort, SC 29902
(843) 525–1946

Port Royal Seafood, Inc.
1111 11th Street
Port Royal, SC 29935
(843) 521–5095

Red Piano Too Art and Gallery
870 Sea Island Parkway
St. Helena Island, SC 29920
(843) 838–2241

Rhett Gallery, Inc.
901 Bay Street
Beaufort, SC 29902
(843) 524–3339

Steamer's Restaurant
168 Sea Island Parkway
Beaufort, SC 29902
(843) 522–0210

What's In Store
853 Sea Island Parkway
St. Helena, SC 29920
(843) 838–7473

TOURS AND NATURE-BASED SERVICES

ACE Basin Tours
One Coosaw River Drive
Beaufort, SC 29902
(843) 521–3099 or (888) 814–3129
info@acebasintours.com

Bicycles-Pedals Rental Sale and Service
71 Pope Avenue
Beaufort, SC 29902
(843) 842–5522

Captain Eddie's Fishing Charters and
Sightseeing Cruises
28 Saltwind Drive
St. Helena Island, SC 29920
(843) 838–3782

Captain Wally's Seawolf
Port Royal Landing Marina
Port Royal, SC 29935
(843) 525–1174
www.scfishnet.com

Greater Beaufort Chamber of Commerce
and Visitors Center
1106 Carteret Street
Beaufort, SC 29902
(843) 986–5400

Gullah Heritage Trail Tour
Hilton Head Island Tour
36 Guntree Road
Hilton Head, SC 29926
(843) 681–7066

Gullah-n-Geechie Mahn Tours
P.O. Box 1248
St. Helena Island, SC 29920
(843) 838–7516
www.gullah-n-geechietours.net

Historic Beaufort Tours by Water
Waterfront Park on Bay Street
Beaufort, SC 29902
(843) 524–4000

The Kayak Farm
1289 Sea Island Parkway
St. Helena Island, SC 29920
(843) 838–2008
www.kayakfarm@islc.net

Lowcountry Bicycles
102 Sea Island Parkway
Lady's Island, SC 29907
(843) 524–9585
www.lowcountrybicycles.com

CHAPTER TWENTY-ONE: LOWER SAVANNAH RIVER VALLEY

ATTRACTIONS
Audubon Newhall Preserve
Palmetto Bay Road
Hilton Head Island, SC 29925

Coastal Discovery Museum
Hilton Head Island Visitors Center
100 William Hilton Parkway/US 278
Hilton Head Island, SC 29925
(843) 689–6767
www.coastaldiscovery.org

Pinckney Island National Wildlife Refuge
Savannah Coastal Refuges
1000 Business Center Drive
Parkway Business Center, Suite 10
Savannah, GA 31405
(912) 652–4415
www.savannah.fws.gov

Savannah National Wildlife Refuge
Savannah Coastal Refuges
1000 Business Center Drive
Parkway Business Center, Suite 10
Savannah, GA 31405
(912) 652–4415
www.savannah.fws.gov

Sea Pines Forest Preserve
Sea Pines Company
32 Greenwood Drive
Hilton Head Island, SC 29928
(843) 363–4530
www.seapines.com

Tillman Sand Ridge Heritage Preserve
South Carolina Heritage Trust Program
South Carolina Department of Natural
Resources
P.O. Box 167
Columbia, SC 29200
(803) 734–3893
www.dnr.state.sc.us

Victoria Bluff Heritage Preserve
South Carolina Heritage Trust Program
South Carolina Department of Natural
Resources
P.O. Box 167
Columbia, SC 29200
(803) 734–3893
www.dnr.state.sc.us

Waddell Mariculture Research and
Development Center
Sawmill Creek Road
Bluffton, SC 29910
(843) 837–3795
www.dnr.state.sc.us

Webb Wildlife Center
1282 Webb Avenue
Garnett, SC 29922
(803) 625–3569

Camping

The Oaks at Point South RV Resort
Route 1, Box 52C
Yemassee, SC 29945
(843) 726–5728

Outdoor Resorts Motor Coach
133 Arrow Road
Hilton Head, SC 29928
(843) 785–7699 or (800) 722–2365
www.hiltonheadmotorcoachresort.com

Outdoor Resorts RV Resort
and Yacht Club
43 Jenkins Road
Hilton Head Island, SC 29926
(843) 681–3256 or (800) 845–9560
www.outdoor-rv.com

Stoney Crest Plantation Campground
419 May River Road/Highway 46
Bluffton, SC 29910
(843) 757–3249

Yemassee Point South KOA
P.O. Box 1760, US 17
Yemassee, SC 29945
(843) 726–5733 or (800) KOA–2948

Neat Places to Stay

Carolina House of Bluffton
800 Fording Island Road
Bluffton, SC 29910
(843) 815–2555
www.southernassisted.com

Palm Key
26 Coosaw Way
Knowles Island, SC 29936
(800) 228–8420 or (843) 726–6468
getawaycottage@palmkey.com
www.palmkey.com

Restaurants and Shops

The Cooper Kitchen
5 Geoffrey Place
SC Highway 46
Bluffton, SC 29910
(843) 815–4555

Crossroads Fine Art and Framing
107 Towne Centre
27 Mellichamp Drive
Bluffton, SC 29910
(843) 757–5551
www.crossroadsfineart.com

Heyward House Historic Center
52 Boundary Street
Bluffton, SC 29910
(843) 757–6293

Hilton Head Factory Stores I and II
1414 Fording Island Road
Bluffton, SC 29910
(843) 837–4339

Jasper's Restaurant
US Highway 17
Hardeeville, SC 29927
(843) 784–5800

Red Piano Art Gallery
220 Cordiollo Parkway
Hilton Head Island, SC 29928
(843) 785–2318
www.artnet.com/redpiano.html

Self Family Arts Center
14 Shelter Cove Lane
Hilton Head Island, SC 29925
(843) 686–3945
www.artscenter-hhi.org

Squat and Gobble
1231 May River Road
Bluffton, SC 29910
(843) 757–4242

Tours and Nature-Based Services

Adventure Cruises
Shelter Cove Marina
Harborside 3, Suite G
Hilton Head Island, SC 29928
(843) 785–4558

Captain Sonny Dolphin and Nature Cruises
Broad Creek Marina
Marshland Road
Hilton Head Island, SC 29926
(843) 681–2522
www.dolphin-watch.net

Cedar Tree Plantation, LLC
1-77 at Exit 34
Ridgeway, SC 29130
(803) 788–8010
arsmythe@msn.com
www.cedartreeplantation.com

Cool Breeze Kayaking
P.O. Box 21896
Hilton Head Island, SC 29925
(843) 683–4040 or (877) 286–5154
www.coolbreezekayaking.com

Harbor Town Lighthouse Legends Tour
149 Lighthouse Road
Hilton Head Island, SC 29928
(843) 671–2810
www.harbortownlighthouse.com

Lawton Stables
Sea Pines Plantation
190 Greenwood Drive
Hilton Head Island, SC 29928
(843) 671–2586

Outside Hilton Head
Plaza at Shelter Cove, Highway 278
Hilton Head Island, SC 29928
(843) 686–6996 or (800) 686–6996
www.outsidehiltonhead.com

Palm Key
Coosaw Way
Knowles Island, SC 29936
(800) 228–8420 or (843) 726–6468
getawaycottage@palmkey.com
www.palmkey.com

Helpful Organizations

SOUTH CAROLINA STATE GOVERNMENT

For general information about South Carolina, visit the State Government Web site at www.myscgov.com.

South Carolina Department of Parks, Recreation, and Tourism
1205 Pendleton Street
Columbia, SC 29201
(803) 734–0173
www.discoversouthcarolina.com/ stateparks
www.sctrails.net
The Division of Park Services operates South Carolina's forty-eight state parks. The South Carolina Trails Program is administered by the department's State Trails Coordinator. Brochures are available on each state park, and *Parkview* is an excellent periodical that lists programs and outings offered at all state parks.

South Carolina Tourism Office
South Carolina Department of Parks, Recreation, and Tourism
P.O. Box 71
Columbia, SC 29202
(803) 734–0126
www.discoversouthcarolina.com
The South Carolina Tourism Office provides a wide variety of tourist information and publishes the annual *South Carolina Travel Guide.*

Office of Heritage Tourism Development
1205 Pendleton Street
Columbia, SC 29201
(803) 734–0141
www.sc-heritagecorridor.org
The Heritage Tourism Development Office is developing South Carolina's Heritage Corridor (which runs up the Edisto River Basin from Charleston to North Augusta, then northwest up the Savannah River Valley) and promoting heritage tourism throughout the state.

South Carolina Department of Natural Resources
P.O. Box 167
Columbia, SC 20202
(803) 734–3883 (general information, hunting and fishing)
(803) 734–3893 (Heritage Trust)
www.dnr.state.sc.us
Contact DNR for information on Heritage Trust, hunting, fishing, Wildlife Management Areas, or *South Carolina Wildlife* magazine.

South Carolina Department of Natural Resources Office
2221 Devine Street
Columbia, SC 29205
(803) 734–9108
Request USGS maps through the DNR's Maps and Information Center. For information on the state's rivers, contact the Environmental Affairs Division.

South Carolina Department of Transportation
Bicycle/Pedestrian Coordinator
Department of Transportation
Park Street, P.O. Box 191
Columbia, SC 29202
(803) 737–1052
www.dot.state.sc.us
doddsdt@dot.state.sc.us
The Bicycle/Pedestrian Program is responsible for creating and extending a bicycle and pedestrian transportation system throughout South Carolina. This office offers technical assistance on bicycle lanes, shoulders, bicycling as transportation, and pedestrian issues. Also contact the DOT for road information and state, county, city, and town maps.

OTHER GOVERNMENT AGENCIES

South Carolina Aquarium
100 Aquarium Wharf
Charleston, SC 29413-9001
(843) 720–1990
www.scaquarium.org

South Carolina Institute of Archaeology and Anthropology
1321 Pendleton Street
Columbia, SC 29208
(803) 734–0567
www.cla.sc.edu/sciaa

South Carolina Forestry Commission
P.O. Box 21707
Columbia, SC 29221
(803) 896–8831
www.forestry.state.sc.us

South Carolina State Library
1500 Senate Street
Columbia, SC 29201
(803) 734–8666
www.state.sc.us/scsl

South Carolina State Museum
301 Gervais Street
Columbia, SC 29201
(803) 898–4921
www.museum.state.sc.us

South Carolina Department of Archives and History
8301 Parklane Road
Columbia, SC 20223
(803) 896–6100
www.state.sc.us/scdah

UNITED STATES GOVERNMENT OFFICES

U.S. Department of Agriculture (USDA) Forest Service
Francis Marion and Sumter National Forests
4931 Broad River Road
Columbia, SC 29201-4021
(803) 561–4000
www.fs.fed/r8/fms

This is the central office for National Forest operations throughout South Carolina.

National Park Service
Congaree Swamp Site
200 Caroline Sims Road
Hopkins, SC 292061
(803) 776–4396
www.nps.gov

PRIVATE SOURCES OF INFORMATION

Center for Carolina Living
4201 Blossom Street
Columbia, SC 29205
(803) 782–7466
www.carolinaliving.com
The center provides information about retirement and relocation.

Hospitality Association of South Carolina
1338 Main Street, Suite 505
Columbia, SC 29201
(803) 765–9000
www.schospitality.org

Nature Conservancy
2600 Devine Street
Columbia, SC 29205
(803) 254–9049
www.nature.org

Palmetto Conservation Foundation and Palmetto Trails
1314 Lincoln Street
Columbia, SC 29201
(803) 771–0870
www.palmettoconservation.org

South Carolina Bed and Breakfast Association
P.O. Box 2020
Georgetown, SC 29442
(888) 599–1234
www.southcarolinabedandbreakfast.com
This organization publishes the South Carolina Bed and Breakfast Association Member Directory.

South Carolina Campground Owners Association
20 Surrey Court
Columbia, SC 29212
(803) 772–5354
www.sccamping.com
Contact the Campground Owners Association for a directory of campgrounds in the state.

Sierra Club
South Carolina Chapter
1314 Lincoln Street
Columbia, SC 29201
(803) 256–8487
www.southcarolina.sierraclub.org

South Carolina Chamber of Commerce
1201 Main Street, Suite 1810
Columbia, SC 29201
(803) 799–4601
www.sccc.org

South Carolina Festival and Event Association Variety Services
P.O. Box 61658
Charleston, SC 29419
(843) 884–6797

South Carolina Nature-Based Tourism Association
Charlie Sweat, President
P.O. Drawer 1763
Walterboro, SC 29488
(843) 549–5591
www.scnatureadventures.com
Request the South Carolina Nature-Based *Tourism Directory*

South Carolina Wildlife Federation
2711 Middleburg Drive, Suite 104
Columbia, SC 29204
(803) 256–0670
www.scwf.org

SOUTH CAROLINA TOURISM REGIONS

The tourism regions provide detailed tourism information and lodging assistance for the counties in their regions.

Discover Upcountry Carolina Association
P.O. Box 3116
Greenville, SC 29602
(864) 233–2690 or (800) 849–4766
www.theupcountry.com
(Anderson, Cherokee, Greenville, Pickens, Oconee, Spartanburg Counties: Drives 1–4)

Myrtle Beach Area/The Grand Strand Tourism Region
Myrtle Beach Area Chamber of Commerce
1200 North Oak Street, P.O. Box 2115
Myrtle Beach, SC 29578
(843) 626–7444 or (800) 356–3016
www.myrtlebeachlive.com
(Horry and Georgetown Counties: Drives 10–11)

Historic Charleston Area Tourism Region
Charleston Area Convention and Visitors Bureau
81 Mary Street, P.O. Box 975
Charleston, SC 29402
(843) 853–8000 or (800) 774–0006
www.charlestoncvb.com
(Charleston and Dorchester Counties: Drives 11, 16–18)

Capital City and Lake Murray Country Tourism Region
2183 North Lake Drive (SC 6)
P.O. Box 1783
Irmo, SC 29063
(803) 781–5940 or (800) 951–4008
www.lakemurraycountry.com
(Richland, Lexington, Saluda, and Newberry Counties: Drives 7, 15)

**Lowcountry and Resort Islands
Tourism Region**
One Lowcountry Lane, P.O. Box 615
Yemassee, SC 29945
(843) 717–3090
www.southcarolinalowcountry.com
(Beaufort, Colleton, Hampton, and Jasper
Counties: Drives 18–21)

Old 96 District Tourism Region
104½ Public Square
Laurens, SC 29360
(864) 984–2233 or (800) 849–9633
www.sctravelold96.com
visitus@sctravelold96.com
(Abbeville, Edgefield, Greenwood,
Laurens, and McCormick Counties:
Drives 4–5)

Olde English District Tourism Region
P.O. Box 1440, 107 Main Street
Chester, SC 29706
(803) 385–6800
www.sctravel.net
sctravel@inforave.net
(Chester, Chesterfield, Fairfield, Kershaw,
Lancaster, Union, and York Counties:
Drives 7–8, 14)

Pee Dee Tourism Region
3290 Radio Road
Florence, SC 29501
(843) 669–0950 or (800) 325–9005
www.peedeetourism.com
info@peedeetourism.com
(Darlington, Dillon, Florence, Lee,
Marion, Marlboro, and Williamsburg
Counties: Drives 8–9)

Santee Cooper Country Tourism Region
9302 Old Highway 6, P.O. Drawer 40
Santee, SC 29142
(803) 854–2131
www.santeecoopercountry.org
(Berkeley, Calhoun, Clarendon,
Orangeburg, and Sumter Counties:
Drives 8, 12–15)

Thoroughbred Country Tourism Region
P.O. Box 850
Aiken, SC 29802
(803) 649–7981 or (888) 834–1654
www.tbredcountry.org
mmellor@lscog.org
(Aiken, Allendale, Bamburg, and Barnwell
Counties: Drive 6)

Bibliography and Further Reading

This appendix lists some of the many excellent sources for learning more about South Carolina's natural resources and other attractions.

DeLorme's *South Carolina Atlas and Gazetteer* is the best single source for finding one's way around the back roads of South Carolina.

Of the several general travel guides to South Carolina, perhaps the most comprehensive, readable, and informative is Henry Leifermann's *Compass American Guides: South Carolina*. Caroline W. Todd and Sidney Wait have compiled an excellent county-by-county guidebook, *South Carolina: A Day at a Time,* focusing heavily on historic buildings.

Good guidebooks for South Carolina's coastal area are William Baldwin's information-packed *Lowcountry Day Trips* and Nancy Rhyne's folksy *Touring the Coastal South Carolina Backroads.*

For guidebooks focusing on natural resources, perhaps the most helpful is Patricia Jerman's *South Carolina Nature Viewing Guide,* which provides detailed descriptions of ninety-three natural viewing sites selected by a steering committee of governmental and private experts. Robin Carter's *Finding Birds in South Carolina* is a superb comprehensive description of birding locations in all forty-six counties. The South Carolina Chapter of the Sierra Club has published a handy county-by-county volume called *South Carolina 2002: Special Places.* This publication, well illustrated with pictures and maps, identifies 116 sites that are naturally unique and in need of greater protection. The Palmetto Conservation Foundation has an outstanding series of short guidebooks on several natural attractions.

Gene Able's *Exploring South Carolina* and Morrison Giffen's *South Carolina: A Guide to Backcountry Travel and Adventure* are exhaustive compilations of outdoor recreation locales.

Hiking South Carolina, by John F. Clark and John Dantzler, provides pictures and detailed maps and descriptions of sixty-three of the state's top hiking trails. Also good, but lacking in maps, is Alan De Hart's *Hiking South Carolina Trails.* Nicole Blouin has written an attractive piece, *Mountain Biking South Carolina.*

Other topflight sources of information about natural attractions are Richard Porcher's *Wildflowers of the Lowcountry and Lower Pee Dee; South Carolina Wildlife* magazine, an excellent bimonthly publication of the South Carolina Department of Natural Resources; *The National Audubon Society Field Guide* series on flora and fauna; and *Birds of the Carolinas,* by Eloise Potter, James Parnell, and Robert Teulings.

South Carolina: A History, by Walter Edgar, is the authoritative work on this subject.

For food, two volumes stand out. Dawn O'Brien and Karen Mulford focus on fifty old and mainly upscale restaurants in *South Carolina's Historic Restaurants and Their Recipes.* Down-home fare is the staple of the eighty-six eateries in Brian Katonak's *A Locals' Guide to South Carolina's Best-Kept Dining Secrets,* which includes at least one restaurant in each of the state's forty-six counties.

FURTHER READING

Able, Gene. *Exploring South Carolina: Wild and Natural Places.* Rock Hill, S.C.: Palmetto Byways Press, 1995.

Able, Gene, and Jack Horan. *Paddling South Carolina: A Guide to Palmetto State River Trails.* Columbia: Palmetto Byways Press, 1986.

Andrews, Judith. *South Carolina Highway Historical Marker Guide,* 2d ed. Columbia: South Carolina Department of Archives and History, 1998.

Baldwin, William P. III. *Lowcountry Daytrips.* Greensboro, N.C.: Legacy Publications, 1993.

Bannon, James, and Morrison Giffen. *Sea Kayaking the Carolinas.* Asheville, N.C.: Out There Press, 1997.

Barry, John M. *Natural Vegetation of South Carolina.* Columbia: University of South Carolina Press, 1980.

Blagden, Tom, and Barry Beasley. *The Rivers of South Carolina.* Englewood, Colo.: Westcliff Publications, 1999.

Blagden, Tom, Jane Lareau, and Richard Porcher. *Lowcountry: The Natural Landscape.* Greensboro, N.C.: Legacy Publications, 1988.

Blouin, Nicole. *Mountain Biking South Carolina.* Helena, Mont.: Falcon Publishing Company, 1998.

Carter, Robin M. *Finding Birds in South Carolina.* Columbia: University of South Carolina Press, 1993.

Clark, John F., and John Dantzler. *Hiking South Carolina.* Helena, Mont.: Falcon Publishing Company, 1998.

Clark, Robert C., and Tom Poland. *Reflections of South Carolina.* Columbia: University of South Carolina Press, 1999.

De Hart, Allen. *Hiking South Carolina Trails,* 5th ed. Guilford, Conn.: Globe Pequot Press, 2001.

DeLorme Mapping Company. *South Carolina Atlas and Gazetteer.* Yarmouth, Maine: DeLorme, 1998.

Duncan, Wilbur H., and Leonard E. Foote. *Wildflowers of the Southeastern United States.* Athens, Ga.: University of Georgia Press, 1975.

Edgar, Walter. *South Carolina: A History.* Columbia: University of South Carolina Press, 1998.

Ewing, Steve. *Patriots Point in Remembrance.* Missoula, Mont.: Patriots Point Development Authority, 1999.

Foothills Trail Conference. *Guide to the Foothills Trail,* 3d ed. Greenville S.C.: The Foothills Trail Conference, 1998.

Fox, William Price. *South Carolina Off the Beaten Path,* 3d ed. Guilford, Conn.: Globe Pequot Press, 2001.

Giffen, Morrison. *South Carolina: A Guide to Backcountry Travel and Adventure.* Asheville, N.C.: Out There Press, 1997.

Isely, N. Jane, William P. Baldwin Jr., and Agnes L. Baldwin. *Plantations of the Low Country: South Carolina 1697–1865.* Greensboro, N.C.: Legacy Publications, 1985.

Jerman, Patricia L. *South Carolina Nature Viewing Guide.* Columbia: South Carolina Department of Natural Resources, 1998.

Katonak, Brian. *A Locals' Guide to South Carolina's Best-Kept Dining Secrets.* Orangeburg, S.C.: Sandlapper Publishing Company, 1999.

Leifermann, Henry. *Compass American Guides: South Carolina.* New York: Fodor's Travel Publications, 1995.

Leland, Elizabeth. *The Vanishing Coast.* Winston-Salem: John F. Blair, 1992.

Manning, Phillip. *Palmetto Journey: Walks in the Natural Areas of South Carolina.* Winston-Salem: John F. Blair, 1995.

McMillan, Cecily. *The Charleston, Savannah & Coastal Islands Book: A Complete Guide,* 3d ed. Lee, Mass.: Berkshire House Publishers, 1998.

Naturaland Trust. *Mountain Bridge Trails.* Greenville, S.C.: Naturaland Trust, 1994.

O'Brien, Dawn, and Karen Mulford. *South Carolina's Historic Restaurants and Their Recipes,* rev. ed. Winston-Salem: John F. Blair, 1992.

Palmetto Conservation Foundation Guide Series. Spartanburg, SC: Palmetto Conservation Foundation Press.

    Audubon Society's Favorite South Carolina Bird Walks. 1998.
    The Audubon Society Guide to Favorite Birding Trails. 1997.
    Palmetto Cycling Coalition Favorite Mountain Bike Trails. 1997.
    The Palmetto Trail Lowcountry Guide. 2000.
    A River in Time: The Yadkin–Pee Dee River System. 2000.
    Scenic Rivers Guide to Favorite Canoe Trails. 1997.
    South Carolina Horsemen's Council Favorite Horse Trails. 1997.
    South Carolina Sierra Club Favorite Day Hikes. 1997.
    The Waterfalls of South Carolina. 2001.

Porcher, Richard. *Wildflowers of the Carolina Lowcountry and Lower Pee Dee.* Columbia: University of South Carolina Press, 1995.

Potter, Eloise F., James E. Parnell, and Robert P. Teulings. *Birds of the Carolinas.* Chapel Hill: University of North Carolina Press, 1980.

Rhyne, Nancy. *Touring the Coastal South Carolina Backroads.* Winston-Salem: John F. Blair, 1992.

Silverman, Jason H., and Judith M. Andrews. *South Carolina Then and Now.* Columbia: South Carolina Department of Archives and History, 2001.

South Carolina 2002: Special Places Identification Project. Columbia: South Carolina Chapter of the Sierra Club, 2001.

South Carolina Association of Naturalists [SCAN]: The First Ten Years. Columbia: SCAN, 1985.

South Carolina Wildlife. A bimonthly magazine published by the South Carolina Department of Natural Resources. Columbia, SC.

Swann, Nancy. *The Complete Walking Tour of Historic Charleston.* Charleston: Charleston Publishing Company, 1997.

The National Audubon Society Field Guide to North American Birds, Eastern Region. New York: Alfred A. Knopf, 2000.

The National Audubon Society Field Guide to North American Reptiles and Amphibians. New York: Alfred A. Knopf, 2000.

The National Audubon Society Field Guide to North American Trees, Eastern Region. New York: Alfred A. Knopf, 2001.

The National Audubon Society Field Guide to North American Wildflowers, Eastern Region. New York: Alfred A. Knopf, 2001.

Todd, Caroline W., and Sidney Wait. *South Carolina: A Day at a Time.* Orangeburg, S.C.: Sandlapper Publishing, 1997.

Whitaker, John O. *The National Audubon Society Field Guide to North American Mammals.* New York: Alfred A. Knopf, 2000.

Wilderness Society. *South Carolina's Mountain Treasures: The Unprotected Wildlands of the Andrew Pickens District of the Sumter National Forest.* Atlanta: The Wilderness Society, Southeastern Office, 1993.

Wright, Louis B. *South Carolina: A Bicentennial History.* New York: W. W. Norton & Company, 1976.

Wyche, Thomas, and James Kilgo. *The Blue Wall: Wilderness of the Carolinas and Georgia.* Englewood, Colo: Westcliffe Publishers, 1996.

index